Police Crime Control Strategies

Larry T. Hoover, Ph.D.

SAM HOUSTON STATE UNIVERSITY

Australia • Brazil • Canada • Mexico • Singapore • United Kingdom • United States

Police Crime Control Strategies
Larry T. Hoover

Vice President, Editorial: Dave Garza

Director of Learning Solutions: Sandy Clark

Senior Acquisitions Editor: Shelley Esposito

Senior Product Development Manager: Larry Main

Senior Product Manager: Anne Orgren

Editorial Assistant: Diane Chrysler

Brand Manager: Kristin McNary

Market Development Manager: Michelle Williams

Senior Production Director: Wendy Troeger

Production Manager: Mark Bernard

Senior Content Project Manager: Jennifer Hanley

Cover design: Riezebos Holzbaur/Tim Heraldo

Cover image(s):

Main Image: Getty Images

Inset images, left to right: Alamy Images; iStockphoto; Alamy Images; Shutterstock Images

Library of Congress Control Number: 2012941388
Student Edition:
ISBN-13: 978-1-133-69162-4
ISBN-10: 1-133-69162-5

Delmar
25 Maxwell Drive
Clifton Park, NY 12065-2919
USA

Cengage Learning is a leading provider of customized learning solutions with office locations around the globe, including Singapore, the United Kingdom, Australia, Mexico, Brazil, and Japan. Locate your local office at: **www.cengage.com/global**

To learn more about Delmar, visit **www.cengage.com/delmar**
Purchase any of our products at your local college store or at our preferred online store **www.cengagebrain.com**

Notice to the Reader
Publisher does not warrant or guarantee any of the products described herein or perform any independent analysis in connection with any of the product information contained herein. Publisher does not assume, and expressly disclaims, any obligation to obtain and include information other than that provided to it by the manufacturer. The reader is expressly warned to consider and adopt all safety precautions that might be indicated by the activities described herein and to avoid all potential hazards. By following the instructions contained herein, the reader willingly assumes all risks in connection with such instructions. The publisher makes no representations or warranties of any kind, including but not limited to, the warranties of fitness for particular purpose or merchantability, nor are any such representations implied with respect to the material set forth herein, and the publisher takes no responsibility with respect to such material. The publisher shall not be liable for any special, consequential, or exemplary damages resulting, in whole or part, from the readers' use of, or reliance upon, this material.

Printed in Mexico
Print Number: 02 Print Year: 2020

Chapter List

Contents

Preface

Philosophically, this book is premised upon the assumption that there is no single superior model of police crime control strategy. Instead alternatives are examined, including the strengths and weaknesses of various "models"—hot spot saturation, broken windows enforcement, community policing, problem-oriented policing, crime-specific interventions, and Compstat. Likewise, this book is designed to provide perspective, not prescription, on allocation and deployment. A conscious effort is made to fairly present all perspectives. Segments of the book which take the form of critique may leave the impression of bias. However, the goal of the critiques is to convey that the appropriateness of the crime control strategy taken depends upon circumstance. For some circumstances community engagement is the best approach, for others it might be problem solving, while for yet other circumstances hot spot saturation patrol is most cost effective. Indeed, for most circumstances, a combination of approaches is preferable. Like all complex social phenomenon, the appropriate police approach to crime reduction is a multi-faced "it depends" question. The phrase *Deployment Without Buzz Words* conveys the perspective taken.

Organization of the Text

While not formally designated as sections, Police Crime Control Strategies is organized into seven topical groupings. Chapter 1–*Police Crime Control Strategy Development*, and Chapter 2–*The Police Effect on Crime* set a historical as well as philosophical context. While community and problem-oriented policing are frequently associated with a police role which transcends crime control, both approaches have gravitated in the last ten years toward the core law enforcement function. Recently emerged formats are discussed in Chapter 3–*The Role of Community Policing,* and Chapter 4–*Focusing Community and Problem-Oriented Approaches on Crime Reduction.*

Chapter 5–*A Typology of Crime Reduction Strategies*, sets the agenda for the next three chapters: *Geographic Targeting Strategies* (6), *Offense Targeting Strategies* (7), and *Offender Targeting Strategies* (8). Nearly all major police agencies have adopted some form of Compstat, if no more than regularly scheduled Crime Strategy Meetings. The role of Compstat is reviewed in detail in Chapter 9–*Compstat and Crime Control* and Chapter10–*Conducting Crime Strategy Meetings*. While Compstat tends to emphasize interdiction by patrol and specialized units, proactive investigations is a critical element of any systematic approach, discussed in Chapter 11–*The Resurrection of Sherlock Holmes*.

A systematic strategic approach to crime control does not just happen. Chapter 12–*Staffing for Crime Control*, Chapter 13–*Deployment for Crime Control*, and Chapter 14–*Limitations on the Police Role* review organizational and deployment issues pertaining to operationalizing an array of crime interdiction strategies.

Finally, Chapter 15–*Evaluating Strategic Impact* reviews the import of structured evaluative research undergirding an evidence-based approach to crime control deployment.

Ancillary Materials

An extensive package of supplemental aids accompanies *Police Crime Control Strategies* and is available for instructor and student use. Supplements are available to qualified adopters. Please consult your local sales representative for details.

FOR THE INSTRUCTOR

Instructor Companion Website To access the password-protected instructor companion website, visit login.cengage.com, sign on using your single sign-on (SSO) login, and add this book to your bookshelf. This will give you access to the Instructor Companion Site that contains the Instructor's Manual, Test Bank, PowerPoint® slides, Lesson Plans, and Real World Resources. ISBN: 9781133692317.

PowerLecture™ This one-stop lecture and class preparation tool makes it easy for you to assemble, edit, and present custom lectures for your course using Microsoft® PowerPoint®. PowerLecture™ includes lesson plans, real-world resources, text-specific lecture outlines, art from the text, and more. The DVD-ROM also contains ExamView® computerized testing, which allows you to create tests in minutes using items from the test bank in electronic format. ISBN: 9781133692287.

CourseMate with Engagement Tracker Criminal Justice CourseMate is available for *Police Crime Control Strategies.*

The instructor version of CourseMate includes Engagement Tracker, a first-of-its-kind tool that monitors student engagement in the course. Instructors also have full access to the interactive eBook and other student CourseMate resources.

To access this CourseMate with Engagement Tracker, go to login.cengage.com, sign in with your SSO (single sign-on) login, and add this title to your bookshelf. (Note: Engagement Tracker monitors students who have purchased access to CourseMate.) ISBN: 9781133691648.

WebTutor™ Advantage Plus on Blackboard® Jumpstart your course with customizable content that's specific to this book. This valuable Course Management System lets you easily add, edit, reorganize, or delete content to meet your needs. You'll find text-specific media assets, quizzing, interactive games and exercises to supplement the classroom experience and ensure students leave with the resources to succeed in law enforcement today. You even can use this resource as an integrated solution for distance learning or a Web-enhanced course with a complete eBook. ISBN: 9781133692362 (Instant Access Code)/9781133692331 (Printed Access Card).

Criminal Justice Media Library WebTutor™ on Blackboard® Offering almost 300 media assets on a wide range of topics, Cengage Learning's Criminal Justice Media Library is available to stream from any Web-enabled computer—and is packed with valuable resources. Career Profile videos feature interviews with criminal justice professionals from a range of roles and locations. Simulations allow students to step into various roles to practice their decision-making skills. Video clips on current topics and animations illustrate key concepts. Interactive learning modules help students check their knowledge of important topics. RealityCheck exercises compare expectations and preconceived notions against the real-life thoughts and experiences of criminal justice professionals. The library also features Interactive Timelines for Criminal Justice Technology and Legal Landmarks. ISBN: 9780495813446 (Printed Access Card).

FOR THE STUDENT

CourseMate Criminal Justice CourseMate is available for *Police Crime Control Strategies*.

This CourseMate includes:

- an interactive eBook, with highlighting, note taking and search capabilities
- interactive learning tools including:
  - Quizzes
  - Flashcards
  - Videos
  - Crossword Puzzles
  - Learning Objectives
  - and more!

To learn more about this resource and access free demo CourseMate resources, go to **www.cengagebrain.com**, and search by this book's ISBN (9781133691624). To access CourseMate materials that you have purchased, go to login.cengagebrain.com, enter your access code, and create an account or log into your existing account.

ADDITIONAL RESOURCES AVAILABLE

Careers in Criminal Justice Website View a demo at academic.cengage.com/criminal justice/careers. This unique website helps you investigate the criminal justice career choices that are right for you with the help of several important tools:

- *Career Profiles* Video testimonials from a variety of practicing professionals in the field as well as information on many criminal justice careers, including job descriptions, requirements, training, salary and benefits, and the application process.
- *Interest Assessment* Self-assessment tool to help students decide which careers suit their personalities and interests.
- *Career Planner* Résumé-writing tips and worksheets, interviewing techniques, and successful job search strategies.
- *Links for Reference* Direct links to federal, state, and local agencies where students can get contact information and learn more about current job opportunities. ISBN: 9780495597216.

Careers in Criminal Justice and Related Fields: From Internship to Promotion, Sixth Edition This comprehensive text, written by seasoned professionals J. Scott Harr and Kären M. Hess, provides students with the invaluable information they need to help them enter and succeed in the field of criminal justice—from finding an internship to identifying the right criminal justice profession for them. ISBN: 9780495600329.

Acknowledgments

A number of my colleagues in the enterprise of improving police effectiveness have had special influence. The substance of the document includes in particular the insight of Jerry Dowling, Gary Cordner and Victor Strecher. Dean Vincent J. Webb of the College of Criminal Justice provided administrative support as part of his commitment to making the College a program of national import. The mix of practitioner and academic perspective is an important attribute of the book. In this respect I want to acknowledge the contribution of the Fort Worth Police Department, and former Chief Ralph Mendoza, the Dallas Police Department and former chief David Kunkle, the Houston Police Department, Chief Charles McClelland, and Assistant Chiefs Timothy N. Oettmeier and Kirk Munden, the Los Angeles Police Department and former Assistant Chief George Gascón, and the Chicago Police Department and former Superintendent Philip J. Cline.

Finally, no professional exceeds in any significant enterprise without the support of family. My wife, Martha, is, of course, first and foremost. But children and grandchildren are also important—Ryan—Tamara, Joe, Rebecca, and Brandon—Gregory, D´Et, Celeste, Ben, and Paige.

REVIEWERS

The author and Cengage Learning would like to thank the following reviewers: Paul R. Bowdre, State University of New York at Canton; Steve Carter, Institute of Technology; Richard Martin, Auburn University—Montgomery; Willard Oliver, Sam Houston State University; Leslie Palmer, Rasmussen College; and Jason Waller, Tyler Junior College.

About the Author

Larry T. Hoover, Ph.D., received his doctorate from Michigan State University, has been on the criminal justice faculty at Sam Houston State University since 1977, and directs its Police Research Center. A former police officer in Lansing, Michigan and training coordinator with the Michigan Law Enforcement Officer's Training Council, he also served on the faculty at Michigan State University from 1972 to 1977. Dr. Hoover, a past president of the Academy of Criminal Justice Sciences, is the recipient of the Academy's *2003* ***Founder's Award*** as well as the ***O. W. Wilson Award*** from the its Police Section. He is also the recipient of the ***Excellence in Research Award*** from SHSU, and was recognized in 2005 by Michigan State University by induction to the School of Criminal Justice "***Wall of Fame***."

His current endeavors include the administration of a statewide police information management system (***CRIMES***), presiding over a Major Cities Chiefs' Seminar Series sponsored by the Law Enforcement Management Institute of Texas, and directing the Texas Major Cities Research Initiative. His publications include articles in the *Journal of Criminal Justice, Police Quarterly, Policing: An International Journal of Police Strategies and Management, Law Enforcement Executive Forum, Public Personnel Management, Monthly Labor Review, Security Administration*, and *Liberal Education*, as well as a research monograph for the National Institute of Justice. He is also editor and chapter author of the anthologies *Police Management: Issues and Perspectives, Quantifying Quality in Policing* and *Police Program Evaluation*, all published by the Police Executive Research Forum; coauthor of *Enduring, Surviving and Thriving as a Law Enforcement Executive*, and coeditor and chapter author of *Improving Police Response to Persons with Mental Illness*, both published by Charles C. Thomas.

Special Acknowledgment by the Author

JAMIE L. TILLERSON played an invaluable role in the composition of *Police Crime Control Strategies*. I want to note her contribution with a special acknowledgment. Her responsibilities included compilation of materials for the book, thorough review of drafts with suggestions for improving content, as well as routine editing.

Ms. Tillerson earned a Bachelor of Business Administration from The University of Texas at Austin in 1974. She began her career at Sam Houston State University in 1983. From 1993 to the present she has served as the Program Manager for the Police Research Center. Her responsibilities include coordination of the Law Enforcement Management Institute of Texas' Major Cities Chiefs' Seminar Series and the Texas Major Cities Research Initiative. In addition, she manages all Police Research Center grants and contracts, and is the administrative manager of the Criminal Research, Information Management & Evaluation System (*CRIMES*) program.

Police Crime Control Strategies

CHAPTER 1

Police Crime Control Strategy Development

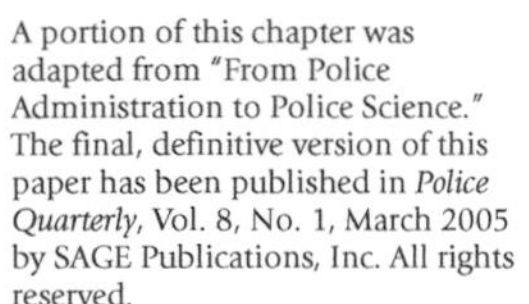

A portion of this chapter was adapted from "From Police Administration to Police Science." The final, definitive version of this paper has been published in *Police Quarterly*, Vol. 8, No. 1, March 2005 by SAGE Publications, Inc.

© iStockPhoto/Christopher Steer

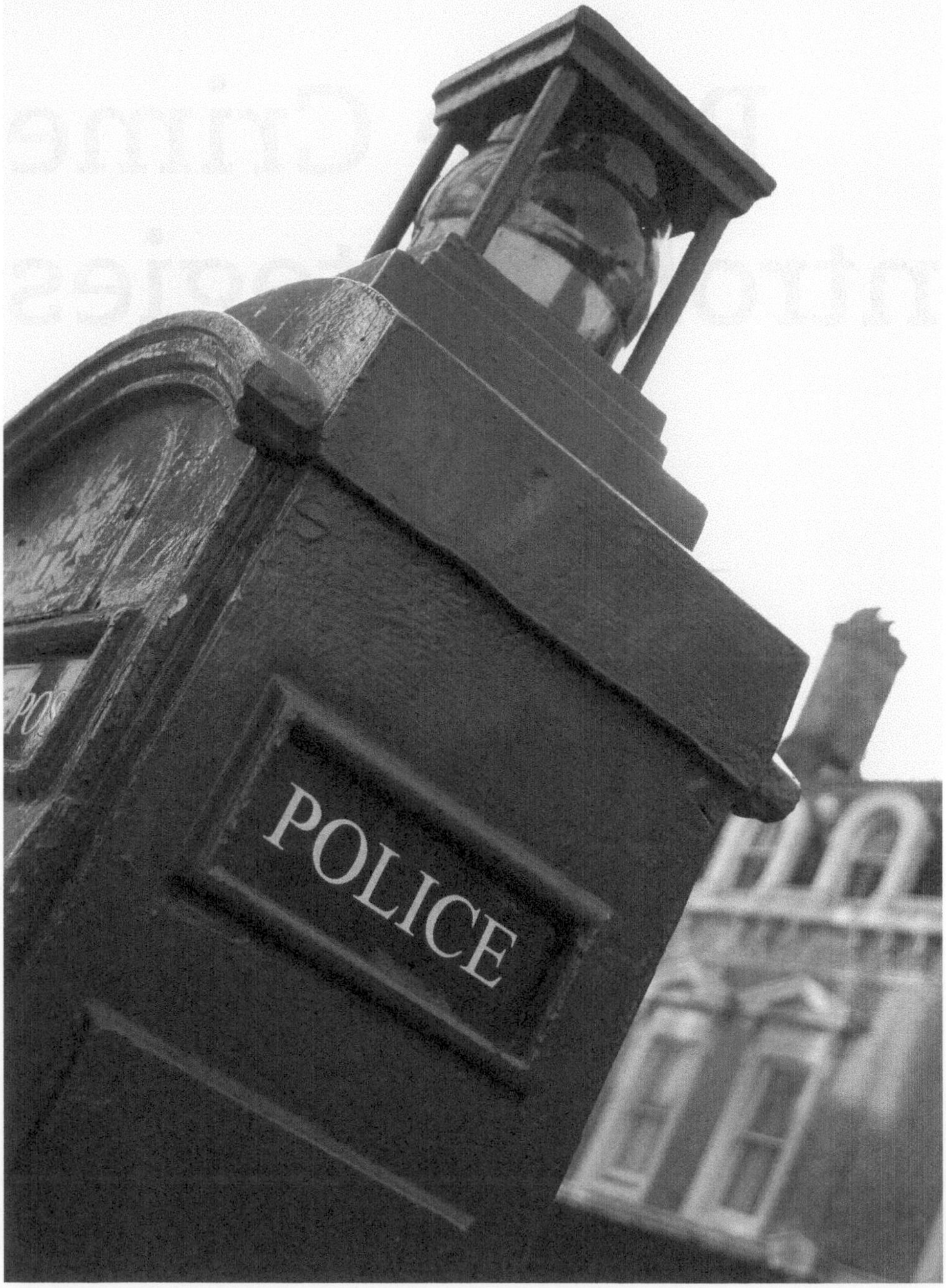

KEY TERMS

"Broken windows" approach
Community policing
Compstat
Crime-specific policing
Differential police response
Directed patrol
Disorderly and nuisance offenses
Effectiveness
Efficiency
Hot spot policing
Law Enforcement Assistance Administration (LEAA)
Managing Patrol Operations
National Victimization Survey
Neighborhood team policing
Police Foundation
President's Commission on Law Enforcement and Administration of Justice
Problem-oriented policing
Property crime
Suppressible street crime
Uniform Crime Reports (UCR)
Violent crime

LEARNING OBJECTIVES

After completing this chapter, you should be able to:

- Identify when and where the first degree programs in the field of criminal justice/law enforcement were created.
- List the six major developments of the 1960s that created a new era in law enforcement.
- Describe why the "nothing works" research of the 1970s is so important.
- Identify the major defining characteristic of community policing.
- Identify the major defining characteristic of problem-oriented policing.
- Contrast the explanations for the unprecedented crime drop during the 1990s.
- Describe the conceptual frameworks that currently mold police strategy.
- Identify the core concepts of each of the fifteen strategic initiatives defining the evolution of police strategy development.
- Explain how the four ground-breaking strategy evaluative studies influenced the development of crime-reduction approaches.
- Characterize evidence regarding the efficacy of hot-spot concentrated patrol.

The phrase may be time worn—those who do not know history are condemned to repeat it—but that does not make it any less true. One cannot understand where we are without understanding where we have been. The first requisite for gaining insight on police crime control effectiveness is understanding how we got to where we are today. An ever-present issue with provision of historical perspective is subjectivity. The subjectivity involved is not so much what a particular author says about the meaning of events—it is usually very clear that this is opinion and should be taken as such—but rather what events are mentioned. The most important issue in establishing historical perspective is indeed deciding what to include—what is of historical significance.

In this chapter, the development of police strategy is first presented chronologically by reviewing the major events occurring by decade since 1950. Unfortunately a chronological perspective tends to imply that there is a discernible order and direction to the developments over recent decades. However, history is never as "ordered" as historical accounts suggest, including the synopsis in this chapter. The chronological review begins with the publication of O. W. Wilson's *Police Administration* (1950). This date was chosen as the true demarcation date of the beginning of the study of police strategy from a "scientific" perspective. Certainly other significant events preceded the publication of *Police Administration*. The emergence of a scientific perspective on forensic evidence at the turn of the century is among them; August Vollmer's work is among them; Bruce Smith's publications are among them. However, Wilson's book marks a true turning point.

This chapter addresses the development of police studies only in the United States. Other publications provide perspective from other nations. Individual people and places are largely ignored. Rather, the concentration is upon the evolution of intellectual perspective. Discussion of the development of an academic establishment is interwoven with that of the development of policing itself, noting their mutual influence. Events are collapsed into six categories to coincide with the last six decades—the 1950s through the 2000s. Collapsing into "eras" is always subjective.

Building upon the "reality of disorderly history," the second half of the chapter is a review from the perspective of the most important strategy initiatives over the same time frame. There are fifteen such initiatives, some of which have endured—but most of which have been abandoned.

The First Perspective: A Chronology of Police Strategy Development

THE 1950s

The primary hallmark of the 1950s was the development of an academic establishment. The development of that establishment must be seen in the context of Wilson's *Police Administration*. The book has had a profound impact on the development of the study of policing and literally set the direction of police management for at least thirty years, from 1950 to 1980. The book was a product of the "principles approach" to administration prevalent in the 1940s. The principles approach to administration is generally recognized as the third major school of thought regarding organization theory in the twentieth century. The century was launched with the scientific management approach; emphasis changed in the 1930s as a product of the Hawthorne experiments to what is often referred to as the Human Relations School, but by the 1940s that perspective had been supplanted by the principles approach. The principles approach to administration assumed there was one best way to run an organization. Its tone was set by authors such as Lyndall Urwick (*Elements of Administration*, 1944), Luther Gulick (*Papers on the Science of Administration*, 1937), and Henri Fayol (*General and Industrial Management*, 1949). The manager from the principles perspective was analogous to the conductor of a symphonic orchestra. Achieving balance was essential. Obtaining the right mix at the right time was critical to success. The manager in this context is seen as more of a coordinator than a leader.

O. W. Wilson, like all of us, was profoundly influenced by the major perspective of his academic discipline, in this case public administration, prevalent in the era. It is therefore hardly surprising that one of the most recognized hallmarks of Wilson's book is the famous, or to some, infamous, 300-item checklist at its conclusion. A checkmark in each of the 300 boxes equates to a well-run police agency.

Wilson's *Police Administration* and its principles were central to the development of police science. The academic programs that were created in the 1950s reflected the Wilson approach to the study of policing—that is, the study of policing was the study of efficient police administration, a subdiscipline of public administration. Students enrolled in police science programs during that era studied policing from what Thomas Kuhn (1996) would call the Wilson paradigm of policing.

Learning Objective

The first academic degree programs in the field were created in 1935, concurrently at San Jose State University in California and Michigan State University (Tenney Jr., 1971). The creation of both programs is directly traceable to August Vollmer and the Berkeley, California, phenomenon. They were both five-year baccalaureate programs, including an administrative internship, and were designed to produce professional police managers. Both were effectively suspended during World War II. By the time the programs geared back up again, *Police Administration* was in print. It was required reading in virtually every academic program in the 1950s, and well into the 1960s. Indeed, the book was the core of every program.

The initial growth of academic programs occurred in California in the 1950s (Ward & Webb, 1984). By 1960, fifty programs could be counted nationally (Saunders Jr., 1970). Although World War II slowed the expansion of academic programs in the field, its aftermath in the form of the G.I. Bill fed it. The development of the community college concept then led to exponential growth.

An academic establishment is an essential component of any occupation seeking professional status—it provides not just preparatory education, but service to the profession and research on improving professional practice. It should be noted that two of the most important approaches to improving law enforcement in recent times—problem-oriented policing and community policing—both emanated from the academic world. The origin of problem-oriented policing is Herman Goldstein at the University of Wisconsin. The root of the community policing philosophy is Robert Trojanowicz at Michigan State University. Both concepts illustrate the point that an academic establishment drives innovation in a profession.

THE 1960s

Learning Objective

The 1960s are important for six reasons:

1. National commission reports recommending professionalization
2. Advent of the "criminal justice" perspective
3. Explosive growth in the number of academic programs in criminal justice
4. "Discovery" of the police by the discipline of sociology
5. Police role and response to the "ghetto riots"
6. Police role and response to Vietnam War demonstrations

First, there was the series of national commission reports in the United States addressing issues of criminal justice administration. They included:

- **President's Commission on Law Enforcement and Administration of Justice** (1967)
- National Advisory Commission on Civil Disorders (1968)

President's Commission on Law Enforcement and Administration of Justice
A national study group convened during Lyndon Johnson's presidency in the 1960s to make recommendations for improvement of policing, court administration, and corrections. Its primary publication is entitled *The Challenge of Crime in a Free Society*.

Which were followed closely in the early 1970s by:

- *Upgrading the American Police* by the Brookings Institution (Saunders Jr., 1970)
- President's Commission on Campus Unrest (1971)
- *Standards Relating to the Urban Police Function* by the American Bar Association (Institute of Judicial Administration, 1973)
- National Advisory Commission on Criminal Justice Standards and Goals (1973)

Virtually all of the reports recommended major changes in policing, all with a slant of professionalizing the police both in terms of administration and academic degree requirements (National Advisory Commission on Criminal Justice Standards and Goals, 1973). An outgrowth of the various commission reports was the advent of federal involvement in criminal justice administration through the **Law Enforcement Assistance Administration (LEAA)**. Federal funds required innovative programming accompanied by evaluation and assessment, as rudimentary as the evaluation and assessment might have been.

Law Enforcement Assistance Administration (LEAA)
A federal agency created in 1968 to provide funding for innovations in state and local law enforcement. The LEAA was superseded in 1982 by the Bureau of Justice Assistance and Bureau of Justice Statistics.

Second, the 1960s saw the advent of the concept of a criminal justice system, or stated differently, a systemic approach to problems of crime and delinquency (Conrad & Myren, 1979). The police was no longer viewed as an isolated agency. One by one existing academic programs changed their titles from *police science* or *police administration* to *criminal justice*. Course content was concurrently broadened, reflecting the title change.

Third, a confluence of factors led to explosive growth in the number of academic programs in the field. The development of the community college had enormous import. For a profession attempting to move from an academic standard of completion of high school to one of college preparation, the advent of the community college was a godsend (Hoover & Lund, 1977). A jump from no degree requirement to a baccalaureate requirement is an enormous leap. The associate degree as an intermediate level provided a reachable goal for working police officers. Second, a central element of the LEAA was the Law Enforcement Education Program (LEEP) (Sherman, 1978). LEEP funds paid for tuition for in-service personnel and provided loans to pre-service personnel, forgiven if they entered law enforcement. Furthermore, one outgrowth of the G.I. Bill in the 1950s was the concept of universal accessibility of higher education. The community college concept was certainly part of this effort, but not its sole product. Until the 1950s, the baccalaureate degree was largely a generic liberal arts degree. After the 1950s, a broad liberal arts degree became the exception. A baccalaureate degree was now seen as preparation for a specific professional area. In this context, the study of criminal justice became academically acceptable in reputable institutions (Hoover, 1975).

The fourth major event affecting police management in the 1960s was the discovery, or recognition, of the complexity of police work by sociologists. Until that time, the only complexity recognized in law enforcement was its identification as a specialized form of public administration—the O. W. Wilson "police science" approach. A series of publications within a span of approximately seven years beginning in 1965 changed dramatically our perception of police work, including:

- Wayne LaFave's *Arrest: The Decision to Take a Suspect into Custody* (1965)
- Cumming, Cumming, and Edell's *Policeman as Philosopher, Guide and Friend* (1965)

- Jerome Skolnick's *Justice Without Trial* (1966)
- John McNamara's *Uncertainties in Police Work* (1967)
- Egon Bittner's *Police on Skid Row* (1967), and later *The Functions of Police in Modern Society* (1970)
- James Q. Wilson's *Varieties of Police Behavior* (1968)
- Arthur Niederhoffer's *Behind the Shield: Police in Urban Society* (1969)
- Albert Reiss Jr.'s *The Police and the Public* (1971)
- Peter Manning's *The Police: Mandate, Strategies and Appearances* (1971), *Observing the Police: Deviants, Respectables and the Law* (1972), and later *Police Work* (1977).

Suddenly, street-level police work became an endeavor legitimate for social science research. The import of this event cannot be overstated. For example, Egon Bittner's *Police on Skid Row* recognized that the goal of an officer in this environment is "maintaining the peace," not enforcing the law. Indeed, the law is used as a tool to maintain the peace, not a goal in and of itself. In this sense, the role of a police officer transcends law enforcement, encompassing the broader goal of order maintenance.

The attention the police were receiving from the academic social science community was, however, far exceeded by the attention police were receiving from the media—and by extension everyone else. The fifth, and unwelcome, source of the attention was civil disturbance. First to occur were the so called "ghetto riots" of the 1960s. Sparked by reaction to an arrest in the Watts section of Los Angeles, widespread civil disturbance in disadvantaged Black inner-city neighborhoods spiraled out of control within days. Arson and looting followed. In the following three "long, hot summers," similar disturbances occurred in numerous major cities, culminating in the Detroit riots in 1968. Although the ultimate cause of the disturbances is traceable to the social plight of Blacks in America, the immediate cause was almost always grievances against the police.

If that were not enough, the late 1960s brought on massive civil protests against the Vietnam War. The character of the Vietnam protests is not comparable in any meaningful way to the character of the inner-city riots. Indeed, it is the distinguishing characteristics that are of importance. Disturbances were frequent. Criticism of police containment tactics was frequent. But at no time during the Vietnam protests did an American police officer kill a protestor. Recall that the deaths at Kent State University emanated from the actions of the Ohio National Guard, not the police. Importantly, however, the Vietnam protests (and in a few cases, riots) begat confrontational melodrama with the collegiate middle class. The police were no longer the invisible enforcers of order in Black inner-city neighborhoods. Their role as keepers of the peace, as the maintainers of the status quo, was played out in full view of the economically privileged.

Taken together, the six major developments of the 1960s genuinely created a new era in policing. **Efficiency** through administration by the principles approach was no longer sufficient. The police were recognized as a complex social institution, with enormous social import. And **effectiveness**—whether defined as community support or crime control—transcended issues of efficiency.

efficiency
Cost per unit of production; in the public sector, generally regarded as the relative cost of achieving a given objective.

effectiveness
The degree to which objectives are achieved.

THE 1970s

Learning Objective

Although one might have entered the 1970s enormously optimistic about the future of police studies, one had to leave them enormously pessimistic. The 1970s was the era of "nothing works" research. The combination of the Kansas City, Missouri, Preventive Patrol Experiment (Kelling, Pate, Dieckman, & Brown, 1974), the RAND Criminal Investigation Study (Greenwood & Petersilia, 1975), and the San Diego Community Profiling Experiment (Boydstun & Sherry, 1975) left everyone discouraged. It certainly appeared by the end of the 1970s that although one might improve the efficiency of police departments through the application of sound principles of public administration, improving their effectiveness might be impossible.

Police Foundation
A not-for-profit organization with headquarters in Washington, D.C.; its goal is fundamental research on police operations; created by the Ford Foundation in 1970.

It should also be noted that this was an era when the **Police Foundation** enjoyed substantial influence. The research sponsored by the Police Foundation included the Kansas City Preventive Patrol Experiment, the San Diego Field Interrogation Experiment, and the San Diego Community Profile Experiment. The contributions to our knowledge base about policing were not being made by an academic establishment. Certainly, the staff of the Police Foundation included individuals with sound academic credentials, but established academic programs in law enforcement and criminal justice were not playing a role. The academic world in the 1970s was still largely in the police administration era, not in the police science era.

THE 1980s

Learning Objective

The 1980s were a reaction to the 1970s. The 1980s were marked by the emergence of the problem- and community policing approaches to policing. Stated as succinctly as possible, **problem-oriented policing** entails employing nontraditional interventions to permanently abate repetitive calls-for-service and/or offense clusters. **Community policing** is broadly defined, but the core is structured community engagement. Both were, in essence, efforts to improve the effectiveness of police agencies in innovative ways. Recognizing that traditional approaches to patrol and investigation did not appear to work, the time for experimentation was right. One of the underlying premises of both the problem- and community policing approaches to policing is that patrol officer creativity and human interaction skills are central to improving police effectiveness. The approaches added a level of complexity to the already complex role of the police officer "discovered" by the sociologists in the 1960s.

problem-oriented policing
An approach or orientation that entails ascertaining root causes of repetitive crime and disorder patterns and using innovative approaches to permanently resolve the issue by changing underlying conditions.

community policing
A philosophy or orientation that emphasizes engagement with citizens and community groups to address issues of crime and disorder.

Importantly, the source of both problem-oriented policing (POP) and community policing (CP) was academe. But this round was very different from the "discovery" of the police by sociologists in the late 1960s. This time the focus was not upon the sociology of a profession, but how to improve the effectiveness of the profession. Herman Goldstein had a background in law enforcement, serving as an aide to O. W. Wilson during his tenure as Superintendent of the Chicago Police Department. However, at the time of his seminal publication, *Improving Policing: A Problem-Oriented Approach* (Goldstein, 1979), Goldstein was on the faculty at the University of Wisconsin. Community policing emerged from Robert Trojanowicz's evaluation of the Flint, Michigan, foot-patrol effort (Trojanowicz, 1982). Trojanowicz was on the faculty of one of the iconic institutions of the field, Michigan State University. Fifty years after the creation of the first academic programs in policing, academe had finally transcended the efficiency issue and was weighing in on the question of police effectiveness. The instigation of both POP and COP was the academic establishment.

THE 1990s

The 1990s in the United States were marked by the incredible drop in crime. There was a precipitous decline in both **property crime** (auto theft, burglary, and theft—three of the seven Part 1 offenses included in the Federal Bureau of Investigation's [FBI's] **Uniform Crime Reports**) and **violent crime** (murder/manslaughter, aggravated assault, sexual assault, and robbery—four of the seven Part 1 offenses included in the FBI's Uniform Crime Reports). Between 1991 and 2001, violent crime measured by the Uniform Crime Reports dropped by 33 percent, property crime by 29 percent (Levitt, 2004). The phenomenon was confirmed as "real" versus an artifact of reporting by data generated from the **National Victimization Survey**, an annual telephone survey of households conducted by the Bureau of Justice Statistics, showing even more dramatic decreases—about 50 percent for violent crime and 53 percent for property offenses (Zimring, 2007).

property crime
Generally refers to auto theft, burglary, and theft—three of the seven Part 1 offenses included in the FBI's Uniform Crime Reports.

Uniform Crime Reports (UCR)
An annual summary of crimes known to the police published by the Federal Bureau of Investigation.

Learning Objective

In the 1990s, there was a booming economy in the United States, and that booming economy certainly accounted for some of the drop in crime. Incarceration rates also increased in the late 1980s and throughout the 1990s, and likely contributed to the drop (Zimring, 2007). But there were no radical transformations of social structure, there were no radical changes in the demographics of the country, and the demographic changes that did occur might suggest increases in crime, not decreases. At the same time, three proactive police efforts all resulted in sudden and dramatic decreases in crime: in the New York City subways in 1990, by the Houston Police Department in 1992, and by the New York City Police Department in 1994 (see Hoover & Caeti, 1994; Kelling & Coles, 1996). No change in incarceration rates or economic-social conditions could explain the suddenness of the dramatic drops. The only variable that changed was police strategy. In New York City in particular the drop was precipitous and far greater than the decline in the rest of the nation's major cities. It defies explanation by any event except the sudden change in police tactics (Zimring, 2007). Those events caused us to reexamine the research on structured police interventions—to give them a second look. Upon a second look it was clear that what did not work were unstructured, untargeted, random interventions at either the patrol or investigative level. But focused, targeted efforts did work. The 1990s pushed us all the way past the paradigm of *efficiency* through police administration and to the paradigm of *effectiveness* through police strategy. Strategy, in turn is associated with experimentation and evaluation, or police science, not prescriptive administrative approaches or models, no matter how politically attractive a particular model may be.

violent crime
Generally refers to murder/manslaughter, aggravated assault, sexual assault, and robbery—four of the seven Part 1 offenses included in the FBI's Uniform Crime Reports.

National Victimization Survey
An annual survey of a sample of households queried regarding household member victimization; conducted by the Bureau of Justice Statistics, a unit of the U.S. Department of Justice.

By the 1990s the academic establishment in law enforcement/criminal justice had developed sufficient sophistication to start making a contribution to the improvement of policing at multiple levels. Reflecting the tripartite function of American higher education—education, service, and research—the American academic establishment now interacted with operational police agencies in three ways. First, as has traditionally been the case, the academic establishment was attempting to improve the educational standard of the field. A baccalaureate degree as a requirement for entry was still sought. Slowly, very slowly, but surely, more and more agencies required at least some college as a requisite for employment, and increasingly the standard was a baccalaureate degree. Second, reflecting the higher-education function of service, educational institutions now participated in assisting and training law enforcement personnel. Third, the academic establishment was doing better at a research contribution—perhaps still not as strong as one would like, but better. Whereas research in the 1970s was conducted by organizations outside the academic establishment, the two dominant ideas of the 1980s, community- and problem-oriented approaches, came from the academic establishment, and by the 1990s academe was driving a wide array of evaluative efforts.

THE 2000s

When we look back at labeling decades, the decade of the 2000s may well be called The Technology Era. Police departments throughout the United States were making increasing use of emergent technology. Mobile computing had a substantial effect, and included field reporting, in-car analytic ability, access to expanded databases, and an integration of global positioning systems into deployment. See Figure 1.1.

Enhanced identification techniques that changed investigations include (1) automated fingerprint identification systems; (2) personal recognition

FIGURE 1.1 Has Technology Changed the Role of Patrol?

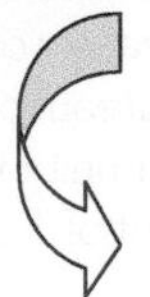

through computer analysis of facial, iris, and voice characteristics; and (3) last, but hardly least, DNA analysis. The police were employing new networks linked through the Internet, including databases linking to both the public and private sector. Real-time computing had begat deployment by analysis. There are several abbreviated descriptions, but regardless of such descriptions, real-time pattern and trend data enhanced by geographic information system display was being integrated into daily operations. Intelligent software and regional databases were yet to become widespread, but were developing. By blending crime analysis with criminal intelligence, it was suggested that crime analysis could provide the what-is-happening picture of the criminal environment, and criminal intelligence could provide the why-it-is-happening perspective (Ratcliffe, 2007, p. 2). Ratcliffe further noted that computer systems with integrated databases could now create intelligence products that supported area commanders and regional operational managers in planning crime-reduction activity and deploying appropriate resources.

THE 2010s

What's next? There is one question in this decade that remains unanswered—whether academe will outgrow advocacy for a particular "style" of policing, substituting neutral, scientific assessment of "what works." The current "evidence-based" perspective is in and of itself "evidence" of encouraging change—ideology does not matter; the issue is what works. But we did not get to this stage overnight.

The next section takes a different perspective, describing the characteristics of fifteen strategy initiatives that postdate O. W. Wilson—most of which have "come and gone," whereas a few are very much alive and well.

The Second Perspective—Characteristics of Major Strategy Initiatives

The most important conceptual frameworks molding innovation and strategy over the last sixty years include community policing, problem-oriented policing, broken windows enforcement approaches, Compstat, hot-spots concentration, and focused- or crime-specific approaches. None of these, of course, parachuted in out of the blue. Some were engendered by closely related research efforts—the Flint, Michigan, Foot Patrol Assessment beget community policing and the Newark (New Jersey) Foot Patrol Experiment beget the broken windows approach. But both approaches transcend the initial reference points, and incorporate both qualitative assessment and pure theoretical conceptual models. Thus, although "quantitative" research has driven some police strategy innovation, hot-spots concentration patrol in particular (Weisburd, 2005), it has not been the only impetus. Importantly, none of the three current pervasive strategy paradigms—community policing, problem-oriented policing, or Compstat—emerged from quantitative data analysis. Table 1.1 is a summary of fifteen of the most important milestones in police crime control strategy development. Table 1.2 lists the major publications describing each of the fifteen initiatives, references to descriptive accounts and/or conceptual works that framed the approach.

Learning Objective

Learning Objective

TABLE 1.1 Major Police Strategy Development Initiatives

1. **Ground-Breaking—The Emergence of Strategy Research**
   Four evaluative studies mark the initiation of focused strategy research in policing: the Kansas City Preventive Patrol Experiment; the RAND Corporation Criminal Investigation study; the San Diego, California, Community Profile Experiment; and the San Diego, California, Field Interrogation Experiment.
2. **Directed Patrol Programs**
   During uncommitted patrol time, units were dispatched to problem locations. Where there was an effect, it tended to be slight.
3. **Managing Patrol Operations**
   In 1977 the U.S. Department of Justice launched a significant nationwide training program entitled Managing Patrol Operations. It introduced police administrators to a new conceptual framework—patrol operations were to be managed, not merely deployed.
4. **Team Policing**
   The concept entailed creating a team of 10 to 20 officers who could be assigned responsibility for total police services for a small geographic area. The strategy was short lived, primarily due to the logistical problems it created.
5. **Managing Criminal Investigations**
   Like patrol operations, the concept that criminal investigations should be managed evolved in the late 1970s.
6. **Foot Patrol**
   The 1980s saw three quality evaluations of effectiveness of foot patrol conducted in Newark, New Jersey; Flint, Michigan; and Edmonton, Alberta. Foot patrol had minimal impact upon area crime rates, but was strongly supported by residents and/or merchants. A more recent evaluation of foot patrol in Philadelphia produced more encouraging results.
7. **Problem-Oriented Policing**
   The core of problem-oriented policing entails employing nontraditional interventions to permanently abate repetitive calls-for-service and/or offense clusters.
8. **Differential Police Response**
   Taking reports of minor offenses over the phone; employing an agency's website for the same purpose is rapidly gaining popularity.
9. **Broken Windows**
   Active enforcement of minor and nuisance offenses and interference with obnoxious behavior. Premised upon supposition that if we tolerate incivilities and minor offenses in an area, there will be an escalation to major crime.
10. **Community Policing**
    Although generally broadly defined, the core of community policing entails structured community engagement programs.
11. **Compstat**
    The core of Compstat is real-time crime analysis coupled with a rigid accountability system for shift/area commanders. Regular strategy meetings are held to review the crime interdiction efforts of shift/area commanders. Proactive enforcement is an assumed overlay.

12. **Crime-Specific**
The fundamental premise is that narrow targeting is more effective than broad-based intervention efforts. Narrow targeting means focusing upon specific offenses committed by specific offender types at specific locations and at specific times.

13. **Hot Spots**
Conceptually, hot spot deployment is premised upon the recognition that crime is not geographically evenly dispersed across the community. There is a subset of criminogenic "places."

14. **Intelligence-Led**
Intelligence-led policing is marked by integrating two elements into crime analysis—offender and/or potential offender data and threat analysis. Although developed initially for information compilation relevant to the terrorist threat, the approach has found a wider application in crime analysis.

15. **Focusing, Data-Driven, and Evidence-Based**
The current era in police strategy development is described as focusing and data-driven. The approaches being employed include geographic, offense, and offender focus. Police intervention strategy is now guided by empirical evidence, not hypothetical conjecture on what the police ought to be doing. Frequently, the term "evidence-based" is used to describe this orientation.

TABLE 1.2 Milestone Research and Development in Police Strategy Evolution

1. **Ground-Breaking—The Emergence of Strategy Research**

1974	The Kansas City Preventive Patrol Experiment: Summary Report (Kelling et al., 1974)
1975	The Criminal Investigation Process—Volume I: Summary and Policy Implications (Greenwood & Petersilia, 1975)
1975	San Diego Community Profile: Final Report (Boydstun & Sherry, 1975)
1975	San Diego Field Interrogation: Final Report (Boydstun, 1975)

2. **Directed Patrol Programs**

1978	An Alternative Approach in Police Patrol: The Wilmington Split-Force Experiment (Tien, Simaon, & Larson, 1978)
1978	Integrating Patrol Assignments: Directed Patrol in Kansas City (Bartch, 1978)
1979	Directed Patrol: An Experiment that Worked (Warren, Forst, & Estrella, 1979)
1981	An Alternative Approach in Police Response: The Wilmington Management of Demand Program (Cahn & Tien, 1981)
1981	The Effects of Directed Patrol: A Natural Quasi-Experiment in Pontiac (Cordner, 1981)
1983	Police Directed Patrol—An Initial National Assessment (Fennessy, 1983)
1988	Directing Patrol Work: A Study of Uniformed Policing (Burrows, Lewis, Stobart, & Tyrer, 1988)

(Continues)

TABLE 1.2 (*Continued*)

3. Managing Patrol Operations	
1977	Managing Patrol Operations–Manual (Cawley & Miron, 1977)
1977	Improving Patrol Productivity: Volume I—Routine Patrol (Gay & Schack, 1977)
1977	Improving Patrol Productivity: Volume II—Specialized Patrol (Schack & Gay, 1977)
1977	National Evaluation Program: Specialized Patrol Projects (Webb, 1977)
1978	Managing Patrol Operations: Program Test Design (Pasciuto et al., 1978)
1985	Synthesizing and Extending the Results of Police Patrol Studies (Larson & Cahn, 1981)
4. Neighborhood Team Policing	
1973	Neighborhood Team Policing (Bloch & Specht, 1973)
1973	Team Policing: Seven Case Studies (Sherman & Milton, 1973)
1975	Full-Service Neighborhood Team Policing: Planning for Implementation (Public Safety Research Institute, 1975)
1977	Neighborhood Team Policing: National Evaluation Program, Phase I Summary Report (Gay, Day, & Woodward, 1977)
5. Managing Criminal Investigation	
1975	Managing Criminal Investigations (Bloch & Weidman, 1975)
1976	Managing Investigations: The Rochester System (Bloch & Bell, 1976)
1976	Three Approaches to Criminal Apprehension in Kansas City: An Evaluation Report (Pate, Bowers, & Parks, 1976)
1978	Integrated Criminal Apprehension Program: Manual for the Design and Implementation of Training (Grassie, Burrows, White, & Waymire, 1978)
1978	The Investigators: Managing FBI and Narcotic Agents (J. Q. Wilson, 1978)
1979	Managing Case Assignments: The Burglary Investigation Decision Model Replication (Eck, 1979)
1983	Solving Crimes: The Investigation of Burglary and Robbery (Eck, 1983)
1986	Catching Career Criminals: The Washington, D.C. Repeat Offender Project (Martin & Sherman, 1986)
1991	An Experimental Evaluation of the Phoenix Repeat Offender Program (Abrahamse & Ebener, 1991)
6. Foot Patrol	
1981	The Newark Foot Patrol Experiment (Kelling, 1981)
1982	An Evaluation of the Neighborhood Foot Patrol Program in Flint, Michigan (Trojanowicz, 1982)
1988	Community-Based Policing and Foot Patrol: Issues of Theory and Evaluation (Greene & Taylor, 1988)
1990	An Evaluation of the Neighbourhood Foot Patrol Program of Edmonton Police Service (Hornick, Burrows, Tjosvold, & Phillips, 1990)
2010	The Philadelphia Foot Patrol Experiment: Research Brief (Ratcliffe et al., 2010)
7. Problem-Oriented Policing	
1979	Improving Policing: A Problem-Oriented Approach (Goldstein, 1979)
1987	Problem Solving: Problem-Oriented Policing in Newport News (Eck & Spelman, 1987)

1990 Problem-Oriented Policing (Goldstein, 1990)
1999 Problem-Oriented Policing in Violent Crime Places: A Randomized Controlled Experiment (Braga et al., 1999)

8. **Differential Police Response**
1978 Response Time Analysis: Executive Summary (Kansas City Police Department, 1978)
1981 Differential Police Response Strategies (Sumrall, Roberts, & Farmer, 1981)
1984 Evaluation of the Differential Police Response Field Test (McEwen, Connors, & Cohen, 1986)
1993 Toward Equity and Efficiency in Law Enforcement: Differential Police Response (Worden, 1993)

9. **Broken Windows Enforcement Style**
1982 Broken Windows: The Police and Neighborhood Safety (J. Q. Wilson & Kelling, March 1982)
1996 Fixing Broken Windows: Restoring Order and Reducing Crime in Our Community (Kelling & Coles, 1996)

10. **Community Policing**
1968 Police and Community Relations: A Sourcebook (Brandstatter & Radelet, 1968)
1973 The Police and the Community (Radelet, 1973)
1988 Community Policing: Rhetoric or Reality (Greene & Mastrofski, 1988)
1990 Community Policing: A Contemporary Perspective (Trojanowicz & Bucqueroux, 1990)
1992 Beyond 911: A New Era for Policing (Sparrow, Moore, & Kennedy, 1992)
1999 The Police and the Community (Carter, 1999)

11. **Compstat**
1998 The Turnaround: How America's Top Cop Reversed the Crime Epidemic (Bratton & Knobler, 1998)
1999 The Crime Fighter (Maple & Mitchell, 1999)
1999 NYPD Battles Crime: Innovative Strategies in Policing (Silverman, 1999)

12. **Crime-Specific**
1974 New York City Police Department Street Crime Unit: An Exemplary Project (Halper & Ku, 1974)
1978 The Effect of Police on Crime (J. Q. Wilson & Boland, 1978)
1984 The Minneapolis Domestic Violence Experiment (Sherman & Berk, 1984)
1988 Deterrent Effects of the Police on Crime: A Replication and Theoretical Extension (Sampson & Cohen, 1988)
1990 Police Crackdowns: Initial and Residual Deterrence (Sherman, 1990)
1994 Crime-Specific Policing in Houston (Hoover & Caeti, 1994)
1995 The Kansas City Gun Experiment (Sherman, Shaw, & Regan, 1995)
1995 Policing Drug Hot Spots: The Jersey City Drug Market Analysis Experiment (Weisburd & Green, 1995)
1999 The Effects of Aggressive Policing of Disorder on Serious Crime (Novak, Hartman, Holsinger, & Turner, 1999)

(Continues)

TABLE 1.2 (Continued)

13.	**Hot Spots**	
	1989	Hot Spots of Predatory Crime: Routine Activities and the Criminology of Place (Sherman, Gartin, & Buerger, 1989)
	1995	General Deterrent Effects of Police Patrol in Crime "Hot Spots:" A Randomized, Controlled Trial (Sherman & Weisburd, 1995)
	1995	Just Enough Police Presence: Reducing Crime and Disorderly Behavior by Optimizing Patrol Time in Crime Hot Spots (Koper, 1995)
	2007	The Effects of Hot Spots Policing on Crime (Braga, 2007)
14.	**Intelligence-Led**	
	2000	Policing By Risks and Targets: Some Dimensions and Implications of Intelligence-Led Crime Control (Maguire, 2000)
	2007	Integrated Intelligence and Crime Analysis: Enhanced Information Management for Law Enforcement Leaders (Ratcliffe, 2007)
	2009	Law Enforcement Intelligence: A Guide for State, Local and Tribal Law Enforcement (Carter, 2009)
15.	**Focusing—Data-Driven—Evidence Based**	
	2010	The Evidence-Based Policing Matrix (Lum, Koper, & Telep, 2010)
	2010	An Evaluation of Compstat's Effect upon Crime (Jang, Hoover, & Joo, 2010)

THE EMERGENCE OF STRATEGY RESEARCH

Learning Objective

Four evaluative studies mark the initiation of focused strategy research in policing. The seminal study is, of course, the Kansas City Preventive Patrol Experiment, conducted in 1972–1973 and published in 1974. The dynamics of that effort are fully discussed in Chapter 2. It should be noted here, however, that the Kansas City experiment did not in and of itself suggest any strategy—it simply indicated that routine preventive patrol as a strategy was ineffectual. What the Kansas City experiment did do is open the door to exploration of alternatives. If routine preventive patrol is not effective, then an agency would have nothing to lose by attempting a different approach. Kansas City opened the door to strategy innovation.

The RAND Corporation Criminal Investigation study is also reviewed in detail in Chapter 11. The RAND Corporation Criminal Investigation study was a mix of "best information available" quantitative analysis with a qualitative overlay. Closely following the results of the Kansas City finding that routine preventive patrol was ineffectual, the RAND study suggested that routine investigative follow-up was likewise ineffectual.

Receiving less attention in the literature base are two studies conducted in San Diego, California, –the Community Profile Experiment and the Field Interrogation Experiment. At its core, the Community Profile endeavor attempted to ascertain whether structured efforts to acquaint patrol officers with social service agencies on their beat would engender more referrals (Boydstun & Sherry, 1975). The effort was actually a bit broader than this, but the core finding is what is important—officer familiarity with social service agencies did not result in more referrals. Indeed, officers reported disillusionment with the ability of social service agencies to offer meaningful intervention into troublesome situations that came to the attention of the police department. Note that the Community Profile experiment was conducted prior to the emergence of community policing as a broad strategy approach. As discussed earlier in this chapter, the fact that the police play an important social service/social counseling role was well documented in the sociological reviews of policing published in the late 1960s. Insightful police managers already recognized that policing was about far more than "fighting crime."

The importance of the San Diego Field Interrogation Experiment is also reviewed in Chapter 2. The significance of this "forgotten experiment" cannot be overstated. A policy of vigorous field interrogations (brief stop-and-question initiations by patrol officers) was found very effectual. Unfortunately, this demonstration of what does work in patrol intervention was overshadowed by the assessments that indicated what did not work. The policy implications were largely ignored.

What the four ground-breaking evaluative studies all demonstrated is that police interventions could be quantified. It is possible to isolate experimental variables, and/or statistically account for intervening variables, and draw strategy conclusions. The years 1974 and 1975 were an auspicious beginning for subsequent assessment efforts.

DIRECTED PATROL PROGRAMS

A predictable reaction to the finding that random routine undirected patrol does not work is to make an effort to direct patrol. Efforts that included some level of assessment were made in Wilmington, Delaware; Kansas City, Missouri; Pontiac, Michigan; and New Haven, Connecticut. Results were mixed. Where there was an effect, it tended to be slight. Further, **directed patrol** looked better on paper than in actual practice. The state of computerization of police records in the late 1970s and early 1980s did not allow real-time crime analysis. Hence patrol officers were frequently directed to last month's, or even last quarter's, problem areas. Patrol officers asserted legitimately that they knew more about problematic locations on their beat than the computer did. Stated differently, "It is my beat, and I know more than headquarters." Second, directed patrol flew in the face of decades of traditional self-directed patrol. Patrol officers did not accept being told to go to a particular location and remain there until the next call for service. The problem was exasperated by the fact that in most cases the so called D-runs were issued by dispatchers. Patrol officers did not accept the legitimacy of receiving "orders" from lower-status dispatchers. It simply offended officers' sense of professionalism. Patrol officers take ownership of their beat; indeed, there have been numerous efforts to encourage such ownership, particularly as part of community policing. For the combination of reasons just cited, directed patrol efforts "fizzled" within a year or two of their implementation.

directed patrol
Consists of dispatching patrol vehicles to problematic locations during uncommitted patrol time.

MANAGING PATROL OPERATIONS

In 1977 the U.S. Department of Justice launched a significant nationwide training program entitled **Managing Patrol Operations**. The titles of the documentation involved say it all—routine patrol, specialized patrol projects, and program test design. The Managing Patrol Operations effort had

Managing Patrol Operations
A training program implemented by the Law Enforcement Assistance Administration designed to train police managers to target patrol resources.

more significance than is commonly attributed to it. Although it was training, not research, it introduced police administrators to a new conceptual framework—patrol operations were to be managed, not merely deployed. O. W. Wilson articulated the basics of controlled deployment in 1950—proportionality to demand for service, both geographically and temporally. But proportionality is a deployment model, not a management model. The Managing Patrol Operations endeavor did not contribute any new strategic approaches, but it did change the mind-set of professional police administration.

NEIGHBORHOOD TEAM POLICING

neighborhood team policing
A precursor to community policing, neighborhood team policing involved assigning a group of officers comprehensive full-time responsibility for a small geographic area.

Neighborhood team policing represented a genuine innovative model of using patrol resources. The concept entailed creating a team of 10 to 20 officers who could be assigned responsibility for total police services for a small geographic area. Typically the team was led by a sergeant who had the authority to make deployment decisions. Additionally, the team was to undertake long-term crime intervention efforts. We do not have an exact count of the number of agencies that attempted the team policing model, but the number probably ranged only between fifty and one hundred. A handful of these were evaluated at some level. Like directed patrol efforts, neighborhood team policing fizzled within a year or two of implementation. Logistical problems plagued its implementation. The model was premised upon geographic stability of officer assignment. But in busy times officers assigned to a particular neighborhood were dispatched to other neighborhoods where urgent calls were pending. That practice, of course, always dominos, such that a subsequent call within the neighborhood team jurisdiction would have to be handled by an outside patrol unit because the neighborhood team unit was tied up elsewhere. Stability of assignment, or lack thereof, was the primary undermining factor. Additionally, however, the neighborhood teams had limited success in implementing meaningful long-term interventions.

One perspective is that neighborhood team policing was simply an idea before its time—that twenty years later the same team deployment framework defined full commitment to community policing.

MANAGING CRIMINAL INVESTIGATIONS

Like patrol operations, the concept that criminal investigations should be managed evolved in the late 1970s. The problem lies in the fact that we still have not figured out how to manage investigations. Although quantifying the effect of patrol interventions is difficult, given enough resources it is possible. That is questionable with the investigative function. The outcome of investigative efforts defies quantification. Developing a predictive model for clearance that would guide the expenditure of investigative effort illustrates the problem. The single strongest predictor of clearance is whether specific suspect information is developed at the initial scene. That factor correlates with the relationship between the offender and the victim—one always has specific suspect information when the offender/victim know one another. Thus if clearance probability determines follow-up effort, all detectives end up investigating are cases involving acquaintances—ignoring what most regard to be the far more serious stranger-to-stranger offenses. A valid model of investigative follow-up decision making has to include the interplay between the inherent seriousness of the offense, impact on a particular victim, victim culpability, and whether a particular offense can be linked to an offense series. The formative evaluations and conceptual frameworks developed around the concept of managing criminal investigations underscored the point that doing so is not as simple as it might initially seem.

FOOT PATROL

The 1980s saw three quality evaluations of effectiveness of foot patrol conducted in Newark, New Jersey; Flint, Michigan; and Edmonton, Alberta. The results were consistent. Foot patrol had minimal impact upon area crime rates, but was strongly supported by residents and/or merchants. A more recent evaluation of foot patrol in Philadelphia produced more encouraging results (Ratcliffe et al., 2010). However, the issue is affordability. Foot patrol is exorbitantly expensive. By and large foot patrol officers cannot respond to calls-for-service, and hence constitute an "overlay" patrol force. And the minute the budget is tight, foot officers are put in patrol cars.

PROBLEM-ORIENTED POLICING

Problem-oriented policing is discussed in several chapters. Stated as succinctly as possible, problem-oriented policing entails employing nontraditional interventions to permanently abate repetitive calls-for-service and/or offense clusters. It is important to note here that the concept is not new—the initial articulation of the concept occurred in 1979—over thirty years ago (Goldstein, 1979). Unlike other strategic approaches, however, problem-oriented policing has not disappeared. What has evolved is our expectations of its potential to ultimately resolve endemic repetitive calls-for-service demand and/or offense clusters. The issue is discussed in Chapter 4.

DIFFERENTIAL POLICE RESPONSE

Differential police response means employing alternatives to sending a patrol unit to every request for service. This has translated primarily to taking reports of minor offenses over the phone, although employing the agency's website for the same purpose is rapidly gaining popularity. The goal is, of course, resource management. If a report can easily be taken over the phone or Internet and the complainant is happy with that response, patrol units can be left free to respond to genuine 911 emergencies. Differential police response is not a strategy in the same sense that foot patrol or problem-oriented policing are strategies. Rather, it is a technique for reserving enough patrol resources that proactive crime control strategies can indeed be undertaken. Some form of differential police response is employed by most major police agencies.

differential police response
Saving patrol resources by taking minor offense reports over the phone or via the Internet.

BROKEN WINDOWS ENFORCEMENT STYLE

As noted earlier in this chapter, the broken windows concept emerged out of the Newark Foot Patrol Experiment. **Broken windows** is a clever metaphor.

"broken windows" approach
Vigorous enforcement of minor and nuisance offenses as well as intervention in obnoxious behavior to prevent the development of a downward spiral of crime and disorder in stressed neighborhoods.

It refers to the fact that if a window is broken in an abandoned building and left unrepaired, soon all the windows will be broken. If, on the other hand, all the windows in a building are intact, they tend to stay intact. The parallel to crime control is that if we tolerate **disorderly and nuisance offenses** in an area (behaviors such as loitering, obnoxious displays, catcalling, and aggressive begging—creating an atmosphere of dangerousness in public places), there will be an escalation to major crime. Broken windows enforcement was one of the underpinnings of New York City's Compstat effort in the 1990s. The current view is that broken windows enforcement is a valid approach to tightly focused geographic efforts, but is more effective in congested areas such as transit systems or downtowns than it is in sprawling suburbs.

disorderly and nuisance offenses Behaviors such as loitering, obnoxious displays, catcalling, and aggressive begging—creating an atmosphere of dangerousness in public places.

COMMUNITY POLICING

The concept of community policing was not an overnight invention. Discussions with residents of Flint triggered Robert Trojanowicz's development of a community engagement framework that came to be called community policing, but its roots go much deeper than the Flint Foot Patrol Evaluation. The need for structured community relations efforts by police agencies was articulated by O. W. Wilson in 1950. In 1968 Arthur Brandstatter and Louis Radelet published the first focused book on the issue, *Police and Community Relations* (Brandstatter & Radelet, 1968). That was followed by Louis Radelet's *The Police and the Community* (Radelet, 1973). Both Brandstatter and Radelet were "founding fathers" of the School of Criminal Justice at Michigan State University. Throughout the 1960s and 1970s, Michigan State University sponsored the annual Police and Community Relations Conference, attended by thousands of police managers. Robert Trojanowicz was among the second generation of Michigan State faculty, and built upon the previous work. This should not be taken as suggestion that Trojanowicz's effort was not innovative and insightful. It was. But the effort built upon the foundation laid by Brandstatter and Radelet.

COMPSTAT

Compstat is described in detail in Chapter 9, Compstat and Crime Control, and Chapter 10, Conducting Crime Strategy Meetings. The core of **Compstat** is real-time crime analysis coupled with a rigid accountability system for shift/area commanders. Regular strategy meetings are held to review the crime interdiction efforts of shift/area commanders. Proactive enforcement, mostly in the form of intense field stops of "suspicious" persons and vehicles, is an assumed overlay. From the perspective of police crime control strategy, what is important to note here is that Compstat was developed as an alternative to community policing, not as a complement to it. Advocates of the Compstat approach generally do not suggest that community engagement is unnecessary, but they do suggest that it has limited applicability, and where applicable has limited effect. Compstat assumes instead that effective crime control is engendered by proactive vigorous police intervention, which includes a broken windows comprehensive enforcement style.

Compstat An approach to crime control originating in the New York City Police Department in the early 1990s. Compstat incorporates up-to-the-minute crime analysis, proactive enforcement, and patrol commander accountability.

CRIME-SPECIFIC APPROACHES

The fundamental premise of **crime-specific policing** is that narrow targeting is more effective than broad-based intervention efforts. Narrow targeting means focusing upon specific offenses committed by specific offenders at specific locations and at specific times. The concept includes a wide diversity of focused efforts, from control of domestic violence and "always-arrest" policies to crackdowns on drug distribution locations to gang enforcement units.

crime-specific policing
Strategies aimed at particular offenses committed by particular offender types at specific times and types of locations.

HOT SPOTS

Hot spot policing efforts might be conceptualized as a subset of crime-specific approaches, but are usually regarded as distinguishable. Current research and approaches are discussed in Chapter 6, Geographic Targeting Strategies. Conceptually, hot spot deployment is premised upon the recognition that crime is not geographically evenly dispersed across the community. There is a subset of criminogenic "places." There are no precisely determined boundaries that define a hot spot. They have been variously defined as ranging from a particular address to a 4- or 5-square-mile area. The evidence is overwhelming that concentrated patrol in hot spots has a significant effect upon "disorderly" offenses—classic broken windows nuisance offenses. The evidence is less firm but tilts toward a definitive effect upon **suppressible street crime**—including auto theft, theft from autos, burglary, robbery, and assaultive behavior in public places. What we do not know is the optimal deployment concentration either in terms of dosage (number of patrol units) or duration (optimal time spent in a hot spot before rotating out).

hot spot policing
Concentrated patrol and other proactive interventions in small geographical areas characterized by inordinately high crime rates or problems of disorder.

Learning Objective

suppressible street crime
Offenses thought to be directly impacted by concentrated or proactive vehicle patrol; includes auto theft, theft from autos, burglary, robbery, and assaultive behavior in public places.

INTELLIGENCE-LED

Although definitions vary, intelligence-led policing is marked by integrating two elements into crime analysis—offender and/or potential offender data and threat analysis. Traditional crime analysis focuses upon events, not people. Intelligence-led efforts emphasize known and potential offenders. Although developed initially for information compilation relevant to the terrorist threat, the approach has found a wider application with integration in crime analysis.

FOCUSING—DATA DRIVEN—EVIDENCE-BASED

Earlier in this chapter it was noted that attaching a name to a current era is risky. Usually the descriptors attached to a particular era by those experiencing it later change. In an effort to be inclusive, the current era in police strategy development is described with three labels—focusing, data-driven, and evidence-based. Samples of publications addressing all three of these orientations are listed in Table 1.1. The approaches being employed include geographic focus, offense focus, and offender focus. Obviously, numerous crime interdiction efforts contain various blends of the three. What is important is that police intervention strategy is now guided by empirical evidence, not hypothetical conjecture on what the police ought to be doing. Frequently the term "evidence-based" is used to describe this orientation.

IMPLICATIONS FOR STRATEGY

No single event can be identified that has "molded" current police crime control strategy. Greater sophistication has been a heuristic process, with developments in one decade setting the stage for the next. The establishment of academic law enforcement/criminal justice programs in the 1950s has engendered diverse effects, most of which cannot be quantified. The 1960s were a decade of import for American policing—with the confluence of national commission reports recommending profound changes, the emergence of the concept of criminal justice as a system, the visibility of police intervention in both Vietnam protests and the inner-city riots, and the "discovery" of the complexity of policing by sociologists. The 1970s were marked by the "nothing works" research, the 1980s by the articulation of the community policing and problem-orienting approaches. The 1990s saw an inexplicable drop in crime. The 2000s can be labeled the technology decade.

A different historical perspective is provided by tracing the development of major strategy initiatives over the same decades. Some innovations failed due to logistical demands. Some failed because they were simply too expensive for prolonged use. Some were ahead of their time. Others simply did not work. What has survived is a blend of strategic approaches. Community engagement is still an integral part of many crime control efforts. Problem solving won't solve every problem, but is relevant to many. Crime-specific approaches now dominate strategy.

This chapter implies that there is direction and purpose to the evolution of police strategy development. There is, but with caveats. There has not been nor is there now an architectural design—a well-thought-out, carefully conceived or guided approach to testing police crime control strategy. Rather than a carefully conceived architectural plan, our progression is more aptly compared to biological species evolution. Although there is continuity, there are also numerous dead-end branches—extinctions have included directed patrol programs and team policing. In other instances, although there is speciation, interbreeding is still common; Compstat includes crime-specific approaches, for example. And as new species arise, although they might acquire new attributes, they do not necessarily shed the functional attributes of their predecessors—an illustration is that a flexible crime-specific approach incorporates community engagement. Finally, to stretch the analogy just a bit more, it should be noted that police crime interdiction strategy is a rapidly evolving species. The final form has not yet arisen.

SUMMARY

- The first academic degree programs in the field were created in 1935, concurrently at San Jose State University in California and Michigan State University (Tenney Jr., 1971).
- The 1960s are important for six reasons:
  1. National commission reports recommending professionalization
  2. Advent of the "criminal justice" perspective

3. Explosive growth in the number of academic programs in criminal justice
4. "Discovery" of the police by the discipline of sociology
5. Police role and response to the "ghetto riots"
6. Police role and response to Vietnam War demonstrations

- The 1970s was the era of "nothing works" research. The combination of the Kansas City, Missouri, Preventive Patrol Experiment (Kelling et al., 1974), The RAND Criminal Investigation Study (Greenwood & Petersilia, 1975), and the San Diego Community Profiling Experiment (Boydstun & Sherry, 1975) left everyone discouraged. It certainly appeared by the end of the 1970s that while one might improve the efficiency of police departments through the application of sound principles of public administration, improving their effectiveness might be impossible.
- One of the underlying premises of both the problem- and community policing approaches to policing is that patrol officer creativity and human interaction skills are central to improving police effectiveness.
- In the 1990s, there was a booming economy in the United States, and that booming economy certainly accounted for some of the drop in crime. Incarceration rates also increased in the late 1980s and throughout the 1990s, and likely contributed to the drop (Zimring, 2007). But there were no radical transformations of social structure or in the demographics of the country. At the same time, proactive police efforts in New York City and Houston resulted in sudden and dramatic decreases in crime in those jurisdictions (see Kelling & Coles, 1996; Hoover & Caeti, 1994). No change in incarceration rates or economic-social conditions could explain the suddenness of the drop. The only variable that changed was police strategy.
- The most important conceptual frameworks molding innovation and strategy over the last sixty years include community policing, problem-oriented policing, broken windows enforcement approaches, Compstat, hot-spots concentration, and focused or crime-specific approaches.
- The fifteen strategic initiatives defining the evolution of police strategy development are:
  1. *Ground-Breaking Evaluative Studies.* Four evaluative studies mark the initiation of focused strategy research in policing: the Kansas City Preventive Patrol Experiment; the RAND Corporation Criminal Investigation study; the San Diego, California, Community Profile Experiment; and the San Diego, California, Field Interrogation Experiment. These four ground-breaking evaluative studies demonstrated that police interventions could be quantified. It is possible to isolate experimental variables, and/or statistically account for intervening variables, and draw strategy conclusions.
  2. *Directed Patrol Programs.* A predictable reaction to the finding that random routine undirected patrol did not work is to make an effort to direct patrol. During uncommitted patrol time, units were dispatched to problem locations. Efforts that included some level of assessment were made in Wilmington, Delaware; Kansas City, Missouri; Pontiac, Michigan; and New Haven, Connecticut. Results were mixed. Where there was an effect it tended to be slight.
  3. *Managing Patrol Operations.* In 1977 the U.S. Department of Justice launched a significant nationwide training program entitled Managing Patrol Operations. Although it was training, not research, it introduced police administrators to a new conceptual framework—patrol operations were to be managed, not merely deployed.
  4. *Neighborhood Team Policing.* Neighborhood team policing represented a genuine innovative model of using patrol resources. The concept entailed creating a team of 10 to 20 officers who could be assigned responsibility for total police services for a small geographic area. The strategy was short lived, primarily due to the logistical problems it created.
  5. *Managing Criminal Investigations.* Like patrol operations, the concept that criminal investigations should be managed evolved in the late 1970s. The problem lies in the fact that we still have not figured out how to manage investigations.

6. *Foot Patrol.* The 1980s saw three quality evaluations of effectiveness of foot patrol conducted in Newark, New Jersey; Flint, Michigan; and Edmonton, Alberta. The results were consistent. Foot patrol had minimal impact upon area crime rates, but was strongly supported by residents and/or merchants. A more recent evaluation of foot patrol in Philadelphia produced more encouraging results.
7. *Problem-Oriented Policing.* The core of problem-oriented policing entails employing nontraditional interventions to permanently abate repetitive calls-for-service and/or offense clusters. Unlike other strategic approaches, problem-oriented policing has not disappeared. What has evolved is our expectations of its potential to ultimately resolve endemic repetitive calls-for-service demand and/or offense clusters.
8. *Differential Police Response.* Differential police response means employing alternatives to sending a patrol unit to every request for service. This has translated primarily to taking reports of minor offenses over the phone, although employing an agency's website for the same purpose is rapidly gaining popularity.
9. *Broken Windows Enforcement Style.* The broken windows concept emerged out of the Newark Foot Patrol Experiment. Broken windows is a clever metaphor. It refers to the fact that if a window is broken in an abandoned building and left unrepaired, soon all the windows will be broken. If, on the other hand, all the windows in a building are intact, they tend to stay intact. The parallel to crime control is that if we tolerate incivilities and minor offenses in an area, there will be an escalation to major crime.
10. *Community Policing.* Although generally broadly defined, the core of community policing entails structured community engagement programs. The concept of community policing was not an overnight invention. Discussions with residents of Flint, Michigan, triggered Robert Trojanowicz's development of a community engagement framework that came to be called community policing, but its roots go much deeper. The need for structured community relations efforts by police agencies was articulated by O. W. Wilson as long ago as 1950.
11. *Compstat.* The core of Compstat is real-time crime analysis coupled with a rigid accountability system for shift/area commanders. Regular strategy meetings are held to review the crime interdiction efforts of shift/area commanders. Proactive enforcement, mostly in the form of intense field stops of "suspicious" persons and vehicles, is an assumed overlay. From the perspective of police crime control strategy, what is important to note here is that Compstat was developed as an alternative to community policing, not as a complement to it.
12. *Crime-Specific Approaches.* The fundamental premise is that narrow targeting is more effective than broad-based intervention efforts. Narrow targeting means focusing upon specific offenses committed by specific offender types at specific locations and at specific times.
13. *Hot Spots.* Conceptually, hot spot deployment is premised upon the recognition that crime is not geographically evenly dispersed across the community. There is a subset of criminogenic "places." There are no precisely determined boundaries that define a hot spot. They have been variously defined as ranging from a particular address to a 4- or 5-square-mile area. The evidence is overwhelming that concentrated patrol in hot spots has a significant effect upon "disorderly" offenses—classic broken windows nuisance offenses. The evidence is less firm but tilts toward a definitive effect upon suppressible street crime.
14. *Intelligence-Led.* Intelligence-led policing is marked by integrating two elements into crime analysis—offender and/or potential offender data and threat analysis. Although developed initially for information compilation relevant to the terrorist threat, the approach has found a wider application in crime analysis.

15. *Focusing—Data-Driven—Evidence-Based.* The current era in police strategy development is described as focusing and data-driven. The approaches being employed include geographic, offense, and offender focus. Police intervention strategy is now guided by empirical evidence, not hypothetical conjecture on what the police ought to be doing. Frequently, the term "evidence-based" is used to describe this orientation.

REVIEW QUESTIONS

1. How did the events of the 1960s change American policing? Is it likely that there was an interactive effect from the events? Which likely exerted the most profound influence?
2. What can/should an academic discipline contribute to field practice? Why in the United States is academe the driving force for "core" research in both the physical and social sciences?
3. It was noted that in controlling the civil rights and Vietnam protestors in the 1960s, American police did not kill a single protestor. At what point in a civil protest are the police in a free society justified in using physical force? If force is used, what limits should be placed?
4. What guidelines should be placed on the use of differential response (taking a report over the phone or Internet)? How should a caller be handled who insists on having a patrol unit respond even when the trivial nature of the complaint does not justify it?
5. To what phenomenon does the metaphor "broken windows" refer? To what enforcement approach does the metaphor apply? What was dramatic about the change in enforcement approach that is associated with broken windows enforcement?

REAL-WORLD SCENARIOS

1. You are a newly hired police chief in a department serving a jurisdiction of 100,000. Your first task is to determine what strategies your predecessor focused on, and then to decide what strategies you will emphasize during your tenure. How will you proceed? How will history and academic studies inform your approach?
2. Regular patrol units assigned to a beat and responsible for responding to all calls-for-service usually find about 40 percent of their time "uncommitted." As a patrol commander, you are aware that the Kansas City study indicated that random, routine patrol is ineffectual in reducing crime. What activities do you suggest to your officers to do during intermittent uncommitted patrol time that might be more effectual?
3. On the release date of the annual Federal Bureau of Investigation (FBI) Uniform Crime Reports, it was noted that nationally both property and violent crime decreased slightly. In your jurisdiction violent crime was likewise down, but property crime showed a modest increase. You are asked by a reporter why this is the case. Your agency has handled property crime in fundamentally the same way for a number of years. Given this context, how might you respond to the reporter's question?

APPLICATION ACTIVITIES

1. In 2011 and 2012 frustration with unemployment and perceived corporate excesses (particularly executive pay) coalesced into national protests dubbed "Occupy Wall Street." Although interactions with the police in most cities remained civil, some violence did occur. Video of officers with the University of California at Davis using OC spray on peaceful sitting protestors triggered repercussions for both the

agency and the university administration. Research police response to the Occupy Wall Street protests, citing successful and less-than-successful regulation strategies.

2. It was noted that in the late 1960s sociologists "discovered" the complexity of police patrol. It is difficult to sort the range of patrol responsibilities into distinct categories, but one perspective employs three broad responsibilities—law enforcement, conflict management, and public safety. Outline what observations of "what patrol officers do" tell us about the complexity of the role.
3. Although the concept of intelligence-led policing emerged prior to 9/11, the terrorist attacks triggered a vitalization of the concept. Every major U.S. city now has a Joint Terrorism Task Force, led by the FBI but staffed with local officers assigned to the entity. The core role of the Task Forces is intelligence. Review the dynamics of law enforcement intelligence gathering in a democracy, both to combat terrorism and to enhance traditional crime analysis efforts.

COURSEMATE

This available CourseMate has an interactive eBook and interactive learning tools, including flash cards, quizzes, and more. To learn more about this resource and access free demo CourseMate resources, go to **www.cengagebrain.com**, and search for this book. To access CourseMate materials that you have purchased, go to **login.cengagebrain.com**.

REFERENCES

Abrahamse, A. F., & Ebener, P. A. (1991). An experimental evaluation of the Phoenix repeat offender program. *Justice Quarterly, 8*(2), 141–168.

Bartch, F. (1978). Integrating patrol assignments: Directed patrol in Kansas City. In *Review of patrol operations analysis: Selected readings from ICAP cities*. Washington, DC: U.S. Department of Justice, Law Enforcement Assistance Administration.

Bittner, E. (1967). The police on skid row. *American Sociological Review, 32*(5), 699–715.

Bittner, E. (1970). *The functions of police in modern society*. Washington, DC: U.S. Government Printing Office.

Bloch, P. B., & Bell, J. (1976). *Managing investigations: The Rochester system*. Washington, DC: Police Foundation.

Bloch, P. B., & Specht, D. (1973). *Neighborhood team policing*. Washington, DC: U.S. Government Printing Office.

Bloch, P. B., & Weidman, D. R. (1975). *Managing criminal investigations*. Washington, DC: U.S. Department of Justice.

Boydstun, J. E. (1975). *San Diego field interrogation: Final report*. Washington, DC: Police Foundation.

Boydstun, J. E., & Sherry, M. E. (1975). *San Diego community profile: Final report*. Washington, DC: The Police Foundation.

Braga, A. A. (2007). The effects of hot spots policing on crime, a Campbell Collaboration systematic review. Available at http://www.aic.gov.au/campbellcj/reviews/titles.html.

Braga, A. A., Weisburd, D., Waring, E. J., Mazerolle, L. G., Spelman, W., & Gajewski, F. (1999). Problem-oriented policing in violent crime places: A randomized controlled experiment. *Criminology, 37*(3), 541–580.

Brandstatter, A. F., & Radelet, L. A. (1968). *Police and community relations: A sourcebook*. Beverly Hills, CA: Glencoe Press.

Bratton, W., & Knobler, P. (1998). *The turnaround: How America's top cop reversed the crime epidemic*. New York: Random House.

Burrows, J., Lewis, H., Stobart, G., & Tyrer, R. (1988). *Directing patrol work: A study of uniformed policing*. London, UK: Her Majesty's Stationery Office.

Cahn, M. F., & Tien, J. M. (1981). *An alternative approach in police response—Wilmington Management of Demand program*. Washington, DC: U.S. Department of Justice.

Carter, D. L. (1999). *The police and the community*. Upper Saddle River, NJ: Pearson Education, Inc.

Carter, D. L. (2009). *Law enforcement intelligence: A guide for state, local and tribal law enforcement agencies* (2nd ed.). Washington, DC: U.S. Department of Justice, Office of Community Oriented Policing Services.

Cawley, D. F., & Miron, H. J. (1977). *Managing patrol operations—manual*. Washington, DC: U.S. Department of Justice, National Institute of Justice.

Conrad, J. P., & Myren, R. A. (1979). *Two views of criminology and criminal justice: Definitions, trends and the future*. Chicago: University of Illinois at Chicago, Joint Commission on Criminology and Criminal Justice Education and Standards.

Cordner, G. W. (1981). The effects of directed patrol: A natural quasi-experiment in Pontiac. In J. J. Fyfe (Ed.), *Contemporary issues in law enforcement* (pp. 37–58). Beverly Hills, CA: Sage.

Cumming, E., Cumming, I., & Edell, L. (1965). Policeman as philosopher, guide and friend. *Social Problems, 12*, 276–286.

Eck, J. E. (1979). *Managing case assignments: The burglary investigation decision model replication*. Washington, DC: Police Executive Research Forum.

Eck, J. E. (1983). *Solving crimes: The investigation of burglary and robbery*. Washington, DC: Police Executive Research Forum.

Eck, J. E., & Spelman, W. (1987). *Problem-solving: Problem-oriented policing in Newport News*. Washington, DC: Police Executive Research Forum.

Fayol, H. (1949, Originally published 1919). *General and industrial management* (C. Stours, Trans.). London: Pitman.

Fennessy, E. F. (1983). *Police directed patrol—an initial national assessment, June 1983*. Washington, DC: U.S. Department of Justice, National Institute of Justice.

Gay, W. G., Day, H. T., & Woodward, J. P. (1977). *Neighborhood team policing, national evaluation program phase I summary report*. Washington, DC: U.S. Government Printing Office.

Gay, W. G., & Schack, S. (1977). *Improving patrol productivity, volume I—routine patrol*. Washington, DC: U.S. Department of Justice, National Institute of Law Enforcement and Criminal Justice.

Goldstein, H. (1979). Improving policing: A problem-oriented approach. *Crime and Delinquency, 25*, 236–258.

Goldstein, H. (1990). *Problem-oriented policing*. New York: McGraw-Hill, Inc.

Grassie, R. G., Burrows, J. W., White, S. M., & Waymire, R. V. (1978). *Integrated criminal apprehension program: Manual for the design and implementation of training*. Washington, DC: U.S. Department of Justice, Law Enforcement Assistance Administration.

Greene, J. R., & Mastrofski, S. D. (Eds.). (1988). *Community policing: Rhetoric or reality*. New York: Praeger.

Greene, J. R., & Taylor, R. (1988). Community based policing and foot patrol: Issues of theory and evaluation. In J. R. Greene & S. D. Mastrofski (Eds.), *Community policing: Rhetoric or reality?* New York: Praeger Press.

Greenwood, P., & Petersilia, J. (1975). *The criminal investigation process—volume I: Summary and policy implications*. Santa Monica, CA: RAND Corp.

Gulick, L. H., & Urwick, L. F. (Eds.). (1937). *Papers on the science of administration*. New York: Columbia University, Institute of Public Administration.

Halper, A., & Ku, R. (1974). *New York City Police Department street crime unit: An exemplary project*. Washington, DC: U.S. Department of Justice, Law Enforcement Assistance Administration.

Hoover, L. T. (1975). *Police educational characteristics and curricula*. Washington, DC: U.S. Government Printing Office.

Hoover, L. T., & Caeti, T. J. (1994). *Crime specific policing in Houston* (Vol. 1). Huntsville, TX: Sam Houston State University. Available at http://www.lemitonline.org/telemasp/index.php#by_volume%201/vol1no9.pdf).

Hoover, L. T., & Lund, D. W. (1977). *Guidelines for criminal justice programs in community and junior colleges*. Washington, DC: American Association of Community and Junior Colleges.

Hornick, J. P., Burrows, B. A., Tjosvold, I., & Phillips, D. M. (1990). *An evaluation of the neighbourhood foot patrol program of Edmonton Police Service*. Edmonton, Canada: Canadian Research Institute of Law and the Family.

Institute of Judicial Administration. (1973). *Standards relating to the urban police function: Project on standards for criminal justice*. New York: American Bar Association.

Jang, H. S., Hoover, L. T., & Joo, H. J. (2010). An evaluation of Compstat's effect upon crime: The Fort Worth experience. *Police Quarterly, 13*(4).

Kansas City Police Department. (1978). *Response time analysis: Executive summary*. Washington, DC: U.S. Department of Justice.

Kelling, G. L. (1981). *The Newark foot patrol experiment*. Washington, DC: Police Foundation.

Kelling, G. L., & Coles, C. M. (1996). *Fixing broken windows: Restoring order and reducing crime in our communities*. New York: Free Press.

Kelling, G. L., Pate, T., Dieckman, D., & Brown, C. E. (1974). *The Kansas City preventive patrol experiment: A summary report*. Washington, DC: Police Foundation.

Koper, C. S. (1995). Just enough police presence: Reducing crime and disorderly behavior by optimizing patrol time in crime hot spots. *Justice Quarterly, 12*(4), 649–671.

Kuhn, T. S. (1996). *The structure of scientific revolutions* (3rd ed.). Chicago: University of Chicago Press.

LaFave, W. (1965). *Arrest: The decision to take a suspect into custody*. Boston: Little, Brown and Company.

Larson, R. C., & Cahn, M. F. (1981). *Synthesizing and extending the results of police patrol studies*. Washington, DC: U.S. Department of Justice, National Institute of Justice.

Levitt, S. D. (2004). Understanding why crime fell in the 1990s: Four factors that explain the decline and six that do not. *Journal of Economic Perspectives, 18*(1), 163–190.

Lum, C., Koper, C. S., & Telep, C. W. (2010). The evidence-based policing matrix. *Journal of Experimental Criminology, 7*, 3–26.

Maguire, M. (2000). Policing by risks and targets: Some dimensions and implications of intelligence-led crime control. *Policing and Society: An International Journal of Research and Policy, 9*(4), 315–336.

Manning, P. K. (1971). The police: Mandate, strategies and appearances. In J. D. Douglas (Ed.), *Crime and justice in America*. Indianapolis: Bobbs, Merrill.

Manning, P. K. (1972). Observing the police: Deviants, respectables and the law. In J. D. Douglas (Ed.), *Research on deviance* (pp. 213–268). New York: Random House.

Manning, P. K. (1977). *Police work*. Cambridge, MA: MIT Press.

Maple, J., & Mitchell, C. (1999). *The crime fighter*. New York: Doubleday.

Martin, S. E., & Sherman, L. W. (1986). *Catching career criminals: The Washington, D.C., repeat offender project*. Washington, DC: Police Foundation.

McEwen, J. T., Connors, E. F., & Cohen, M. I. (1986). *Evaluation of the differential police response field test*. Alexandria, VA: Research Management Associates, Inc.

McNamara, J. H. (1967). Uncertainties in police work: The relevance of police recruits' backgrounds and training. In D. J. Bordua (Ed.), *The police: Six sociological essays* (pp. 163–252). New York: John Wiley and Sons.

National Advisory Commission on Civil Disorders. (1968). *Report*. New York: Bantam Books.

National Advisory Commission on Criminal Justice Standards and Goals. (1973). *Report on police*. Washington, DC: U.S. Government Printing Office.

Niederhoffer, A. (1969). *Behind the shield: Police in urban society*. New York: Anchor Books.

Novak, K. J., Hartman, J. L., Holsinger, A. M., & Turner, M. G. (1999). The effects of aggressive policing of disorder on serious crime. *Policing: An International Journal of Police Strategies and Management, 22*(2), 171–190.

Pasciuto, A., et al. (1978). *Managing patrol operations—program test design*. Washington, DC: U.S. Department of Justice, National Institute of Law Enforcement and Criminal Justice.

Pate, T., Bowers, R. A., & Parks, R. (1976). *Three approaches to criminal apprehension in Kansas City: An evaluation report*. Washington, DC: Police Foundation.

President's Commission on Campus Unrest. (1971). *The report of the President's Commission on Campus Unrest*. New York: Avon Books.

President's Commission on Law Enforcement and Administration of Justice. (1967). *The challenge of crime in a free society*. Washington, DC: U.S. Government Printing Office.

Public Safety Research Institute. (1975). *Full-service neighborhood team policing: Planning for implementation*. St. Petersburg, FL: Public Safety Research Institute Inc.

Radelet, L. A. (1973). *The police and the community* (1st ed.). Encino, CA: Glencoe Press.

Ratcliffe, J. H. (2007). *Integrated intelligence and crime analysis: Enhanced information management for law enforcement leaders*. Washington, DC: U.S. Department of Justice, Police Foundation and Office of Community Oriented Policing Services.

Ratcliffe, J. H., Groff, E., Wood, J., Taniguchi, T., Johnson, L., McGuire-Taylor, C., et al. (2010). *The Philadelphia foot patrol experiment: Research brief*. Philadelphia: Temple University and Philadelphia Police Department.

Reiss Jr., A. J. (1971). *The police and the public*. New Haven: Yale University Press.

Sampson, R., & Cohen, J. (1988). Deterrent effects of the police on crime: A replication and theoretical extension. *Law and Society Review, 22*, 163–189.

Saunders Jr., C. B. (1970). *Upgrading the American police*. Washington, DC: The Brookings Institution.

Schack, S., & Gay, W. G. (1977). *Improving patrol productivity, volume II—specialized patrol*. Washington, DC: U.S. Department of Justice, National Institute of Law Enforcement and Criminal Justice.

Sherman, L. W. (1978). *The quality of police education*. San Francisco: Jossey-Bass.

Sherman, L. W. (1990). Police crackdowns: Initial and residual deterrence. In M. Tonry & N. Morris (Eds.), *Crime and justice: An annual review of research* (Vol. 12). Chicago: University of Chicago Press.

Sherman, L. W., & Berk, R. A. (1984). *The Minneapolis domestic violence experiment*. Washington, DC: Police Foundation.

Sherman, L. W., Gartin, P. R., & Buerger, M. E. (1989). Hot spots of predatory crime: Routine activities and the criminology of place. *Criminology, 27*(1), 27–56.

Sherman, L. W., & Milton, C. H. (1973). *Team policing—seven case studies*. Washington, DC: Police Foundation.

Sherman, L. W., Shaw, J. W., & Regan, D. P. (1995). *The Kansas City gun experiment*. Washington, DC: National Institute of Justice.

Sherman, L. W., & Weisburd, D. (1995). General deterrent effects of police patrol in crime "hot spots": A randomized, controlled trial. *Justice Quarterly, 12*(4), 625–648.

Silverman, E. B. (1999). *NYPD battles crime: Innovative strategies in policing*. Boston, MA: Northeastern University Press.

Skolnick, J. H. (1966). *Justice without trial: Law enforcement in a democratic society*. New York: John Wiley and Sons.

Sparrow, M. K., Moore, M., & Kennedy, D. M. (1992). *Beyond 911: A new era for policing*. New York: Basic Books.

Sumrall, R. O., Roberts, J., & Farmer, M. T. (1981). *Differential police response strategies*. Washington, DC: Police Executive Research Forum.

Tenney Jr., C. W. (1971). *Higher education programs in law enforcement and criminal justice*. Washington, DC: U.S. Government Printing Office.

Tien, J., Simaon, J., & Larson, R. (1978). *An alternative approach in police patrol: The Wilmington split-force experiment*. Washington, DC: U.S. Government Printing Office.

Trojanowicz, R. (1982). *An evaluation of the neighborhood foot patrol program in Flint, Michigan*. East Lansing, MI: Michigan State University.

Trojanowicz, R., & Bucqueroux, B. (1990). *Community policing: A contemporary perspective*. Cincinnati, OH: Anderson Publishing Co.

Urwick, L. F. (1944). *Elements of administration*. New York: Harper.

Ward, R. H., & Webb, V. J. (1984). *Quest for quality*. New York: University Publications.

Warren, J., Forst, M., & Estrella, M. (1979). Directed patrol: An experiment that worked. *The Police Chief, 48*, 78.

Webb, K. W. (1977). *Specialized patrol projects, phase 1: Summary report*. Washington, DC: U.S. Department of Justice, National Institute of Law Enforcement and Criminal Justice.

Weisburd, D. (2005). Hot spots policing experiments and criminal justice research: Lessons from the field. *Annals of the American Academy of Political and Social Science, 599*(5), 220–245.

Weisburd, D., & Green, L. (1995). Policing drug hot spots: The Jersey City drug market analysis experiment. *Justice Quarterly, 12*(4), 711–734.

Wilson, J. Q. (1968). *Varieties of police behavior: The management of law and order in eight communities*. Cambridge, MA: Harvard University Press.

Wilson, J. Q. (1978). *The investigators: Managing FBI and narcotic agents*. New York: Basic Books.

Wilson, J. Q., & Boland, B. (1978). The effect of police on crime. *Law and Society Review, 12*(3), 367–390.

Wilson, J. Q., & Kelling, G. L. (March 1982). Broken windows: The police and neighborhood safety. *Atlantic, 249*, 29–38.

Wilson, O. W. (1950). *Police administration*. New York: McGraw-Hill.

Worden, R. E. (1993). Toward equity and efficiency in law enforcement: Differential police response. *American Journal of Police, 12*(1), 1–32.

Zimring, F. E. (2007). *The great American crime decline*. New York: Oxford University Press.

CHAPTER 2

The Police Effect on Crime

© Michael Matthews–Police Images/Alamy

Given two communities with exactly the same demographics, one policed by the worst agency in the country while the other is policed by the best, what will be the difference in crime rates? We simply do not know. This chapter reviews the evidence that does exist regarding the impact of the police upon crime. But it must be understood at the outset that there is far more that we do not know than what we do know. There is a wealth of anecdotal evidence—single case studies—indicating that police make a substantial difference. There are a handful of experimental designs testing a particular police strategy, for example, problem-oriented approaches or hot spot saturation, which indicate that at the very least the police make a measurable difference. But to paraphrase the findings of Robert Martinson (1975) in his review of correctional treatment interventions, *no prevailing mode of law enforcement intervention has demonstrated a substantial and enduring impact upon crime rates*. It must be emphasized that the assertion is a commentary on the lack of sustained research, not a characterization of potential police effectiveness.

KEY TERMS

CPTED
General deterrence
Incapacitation
Random routine preventative patrol
Reintegration
Specific deterrence

LEARNING OBJECTIVES

After completing this chapter, you should be able to:

- Characterize our state of knowledge of police impact upon crime.
- Describe why there has been pessimism regarding the potential of police impact upon crime.
- Identify the strategic approach with the most evidence for effectiveness.
- Identify the two cities where considerable drops in crime were likely produced by dramatically increased enforcement activity.
- Identify the city where cessation of police enforcement immediately resulted in a surge in crime.
- Describe the conclusions that can be drawn from the Kansas City Preventive Patrol Experiment.
- Describe the conclusions that can be drawn from the San Diego Field Interrogation Experiment.
- Identify the intervention suggested by the Minneapolis Domestic Violence Experiment.
- Cite the evidence for the clustering of crime in hot spots.
- Explain why the results of the Indianapolis Directed Patrol Program are perplexing.
- List what we do *not* know regarding place-based extra patrol deployment (hot spot saturation).

Learning Objective

This chapter reviews the evidence regarding the effect of the police on crime. Conceptually, the underlying premise is that indeed the police make a difference. In some cases, police intervention can make a substantial difference. Most scholars attribute at least some of the crime drop since 1992 to innovative, crime-focused police strategies. Indeed, we have come to recognize that focused efforts make far more of a difference than vaguely conceived and diffused interventions. Early research indicating that neither traditional patrol nor investigations had substantial impact on crime ushered in an era of experimentation. Evolving out of this era were the community policing and problem-oriented approaches. Later, the success of the New York City Police Department with its Compstat strategy led to the current popularity of hot spot concentrated deployment.

Do the Police Make a Difference?

It is simply illogical to assert that the police make no difference at all. It is an unfortunate commentary on human nature that looting almost always accompanies natural disasters. When a portion of the public knows or perceives that the police are unable to respond, crime runs rampant. One of the reasons we routinely mobilize the National Guard during natural disasters is to maintain order. Does anyone doubt that if one of the five area commands of Chicago were to simply shut down that criminal gangs would very quickly take over that area? From a different perspective, think of a police agency shutting down its detective division. Although the efficacy of investigative divisions in clearing unknown suspect cases has been questioned (Greenwood & Petersilia, 1975), no one suggests that it is a waste of time for detectives to prepare cases with known suspects for prosecution. Without that preparation, a high proportion of offenses would simply be dismissed. Again, the question is not whether the police make a difference, but how much difference.

Learning Objective

Incredibly there was an era when numerous criminologists asserted that police make no difference. In its more logical form, the myth asserted that the difference in crime rates in a community policed by the worst agency and one policed by the best was miniscule. The myth was born of two phenomena: (1) the fact that variation in police/citizen ratios across the United States does not appear to correlate with differences in crime rates, and (2) the double-barreled impact of the Kansas City Preventive Patrol Experiment (Kelling, Pate, Dieckman, & Brown, 1974) and the RAND Criminal Investigation Report (Greenwood & Petersilia, 1975).

The issue of police/citizen ratios is discussed more thoroughly in Chapter 12, Staffing for Crime Control. What needs to be noted here is that ratios do indeed vary substantially across the United States. East Coast and upper Midwest cities typically have police/citizen ratios exceeding 3.5 officers per thousand populations. As one moves across the country in a diagonal line from Bangor, Maine, to San Diego, California, ratios decrease. By the time one gets to the country's midsection, ratios are down to 2.5 per thousand, and in the Southwest and California typical major cities' ratios drop as low as 1.7 per thousand. There are several reasons for this phenomenon. It is generally accepted that densely populated vertical cities, such as those on the East Coast, require more officers. Density of populations equates to greater regulatory needs. Second, it has generally been the case that East Coast and Midwest cities expect a broader range of functions from their police agencies. Third, placing two officers in every patrol car is a more widespread practice in the East—due to, at least partially, the strong influence of police unions in that part of the country. In addition to these tangible phenomena it is also possible that there is a more abstract confusing factor. If more crime leads communities to hire more police, then it will be difficult to statistically establish that more police will cause less crime. In the macro picture, as crime decreases, communities may decrease the size of their police departments—witness the reduction in recent years in the number of officers in the New York City Police Department. When crime begins to climb again, more police will be hired.

So we have three tangible factors and one abstract argument that explains, or at least helps explain, why we do not find an immediate obvious statistical inverse correlation between the number of officers and the amount of crime. Keep in mind as well the necessity to compare the statistics only among similarly constituted jurisdictions. Running statistical correlations between officer/citizen ratios and crime rates that compare central cities to suburbs is invalid on its face. Suburbs always have less crime and they concurrently have fewer officers.

We then get to the question of what is a similarly constituted city: Can Boston be compared to San Diego? Can Philadelphia be compared to Los Angeles? The relationship between police/citizen ratios and crime rates is more complex than it might seem on the surface.

The second source of the myth that police make no difference is the results of two of the earliest efforts to measure the effectiveness of police strategy—the Kansas City Preventive Patrol Experiment and the RAND Criminal Investigation Study. What we do know about the effectiveness of various police approaches to reduce crime can be captured in a single word: targeted. Crime-specific strategies are targeted strategies, targeting specific offenses committed by specific types of offenders at specific times and places. The antithesis of this approach is best captured by a phrase that emanated from New York City during the early days of Compstat: random patrol produces random results. As described in Chapter 5, The mixture of targeting and tactics produces ten commonly employed approaches to crime control/reduction.

There is consistently accumulating evidence that focused police efforts to reduce particular crimes committed by particular offenders at particular times and places are effective. In this chapter, we refer to such approaches as *crime-specific strategies.* The vast majority of controlled experiments entailing crime-specific interventions have yielded positive results; that is, crime went down. In other words, when the police concentrate resources on a particular crime, the incidence of that crime drops.

Several well-known "legacy" studies, reviewed later in this chapter, illustrate the point. The San Diego Field Interrogation Experiment (Boydstun, 1975) demonstrated the efficacy of proactive stop-and-question techniques. Eck and Spelman's (1987) evaluation of problem-oriented techniques in Newport News, Virginia, launched an approach almost universally regarded as having the potential not only to reduce calls-for-service, but also to reduce crime. The Minneapolis (Minnesota) Recap Experiment (Sherman, Gartin, & Buerger, 1989) confirmed the short-term effect of problem-oriented approaches directed toward problem locations. The Kansas City Gun Reduction Experiment (Sherman, Shaw, & Regan, 1995) illustrated the effectiveness of focusing street enforcement on a specific problem. Indeed, perhaps more than any other research study conducted prior to the year 2000, the 1993 Kansas City Gun Reduction Experiment demonstrated the very narrow effect of a particular police strategy. One might reasonably expect that with additional units aggressively patrolling target areas, overall crime in those areas would drop. But while there was a very dramatic effect on the targeted gun crimes in the Kansas City targeted beat, there was no measurable impact on other offenses. Police efforts targeted at particular offenders committing particular crimes produced results in the Kansas City Gun Reduction Experiment, as it did in more recent hot spot deployments. But unfocused strategies have produced few results.

Learning Objective

Crime Rates Since 1992

In the United States, we now find ourselves in the midst of a historically unprecedented drop in crime rates. From 1992 to the present every type of crime has decreased dramatically. Since 2000 crime rates have leveled, but still continue on a downward slope. Granted, there is some unevenness. Although crime has dropped precipitously in some cities, it has actually increased in a few others. But the exceptions are indeed few. There are five possible explanations for the decrease:

Social-Demographic Trends. Criminologists generally regard social-demographic trends as the strongest influence on crime rates—more important than structured social response (police/courts/corrections). A high proportion of fourteen- to twenty-five-year-olds equals a high overall crime rate. Factors such as migration patterns also influence crime. Mobile, disrupted groups tend to commit more crimes than settled, stable groups.

Economic Conditions. The economy is recognized as influencing the rate of both violent and property crime. Extreme economic stress, for example, breeds social violence, particularly spouse abuse. Obviously, property crime is likewise influenced by changing economic conditions. However, the relationship is not necessarily a straightforward one. Property crime may increase in an improving economy, particularly if increases in wealth are unevenly distributed.

Drug Use Prevalence. Crime is linked in complicated ways to the supply of illicit drugs. Scarce supplies raise street prices, potentially increasing crime, but may also mean fewer users, thus decreasing crime. Drug supply and drug use prevalence interact.

incapacitation
The inability of confined offenders to commit additional offenses as a result of simply being locked up.

reintegration
Processes involved in an offender reestablishing a legitimate role in the community.

Incarceration Rates. In the late 1980s and early 1990s, states built new prisons at record rates. The most obvious effect is **incapacitation**—the inability of confined offenders to commit additional offenses as a result of simply being locked up. We wish that **reintegration** success—improved rates of offenders reestablishing a legitimate role in the community—might have had an influence. However, simple incapacitation appears, at least on the surface, to offer one of the best explanations for decreasing street crime.

Police Programs. Decreases in crime have not been evenly distributed. Where agencies have implemented aggressive intervention styles, crime has dropped precipitously. Clearly, the police make a difference.

There is no way to determine the relative contribution of these factors to the current downward trend. However, one may certainly argue that of the five, two have had the greatest effect—incarceration rates and police programs. A review of the issue in 2010 by *Time Magazine*, "Why Crime Went Away," focused upon these two explanations—referring to them as "The Lockup Factor" and the "Data Processing Factor" (von Drehle, 2010). The impact of law enforcement was referred to as a revolution—premised upon crime analysis driven by Compstat. The other factors tend to have longer-term effects on crime rates. James Q. Wilson argued as well for several converging effects, primary among them were incarceration rates and proactive policing (J. Q. Wilson, 2011). Wilson suggested as well that an immeasurable change in culture may account for a significant part of the crime rate decline.

When crime drops in a particular city by 30 percent in one year, it is not likely that changes in demographics are the explanation. And indeed, there have been no dramatic shifts in the nation's demographics since the start of the decline in 1992. Although the median age increased from thirty-two in 1990 to thirty-six in 2010, with a hypothetical decrease in the proportion of the population in the crime-prone youthful years, nonetheless, the crime rate within the juvenile segment of the population is the lowest in twenty years (von Drehle, 2010). Changes in economic conditions also do not appear to have had a dramatic effect. With the exception of two or three mild recessions, the nation experienced slow but steady economic growth from 1970 until the onset of recession in 2008. Unemployment rates varied during that period within a range of 2 percent. In fact, if one were to look to economics for any type of explanation, one might argue that changes in the distribution of wealth in the 1990s would beget more crime, not the drop in crime that occurred. Further, crime did not increase with the economic downturn, labeled the "Great Recession," which started in 2008 (J. Q. Wilson, 2011). Indeed crime has continued its gradual downward slope.

Like trends in demographics and economics, trends in drug use do not offer any apparent explanation for the decrease in crime. Although the use of some drugs decreased in the late 1980s and early 1990s, the use of others remained steady. Further, in the mid-1990s, drug experimentation surveys of high school students indicated increases in use, or at least in experimentation. Statistics on drug seizures indicated that trafficking continued unabated. The war on drugs has not caused the dramatic decreases in crime.

Unlike demographics, economics, and drug use prevalence, incarceration rates should be considered as a possible explanation for the drop in crime. Over the past twenty-five years, prison capacity has increased dramatically; the incarceration rate rose from 300/100,000 in 1990 to over 500/100,000 in 2010 (Bureau of Justice Statistics, 2010). Fed up with persistent high crime rates, the public has demanded that chronic offenders, particularly violent offenders, be locked up for long periods. Thus, a prison building boom has accompanied changes in sentencing laws. We have no way of knowing the relative import of incarceration in terms of **general deterrence** (the propensity of the general public to obey the law out of fear of punishment) versus **specific deterrence** (the propensity of a particular potential offender to obey the law out of fear of punishment) versus incapacitation, but incapacitation is the most evident. And the effect is undoubtedly substantial.

general deterrence
The propensity of the general public to obey the law out of fear of punishment.

specific deterrence
The propensity of a particular potential offender to obey the law out of fear of punishment.

The Police and the Drop in Crime

Learning Objective

Although there is uncertainty over what caused the crime drop in the 1990s, many police executives, police scholars, and laypeople looked to new policing practices as a primary explanation (Weisburd & Eck, 2004). Although focused or targeted enforcement produces the best results, we nevertheless must be cautious about dismissing broad proactive arrest efforts. Dramatically increased enforcement activity in Houston and New York City in the early 1990s produced considerable drops in crime. The most likely explanation is that the effectiveness of particular police strategies depends on environmental circumstances. When enforcement is lacking for long periods and there is a sudden and dramatic turnaround in general enforcement effort, results are measurable. To better understand the effect of police enforcement "turnarounds," this author and the late Tory Caeti compared the sharp drop in crime in Houston in 1992 with crime rate changes in other major Texas cities. While crime was declining in all of the state's major cities, as it was nationally, a sudden and dramatic drop in crime occurred only in Houston. This drop correlated month by month with dramatically increased arrests (Hoover & Caeti, 1994).

The argument that most of the drop in crime in Houston was the product of police agency proactivity was bolstered by a similar drop in New York City two years later. Like Houston, New York elected a new mayor who brought in a new Police Chief determined to use different approaches to crime. As in Houston, both the mayor and the Police Chief dismissed the fluff elements of community policing. Instead, they mandated that precinct commanders take personal responsibility for crime rates in their area. In turn, commanders ordered patrol officers to make arrests. In New York, long-standing policies prohibiting patrol officers from enforcing vice and narcotic offenses were lifted (those policies were meant to control corruption at the beat level). Crime started dropping immediately (Walsh, 2001).

College students are taught in their first research methods class that correlation does not equal cause and effect. Indeed, instructors usually go out of their way to find historical accounts of the misinterpretation of correlation as cause and effect. The experimental design is, of course, offered as the ultimate solution to isolating cause and effect from correlation. Unfortunately, many criminologists who have spent their careers cautioning undergraduates about this phenomenon have allowed their own perspective to become distorted. They can no longer accept obvious links between phenomena in the real world. Absent an experimental design, nothing is accepted as causal. It is true that we can always find absurd examples of correlation. The viscosity of asphalt on a given day in a beach community correlates with the number of drownings. Obviously, there is no cause-and-effect linkage between these phenomena—more people swim on a warm day. But the link between increasing enforcement efforts and a drop in crime is not *prima facie* absurd; indeed, it is *prima facie* logical. And when a major city dramatically increases enforcement efforts, and the crime rate immediately drops precipitously, it is illogical to dismiss the relationship as spurious.

In addition to Houston and New York City, there was Chicago in 2004. The Chicago Police Department launched an intensive and innovative crime-reduction effort focused upon homicide reduction. The city had the dubious distinction of being labeled the "Homicide Capital of the World" by the local news media. Nearly 600 homicides in 2003 did indeed place Chicago at the top of major American cities (although homicides peaked in Chicago in 1992 at 943.) To reduce the rate, the Chicago Police Department launched an array of interventions. Most were intended to reduce the prevalence of drug distribution and gang influence. The number of homicides decreased to an average of 450 annually—a 25 percent reduction.

Supporting the program initiatives listed in Table 2.1 was a Deployment Operations Center (DOC) responsible for gathering and analyzing information needed for deployment, and mobile response teams, such as the Targeted Response Unit (TRU) and Area Narcotics Enforcement Teams (ANET). The department consolidated some units to get more officers on the street; increased the number of narcotics officers working the streets, and reinstituted and doubled the size of the gang intelligence unit to gather better information (Rosenbaum & Stephens, 2005).

The Chicago Police Department also implemented its own form of a Compstat Crime Reduction Strategy meeting, VISE (Violence Initiative Strategy Evaluation)—a form of a management accountability process that focused just on public violence. VISE meetings involved rotating presentations by the

TABLE 2.1 Chicago Police Department (CPD) Crime-Reduction Initiatives in 2004

1. **Police Observation Devices (PODs)**
   Chicago broke new ground in the United States with the deployment of 20 outdoor surveillance cameras at high-crime locations in the fall of 2003. Since their deployment, innumerable American police agencies have replicated Chicago's effort. Additionally, at the insistence of Chicago residents, camera deployment has been expanded significantly in the city.

2. **Roadside Safety Checks**
   The Chicago Police Department established roadside "pull-over" check lanes at stipulated locations. The check lanes were in place to check seat-belt use and driving under the influence (DUI) status. However, the Roadside Safety Checks were placed at strategic locations also designed to intercept vehicle transport of drugs from one neighborhood to another. Vehicles attempting to evade the check lanes (turnarounds) were particularly targeted.

3. **Neighborhood-Focused Crackdowns (Back to School, Spring Cleaning)**
   Classic neighborhood saturation efforts, Back to School, and Spring Cleaning, were focused upon blighted residential areas in which extensive drug sales were conducted, and gang control of the streets was pervasive. CPD would pick one district of each (several miles square)-south and west. The multi-agency effort included intensive parole compliance checks, increased warrant checks, and fugitive apprehension coordinated with narcotics, gangs, and tactical. Other city departments were involved in follow-up neighborhood clean-ups, including sanitation, streets, and parks.

4. **Street Corner Conspiracies**
   A fresh approach to control of open-air drug markets, the Street Corner Conspiracy effort combined several intervention tactics. Concealed camera surveillance established the sale pattern, including the identification of sellers. Second, buys were made-but arrests deferred. Finally, numerous arrests were made on-site after irrefutable evidence of sales was achieved and "area" distributors identified. An important component was linking the cases in court. Defendants were charged with criminal drug conspiracy, with a six-year minimum sentence (three years after good time, parole). An exception to the hearsay rule for conspiracy allowed statements by one defendant to be used against others. About 90 percent of sale cases ended in pleas. Coordinated flow of intervention: Street Corner Conspiracy → Reverse Sting → Saturation Patrol → Camera → Neighborhood Revitalization.

5. **Reverse Narcotics Sale Stings**
   Following completion of a Street Corner Conspiracy, undercover Chicago police officers were immediately substituted for the arrested sellers. They continued feigned sales for one day, arresting buyers. Buyers were charged with "attempted possession of a controlled substance." If the buyer lived in a suburban community, the chief of police of that community was notified of the arrest.

(continues)

TABLE 2.1 (*Continued*)

6. **Parole Restrictions (Operation Windy City)**
   Operation Windy City entailed the establishment of a close working relationship with the Illinois Department of Corrections. It included notification of the CPD when gang members involved in drug trafficking were released from imprisonment to parole. Notorious gang members were sometimes placed under surveillance by the police department. Another program element was the imposition of a parole condition by the board that prohibited the parolee from being in areas of the city where the parolee had previously engaged in drug distribution or gang activity. Through both surveillance of gang leaders and vigorous field interviews, parolees found violating this condition were returned to the penitentiary system. Additionally, CPD accompanied parole officers on house visits. Finally, the Illinois Department of Corrections provided CPD with lists of parolees living in areas experiencing intensified problems. Area Command gang personnel conducted debriefings of the parolees for information on active offenders and gang conflict.
7. **Main 21/Area Top Ten**
   The Chicago Police Department divides the city into five Area Commands. The five Area Commands subsume twenty-five Districts. Chicago's version of the FBI's Most Wanted list, the Main 21/Area Top Ten program, involved identification of the city's "worst" offenders citywide—generally powerful gang members immersed in drug distribution. Each Area Command generated a "Top Ten" list. The worst of these were moved to the citywide Main 21 list. The program enlisted the support of other local law enforcement agencies, the Department of Corrections, and several federal law enforcement agencies. Monthly meetings were employed to track the combined agency effort to "make a case" against Main 21 offenders.
8. **Retaliatory Homicide Intervention**
   A killing of one gang member by a rival gang almost always begets a retaliatory effort by the offended gang. To attempt to reduce the prevalence of retaliatory killings (driving much of the high homicide rate), the department made a special saturation effort to identify and arrest the original perpetrator. An especially successful approach was intense efforts at buy/busts in affected neighborhoods. Arrested sellers were then "squeezed" for information about the murder. Area drug dealers almost always knew who had done the killing and why—usually dispute over control of drug distribution locations.
9. **Targeted Response Unit**
   A Targeted Response Unit was available for rapid deployment anywhere in the city to hot spot areas. Consisting of 240 officers assigned to one of three "companies," the units employed a variety of intervention strategies targeting high-crime locations—termed "level-two deployment areas" by the department. The Deployment Operations Center determined where to deploy. All were deployed in uniform, with marked cars.

10. Intense Field Interview

The CPD employed intensive field interviews (FIs) in conjunction with several of its street-level strategies. Targeted Response Units were expected to conduct numerous FIs. The neighborhood crackdowns entailed extensive street stops designed to interdict or at least disrupt drug distribution. The Roadside Safety Checks were essentially structured but random FIs. Regular patrol units were provided extensive suspect information with the expectation that they would conduct numerous FIs to attempt to apprehend gang members with drugs or weapons.

Crime Control Deployment Resources:

Each of the five areas had about five districts, plus two downtown districts.
Each area had saturation teams in uniform, marked cars.
Each area had a gun team-focused upon gun distribution.
Each area had a gang intelligence unit. Assigned under narcotics to eliminate conflict.
Each district had three tactical teams-one assigned days (9–5 or 10–6), one evenings (6–2), and one as relief so there was always a tactical team on duty. One sergeant, 10 members.
Additionally, each district had two gang teams-limited to gang-related issues. Gang teams could be pulled from assigned district to other assignments by area commanders.

Source: From *Making Chicago the Safest Big City in America* (2007). Reproduced with permission of the Chicago Police Department. Supplemented by personal correspondence with Philip J. Cline, retired Superintendent of the Chicago Police Department.

commanders of all of the districts in one of the five police areas, plus their area deputy chief. These one-hour review sessions closely examined trends in specific crimes, including district homicides, aggravated battery with firearms, and other public violence involving the use of firearms (Rosenbaum & Stephens,.2005). The VISE meetings' focus was typically confined to the four-week period prior to the meeting—a classic Compstat model. The immediate 25 percent reduction in homicides—an offense typically regarded as beyond the influence of police crime suppression—strongly reinforces the theme of this chapter: The police can make a difference in crime rates.

Is there evidence in the opposite direction—that police cessation of enforcement begets more crime? Yes—overwhelming evidence from a city better known for being misspelled, Cincinnati, Ohio. In 2000–2001 there was a series of police shootings of Black males with tension mounting. On April 7, 2001 an officer shot and killed an unarmed African-American youth. News of the young man's death set off three days of rioting, in which arson, looting, property destruction, and shooting took place. The riots brought heavy media attention to the Cincinnati Police Department. In May 2001, the U.S. Department of Justice began a civil rights investigation of the department, and the shooting officer was indicted with criminal charges. These events caused an abrupt and large increase in the perceived cost for officers of committing another error (Shi, 2009). Monthly misdemeanor arrests decreased by 42 percent after April 2001. There was a clear surge in felony offenses in the months after April 2001. Post-riot violent crime increased by 38 percent compared with that before November 2000. Property crime increased by 22 percent (Shi, 2009, p. 109). When proactive enforcement stops, crime surges.

Learning Objective

What we do not know is "how many police make how much difference." Weisburd and Eck (2004) note: ". . . removing all police will lead to more crime does not answer the primary question that most scholars and policy makers are concerned with—that is, whether marginal increases in the number of police officers will lead to reductions in crime, disorder, or fear" (p. 49).

An analogous international problem may be relevant here. The 1990s saw a different kind of violence in Bosnia. In an effort to stop the killing, United Nations (UN) troops were dispatched. However, commanders were hamstrung—ordered not to use force unless in immediate danger. The killing went on. Finally, fed up with the genocide, NATO took over—dispatching troops with orders to shoot to stop the killing. And the killing stopped. It is perhaps stretching the point a long way, but the parallel between crime in major U.S. cities and the situation in Bosnia is striking. When the police are merely present, but passive, crime continues. When the police suddenly and decisively change their approach to one of proactive intervention, crime starts dropping.

Our Research Legacy: A Brief Synopsis Pre-2000

Summarized in this section are the major experimental or quasi-experimental strategy evaluation efforts conducted prior to the year 2000. More recent research is described in the next section and subsequent chapters. Not all research conducted prior to 2000 is described here. Selected for review are those studies that made "original" contributions, are frequently cited, and are directly relevant to control of suppressible street crime. They are reviewed together here, rather than scattered among various chapters, in order to provide perspective on the baseline upon which we now build.

KANSAS CITY PREVENTIVE PATROL EXPERIMENT

The granddaddy of all police research is the Police Foundation's Kansas City Preventive Patrol Experiment (Kelling et al., 1974). Conducted in Kansas City from 1972 to 1973, the research is also the most frequently misinterpreted. To understand this misinterpretation, a quick review of the research design is necessary. The south patrol district contained 15 beats. Five of these beats were designated as controls, where the level of routine preventive patrol for a year was to remain constant with past practice. Five of the beats were designated reactive. On these beats, patrol units would enter to handle calls-for-service, then immediately leave. In effect, routine preventive patrol was withdrawn. Five of the beats were designated proactive. The patrol units from the reactive beats were instructed to conduct routine preventive patrol in the proactive beats, in effect doubling the amount of patrol in these areas. Moreover, additional patrol officers were assigned to the south district, such that the patrol level on the proactive beats was two to three times what it had been. Everyone in the police field knows the results. Over the course of a year, no change was detected in reported crime, crime as measured by victimization surveys, citizen satisfaction with the police, or several other measures. Researchers, chief among them George Kelling, appropriately and conservatively concluded that routine preventive patrol as practiced in Kansas City had no effect on crime (Kelling et al., 1974). Unfortunately, the very conservative conclusions drawn were inappropriately and grossly overgeneralized in subsequent years. The conservative conclusion that *routine preventive patrol within the limits tested in Kansas City has no measurable effect on crime* became *the police don't make a difference.*

To fully appreciate just how wrong such an overgeneralization is, one must carefully consider what was tested in Kansas City. In 1972, routine preventive patrol was not a sharp, focused tactic. Typically, in urban areas, between 40 percent and 60 percent of patrol time is uncommitted (as opposed to committed to responding to calls-for-service). Analysis in several jurisdictions indicates that of the uncommitted patrol time, only about half is spent cruising through a beat. The other half is spent on administrative matters or breaks. Thus, for a typical beat, about two hours out of every eight are spent on nondirected cruising. This was the case in Kansas City.

There could not be a more generic approach to policing than **random routine preventive patrol**. The individual patrol officer decides what merits attention. If an officer likes to engage in traffic enforcement, or is under pressure to do so, then that will occupy a substantial portion of routine preventive patrol time. If an officer is inclined to make a round of visiting on the beat, then that becomes routine preventive patrol. And so it goes. The individual patrol officer accounts for most of the variation in the specific activities conducted during routine patrol. However, patterns also vary by the nature of the beat, the time of the day, and the day of the week. No police strategy could be more diffuse. One must truly believe that the mere occasional presence of a patrol car cruising by deters crime to believe that routine patrol makes any difference.

random routine preventive patrol
Unstructured, unguided cruising of a patrol beat; associated with the concept of systematically unsystematic patrol.

Further, one must visualize the design of the Kansas City experiment. On the one hand, the decision to concurrently test decreases in routine preventive patrol and increases in adjoining beats had its strengths, particularly in an era when there was virtually no research on police strategy. In concurrently withdrawing and increasing routine preventive patrol in the south district, the researchers assumed that citizens perceived the amount of preventive patrol, and reacted to it, within the confines of beat boundaries. In other words, someone living in a designated reactive beat would hypothetically conclude there was less preventive patrol based solely on the fact that there was less preventive patrol on that particular beat. Similarly, someone in an adjoining proactive beat would hypothetically conclude there was more preventive patrol based solely on the increase on that beat, ignoring adjacent beats. See Figure 2.1. With rare exception, citizens do not know where beat boundary lines are drawn. So our assumption is that most south district citizens would perceive more or less preventive patrol, and alter their behavior accordingly, within a living/working area bounded by a single beat.

However, someone residing in one beat and working and/or playing in another would in effect live in both a proactive and a reactive area. Indeed, any mobility at all would result in citizens experiencing all three levels of patrol—proactive, reactive, and control. Thus, a necessary assumption is that most citizens would perceive variation, if it were to be perceived, independently and without overlap within the boundaries of the fifteen police beats. No one would propose that *every* citizen perceived the levels of preventive patrol exclusively within the boundaries of a single beat. Kansas City is a horizontal municipality. The south district contains a range of residential, business, and shopping/recreation areas. Everyone recognized that a lot of citizens routinely crossed beat

FIGURE 2.1 Preventive Patrol Experiment Beat Configuration

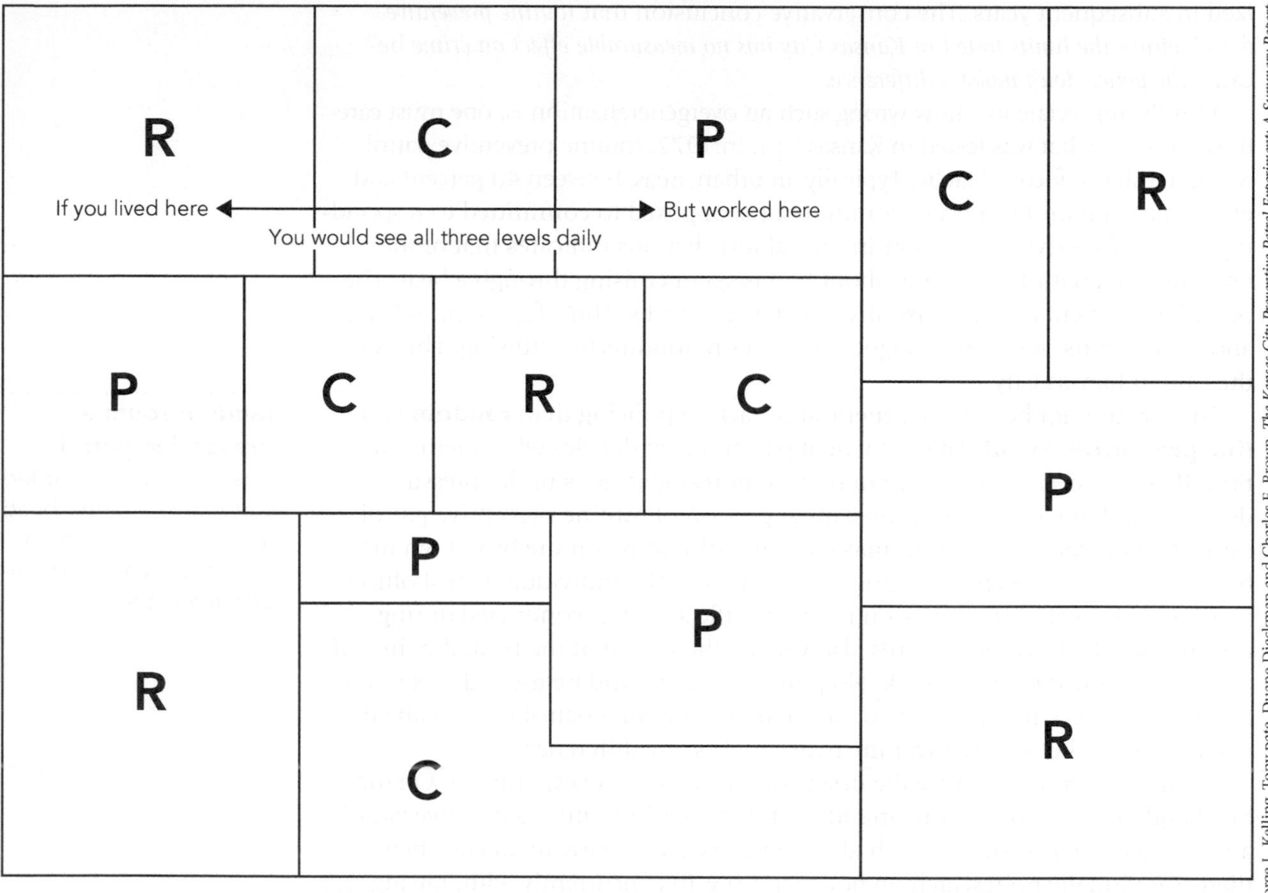

R = Reactive Beat
P = Proactive Beat
C = Control Beat

Source: George L. Kelling, Tony pate, Duane Dieckman and Charles E. Brown, *The Kansas City Preventive Patrol Experiment: A Summary Report.* Washington, D.C., Police Foundation, 1974. Reprinted with permission of the Police Foundation. www.policefoundation.org/pdf/kcppe.pdf

boundaries. The issue is perceptual effect. Would a lack of preventive patrol in a particular area, or an increase in another area, be perceived by enough people to change their behaviors?

Now, from one perspective, that was the whole point of the experiment. It was designed to test such perception. But is it not possible that the perception of withdrawal was canceled by the perception of enhancement? In other words, is it possible that most citizens could not detect any difference in preventive patrol because, overall, in the south district there was no difference in the level?

This is not to suggest that the experiment was flawed. It was well conceived and carefully designed and monitored. The researchers drew conservative conclusions. The issue is overgeneralization of results. Like any good piece of research, the experimental variable in Kansas City was very narrowly drawn. It demonstrated that citizens did not perceive variation in routine preventive patrol across beats. It did *not* demonstrate that police activities directed at particular targets made no difference. It did *not* demonstrate that withdrawal of patrol across a broadly defined area made no difference. It did *not* demonstrate that increasing routine preventive patrol across a broad area made no difference. It says nothing

Learning Objective

about potential patrol saturation effect, regardless of the nature of the patrol activity (given the size of police beats in Kansas City's south district, two to three patrol units in one of those areas is hardly saturation). Most important, the Kansas City Preventive Patrol Experiment says nothing about the efficacy of planned, focused police field intervention. One must be very conservative drawing conclusions about police effectiveness from this study.

SAN DIEGO FIELD INTERROGATION EXPERIMENT

Learning Objective

Following close on the heels of the Kansas City Preventative Patrol Experiment was the San Diego Field Interrogation Experiment (Boydstun, 1975). The contrast in results is striking, and it supports the principle that proactive patrol interventions reduce crime. To the extent that the Kansas City experiment demonstrated that a passive police presence made no difference, the San Diego experiment demonstrated that an active police presence makes a dramatic difference. Conducted in 1973, the experiment involved varying the intensity of police stop-and-question activities. Three areas in San Diego were compared. One group of beats was designated control, where field interrogations during the experimental period were maintained at the same intensity as before. In a second group of beats, officers were trained to conduct field interrogations with more courtesy (it was felt that an increase in the already high levels of field interrogations would infringe upon civil rights). A third group of beats was designated as "no field interrogations." Actually, field interrogations were allowed on these beats, but officers were to conduct them only when extreme suspicion existed. The level of field interrogations in the experimental beats dropped tremendously. Suppressible street crime was measured for seven months before the experiment, for nine months during which experimental conditions were maintained, and for five months as follow-up. Suppressible crime was defined as robbery, burglary, auto theft, street theft, street rape, other sex crimes, malicious mischief, and disorderly conduct.

There was no change in crime in the control beats and in those where officers were specially trained. However, on the beats where field interrogations were withdrawn, the average number of suppressible crimes jumped from 75 to 104 per month. When field interrogations were reestablished, suppressible crime dropped down to 81 offenses per month. There was about a one-month lag time between the change in the number of field investigations and the change in crime rates.

Whereas the passive police activity characterized as routine preventive patrol had no effect in Kansas City, the proactive activity characterized by field interrogation had a dramatic effect in San Diego. Interestingly, officers conducted most field interrogations after observing suspicious behavior while on routine preventive patrol. But some officers engaged in routine preventive patrol and never initiated a field interrogation. Thus, researchers must test these activities independently. The implications of the San Diego Field Interrogation Experiment are more thoroughly discussed in Chapter 8.

DIRECTED PATROL IN NEW HAVEN AND PONTIAC

As a result of the Kansas City Preventive Patrol Experiment, many agencies implemented directed patrol programs in the late 1970s. The idea was to use uncommitted patrol time to focus on particular problems, for example, thefts from autos in shopping area parking lots. Evaluations of directed patrol efforts were conducted in New Haven, Connecticut (Warren, Forst, & Estrella, 1979) and Pontiac, Michigan (Cordner, 1996). Some crime reduction was noted. However, it must be observed that the assessments did not employ experimental designs. Further, the evaluators noted that implementing directed patrol was problematic.

SPLIT-FORCE PATROL IN WILMINGTON

Another effort to use uncommitted patrol time in a structured strategy was launched by the Wilmington, Delaware, Police Department in 1975 (Tien, 1978). The department divided its patrol division into a basic patrol force, consisting of approximately 70 percent of the officers, and a structured patrol force, consisting of 30 percent of the officers. The structured patrol force was not to respond to calls-for-service except in emergencies, allowing them to conduct proactive crime intervention activities. The structured patrol force spent their time on problem areas and initial follow-up investigations of all crime-in-progress calls. The patrol division's overall arrest rate increased by 4 percent, charges per arrest increased by 13 percent, and clearances increased by 105 percent. However, the detective division's clearance rate dropped by 61 percent, producing an overall drop of 28 percent for the department. The agency abandoned the split-force approach partially due to the impact on investigative clearance rates, and partially because of disillusionment in the patrol force. In particular, the officers in the basic patrol force deeply resented the freedom given to the other officers.

MINNEAPOLIS DOMESTIC VIOLENCE

Most patrol research addresses the effect of various patrol deployment approaches to suppressible street crime. The Minneapolis Domestic Violence Experiment (conducted in 1982), measured something quite different—the comparative effect of patrol responses to a common offense—domestic physical assaults. Domestic disturbance calls where there was evidence that a physical assault had occurred were randomly assigned to one of three interventions: mediate, arrest of the assailant, or separate (send the alleged assailant away). Arrest proved to have the strongest deterrent effect, measured both by subsequent calls to the police and a follow-up telephone survey—re-occurrence was measured at 10 percent and 19 percent respectively. In contrast, re-occurrence was measured at 19 percent/37 percent for mediation, and 24 percent/33 percent for separate (Sherman & Berk, 1984).

Learning Objective

Replications were conducted in Atlanta, Milwaukee, Omaha, Metro-Dade, Charlotte, and Colorado Springs between 1986 and 1989. The multi-city replication failed to demonstrate the efficacy of arrest. Indeed, at three sites—Charlotte, Milwaukee, and Omaha—arrest begat the worst repeat violence rate. The results obtained in Minneapolis may be limited to cities with similar social, economic, and demographic characteristics (Schmidt & Sherman, 1993).

NEWARK AND FLINT FOOT PATROL

The early 1980s saw the emergence of two of the most influential police strategies ever conceived—community policing and broken windows enforcement. The community policing conceptual framework emerged from Robert Trojanowicz's evaluation of the Flint, Michigan, Foot Patrol Program (Trojanowicz, 1982). Although the analysis indicated only marginal effects on crime—a 9 percent reduction in a single offense category, burglary—there was overwhelmingly strong citizen support for the endeavor. Likewise, an assessment of the effect of foot patrol in Newark indicated no substantive impact upon crime. However, the qualitative assessment of the program engendered the broken windows approach—control of street "incivility" will lead to reductions in serious crime (J. Q. Wilson & Kelling, 1982). The inverse is also true—tolerance of drug dealing, street-corner prostitution, gang congregation, and threatening and/or obtrusive behavior begets serious crime.

PROBLEM-ORIENTED POLICING IN NEWPORT NEWS

Nearly 15 years after the Kansas City Preventive Patrol Experiment, the first truly innovative alternative use of uncommitted patrol time was developed in Newport News, Virginia (Eck & Spelman, 1987). Darrel Stephens, then chief of the police department, implemented problem-oriented policing. Refined by Herman Goldstein, the technique involves making patrol officers responsible for finding longer-term solutions to recurrent police problems (Goldstein, 2003). Eck and Spelman (1987) documented the success of problem-oriented policing in Newport News with regard to three issues: (1) thefts from autos in the parking lots adjoining the shipyards, (2) robberies associated with a deteriorating downtown area, and (3) burglaries and other problems associated with the New Briarfield housing project. For all three problems, patrol officers attacked underlying conditions and substantially reduced crime rates. The degree to which nontraditional approaches were employed varied substantially (see Figure 2.2).

The Washington Avenue robbery problem was dealt with by largely traditional, albeit focused, law enforcement approaches. There was, however, employment of code enforcement targeting problematic businesses. Additionally, the police department persuaded judges to prohibit arrested prostitutes from returning to the area as a condition of probation. The shipyard thefts were addressed with classic Crime Prevention Through Environmental Design **(CPTED)**, the altering of the physical environment to assist in deterring crime. In this case the city required the owners to make the parking lots more secure through city ordinances. The New Briarfield housing project was a different story. For all intents and purposes the Newport News Police Department took over management of the development.

CPTED
An acronym representing Crime Prevention Through Environmental Design, or the altering of the physical environment to assist in deterring crime.

FIGURE 2.2 Newport News Problem-Solving Approaches

Problem	Use of Nontraditional Approaches
• Washington Avenue Robberies	None to Nominal
• Shipyard Thefts from Vehicles	Intermediate
• New Briarfield Burglaries	Extensive

The phenomenon illustrates one of the underlying issues with problem-oriented policing—the problem becomes the police department's problem. Nonetheless, problem-oriented policing is still one of the most popular crime intervention strategies, discussed extensively in subsequent chapters.

MINNEAPOLIS REPEAT CALL ADDRESS POLICING (RECAP)

Learning Objective

In 1988, the city of Minneapolis, Minnesota, determined that 3 percent of the city's 1,115 addresses accounted for 50 percent of police calls-for-service. Five percent of those addresses generated 64 percent of the calls, and during the time frame analyzed, nearly 60 percent of the city's addresses generated no calls. Minneapolis formed a special unit of five officers who were assigned 125 residential and 125 commercial addresses. They were to use problem-oriented techniques to reduce the calls-for-service coming from those addresses. After six months, the target addresses had 15 percent fewer calls-for-service (Sherman, 1990). However, after one year, all the gains were erased; indeed, the residential addresses were actually producing more calls-for-service. The conclusion was reached that target rotation may be the best police strategy when dealing with problematic addresses.

MINNEAPOLIS HOT SPOTS

Hot spots were identified that consisted of clusters of addresses with high crime rates, high volumes of calls-for-service, and "disorder" problems. A total of 110 areas identified as hot spots were randomly assigned to treatment (55 locations) or control (55 locations). Each hot spot was one city block or less. Extra patrol was assigned to the treatment zones, generally two to three additional hours per day during problem times, for the one-year period from December 1988 through November 1989. Although serious crime decreased more in the experimental zones, the differences were not statistically significant. There was a modest, but statistically significant reduction in calls-for-service related to petty crime (disorder) in the treatment zones. More optimistically, observed disorder problems were cut in half in the treatment areas compared to the controls (Sherman & Weisburd, 1995).

KANSAS CITY GUN EXPERIMENT

From July 1992 to January 1993, patrol overtime hours from 7 p.m. to 10 p.m. were directed at detecting concealed weapons in beat 144 of Kansas City. A total of 4,512 officer hours (2,256 patrol car hours) were concentrated in the beat during the six months. Typically, two extra patrol units were in the beat each evening. Beat 144 is an eight-by-ten-block area with a 1991 homicide rate of 177 per 100,000, about twenty times the national average. The beat was 92 percent non-White, but 66 percent of the residents were homeowners.

Police gun seizures in the target area increased by more than 65 percent, and gun crimes declined by 40 percent (Sherman et al., 1995). Neither gun seizures nor gun crimes changed significantly in a similar beat several miles away, where directed patrol was not used. Further, there was no measurable displacement of gun crimes to patrol beats adjacent to the target area. Whereas drive-by shootings dropped from seven to one in the target area, they doubled from six to twelve in the comparison area. Again, there was no displacement to areas adjacent to the target beat. Homicide showed a statistically significant reduction in the target area, but not in a comparison area (McGarrell, Chermak, Weiss, & Wilson, 2001). The investment of 4,512 police officer-hours was associated with 29 more guns seized and 83 fewer gun crimes, or about 55 patrol hours per gun crime and almost three gun crimes prevented per gun seized. Traffic stops were the most productive way to find guns, with an average of one gun found for every 28 stops. Interestingly, two-thirds of the people arrested for carrying guns lived outside the target area. Only gun crimes were affected by directed patrols, with no changes in the number of calls-for-service or the total number of violent and nonviolent crimes reported.

INDIANAPOLIS DIRECTED PATROL

The Indianapolis Police Department targeted two high-crime beats in the summer of 1997. For 90 days the intensity of patrol was increased, adding about 100 patrol unit hours per beat per week (McGarrell et al., 2001). In the North Beat homicides were reduced from eleven during the comparable months in 1996 to one in 1997. Aggravated assault with a gun and robbery were down about 40 percent. However, in the sister East Beat, aggravated assault was up by 58 percent compared to the summer of 1996, and robbery increased by 16 percent. In the two control beats, violent crime was up slightly. There was no significant displacement or diffusion effect in the beats surrounding the two experimental areas.

The findings are characterized as perplexing. The authors of the evaluation offer as explanation the possibility that officers in the North Beat were more selective in their stops—targeting suspicious persons. In the East Beat there were twice as many traffic stops, and more citations written. In the North Beat there were fewer stops, but more citations, weapons seized, and arrests per stop. Officers assigned to the East Beat indicated that only 3 percent of the stops they made were for suspicious behavior, compared to 19 percent in the North Beat (McGarrell et al., 2001). In short, the North Beat officers made fewer stops, but were more "intrusive" during the stops they did make.

Learning Objective

What to make of this? It is difficult to draw any definitive conclusions. Although the results in the North Beat offer definitive support for the efficacy of hot spot strategy, the East Beat does the opposite. It is a cliché to say that "more research is needed," but the results do underscore the need for testing directed patrol variation in a variety of environments.

Conclusions from Our Research Legacy

Perhaps more than any other study, the 1993 Kansas City Gun Experiment demonstrates the very narrow effect of a particular police strategy; although there was a very dramatic effect on the target—gun crimes—there was no measurable impact on other crimes. Police efforts targeted at particular offenders committing particular crimes produced results in Kansas City, as they did in Newport

News and San Diego. And crackdowns conducted in situations previously lacking enforcement may produce results. But mere police presence does little. Further, defused strategies without a sharp focus have produced little results. Directed patrol in Pontiac and New Haven consisted of targeting various crimes committed by various offenders at various times of the day—and no definitive results materialized. The same held true for the Wilmington Split-Force Patrol Experiment. Likewise, research on the efficacy of investigations leads to precisely the same conclusion—it is focused police efforts that make a difference.

Confirming the Legacy: Post-2000 Research

More recent research is described in detail in subsequent chapters (including Chapter 6, Geographic Targeting Strategies; Chapter 7, Offense Targeting Strategies; and Chapter 8, Offender Targeting Strategies). But it should be observed here that the results of more recent research are consistent with the research legacy of the 1970s through the 1990s. A "focused and aggressive enforcement" strategy reduces crime. To some extent aggressive enforcement even without specific focus appears to work. The Houston, New York, and Chicago experiences described earlier are certainly cases in point.

"MACRO-ANALYSES"

An initial "macro-analysis" of the linkage between aggressive patrol and serious crime used traffic citation issuance among thirty-five cities as a measure of "aggressive patrol." Wilson and Boland (1978) concluded that aggressive patrol reduced robbery. Sampson and Cohen (1988) extended this analysis to a sample of 171 cities with populations over 100,000, and confirmed the correlation. More broadly, MacDonald found in an analysis of data from 164 agencies that agencies whose officers more aggressively enforced disorderly conduct and driving under the influence had significantly lower robbery and homicide rates (MacDonald, 2002)—a finding supportive of the broken windows model. More recently, Kubrin, Messner, Deane, McGeever, and Stucky (2010) revisited the deterrent effects of proactive policing on robbery rates between 1996 and 2003 by analyzing panel data from large cities. Following Sampson and Cohen, the authors measured proactive policing as an arrest rate of driving while intoxicated and disorderly conduct divided by the number of sworn police officers. Controlling for the influence of other community-level predictors, the models supported the findings from previous studies—as minor offense enforcement increased, robbery decreased.

FOCUSED APPROACHES

Nonetheless, results are even more definitive for focused aggressive interventions. Weisburd and Eck (2004) emphasized the effectiveness of focused efforts in their review of strategies based upon a typology of approaches: the "standard model" (random patrol, higher police/citizen ratios, rapid response) contrasted to recent approaches (community policing, problem solving, hot spots). The authors asserted that focused efforts employing proactive approaches appeared to have the greatest crime-reduction effect. Further, Weisburd and Mazerolle (2000) concluded that geographic (place-oriented) efforts had the greatest effect on specific crimes. Braga's (2001) analysis of hot spot saturation deployment found that seven of nine resulted in measurable crime reduction. In a subsequent and more rigorous review, a Campbell Systematic meta-analysis, Braga (2007) reported that focusing police efforts at high-activity crime places can be effective in preventing crime. Richmond, Virginia, was not included in Braga's reviews, but reported as well a significant reduction in violent crime after concentrated patrol in hot spots (Smith, 2001). Lum (2009) notes that evidence-based policing was engendered by (1) integrated information technology and sharing systems, (2) crime mapping for directing hot spot and problem-oriented approaches, and (3) employment of crime analysis for long-term strategic planning. She concludes that "a promising realm of effectiveness is the intersection of focused, place-based and highly proactive dimensions" (p. 8).

IMPLICATIONS FOR STRATEGY

Learning Objective

We still do not know in any detail the relative efficiency of macro strategy, much less micro strategy. For example, although hot spot saturation deployment appears effective overall, we do not know the relative effect of how many patrol units (how high the dosage), focused upon what—offenses, offenders, or targets—using what strategies, assigned for what duration (hours, days, weeks, months). Will one extra patrol unit in a square mile make a difference, or are more required? How about in two or three city blocks instead of a square mile? Or more broadly in an entire beat? For how many hours a day? Remaining for a week, or a month, or is a year required to have an effect? We don't know. Controlled experiments are, of course, both complex and expensive. It is difficult to manipulate police field strategies. It is extraordinarily difficult to withdraw a service from a geographic area or clientele. Indeed, not since the San Diego Field Interrogation Experiment in 1975 has any research design included withdrawal of any type of police activity. It is a bit easier to differentially distribute new services, for example, conduct saturation patrol in some beats but not in others. Even then, however, police managers face the dilemma of equity in distributing resources to the citizens they serve. If differential distribution might harm some citizens, ethical questions are obviously raised. Additionally, the situations for which excess resources are available for differential distribution, although not rare, are not common either. Beyond these difficulties, for a field experiment to occur, there must be a confluence of research expertise, a motivation to conduct the experiment, and a police administrator's willingness to take the risk involved. We can only hope that future years see more such experiments. First, however, we must be convinced that the police do make a difference.

SUMMARY

- Police can impact crime rates. What we do not know is specificity in this respect—what interventions work best for particular types of offenses and the degree of difference a particular intervention makes.

- It took the development of Compstat in New York City to "seal the case" that the police can indeed have a substantial effect on crime rates. Until that event there was considerable pessimism regarding the potential of police impact. That pessimism was caused by the lack of correlation between police/citizen ratios and crime rates (a higher ratio did not correlate with lower crime rates), and the "nothing works" research of the early 1970s. The substantial impact on crime in both Houston and New York City with the revitalization of those agencies in the early 1990s engendered a new era of optimism regarding the potential police effect on crime. Reinforcement came from Cincinnati, Ohio, where criticism of the police department led to cessation of enforcement, immediately resulting in a surge of serious crime.
- The first true experimental design measuring the effectiveness of police strategic approach was the Kansas City Preventive Patrol Experiment conducted in 1971–1972. Although the results indicated that random routine patrol did not affect crime, the experiment did not indicate that police presence made no difference or indicate whether alternative strategic approaches might make a difference. The San Diego Field Interrogation Experiment conducted three years later indeed indicated that proactive police intervention does reduce suppressible street crime. The fact that focused police interventions are effective was reinforced by the Minneapolis Domestic Violence Experiment, which indicated that arrest of an aggressor reduced subsequent violent incidents.
- The "broken windows" conceptual framework originated from qualitative assessment of the Newark Foot Patrol Experiment. Broken windows is a metaphor referring to the fact that if all of the windows in an abandoned building are intact, they tend to remain intact. However, if one window is broken at the same site, soon all will be broken. The extension is that if obnoxious behavior and nuisance offenses are tolerated in a neighborhood, soon serious crime will follow—"all of the windows will soon get broken." Evidence for the efficacy of broken windows approaches is mixed. It appears to be an effective strategy in densely populated areas, but is less relevant as density decreases.
- There is overwhelming evidence that crime clusters in so-called "hot spots." A hot spot is defined as a location or an area of a jurisdiction where the crime rate is substantially above the norm. Police agencies have attempted various approaches to reducing crime in hot spots, but most frequently employ saturation patrol with intense field interviews. Evidence tends to support the efficacy of hot spot saturation patrol, but there are mixed results, illustrated by the Indianapolis Directed Patrol Program, in which one targeted beat experienced crime reduction while a parallel targeted beat actually saw crime increases. What we don't know about effective saturation patrol exceeds by a considerable margin what we do know. We don't know the optimum level of saturation for a given hot spot zone; we don't know the optimal zone size—definitions of a hot spot vary from a single address to a city block to a square mile to an entire four- to five-square-mile police beat; we don't know what the optimal duration of saturation patrol is; related to this issue we don't know what the residual effect of a saturation might be.

REVIEW QUESTIONS

1. What most likely explains the precipitous drop in crime in the 1990s, as well as its continued gradual decline since then? Why is a definitive explanation so difficult to come by?
2. Contrast the findings of the Kansas City Preventive Patrol Experiment and the San Diego Field Interrogation Experiment. What explains the dramatically different results?
3. What characteristics of foot patrol might explain why two significant strategies—community Policing and broken windows enforcement—emerged from evaluations of foot patrol experiments?

4. The most perplexing of the hot spot deployment assessments are the contradictory results of the Indianapolis Directed Patrol program. What might explain the contrasting crime trends in the two beats? What is implied?
5. What **don't** we know about the characteristics of hot spot deployment that might increase its cost-effectiveness?

REAL-WORLD SCENARIOS

1. You are a district police commander in a large agency. Within your district is a one-mile strip of largely entertainment businesses, anchored by three large night clubs. The one-mile strip is a classic "hot spot" of crime. You decide to launch a saturation patrol effort focused on the evening hours. What decisions do you have to make regarding the characteristics of the intervention?
2. An organization concerned about the welfare of victims of domestic violence has publically criticized the police department for inadequate response. Among the organization's assertions is that officers should be required to arrest a possible assailant when there is even the slightest suspicion of assaultive behavior—indeed even if the victim says a physical assault did not occur. Given what you know about evaluations of the relative effectiveness of domestic violence interdiction, how might you respond?
3. You are the chief of police of an agency for which a strong police association engages in collective bargaining for wages and benefits with the parent jurisdiction. An impasse in the process of reaching an agreement has occurred. The association leadership "grumbles" that perhaps officers should stop arresting except in the most grievous situations. Taking into account what you know about the effect of cessation of enforcement, how do you respond?

APPLICATION ACTIVITIES

1. It is asserted that it is absurd to believe that the police make no difference in crime rates. Review this issue in terms of what the Kansas City Preventive Patrol Experiment does and does not tell us about the effect of police presence. Distinguish between police presence and random routine patrol. Include discussion of the experimental conditions in Kansas City, including presence in the reactive beats and concentrated presence in adjoining proactive beats.
2. The San Diego Field Interrogation Study has been called the "forgotten experiment." Discuss the hypothetical import of this evaluation contrasted to the actual minimal import. Why the difference? What developments may have transcended the San Diego findings? What is the relevance of the findings to today's deployment patterns?
3. The last strategy evaluation that entailed actual withdrawal of a police activity was the San Diego Field Interrogation Experiment in 1975. Although numerous studies since then have varied the "dosage" of a particular intervention, none have gone so far as to deliberately eliminate entirely a particular program or tactic. Discuss the issues involved in deliberatively "manipulating" the degree of police effort, whether in total or in part and whether in general or a specific tactic. Consider diminution of service to either a geographical area, offense type, or citizen type.

COURSEMATE

This available CourseMate has an interactive eBook and interactive learning tools, including flash cards, quizzes, and more. To learn more about this resource and access free demo CourseMate resources, go to **www.cengagebrain.com**, and search for this book. To access CourseMate materials that you have purchased, go to **login.cengagebrain.com**.

REFERENCES

Boydstun, J. E. (1975). *San Diego Field Interrogation: Final report.* Washington, DC: Police Foundation.

Braga, A. A. (2001). The effects of hot spots policing on crime. *Annals of the American Academy of Political and Social Science, 578,* 104–125.

Braga, A. A. (2007). The effects of hot spots policing on crime, a Campbell Collaboration systematic review. Available from http://www.aic.gov.au/campbellcj/reviews/titles.html.

Bureau of Justice Statistics. (2010). *Correctional populations in the United States: Imprisonment rate.* Washington, DC: U.S. Department of Justice, Bureau of Justice Statistics.

Chicago Police Department. (2007). *Making Chicago the safest big city in America, Chicago Police Department crime reduction initiatives: 2003–2007.* Chicago, IL: Chicago Police Department.

Cordner, G. W. (1996). Evaluating tactical patrol. In L. T. Hoover (Ed.), *Quantifying quality in policing.* Washington, DC: Police Executive Research Forum.

Eck, J. E., & Spelman, W. (1987). *Problem-solving: Problem-oriented policing in Newport News.* Washington, DC: Police Executive Research Forum.

Greenwood, P., & Petersilia, J. (1975). *The criminal investigation process-Volume I: Summary and policy implications.* Santa Monica, CA: RAND Corp.

Goldstein, H. (2003). On further developing problem-oriented policing: the most critical need, the major impediments, and a proposal. *Crime Prevention, 15, 13–47.*

Hoover, L. T., & Caeti, T. J. (1994). *Crime specific policing in Houston* (Vol. 1). Huntsville, TX: Sam Houston State University. Available at www.lemitonline.org/telemasp/index.php#by_volume%201/vol1no9.pdf.

Kelling, G. L., Pate, T., Dieckman, D., & Brown, C. E. (1974). *The Kansas City Preventive Patrol Experiment: A summary report.* Washington, DC: Police Foundation.

Kubrin, D. E., Messner, S. F., Deane, G., McGeever, K., & Stucky, T. D. (2010). Proactive policing and robbery rates across U.S. cities. *Criminology and Public Policy, 48,* 57–91.

Lum, C. (2009). *Translating police research into practice.* Washington, DC: Police Foundation.

MacDonald, J. M. (2002). The effectiveness of community policing in reducing urban violence. *Crime & Delinquency, 48*(4), 592–617.

Martinson, R. (1975). The effectiveness of correctional treatment: A survey of treatment evaluation studies. In *The State of Corrections,* American Correctional Association.

McGarrell, E. F., Chermak, S., Weiss, A., & Wilson, J. M. (2001). Reducing firearms violence through directed police patrol. *Criminology & Public Policy, 1*(1), 119–148.

Rosenbaum, D. P., & Stephens, C. (2005). *Reducing public violence and homicide in Chicago: Strategies and tactics of the Chicago Police Department.* Chicago: University of Illinois at Chicago, Center for Research in Law and Justice.

Sampson, R., & Cohen, J. (1988). Deterrent effects of the police on crime: A replication and theoretical extension. *Law and Society Review, 22,* 163–189.

Schmidt, J. D., & Sherman, L. W. (1993). Does arrest deter domestic violence? *American Behavioral Scientist, 36*(5), 601–609.

Sherman, L. W. (1990). Police crackdowns: Initial and residual deterrence. In M. Tonry & N. Morris (Eds.), *Crime and Justice: An Annual Review of Research* (Vol. 12). Chicago: University of Chicago Press.

Sherman, L. W., & Berk, R. A. (1984). *The Minneapolis Domestic Violence Experiment.* Washington, DC: Police Foundation.

Sherman, L. W., Gartin, P. R., & Buerger, M. E. (1989). Hot spots of predatory crime: Routine activities and the criminology of place. *Criminology, 27*(1), 27–56.

Sherman, L. W., Shaw, J. W., & Regan, D. P. (1995). *The Kansas City Gun Experiment.* Washington, DC: National Institute of Justice.

Sherman, L. W., & Weisburd, D. (1995). General deterrent effects of police patrol in crime "hot spots": A randomized, controlled trial. *Justice Quarterly, 12*(4), 625–648.

Shi, L. (2009). The limit of oversight in policing: Evidence from the 2001 Cincinnati riot. *Journal of Public Economics, 93,* 99–113.

Smith, M. R. (2001). Police-led crackdowns and cleanups: An evaluation of a crime control initiative in Richmond, Virginia. *Crime and Delinquency, 47*(1), 60–83.

Tien, J., Simaon, J., & Larson, R. (1978). *An alternative approach in police patrol: The Wilmington split-force experiment.* Washington, DC: Government Printing Office.

Trojanowicz, R. J. (1982). *An evaluation of the Neighborhood Foot Patrol Program in Flint, Michigan.* East Lansing: Michigan State University.

von Drehle, D. (2010, February 22). Why crime went away: The murder rate in America is at an all-time low. Will the recession reverse that? *TIME Magazine.*

Walsh, W. F. (2001). Compstat: An analysis of an emerging police managerial paradigm. Policing: *An International Journal of Police Strategies and Management, 24*(3), 347–361.

Warren, J., Forst, M., & Estrella, M. (1979). Directed patrol: An experiment that worked. *The Police Chief, 48*, 78.

Weisburd, D., & Eck, J. E. (2004). What can police do to reduce crime, disorder, and fear? *Annals of the American Academy of Political & Social Science, 593*(5), 42–65.

Weisburd, D., & Mazerolle, L. G. (2000). Crime and disorder in drug hotspots: Implications for theory and practice in policing. *Police Quarterly, 3*(3), 331–349.

Wilson, J. Q. (2011). Hard times, fewer crimes. *Wall Street Journal*. Retrieved May 28, 2011, from http://online.wsj.com/article/SB10001424052702304066504576345553135009870.html.

Wilson, J. Q., & Boland, B. (1978). The effect of police on crime. *Law and Society Review, 12*(3), 367–390.

Wilson, J. Q., & Kelling, G. L. (1982). Broken windows: The police and neighborhood safety. *Atlantic Monthly, 249*(March), 29–38.

CHAPTER 3

The Role of Community Policing

© Jim West/Alamy

KEY TERMS

Bureau of Justice Statistics
Citizens on patrol
Citizens' police academies
Civil service commissions
Court watch programs
Evidence-based policing
Intelligence-led policing
Neighborhood watch
Police Executive Research Forum (PERF)
Storefront police stations

LEARNING OBJECTIVES

After completing this chapter, you should be able to:

- Describe the naïve imagery of policing as the way "it should be."
- List the three community policing programs reported as implemented by almost all respondents on a Police Executive Research Forum survey, and a second grouping of activities for which about 50 percent of the departments indicated some level of implementation.
- Identify activities or programs on the Police Executive Research Forum survey that may be inappropriate or questionable.
- Cite the primary components of an appropriate model of community policing.
- Explain the ramifications of integrating the term "policing" into a descriptive phrase of a strategic approach.
- Characterize the outcomes of four attempted evaluations of the effect of community policing upon crime.
- Explain why police officers typically place a higher importance upon traditional crime control than do citizens.
- Explain why it is so difficult to measure the outcomes of community policing approaches and programs.
- Distinguish the universal attribute of community policing from programs or approaches that should not be characterized as community policing.
- Identify the recent trend of agency sponsorship of specialized community policing roles.

The development of both community and problem-oriented approaches can be characterized as classic case studies in fast-paced change following organizational stress. In the 1970s the police were stressed in two major ways. First, the combination of the inner-city riots and Vietnam War protests of the 1960s brought the police to the forefront of public attention. The inner-city riots sprang from a long history of social and economic stress for American Black citizens. But as noted in Chapter 1, a confrontation between police and Black citizens was almost always an instigating immediate factor. And, interestingly, as noted in Chapter 1, by and large the police handled the Vietnam protests (riots) extraordinarily well. However, the excessive reaction of the Chicago Police Department toward war demonstrators during the 1968 Democratic Convention triggered calls for reform. Additionally, crime began to rise in the United States precipitously in the early 1960s, becoming a national political issue for the first time. The federal government became involved in assisting local law enforcement in 1965 through the Office of Law Enforcement Assistance, later the Law Enforcement Assistance Administration (LEAA). Sudden national attention was also manifested in a series of national commissions that examined law enforcement, all calling for dramatic reform. Reinforcing the political discontent with the police was the "nothing works" research of the Kansas City Preventive Patrol experiment and the RAND Criminal Investigation study, described previously. The stage was set for new approaches. Of particular appeal was the core component of community policing—community engagement.

There is nothing inherently wrong with community engagement. Chapter 4 is focused upon linkage of meaningful community engagement to crime control. This chapter addresses the range of programming commonly accepted as components of community policing. Conversely, the "misuse" of community policing as a rhetorical tool is first addressed.

Learning Objective

Misuse of the Community Policing Concept

There exists among some a naïve imagery of policing the way it should be:

> *Small town America on the Fourth of July, waving the red, white and blue. Neighbors sitting on one another's porches visiting about a bake sale to raise money for playground equipment. Officer Gonzales strolling by on a residential walking beat, first frolicking with the children in a game of hopscotch, then joining the adults on the porch for an iced tea.*

This imagery is appealing, but in reality is a Norman Rockwell picture of an America that disappeared on December 7, 1941.

Peter Manning (2003) characterized community policing as a term that fits in the category of a rhetorical sponge—a word that absorbs whatever meaning one wants to ascribe to it. Like globalization, the new economy, or American interest, community policing means different things to different people. Too frequently, the concept is mischaracterized.

Police Executive Research Forum (PERF)
An association of police chiefs from large agencies and other police professionals; incorporated in 1977; offices in Washington, D.C.

Potential abuse of community policing terminology is illustrated by a **Police Executive Research Forum (PERF)** survey conducted in 1992, 1997, and 2002 that intended to measure "progress" in the implementation of community policing (Fridell & Wycoff, 2004). There are a number of characteristics of community policing listed in the survey. Responding agencies were asked to indicate whether their department had implemented these "reforms." The sample was 240 agencies surveyed in 2002 that had indicated in a parallel survey done in 1997 that they had either implemented or were implementing community policing.

Learning Objective

Three activity categories were reported as implemented by almost all respondents: attending police community meetings, participating in neighborhood watch, and helping police identify and resolve problems. These are widely accepted appropriate means to engage citizens with their police department.

There was a second grouping of activities for which about 50 percent of the departments indicated some level of citizen engagement: serving on jurisdiction advisory councils, serving on neighborhood advisory councils, serving on advisory groups for chiefs or other managers, serving as volunteers in the police agency, serving on **citizens on patrol** programs coordinated by police agencies, and attending **citizens' police academies**. This grouping of endeavors can be characterized as structured community contact and participation. Again, these are solid components of community engagement.

At this juncture, however, the suggested components of community policing becomes problematic. About 20 percent of the responding agencies reported that citizens participated in their promotional process. One must be surprised that any agency reported this. We do not know, of course, what the respondents were thinking about when they said "yes." More than likely these were agencies with formal **civil service commissions**. Typically, the actual commission members are citizens appointed to serve in that role and hence the "yes" is technically a correct response. But this is certainly not a new component of policing engendered by the advent of the community policing concept. Civil service commissions date back 100 years.

Finally, there is the inappropriate. **Court watch programs** are listed as a component of community policing. Very few agencies indicated that citizens participated in a court watch program. But why in the world would a professional public administrator from the executive branch of government, a.k.a. a police chief, form a coalition of citizens and police conducting a court watch program in the first place? Court watch programs are intended to bird-dog presumably liberal judges, coercing them into administration of nothing but draconian sentences. Other systems are in place to assure the judiciary reflects the will of the majority of people in a democracy. That is not a role for the police department. Court watch programs are not and should not be a component of community policing.

There are other questionable endeavors listed as representing movement toward community policing, for example, "citizens helping review complaints against police" and "helping evaluate officer performance" (Fridell & Wycoff, 2004). It is important to point out that the 2004 publication was a continuation of a longitudinal survey begun in 1992. The early 1990s were the high-water mark of community policing as the "reinvention" of policing. Few today would place endeavors such as court watch as a desirable feature of community engagement. But the exaggerated range of identified community policing components originally listed in 1992 exemplifies the inappropriate "rhetoric" of community policing.

Brogden (1999) notes the misguided "religious fervor" characterizing the worldwide diffusion of community policing:

> New missionaries have spread a particular policing creed. A uni-linear perception of police development has been assumed, a process occurring largely independently of local police mandates, cultures and patterns of organization. What appeared to offer promise in small-town America, and in the prosperous white suburbs, is being exported by a new brand of academic and police salespeople to all and sundry. (p. 179)

The truly critical issue is neighborhood management. Inappropriate versions of community policing see the police woven into the very fabric of neighborhoods. Neighborhoods are envisioned as relatively autonomous, cohesive, identifiable, distinct subunits of larger communities. The vision is our small-town America on the Fourth of July, but that vision cannot be transposed to places like the Southern California Megaplex.

citizens on patrol
Volunteer groups sponsored by police agencies that drive around neighborhoods, usually during evening hours, reporting anything suspicious to police communications; always unarmed with instructions to never attempt intervention.

Learning Objective

citizens' police academies
Abbreviated versions of police basic training offered to interested citizens to acquaint them with the challenges of a law enforcement role; typically one evening a week for ten weeks.

civil service commissions
Official entities of government responsible for administration of personnel policies; typically commissions set standards for employment and competitive promotion of police and fire departments; the purpose of employing commissions is to separate public safety personnel administration from partisan political influence.

court watch programs
Informal volunteer efforts to monitor judicial sentencing practices; ostensibly neutral but in practice nearly all court watch programs are premised upon elimination of what is perceived as lenient sentencing practices.

Appropriate Models of Community Policing

In the middle of the Dallas/Fort Worth, Texas, Metroplex is the city of Euless. Euless is classic suburbia. It certainly has an economic mix, but it is dominantly middle class. Several major roadway arteries of the Dallas/Fort Worth Metroplex run through it. There are a number of strip shopping centers, a mall, and some light industry. The city is dominantly single-family residences, but substantial numbers of residents in Euless live in apartments. There are a few residents who have lived in Euless all their lives, and strongly identify with the city as an entity, but very few. The majority of residents moved into the city in recent years, and will at some point in their lives move back out again. Identifiable, clearly bounded neighborhoods are difficult to even discern. Further, less than half of the residents are in households premised upon the classic American model of mother, father, and two children. Of such households, in over 70 percent both parents are working.

Learning Objective

The Euless Police Department sponsors a citizens' police academy, and the academy has fed a volunteer law enforcement program—mostly senior citizens. There are citizens on patrol programs in some neighborhoods, and they are supported by the police department. In the 80-person police department there are four officers assigned as community policing specialists, each with a quadrant of the city. They engage in structured community contact, mostly neighborhood watch support, school liaison, and very occasionally in problem solving. They spend a great deal of their time providing direct assistance to patrol services. If this is what we mean by community policing, then certainly the Euless Police Department is "doing" community policing.

However, the Euless Police Department and the citizens it serves are not interwoven. Citizens do not decide who is promoted, or who gets a good performance evaluation. Complaints are handled by an internal investigation, not at a meeting of participants at a neighborhood association. Most important, police officers are not managing the neighborhoods of Euless. To the extent that neighborhood management occurs at all, it is a function of several other city departments, not the police department. And the Euless Police Department spends substantially all of its time on issues of crime and disorder, not quality of life. There are innumerable other entities in the city of Euless to address quality of life issues, from the parks and recreation department to the Euless Independent School District. And no officer walks anywhere. Every one of them drives a motor vehicle.

If a small, tightly integrated, autonomous, self-identified neighborhood interwoven with its police department is what is envisioned, you are hard pressed to find it in the mix of single-family residences, apartment complexes, strip shopping malls, and major highways within Euless. Moreover, the citizens of Euless seem perfectly happy with this arrangement. After both mom and dad have put in an eight-hour work day and arrive home at 6 p.m., they are not very enthused about going down to help the police chief run the Euless Police Department. They have a soccer game to attend, there are school functions, the kids have homework they need help with, and the grass needs to be cut. Sometime during the evening they would like a few minutes to just sit and relax. However, they do have a few simple demands of the police department. They would like to see a patrol car drive down their street once in a while. They want the assurance that the department is competent should they become a victim of a serious crime. When they do encounter a patrol officer, they expect to be treated with dignity and courtesy. When their eighteen-year-old is caught with a six-pack of beer, they hope he will not be treated as a dangerous predator upon society.

There are innumerable publications on global urbanization and its effects on human interaction. Indeed there are whole departments in universities on urban studies. The important issue here is whether in a metropolitan environment or not, the development of small, cohesive, integrated, interactive neighborhoods is possible. Yes, you can give names to areas of a city (The Oaks, The Hills, The Arts District). One can even reach reasonable consensus about what the boundaries of those areas might approximately be. But does that make such areas an integrated and interactive neighborhood, and more particularly, an integrated, interactive neighborhood interwoven with its police department?

Even if it were possible to accomplish an interwoven model from a structural perspective, it cannot be reasonably accomplished from an economic perspective. There are a handful of police departments in the United States staffed with as high as four or five officers per thousand residents. For the vast majority of agencies, a staffing level of two per thousand is typical. Indeed in many southwestern and western cities it is considerably less than that. At anything approaching reasonable staffing levels, the typical staffing level of two per thousand that citizens are willing to pay for, one cannot afford to convert the police department to the role of neighborhood managers. There is a never-ending stream of service calls that must be answered. There is a never-ending stream of burglaries that must be investigated. There is a never-ending flow of traffic accidents that must be cleared. There is a demand for a presence in schools, in shopping areas, and on multi-agency drug, gang, violent crime, and now terrorism task forces. This is in reality a public administration issue—it is a choice among expenditures of public resources.

The Effect of Inappropriate Terminology

We need to stop tagging "policing" onto a descriptive phrase of a strategic approach. Enormous harm has occurred by using the term "policing" as part of the titling of problem-oriented and community approaches. We are repeating the error with "**intelligence-led policing**," "**evidence-based policing**," and the like. When we describe an approach, or set of strategies, with the term "policing," we imply that that is the way law enforcement is done, and—this is how the harm occurs—that the "policing" approach named is the *only* way law enforcement is done. Hence as Compstat emerged there was vehement, and indeed irrational, criticism of the approach. Compstat violated the premise that there was one and only one way to do policing.

Both structured and unstructured community engagement should be an important element of every police department's operations. Likewise, use of problem-oriented interventions, attempting to find alternative ways to effect long-term resolutions to chronic but focused issues of crime and disorder, approaches common sense. But because these approaches are appropriate under some circumstances does not mean that vigorous enforcement is inappropriate. Vicious and ruthless gang leaders spraying intersections with automatic weapons, fire need to be locked up, period. The perception that arrest is only a last resort,

intelligence-led policing
A broad strategic approach emphasizing, in addition to traditional crime analysis, linkage of known offenders to crime patterns; also incorporates the concept of anticipating crime or security issues by risk assessment.

Learning Objective

evidence-based policing
A conceptual framework emphasizing basing crime and disorder interdiction strategies upon structured, sophisticated research regarding the relative effectiveness of alternatives.

and always an undesirable outcome, is borne from individuals living in relatively crime-free environments.

Retired Superintendent Cline characterized the adult gangs in Chicago as "the new form of organized crime." These were not youth gangs flashing colors—these were organized criminal networks marketing drugs. Like traditional organized crime, they were beginning to branch out into other enterprises, sometimes just to conceal the enormous profits they were making from the drug trade. Community engagement became irrelevant in such situations. Police resources were mobilized to combat street executions conducted by the new form of organized crime. Just as with Al Capone's reign of terror in Chicago, you arrest your way out of the problem.

Community Policing Evaluations

An accepted definition of community policing never developed during its formative stage (Eck & Rosenbaum, 1994). The closest is a vague "engaging the community." Nonetheless, there are assessments of components of community policing that merit comment. Cordner reported the crime reduction effect as mixed, premised upon his assessment of published reports of the effect of community policing upon crime (Cordner, 2001). It should be noted that reported drops in crime "due to community policing" occurred during the 1990s, when crime was decreasing everywhere nationally. Indeed the comparative drop in major cities nationally is one of the strongest criticisms of the attribution of the homicide drop in New York City to Compstat.

Learning Objective

Four empirical assessments merit further discussion, as they exemplify the difficulty in measuring the impact of community policing. Three of the four found no impact. Although one reports a positive impact upon crime, the "treatment" is never defined beyond stability of geographic patrol assignment—hardly a unique attribute of community policing.

In a macro-analysis of the effect of community policing on homicide and robbery, MacDonald (2002) concluded that "Overall, the results from the series of regression analyses indicated that community policing planning or community and problem-solving training and operations had little effect on the change in urban violence across major American cities" (p. 609). The study compared the extent of community policing implementation as measured by the **Bureau of Justice Statistics**' Law Enforcement Management and Administrative Statistics program (LEMAS) to changes in homicide and robbery rates in 164 cities over 100,000 populations from 1993 to 1998. Nearly 70 percent of the agencies reported some level of operationalization of community policing—the degree was measured by a summative scale from five questions on the LEMAS survey. MacDonald reported that the level of community policing training (a measure of community policing implementation in its own right, but also a surrogate measure of operationalizing community policing) had no effect on homicide and robbery. Indeed, agencies that reported having a community policing plan in place had significantly higher rates of robbery, even after controlling for demographic variables.

Bureau of Justice Statistics
Federal agency in the U.S. Department of Justice responsible for compiling a range of statistical reports pertaining to state and local criminal justice administration.

Evaluation of an extensive single site community partnership effort yielded a similar finding—no effect from community policing. Weisburd, Morris, and Ready (2008) assessed the impact of a two-year effort by the Redlands,

California, Police Department to affect the social views of youth in stressed neighborhoods. Thirty-two census block groups were identified as stressed neighborhoods. Sixteen of these were assigned to treatment and sixteen assigned to control. Over a two-year period the Redlands Police Department conducted seventy-four different "community engagement" programs in the sixteen experimental census block groups. At both the initiation and conclusion of the program, a battery of social attitude survey instruments was administered by Weisburd et al. (2008). No differences in citizen attitudes were found between the experimental and control areas. Because the census block groups were relatively geographically small, approximately 300 households and 1,000 persons, and because the treatment in comparison block groups was interspersed throughout the community, no effort was made to measure impact upon crime rates.

The treatment in this case included a wide range of community engagement efforts. Some were fairly traditional, such as **neighborhood watch**. Others were classic "soft" community policing efforts, including Easter parties, a cyber café, and parenting classes. The Redlands engagement is precisely the type of community policing that draws criticism for overextending the role of the police. Easter parties and parenting classes may or may not strengthen the social fabric of a community, but it is rare to find a police department budget sufficient for such indirect and long-term forms of crime prevention.

neighborhood watch Volunteer groups sponsored by a police agency that commit to monitoring activity in their own residential vicinity; receiving emphasis is observing neighbors' homes during absences for indications of burglary.

Positive results were obtained from a third "community policing" assessment (Connell, Miggans, & McGloin, 2008). In this instance an unidentified police agency targeted a geographic area with an unusually high crime rate. A team of officers was assigned responsibility for patrolling the area. Each officer in the team had a designated geographic subset for which he or she was particularly responsible. Two control areas were identified for comparative evaluation. The authors assured us that all four components of community policing as identified by Cordner (2001) were incorporated. However, they failed to identify any specific intervention other than assigning long-term geographic responsibility to a patrol team. Crime rates in the treated area declined statistically more than in the control areas (Connell et al., 2008).

There are numerous conceptual problems with this report. First, the demographics of the treated versus control area were never reported—so we do not know how comparable they were. Second, agency-wide offense data during the experimental period were not reported, so we do not know whether what occurred in the experimental area might have been part of a larger trend, albeit not specifically affecting the stipulated control areas. Indeed, crime did decline in the two control areas during the experimental areas—suggesting that the crime decline in the experimental areas may well have simply been part of a larger trend. Third, the findings are grossly overgeneralized. There may have been a range of community engagement efforts, there may have been a range of problem-solving projects, but they're not reported.

A fourth evaluation addressed community engagement process rather than impact, but with important implications for impact assessments. Famega (2007) addressed the issue of "what indeed is the treatment" by comparing the activities of "regular" patrol officers with those operating under a community policing model. The findings from Baltimore indicated that no significant difference in mean patrol time was found by type of officer, and both "post" (regular patrol) and community officers spent less than 2 percent of time on foot patrol. Regular officers spent less than 1 percent of time engaged in casual conversation with the public, and only 1.4 percent of time gathering information from citizens. Community officers spent less than 1 percent of time on both of these activities combined. Communication between community officers and citizens appeared to be primarily within the context of prearranged neighborhood/housing meetings (5.4 percent of community officer time) (p. 27).

An Alternative Goal—Citizen Satisfaction

It is difficult if not impossible to directly link crime reduction, or the lack thereof, to either community policing or problem-oriented efforts. That noted, there is a valid measure of community policing success that does not require crime reduction. If citizens are happy with police partnerships, it can be argued that this outcome alone justifies the required investment of resources. A case in point is Fort Worth.

storefront police stations
Small offices usually located in commercial strip centers designed primarily to provide citizens "walk-in" convenience to report issues; staffing levels vary, but typical is a single police agency employee during business hours; patrol units do not deploy from storefronts, but may use the facility to complete reports.

Citizens and a sample of police officers were asked to assess the importance of three distinct Fort Worth Police Department community policing programs—neighborhood patrol officers (community policing specialists), **storefront police stations**, and citizens on patrol programs. The success of the Fort Worth Police Department's community policing effort was affirmed in a telephone survey of 400 randomly selected Fort Worth residents (Liederbach, Fritsch, Carter, & Bannister, 2007). Liederbach et al. (2007) noted that Fort Worth residents were genuinely satisfied with the police and believed the department was competent. Interestingly, citizens viewed these three community engagement programs as more important than was perceived by officers. Citizens' mean scores were significantly greater than officers' mean scores for all three. Further, a higher proportion of police officers indicated that these three community programs were "not valuable." Indeed, fully one-third of the officers indicated that the neighborhood patrol officer program was not valuable. Liederbach et al. (2007) concluded that "the findings appeared to tell two different stories regarding the impact of community policing in Fort Worth" (p. 286). Although recognizing the success of the programs with citizens, the authors noted that "street level officers in Fort Worth still appeared to be resistant in many respects to community policing, at least when their views were compared to those of citizens." They went on to suggest that officer resistance was likely a by-product of traditional police culture that continued to hold sway over police officers.

Learning Objective

There is, however, another explanation. Literally on a daily basis police officers are exposed to the harm and suffering of victimization. Occasionally the consequences of victimization are horrific. More typically, although less than horrific, the consequences of victimization are disruptive and disturbing. The literature is replete with references to the trauma of having one's home burglarized, for example. Dealing with the trauma of victimization has a deep and profound impact upon police officers. William Muir addressed the phenomenon in detail in his landmark book *Police: Streetcorner Politicians* (1977). Muir asserted that human beings cannot cope with the job of policing without developing a tragic sense of human existence. Stated differently, one must come to accept the fact that bad things happen to good people in order to maintain one's psychological health as a police officer. Officers who assert that dealing with the tragedy of victimization does not bother them are in denial.

The relevance here is that police officers in any comparative survey, such as the one completed in Fort Worth, are going to place higher importance upon traditional crime control than citizens. The amount of tragic victimization experienced by any randomly selected 400 households in Fort Worth is not likely to be high. Most citizens will respond to ratings of the importance of traditional crime control versus public order and community programs in the context of never having experienced traumatic victimization. As usual, they want the kids to stop speeding down the street, gang graffiti in the area eliminated, unsightly properties cleaned up, and so forth. In contrast, on rating or ranking scales assessing the relative import of traditional crime control and quality-of-life initiatives, police officers who deal with victimization will inevitably rate traditional crime control higher. They are not responding as mere puppets socialized into traditional police culture; they are responding as human beings angry over the tragedy of victimization caused by callous street predators.

Limitations on Community Policing Validation

The discipline of theoretical physics is struggling with a dilemma surprisingly similar to our inability to "test" the efficacy of community policing—the inability to test the veracity of string theory. String theory holds that all matter and energy in the universe is composed not of minuscule particles, but extraordinarily small "vibrating" energy strings, less than a trillionth of a trillionth the size of an atom. String theory holds the promise of uniting Einstein's relativity with Bohr's quantum mechanics—the conflicting products of a century of physics. But it is at present only a mathematical concept—and frustratingly requires the existence of several additional physical dimensions unobservable to anyone. There is unhappiness among an increasing number of physicists with the very concept:

> The main problem with string theory—acknowledged by critics and supporters alike—is that no one knows if it will ever generate testable predictions that can be addressed by experiment (a process that essentially defines the practice of science). The basic equations of string theory have more solutions than there are atoms in the universe. Since the theory can't be disproved, there may never be a way to tell if it is right or wrong. (D'Agnese, 2006, p. 68)

We struggle with a similar dilemma when attempting to measure a conceptual framework in policing. Strategies are testable; philosophies are not. Conceptual frameworks defy measurement. One can certainly argue that both community policing and problem-oriented policing are conceptual frameworks, not strategies.

Learning Objective

If we move to a narrower definition of community policing, resources expended upon formal, structured community contact, then in theory the concept might be scientifically testable. The problem here, however, is that a scientific test in policing requires Treatment A versus Treatment B versus, ideally, Control. Think the Kansas City Preventive Patrol Experiment: Reactive Patrol Beat, Proactive Patrol Beat, Control Beat; or in San Diego, Field Interrogation Area versus No Field Interrogation Area. If the community policing paradigm is Treatment A, then what is Treatment B? No community engagement? That is hardly a reasonable alternative.

The only real potential Treatment B is expending the scarce resources spent on structured community contact on something else—tactical units, surveillance units, special proactive investigative units. After one year, the researcher measures crime in the community policing sector against crime in the repression area. However, no police chief is going to authorize such an "experiment" and no responsible researcher would agree to undertake it.

Learning Objective

As a strategic approach, the only universal attribute of community policing is structured community contact. Importantly, there are a number of things community policing is not. Community policing is not problem-oriented policing. Structured community contact and structured problem solving are two different strategies, two different approaches. Selected citizens may be engaged as part of a problem-solving effort, but that does not make the two concepts synonymous. Of even greater import, community policing is not everything that works in policing. There are lots of approaches in law enforcement that are better than others. Deployment by analysis works far better than unstructured, nondirected deployment. Monitored investigative caseloads work better than simple rotational assignments of cases to new detectives. Providing patrol officers with detailed information about problem locations and problem persons on their beat works better than depending solely upon their accumulated street knowledge. Use of civil nuisance abatement statutes to deal with problem locations works very well. None of these are inherently embedded in community policing.

IMPLICATIONS FOR STRATEGY

Community policing is more than a strategy—but it is not everything that works in policing either. An agency should have a broadly based community engagement approach. But the dedication of more extensive resources is subject to classical cost-benefit analysis. An Urban Institute publication notes:

> Even when an intervention is effective (i.e., it is known to prevent crime), the analysis of costs and benefits is necessary since the cost of the intervention might outweigh the benefits associated with the reduction in crime. (Roman, Dunworth, & Marsh, 2010, p. 1)

This is certainly the case with resource-hungry community engagement efforts, as well as problem-oriented initiatives. The same holds true, of course, for all strategic approaches. The point here is that community policing is not an exception from cost-benefit analysis. This is particularly the case with agency sponsorship of specialized community policing roles. Both formally and informally since the year 2000, agencies have conducted such analyses, and reduced resources dedicated to community policing. Survey data compiled by the Bureau of Justice Statistics indicated that from 2000 to 2003, the number of community policing officers declined by almost half—from about 103,000 to about 55,000. From 2003 to 2007, the downward trend continued, dropping to 47 percent of departments and 47,000 officers. In 2007, overall only 14 percent of local police departments had a separate specialized unit with full-time officers dedicated to community policing activities. From a different perspective, however, it should be noted that 85 percent of departments serving 1 million or more residents had a specialized community policing unit, and about 60 percent of those serving a

Learning Objective

population of 50,000 to 999,999 had such a unit (Reaves, 2010, p. 28). One can certainly argue that the creation of specialized units or even roles in small agencies was never envisioned as appropriate implementation of community policing in the first place. Regardless, a "happy medium" appears to have evolved over the last decade. In the next chapter, the role of community and problem-oriented approaches as a component of crime reduction strategy is discussed.

SUMMARY

- Misuse of the community policing concept is common. There exists among some a naïve imagery of policing the way it should be; the imagery is appealing but is a Normal Rockwell picture of an America that disappeared on December 7, 1941. Potential abuse of community policing terminology is illustrated by a survey conducted in 1992, 1997, and 2002 that intended to measure "progress in the implementation of community policing." Although a number of potential characteristics of community policing listed in the survey are perfectly appropriate, also included are some that are inappropriate.
- Appropriate models of community policing include endeavors such as community policing specialists engaging in structured community contact, supporting neighborhood watch programs, serving in a school liaison role, and implementing problem-solving efforts. Other programs can exist independent of an agency having a community policing specialist, including citizen advisory groups, citizens' police academies, citizens on patrol, and active neighborhood watch programs.
- A common practice is to tag the word "policing" onto a descriptive phrase as part of the naming of a strategic approach. For example, currently circulating are the terms "intelligence-led policing," "evidence-based policing," as well as the enduring use of the terms community policing and problem-oriented policing. The problem is that when we describe an approach or set of strategies with the term "policing," we imply that that is the way law enforcement is done, and—this is how the harm occurs—that the policing approach named is the only way that law enforcement should be done.
- Four empirical assessments attempted to link components of community policing to crime reduction. Three of the four found no impact. Although one reported a positive impact upon crime, the treatment was never defined beyond stability of geographic patrol assignment—hardly a unique attribute of community policing. However, it must be noted that it is methodologically nearly impossible to directly link the kinds of efforts conducted under the auspices of community policing to specific crime reduction. The intermediate measure of citizen satisfaction and support for such programming is more realistic, and potentially just as valuable.
- Police officers are often faulted for being less than fully supportive of generic quality-of-life endeavors implemented under the auspices of community policing. However, this is best explained by the fact that on a daily basis police officers are exposed to the harm and suffering of criminal victimization. In contrast, the amount of tragic victimization experienced by any randomly selected group of surveyed households is not likely to be high. The result is that police officers will always place higher importance upon traditional crime control than citizens.
- Community policing should not be characterized as everything that works in policing. The universal attribute of community policing is structured community contact. Community policing likewise is not synonymous with problem-oriented policing. Although problem-oriented policing frequently includes a citizen engagement component, it is a distinguishable strategy.
- The Bureau of Justice Statistics reports that since the year 2000 there has been a significant decline in the number of community policing specialists, dropping from 103,000 in 2000 to 47,000 in 2007. Nevertheless, it should be noted that 85 percent of departments serving 1,000,000 or more residents have a specialized community policing unit, and 60 percent of those serving a population between 50,000 and 1,000,000 have such a unit.

REVIEW QUESTIONS

1. The Police Executive Research Forum survey of characteristics of community policing implementation includes programs that are characterized as appropriate, as well as some characterized as inappropriate. Briefly describe the hypothetical components of community policing that are characterized as appropriate, and additionally three components that are characterized as inappropriate or questionable.
2. It is suggested that small, tightly integrated, autonomous, self-identified neighborhoods interwoven with their police departments is mythology. What characteristics of a typical suburban city and its residents argue against the mythological image?
3. What harm occurs by tagging the term "policing" onto a descriptive phrase of a strategic approach, that is, community policing, problem-oriented policing, intelligence-led policing, evidence-based policing, and the like?
4. Describe which components of community policing were tested in each of the four empirical assessments that attempted to link the implementation of the respective component to crime reduction.
5. The Bureau of Justice Statistics periodically surveys major police departments to ascertain a range of information, from policies to staffing. Summarize recent results in terms of both the number of community policing specialists reported by surveyed agencies as well as the proportion of agencies reporting the existence of a designated community policing organizational unit.

REAL-WORLD SCENARIOS

1. You are the chief of police of a suburban agency of 50,000 residents. The former chief had been in the position for nearly twenty years, and believed that appropriate communication with the community was via the community's elected representatives—the city council. You see a need to broaden the range of community contact. List and briefly describe at least five programs that you might consider that would accomplish this purpose.
2. One component of your community is a "retirement village" with nearly 1,000 residents. You have received a letter from the president of their community association indicating that a number of residents would like to volunteer to assist the police department in whatever way possible. Prepare a descriptive list of at least three appropriate volunteer activities.
3. You are a lieutenant in charge of special services, which includes four officers assigned as community policing specialists. Your chief of police approaches you, noting that some agencies in the area have eliminated these roles. She asks you to prepare a briefing document on the range of endeavors that might be undertaken by community policing specialists, beginning with those that are directly relevant to crime control and progressively descending to those that pertain to community quality-of-life issues that may or may not directly affect the incidence of crime. Prepare such a rank-ordered list.

APPLICATION ACTIVITIES

1. The term "intelligence-led policing" is used in this chapter. Using standard library resources, locate a minimum of three documents that describe this approach. Construct a descriptive synopsis of the concept from these resources.
2. Go to the National Association of Citizens on Patrol website, http://www.nacop.org/. Using the links provided, list five important components of such programs.
3. Using a web search engine, find descriptive information about police school liaison programs. From the information provided, develop a list of five significant functions of police school liaison officers.

COURSEMATE

This available CourseMate has an interactive eBook and interactive learning tools, including flash cards, quizzes, and more. To learn more about this resource and access free demo CourseMate resources, go to **www.cengagebrain.com**, and search for this book. To access CourseMate materials that you have purchased, go to **login.cengagebrain.com**.

REFERENCES

Brogden, M. (1999). Community policing as apple pie. In R. I. Mawby (Ed.), *Policing across the world* (p. 179). London: University College London Press.

Connell, N. M., Miggans, K., & McGloin, J. M. (2008). Can a community policing initiative reduce serious crime? *Police Quarterly, 11*(2), 127–150.

Cordner, G. (2001). Community policing: Elements and effects. In R. G. Dunham & G. P. Albert (Eds.), *Critical issues in policing: Contemporary readings* (4th ed., pp. 493–510). Prospect Heights, IL: Waveland.

D'Agnese, J. (2006, September). Book review: Not even wrong and the trouble with physics. *Discover Magazine*, p. 68.

Eck, J. E., & Rosenbaum, D. (1994). The new police order: Effectiveness, equity and efficiency in community policing. In D. P. Rosenbaum (Ed.), *Community policing: Testing the promises*. Thousand Oaks, CA: Sage.

Famega, C. N. (2007). A comparison of patrol officers' and community policing specialists' time allocation. Paper presented at the Academy of Criminal Justice Sciences 2007 meeting.

Fridell, L., & Wycoff, M. A. (2004). *Community policing: The past, present, and future.* Washington, DC: Police Executive Research Forum.

Liederbach, J., Fritsch, E. J., Carter, D. L., & Bannister, A. (2007). Exploring the limits of collaboration in community policing: A direct comparison of police and citizen views. *Policing: An International Journal of Police Strategies and Management, 31*(2), 271–291.

MacDonald, J. M. (2002). The effectiveness of community policing in reducing urban violence. *Crime & Delinquency, 48*(4), 592–617.

Manning, P. K. (2003). Personal communication during International Police Studies Conference, Eastern Kentucky University. Richmond, KY.

Muir, W. K. (1977). *Police: Streetcorner politicians*. Chicago, IL: University of Chicago Press.

Reaves, B. A. (2010). *Local police departments, 2007*. Washington, DC: U.S. Department of Justice, Office of Justice Programs, Bureau of Justice Statistics.

Roman, J. K., Dunworth, T., & Marsh, K. (Eds.). (2010). *Cost-benefit analysis and Crime control*. Washington, DC: The Urban Institute Press.

Weisburd, D., Morris, N. A., & Ready, J. (2008). Risk-focused policing at places: An experimental evaluation. *Justice Quarterly, 25*(1), 163–200.

CHAPTER 4

Focusing Community Policing and Problem-Solving on Crime Reduction

KEY TERMS

Beat team concept

"Every officer is a community policing officer" model

GIS

Meta-analysis

SARA model

Specialist model of community policing

Three Citizens Model

LEARNING OBJECTIVES

After completing this chapter, you should be able to:

- Characterize the totality of research evidence regarding whether community policing impacts strongly on crime and disorder.
- Cite the reason neighborhood deployment is necessary regardless of research evidence regarding its effectiveness.
- Define the term *neighborhoods* in the context of neighborhood deployment of the police.
- Describe three models of neighborhood deployment, including issues of efficacy associated with each.
- Distinguish the definition of community policing from that of problem-oriented policing.
- Identify the components of the "Three Citizens' Model."
- Characterize the degree of success of total restructuring of patrol deployment in order to implement community policing.
- Characterize in general terms the status of problem-oriented policing.
- Describe the primary "problem" with problem-oriented policing.
- Explain why bias in reporting of the success of problem-oriented policing exists.
- Contrast the nature of conflicting views regarding the utility of the SARA model.
- Describe why it is difficult to construct experimental designs to test the efficacy of problem-oriented policing.
- Cite the relevance of research conducted in Jacksonville, Florida, comparing concentrated patrol to problem-oriented interventions.
- Describe the nature of both congruence and conflict between problem-solving and enforcement-focused efforts.
- Identify the range of specific actions that might be undertaken as part of an enforcement crackdown.
- Explain why permanent resolution of issues is an unrealistic expectation for problem-oriented policing approaches.
- Describe the role of community policing specialists in a Compstat environment.

A focus upon crime control does not mean that neighborhood-centered efforts should be eliminated. The criticism of community policing described in Chapter 3 is directed at the "reinvention-of-policing" model of community policing, not the citizen engagement model. A deteriorating neighborhood with vacant homes used as shoot-up galleries, abandoned cars, overgrown vacant lots, and burglar bar windows—all scarred by gang graffiti—requires innovative and broadly defined interventions. It is appropriate that police agencies not only be involved in such efforts, but when necessary lead them. At the same time, police departments are not neighborhood management departments. Crime control must remain the focus.

Research Evidence: An Irresolvable Problem

Learning Objective

The near impossibility of empirically linking community policing to crime reduction has already been discussed. According to Weisburd and Eck (2004, p. 52), evidence that does exist does not provide strong support for the position that community policing impacts strongly on crime or disorder. Weisburd and Eck elaborate regarding the lack of evidence linking community policing to crime reduction, including research failing to find a linkage for (1) community meetings, citing Wycoff and Skogan (1986); (2) neighborhood watch, citing Rosenbaum (1989); (3) storefront offices, citing Skogan (1990) and Uchida, Forst, and Annan (1992); and (4) newsletters, citing Pate and Annan (1989).

Learning Objective

Learning Objective

Nonetheless, community demand for neighborhood deployment cannot be ignored. Regardless of the lack of research evidence substantiating effects, citizens expect to see police officers on patrol in their neighborhood. The most frequent complaint on surveys of citizen satisfaction is that "we never see the police." By neighborhood deployment, what is meant is the direction of patrol resources to be responsive to the particular requirements and demands of a geographic subdivision of a jurisdiction. We most often describe a jurisdictional subdivision as a neighborhood. However, jurisdiction subdivisions are not necessarily neighborhoods in the classic sense; they may also be central business districts, retail commercial areas such as a mall and its environs, or even schools.

Models of Neighborhood Deployment

Learning Objective

Specialization by geography, or neighborhood responsiveness specialization, takes three essential forms (see Figure 4.1). By far the most popular is the overlay model. In an overlay model the agency continues to deploy regular patrol units that respond to calls-for-service and use uncommitted patrol time for proactive enforcement efforts. As an overlay to these regular patrol units, specialist officers engage in structured community contact and problem solving. Stated differently, this is the **specialist model of community policing**. A community resource officer is assigned to some aggregation of regular patrol beats, typically four or five regular patrol beats, works flexible hours, and hypothetically provides support to regular patrol through community engagement and problem solving.

specialist model of community policing Assignment of officers to concentrate on community engagement and problem solving; normally a full-time assignment.

FIGURE 4.1 Three Basic Models of Community Policing

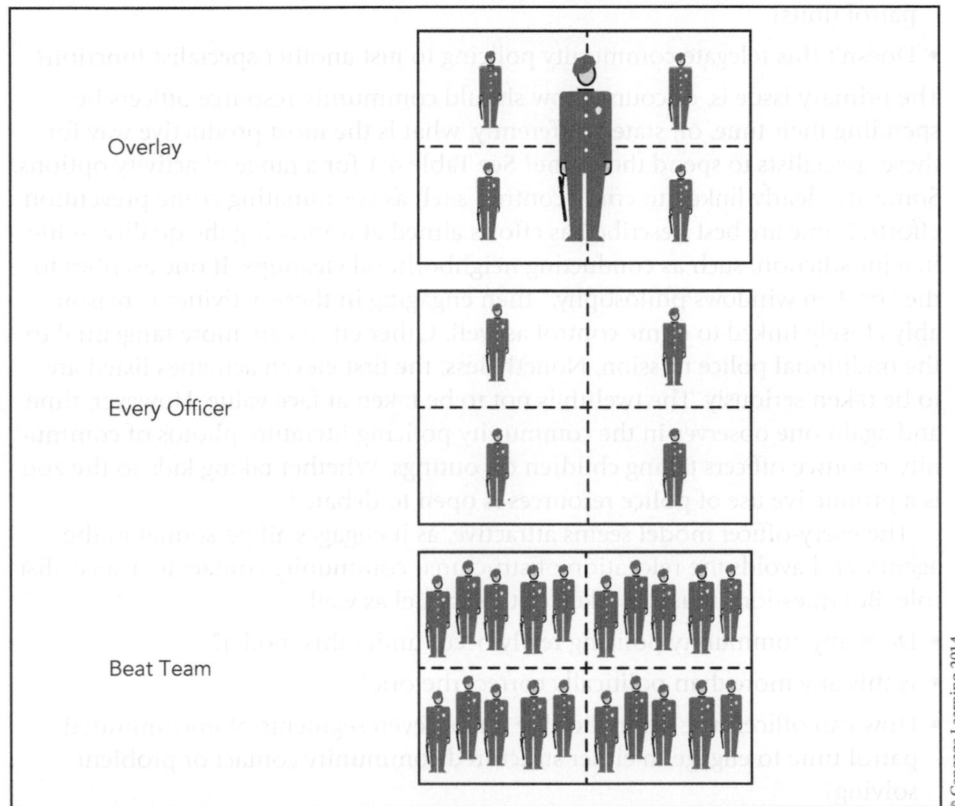

A second of the three models is the **"every officer is a community policing officer" model**. Using this scheme, patrol is staffed at a level sufficient that officers cannot only meet the responsibilities for responding to calls-for-service and proactive enforcement, but also engage in structured community contact and problem solving. The every-officer model assumes that there will be sufficient staffing—that some flexibility exists in relieving officers from immediate responsibility for call-for-service response during periods of a shift, or at least during a period of a month.

"every officer is a community policing officer" model
Hypothetical commitment to having every officer responsible for community engagement; most frequently an emphasis upon a philosophy of neighborhood responsiveness rather than structured positive engagement programs.

The third model is the **beat team concept**. The beat-team concept is a deployment scheme that harkens back to the 1970s neighborhood team policing movement. A group of officers is assigned to a geographic subdivision of a jurisdiction. Typically, a sergeant is in charge of that geographic subdivision, with 24/7 responsibility. The group of officers assigned permanently to that area assumes responsibility not only for regular patrol services, but for structured community contact and problem solving as well. Individual officers on the team may work for three weeks in a regular response patrol capability, and then draw a week's worth of relief from such responsibility while they engage in structured community contact or problem solving.

beat team concept
Assignment of a team of officers, usually ten to fifteen, for providing all services to a designated area, typically a cluster of three to five beats; supervised by a sergeant and granted broad leeway to establish its own engagement and problem-solving endeavors.

Learning Objective

Issues exist with each of the three models. For the overlay model, the questions that might be asked include:

- What are community policing overlay specialists supposed to be doing?
- How do we measure their productivity?

- What is the proper ratio between community policing specialists and regular patrol units?
- Doesn't this relegate community policing to just another specialist function?

The primary issue is, of course, how should community resource officers be spending their time, or, stated differently, what is the most productive way for these specialists to spend their time? See Table 4.1 for a range of activity options. Some are clearly linked to crime control, such as coordinating crime prevention efforts. Some are best described as efforts aimed at improving the quality of life in a jurisdiction, such as conducting neighborhood cleanups. If one ascribes to the "broken windows philosophy," then engaging in these activities is reasonably closely linked to crime control as well. Other efforts are more tangential to the traditional police mission. Nonetheless, the first eleven activities listed are to be taken seriously. The twelfth is not to be taken at face value. However, time and again one observes in the community policing literature photos of community resource officers taking children on outings. Whether taking kids to the zoo is a productive use of police resources is open to debate.[1]

Learning Objective

The every-officer model seems attractive, as it engages all personnel in the agency and avoids the relegation of structured community contact to a specialist role. But questions must be asked of this model as well:

- Does any community policing really occur under this model?
- Is this any more than politically correct rhetoric?
- How can officers use unpredictable and uneven segments of uncommitted patrol time to engage in either structured community contact or problem solving?

Is the every-officer model just another way of saying "we've been doing community policing all along" without effecting any change at all? Or, from a more sympathetic perspective, does the every-officer model represent sincere commitment to community engagement and problem solving as opposed to putting a box in the organization chart? It is probably the former.

The final model is the beat-team approach. Relatively few agencies have attempted this model. Among those that have are Arlington, Texas;

TABLE 4.1 A Dozen Activity Options for Community Resource Officers

1. Directing problem-oriented policing projects
2. Attending community meetings
3. Assisting neighborhood associations
4. Coordinating crime-prevention efforts
5. Coordinating family assistance
6. Assisting persons with special problems
7. Coordination with social and mental health agencies
8. Helping youths with their lives
9. Conducting neighborhood cleanups
10. Demolishing abandoned structures
11. Assisting the homeless
12. Taking kids to the zoo

Charlotte-Mecklenburg, North Carolina; Lansing, Michigan; and Reno, Nevada. The issues raised by the beat-team model include:

Learning Objective

- Can agencies afford the cost of neighborhood teams?
- Is this really any different than the "every officer is a community policing officer" model?
- Who among the seven to ten team members is responsible for what?
- Does the model fragment and isolate patrol services within artificial beats or district boundaries?

The Arlington, Texas, agency has made some modifications to the model since its implementation, including the restoration of shift responsibility to lieutenants. Nevertheless, the agency still believes strongly in its viability.

The Question Remains: Rhetoric or Reality

Thirty years after the development of the community policing concept, a great variety of initiatives have been created and described. Many, however, have had little relationship to the original concept (Goldstein, 2003). In short, how to best accomplish structured community communication and problem solving is still an unanswered question. Further, it appears that the community policing effort post-09/11 is a lower priority (deGuzman, 2002; DeSimone, 2003).

Learning Objective

As noted in Chapter 3, the term *community policing* as used herein refers to structured community contact efforts by police agencies. The term is *not* used to mean generic community responsiveness, being nice to people, or operating under total quality management principles. The term *problem-oriented policing* (POP) is used to denote defined, long-term, typically atypical responses to specific crime and disorder issues. In this sense, POP includes endeavors such as a multifaceted intervention at a high-crime apartment complex, most Crime Prevention Through Environmental Design (CPTED) projects, and efforts to reduce repetitive calls-for-service from the same location. In this context, POP does *not* include investigations of a single incident or incident series, generic efforts to make referrals to social service agencies when appropriate, or the creation of a police athletic league because there is a perception that such engagement will ultimately reduce youth crime. Most important, POP is not the equivalent of Compstat. Compstat is a separate and distinguishable approach to crime and disorder problems, usually incorporating POP projects, but only as one tactic among many.

Definitions are important here because there is so much ambiguity regarding the terms *community policing* and *problem-oriented policing*. Indeed, it has become popular to use the abbreviation CPOP as a term to describe the integration of both. However, as described later in this chapter, it is clear that the two have not been integrated in practice.

Community Policing

THE BIG PICTURE

All police managers say that they are "doing community policing." It is politically inept for a police chief or sheriff to indicate "I don't believe in community policing." Such a police chief or sheriff could immediately add, "and I'll be leaving this position soon." In its broadest sense, *doing community policing* is simply defined as being responsive to the community served. But when wasn't American law enforcement responsive to the communities it served? We need to move beyond that simple-minded response and define community policing as structured programs to engender broadened community contact.

Learning Objective

Three Citizens' Model
Structured community engagement consisting of citizen advisory groups, citizens' police academies, and citizens-on-patrol programs.

Virtually every police department in the United States has some type of structured program that engenders routine and repetitive community contact. The most common form is the "**Three Citizens' Model**"—citizens' advisory groups, citizens on patrol, and citizens' police academies—frequently abbreviated to the "Three C's." All three are widely employed. Indeed, citizens' police academies are almost universal among large agencies. There are even specialized variants of citizens' police academies. Agencies report conducting citizens' police academies in Spanish, and some have youth citizen police academies. A frequent model is to use the citizens' police academy to "feed" citizens into a citizens on patrol program, volunteers in law enforcement program, or advisory groups. A mere handful of agencies indicate that they once had a citizens' police academy, but had eliminated it.

Community Communication

As social networking websites expanded to include organizations, police agencies rapidly responded. The creation of Facebook or Twitter pages by police agencies is common. Surprising even the optimists, very substantial numbers of citizens join as "fans" or "friends."

Citizen advisory groups come in all shapes and sizes. Some agencies employ a jurisdiction-wide citizen advisory group, some employ neighborhood advisory groups, some employ special-interest advisory groups, and some employ combinations of all of these. Fewer agencies sponsor citizens on patrol programs.

When we get to regularly scheduled generic citizens' meetings or forums, it is another story. Numerous agencies report difficulty in sustaining interest in scheduled neighborhood meetings. Most often, police agencies report that the strongest participation in neighborhood association meetings is from neighborhoods that need police intervention the least.

If one excludes endeavors conducted by community policing specialists, then it is safe to say that about 90 percent of the structured community contact conducted by agencies consists of a combination of the Three Citizens' Model. However, that leaves a large number of programs that are not part of that model. After the Three Citizens' Model, by far the most popular program is neighborhood watch. The Three Citizens' Model, combined with neighborhood watch, is testimony to commitment by U.S. police agencies to engender structured community communication. Beyond these efforts, however, is the creation of community policing specialist roles.

Citizen Input

A time-tested axiom is "don't ask for advice unless you are prepared to take it." The warning applies to the use of neighborhood advisory groups. Many agencies report difficulty in achieving communication and input without relinquishing control of policing in the neighborhood.

A useful comparison is citizen input into public school systems. Although we certainly want Susie's mother to be able to communicate freely with her daughter's first-grade teacher, and indeed to confer with her if problems develop, we do not relinquish control of the classroom to Susie's mother. It is the first-grade teacher's responsibility to promulgate what is to be taught and the fundamentals of how it is to be taught. There may be times when an adjustment and accommodation is necessary given a particular child's learning style or given a particular child's problematic family environment. But "control" remains with the teacher. The same holds true for policing a beat.

COMMUNITY POLICING SPECIALISTS

It is clear that community policing has become a specialist function. A preponderance of medium and large police agencies designate at least some proportion of their officers as full-time specialists in community policing. Willis (2011) notes that not one of six sites he reviewed expected generalist patrol sergeants and their officers to attend community meetings and collaborate closely with community members or organizations to address neighborhood problems: this was the domain of community policing units.

Community Policing Efforts—The Bright Side

Comments from police chiefs:

- Police have become the face of local government.
- One of the benefits of community policing is a city council lobby.
- District area representatives (DRs) are assigned to area commands. They perform:
  - Crime prevention
  - Bicycle patrol
  - Safety education
  - Code enforcement
  - Neighborhood cleanups
  - Call response—if short in patrol

DRs have even cut grass and installed handicap ramps in homes. There is a strong neighborhood association identification with district representatives, with citizens commonly referring to them as "my DR."

- The community networking center became a city hall substation.
- Town hall meetings are held twice a year in each of four districts. Attendance is increasing, and all city departments are present. Most issues concern public works and code enforcement.
- An apartment managers coalition meets monthly.
- A strong citizens' police academy and alumni association exists. Volunteers are paid for parking control at special events, with funds donated to the police department.
- Vehicles have been donated for citizens on patrol programs.
- Linkages of neighborhood watch to other programs include:
  - Citizens on patrol
  - Community associations

(Continues)

(Continued)

- Citizens' police academies
- Senior citizens groups
- A newly initiated volunteer program has taken over order-maintenance jobs, such as:
  - Vacation checks
  - Code checks
  - Abandoned vehicles
  - Speed check points
  - Filing microfiche

The Three Citizens' Model commingles with the role of community policing specialists. That is, in many agencies, designated community specialists are responsible for coordinating the citizens' police academy, citizens-on-patrol program, citizens' advisory groups, neighborhood watch programs, and similar endeavors. At the same time, in most agencies that employ specialists, their role transcends the coordination of these structured community contact efforts. As noted previously, the most common model is to divide a jurisdiction into areas that contain four to six regular patrol beats and assign a specialist to each area. The specialist is then responsible for addressing quality-of-life issues and using problem-oriented intervention techniques to resolve both repetitive calls-for-service and crime issues within that cluster of beats.

Mobile Unit

Programs involving purchase of a mobile trailer that is pulled to problem neighborhoods and parked for a while to establish a police presence have not proven sustainable. Agencies report initial success, but rapidly waning interest. Very quickly, a situation develops where the mobile trailer is pulled to a neighborhood, parked, and virtually no one stops by.

However, the role of community policing specialists is clearly evolving. As noted in Chapter 9, agencies are increasingly focusing the efforts of community policing specialists upon crime control. This trend is captured by the police chief comments in the accompanying inset, "Community Policing Efforts—The Problematic Side." Feedback from police chiefs does not provide a clear and unequivocal reason why this is occurring. Certainly in some instances, disillusionment with such efforts is cited. Other agency representatives mention the strain on resources. Some administrators mention the internal stress that is generated when a portion of the patrol force is removed from normal police responsibilities and reassigned to quality-of-life and social service efforts.

Community Policing Efforts—The Problematic Side

Comments from police chiefs:

- We need to overlay aggressive policing onto community policing.
- Community policing (CP) has become a substation commander saying to a CP officer "keep these problem people off my back."
- Community engagement needs to be crime/disorder oriented—not quality of life, youth education, and/or community infrastructure.

- Community policing officers are resented by regular patrol. They are now occasionally used as a saturation unit.
- Visits with St. Petersburg indicated that NPOs all moved to day shift and patrol officers "flipped" "nonpolice" problems to the NPOs.
- We had created overlay officers, but eliminated them because of resentment by patrol.
- Community policing officers have sometimes become "errand runners."
- We had assigned CP officers to specific neighborhoods. Once assigned, they were very difficult to withdraw—neighborhoods go to the media. CP officers were very successful in eliminating crime. However, after the crime problem is solved, there is no one to replace the police. (Note to the reader: This, of course, could be alternatively interpreted as evidence of community policing success.)
- Evolution has taken place, from an approach of "all things for all people" to swinging back to crime control—the core police function.
- We have three area coordinators—east, west, and business. Originally, they were totally service oriented—literacy classes, boys/girls clubs, bilingual assistance, and so on. The effort of officers was "lost" to the police role. Now the program is reoriented to patrol support—for example, checking compliance of registered sex offenders, monitoring graffiti, and so on.
- We tried the beat-team model, with the city divided into three areas, three shifts per area. It was a "disaster" and was eliminated after three years.
- Community policing initially was implemented by having a couple of officers go out and drink coffee with senior citizen groups—there was no connection to crime. This format was abandoned.
- Efforts to clean up apartment complexes have been successful, but the properties rapidly decay—a six-month effect at most. Ongoing maintenance is required.
- Community policing is now more of a "quality" approach rather than specific projects.
- Community policing is too frequently just traffic patrol.
- Generally, CP is reactive; we have had difficulty in engendering proactive efforts.
- Police area representatives were reduced from six to three, and re-titled community resource officers.
- We cut storefronts from three to one, due to budget cuts and stronger needs in patrol.
- Two community policing officers were appointed, but they were resented by other officers because they were unsupervised. Both eventually left the agency.
- We tried bicycle patrol, but there were not enough resources. Also, we had problems with assigned officers isolating themselves.
- The idea that "every officer is a community officer" is a myth.
- Community meetings—dropped from twenty people attending to one or two. A lot of the tough issues have been dealt with. The public safety advisory board absorbs most of the problems.

(Continues)

(Continued)

- We tried community-oriented policing geographic deployment several years ago:
  - Split city into sixty beats, with one officer per beat.
  - Beats were not staffed twenty-four hours, but lieutenants were assigned twenty-four-hour responsibility over a district.
  - Used the every-officer model.
  - Citizens loved it—would call them "their" officers, but if officer was on vacation, would not get response for days.
  - Ultimately, the deployment did not work.
- The program has changed dramatically. We now have six beats, staffed with four to six officers per shift. Regular patrol has no specific community policing responsibility.
- We also tried two officers per beat; one answered calls, the other did COPS. It did not work; we didn't have enough personnel.

Additionally, during recent years there has been a decrease in the number of individuals assigned to community policing specialists' roles. Numerous agencies use variants of the phrase, "We used to have *x* number of community policing officers, but now we only have *y*." More than a few agencies indicated that they once had specialist roles, but have completely eliminated them. Statistical confirmation of the phenomenon was described in Chapter 3—citing the Bureau of Justice Statistics survey data. At the same time, it must be emphasized that, overall, although there has been some reduction in numbers, there appears to be commitment to maintaining these roles among the majority of agencies. Numerous descriptions of efforts by community policing specialists were positive. Nevertheless, there is also cynicism about the role of community policing specialists.

Starting with Youth

The observation has been made that "kids are the key to a neighborhood." What this means is that working with a neighborhood initially on youth programs brings involvement and commitment by parents. Once that involvement and commitment is established, the range of programs can be expanded.

Learning Objective

However, implementation of community policing by total restructuring of patrol deployment has failed. Innumerable agencies have tried "community policing" patrol deployment schemes, only to abandon them.

Resident Officers

Among the fifteen "community service" officers in the Pasadena, Texas, Police Department, two are resident officers. These officers live in distressed neighborhoods in homes paid for by the city. Each home includes an office area. The cost to the city includes a price of $75,000 to $100,000 for the home itself, and the city pays the utility bills. The program is regarded as very successful by the agency. The focus of the resident officers is upon "broken windows" issues. Interestingly, after assignment of a resident officer to a neighborhood, crime initially went up, then decreased. The initial increase was attributed to increased reporting of offenses by citizens to the assigned resident officer.

Problem-Oriented Policing

THE DISCOURAGING SIDE

Learning Objective

Although structured community contact programs are entrenched in almost all police agencies, and although a community policing specialist role has emerged in most agencies, problem-oriented policing (POP) is still in flux. Many agencies report difficulty with sustaining POP efforts. Some do mention that their community policing specialists conduct POP projects. The difficulty in maintaining POP is not due to a lack of effort or commitment. Numerous agencies have brought in outside trainers to assist with POP, and still are unable to maintain a long-term effort.

Problem-Oriented Policing—The Problematic Side

Comments from police chiefs:

- We trained everyone in POP and total quality management (TQM). Training included representatives from Reno and San Diego. POP fizzled. The structured "Scanning Analysis Response Assessment" (SARA) process proved too cumbersome. We had a few real successes with SARA, but it was not widely employed. What has survived is Compstat. The Compstat process has replaced the SARA process.
- We brought in instructors from the National Institute of Justice (NIJ), who trained all officers. However, no success resulted among officers on regular shifts.
- Officers have been trained in CPOP, but at best it has only sensitized them to being more concerned about "quality-of-life" calls, for example, mental health.
- When it started, the philosophy was that everyone has to have a POP project. Now we have decided that not every officer will participate consistently.
- SARA is too complex; it wraps officers up in process rather than resolution.
- We have trained in POP. We have tried to involve other city departments, particularly for housing issues, but have experienced very limited success.
- Problem solving has been mixed. The specialized units have had more success.
- POP has been almost exclusively oriented toward nuisance abatement.
- Efforts to encourage problem-oriented policing have had little effect.
- We have a crime analyst, but it has resulted in few problem-oriented approaches.

Learning Objective

The primary "problem" with problem-oriented policing is unrealistic expectations by its advocates. From an analysis of Compstat implementation among six agencies, Willis suggests that a department's traditional 911 response system undermines the ability of sergeants to engage in problem-solving efforts with their officers; patrol focuses on responding to individual crime incidents and engaging in traditional law enforcement activities at "hot spots" (Willis, 2011). Innes (2005) observed that although POP can, given the right circumstances, significantly reduce crime and/or disorder, such circumstances are the exception rather than the rule. On a macro level there is not an infinite number of strategy options for law enforcement interdiction of crime. A great deal of the community and problem-oriented policing literature implies that there is. There is not. Despite exultations to law enforcement managers to be creative, innovative, engage other governmental entities, engage "the community," and to always attempt the full **SARA model** (scanning, analysis, response, assessment), the list of cost-effective alternatives available to intercede is limited. Yes, success of nontraditional interventions is celebrated at the annual Problem-Oriented Policing conference. The successes are real. But the truly unusual approach that works effectively to reduce a particular type of crime at a particular location is the rare exception, and not the day-to-day rule. The presentations at the conference do not consist of a random selection out of thousands of structured efforts to reduce crime across the United States, Canada, and Britain. The presentations represent a self-selected group attuned to appropriate documentation. These presenters should be rightfully proud of their success. But what do not make it to the conference are stories of the hundreds of similar efforts that went nowhere.

SARA model
A recommended approach to formal problem solving premised upon scanning, analysis, response, and assessment.

Noted in the Campbell Systematic Review of problem-oriented policing (Weisburd, Telep, Hinkle, & Eck, 2008) is the fact that substantial bias exists in reported problem-oriented success stories. The Goldstein Awards began in 1993, and are given by the Center for Problem-Oriented Policing at the conference just mentioned. Submissions come from American departments, although there are also entries from the United Kingdom, Canada, and Australia. Since their inception in 1999, the Tilley Awards are given to departments only in the United Kingdom by the Home Office. Failed efforts are not in the competitions, only successful problem-oriented policing interventions. It would be illogical for departments to attempt to win a problem-oriented policing award with a project that was not effective... hence the success bias.

Learning Objective

The Problem with Problem Solving from the Private Sector

1. *Actions will not be taken to move us toward our aspirations.*
   Instead, they will be a reaction to the problems. People will be motivated by what they do *not* want, rather than what they *do* want.
2. *There is a difference between building demolition and architecture.*
   One is taking action to have something go away; the other is taking action to have something come into being. This is the difference between problem solving and driving the organization by a vision of what we want to accomplish.
3. *Organizational learning is limited to how to eliminate unwanted situations, not how to bring about desired situations.*

Therefore, learning would not provide the organization with added competency and capacity. And, if the problem-solving tactic is truly successful, the problem will go away, leaving little application for learning in the future.

4. *Motivation for action shifts from one problem to another as problems change in importance over time.*
5. *A false impression of effectiveness is created within the organization, leading to questionable values (for example, that the time to act is when there is a crisis).*

During the heyday of problem-based management styles in the 1970s and early 1980s, many companies discovered that some of the best firefighters within their organizations also turned out to be the pyromaniacs! The more rewards that were given for dealing with crises, the greater the number of calamities. Some companies found that if they got rid of the firefighters, many of the fires went out.

6. *Problems dictate a biased viewpoint.*

Problem solving tends to bias our viewpoint and prejudice our choice of process.... By using this form, people begin to arrange their activities around a search-and-destroy mission against problems. Too often this way of thinking gives people the impression that they are doing something important, but in actuality they are usually filling their time correcting the effects created by faulty structural design.... Of course, organizations do have problems and do need to deal with them well. But the better designed the business is, the less likely it will be that problem solving is its primary orientation.

Among departments that report any POP effort at all, the typical response is that few regular (nonspecialist) officers ever suggest a project. One reason is that officers pulled from regular patrol to work on a POP project are resented by other officers on patrol. Rather than garnering respect for being innovative, a typical response is "We're doing your work for you." Clearly, the patrol officer subculture very quickly dampens any enthusiasm that might have existed among some officers for POP.

Learning Objective

POP has intrinsic appeal to academics. The components of the SARA model—scanning, analysis, response, assessment—parallel those of the scientific method. It is an analogue to the fundamental approaches that researchers employ (Innes, 2005). However, among police managers, few are supportive of the SARA model. The universal response is that the SARA approach is too complex, too cumbersome, and too time-consuming. Interestingly, the negative view is strongest among participants from agencies that had brought outside SARA trainers to their departments at the initiation of POP. Indeed, it should be noted that in an evaluation of problem-oriented policing in San Diego, California, Cordner and Biebel found that officers there responded in the same way. They simply found SARA to be superfluous to POP efforts. Officers in San Diego related succinctly, "We know what the problem is, the problem is solving the problem" (Cordner & Biebel, 2004).

THE ENCOURAGING SIDE

meta-analysis
Research that includes scanning all previous related evaluations to ascertain patterns in the findings.

Evaluative research supports the efficacy of problem-oriented policing, albeit with limitations. A Campbell Systematic Review **meta-analysis** was conducted by George Mason University's Center for Evidence-Based Policing (Weisburd et al., 2008). Eligible studies met three criteria: (1) the SARA model was used; (2) a comparison group was included; and (3) at least one crime or disorder outcome was a dependent variable. Over 5,500 articles and reports on problem-oriented policing were screened, but only ten met all three criteria (p. 6).

The good news is that the evaluations reported "an overwhelmingly positive impact of problem-oriented policing." The caveat is that the authors cautioned that the number of eligible studies—meeting minimum criteria for a quasi-experimental design—was very small (.002 percent), and those that did meet the criteria included a diverse group of problems. Even more sobering was the observation that "...experimental studies all employed, at least to some extent, a hot spot approach to using problem-oriented policing, which suggests that problem-oriented policing may be particularly effective when used in concert with hot spot policing" (Weisburd et al., 2008, p. 21).

Learning Objective

To balance the perspective, however, it must be noted that the vast majority of problem-oriented policing projects do not lend themselves to inclusion of comparison groups—whether geographic areas, specific locations, or "problematic" people/groups. An illustration is budget motel programs. Because such facilities offer low rates, accept cash, and often involve an unrestricted environment, customers with illicit intentions find them attractive (Schmerler, 2005). The worst of budget motels do not ask for identification, rent rooms by the hour, and are frequently in profit-sharing arrangements with drug dealers and prostitutes. A study of Chula Vista, California, motels found that those charging $40 or less per night had twice the number of police service calls per room, and two and a half times the number of arrests per room (Schmerler, 2005). An agency mounting a multifaceted "attack" on such businesses is going to choose the worst of the worst for concentrated effort. Random assignment of some motels to treatment and others to no treatment (controls) will make little sense to a police chief under political pressure to clean up these premises.

Learning Objective

A notable exception to the problem of including control areas is research conducted in 2009 in Jacksonville, Florida (Taylor, Koper, & Woods, 2011). A total of eighty-three violent crime hot spots (measured violent crime excluded domestic violence) were randomly assigned to one of three conditions: forty to control (no changes), twenty-one to saturation/directed patrol, and twenty-two to problem-oriented interventions. Each of the three conditions was maintained for a ninety-day period. Total officer-hours at the saturation/directed patrol locations averaged about fifty-three per week. Sixty officers and four crime analysts were assigned to the POP intervention sites, averaging ninety-five officer-hours per week per hot spot. There were no statistically significant effects from either saturation patrol or POP efforts *during* the intervention period, although the crime measures did decline by up to 20 percent in the saturation/directed patrol locations. However, problem-solving interventions were associated with a 33 percent reduction in the count of "street violence" during the ninety-day post-period—the ninety days following the intervention. In contrast, crime immediately rebounded at the sites receiving saturation patrol—that is, once the police left, crime rates immediately returned to pre-intervention levels. The results argue for the durability of POP intervention versus simple saturation patrol.

Problem-Oriented Policing—The Bright Side

Comments from police chiefs:

- We have had success with the evening overlap shift. SWAT team officers are also used for directed efforts during evening hours.
- Each unit is supposed to employ POP. Emphasis is placed on removing boundaries between divisions. We send a team to POP Conference every year. Reduction of service demand is the focus.
- We have four full-time neighborhood police officers; they are occasionally assigned complaints as part of their POP projects.
- We brought in outside trainers, and included PERF. We trained in SARA. We concentrated on hot spots and "broken windows" issues (we bulldozed a lot of houses). Still using SARA, crime analysis, and CPTED.
- We have storefront personnel who also do POP. Based upon input from shift commanders, they do a good job.
- We send four officers a year to POP Conference. We play up POP successes with PowerPoint® presentations and other activities. A success ex ample is the Blue Cross Headquarters, where through classic CPTED we reduced crime to zero.
- We attempt to have every officer participate in POP.
- POP has been attempted, with some successes, particularly against blight.
- From initiation in 1995 to today, POP has replaced community policing.

Low-cost or "Section Eight" housing is another perennial police problem. Criminal offenders and drug dealers gravitate to such locations. Such housing projects are frequently classic cases of the "broken windows" phenomenon—literally, not figuratively. In some cases, every window is broken. Some jurisdictions insist that funding for the police department is built into all Housing and Urban Development (HUD) community development block grants. Thus, for example, in a $2 million grant, the police department might get $100,000 to provide the housing complex focused attention. Problem-oriented policing approaches are often employed in such circumstances. Indeed, the situation parallels that described in the New Briarfield apartment complex in Newport News, Virginia, in the landmark publication *Problem Solving: Problem-Oriented Policing in Newport News* (Eck & Spelman, 1987). In low-cost housing, whether government subsidized or simply private apartments, the complaints are about drug dealers, prostitutes, and the real crime that accompanies them. The most frequently reported type of success story with POP entails long-term intervention at crime-ridden apartment complexes.

If repetitive citizen complaints about an issue are used as a measure of a community definition of problems, then the frequently reported problem is simply traffic. Agency after agency reports that the most troublesome issue that is reported by citizens is traffic problems. Traffic issues were reported as the most frequent type of repetitive calls to police departments and the most frequently mentioned issue during neighborhood meetings. After traffic, complaints about animals come next. Animal complaints are almost always in the form of "dogs running loose." These responses reinforce what we have heard so many times before: If one asks citizens what bothers them, police managers do not hear "murder, rape, and robbery;" what they hear is "teenagers speeding and dogs running loose." At the same time, one must be careful about overgeneralizing this characterization. These are the problems of middle-class neighborhoods, not low-cost housing projects. To relegate problem-oriented policing to control of dogs running loose is, to say the least, degrading to the concept.

PROBLEM-ORIENTED POLICING AND ARREST-FOCUSED ENFORCEMENT

Learning Objective

Variation in approach in policing, as well as in any other organization, will generate both congruence and conflict among alternatives. This is the case in comparing problem-solving and enforcement-focused efforts. First, the congruence:

- POP is premised upon ultimately saving resources, not consuming them.
- POP "properly applied" focuses upon crime and disorder—not taking over the responsibilities of parks and recreation or the school district.
- POP "properly applied" engages multiple units in a police department (like Compstat) but expands engagement where appropriate outside of the police agency (unlike Compstat).
- Infusion of POP into Compstat crime strategy meetings is a counter to the short-term bias and limited response mode of Compstat.

As noted by David Kennedy, "If you watch what goes on in Compstat, and spend time in the precincts and boroughs.... you see a lot of what would now be called community policing and problem-solving policing" (Gurwitt, 2007). The point was reinforced by Gurwitt, noting that upon taking over Providence, Rhode Island, Dean Esserman "... instituted the Brattonite playbook: Compstat; spinning the department off into nine districts with substations in each; walking or biking beats; re-orienting the department's philosophy toward problem solving and crime prevention, not reaction..." (Gurwitt, 2007).

In making any comparison, it is assumed that an ideal or "high-quality" form of each is being employed. One can, of course, make the case for one approach versus the other if, on the one hand, you use the best form of one and, on the other hand, use the worst form of the other. If POP is paralysis by analysis, then enforcement-focused efforts will always look better. If enforcement-focused efforts consist of nothing more than running from one collection of **GIS** dots to another with five patrol units, then POP will always look better. A fair comparison demands that the playing field be level, and in this case the leveling is the assumption that they both are quality forms of the approach.

GIS
Geographic Information System, or computerized mapping.

Learning Objective

On the other hand, there are inconsistencies between POP and arrest-focused enforcement, as shown in Table 4.2.

Importantly, both POP and enforcement efforts, properly applied, engage top management in structured analysis of crime and disorder. They both force management to think in terms of delivery of services to the community, not merely internal administrative issues. Both force resource analysis. All police agencies operate with limited resources, albeit some more limited than others. Both POP and an enforcement focus engage management in discussing how scarce discretionary resources can best be allocated.

TABLE 4.2 Problem-Oriented Policing and Compstat

Conflict		
Problem-Oriented Policing		**Compstat**
Analytic base emphasizes cross-sectional data	→	Analytic base emphasizes longitudinal data
Long-term perspective—months or years	→	Short-term perspective—days or weeks
Emphasizes disorder reduction	→	Emphasizes Part I crime reduction
Includes some quality-of-life concerns	→	Eliminates quality-of-life issues from police agenda
Tends to become responsibility of specialists	→	Tends to employ only uniformed patrol and tactical units
Collaboration with other agencies and community	→	Response by police department only
Deflection of effort to "nonpolice" issues a risk	→	Fixation upon Part I offenses a risk

This observation brings us back to the observation of Weisburd et al. (2008) that POP frequently comingles with hot-spot enforcement. A co-employment model might also be called a crackdown, defined by Scott (2003) as "sudden and dramatic increases in police officer presence, sanctions and threats of apprehension either for specific offenses or for all offenses in specific places" (p. 1). Scott suggests that specific actions officers might take as part of a crackdown include:

Learning Objective

- Arresting offenders
- Issuing citations
- Conducting field interviews
- Issuing written or verbal warnings
- Taking juvenile offenders into custody for status offenses (for example, for truancy or curfew violations)
- Conducting highly visible patrols
- Conducting traffic stops
- Serving search warrants
- Serving arrest warrants
- Inspecting licenses (liquor, business, driver's)
- Inspecting property for code violations, and enforcing them
- Establishing mobile police command posts/booking stations/neighborhood offices
- Conducting "knock-and-talk" operations (to gain information from citizens who are hesitant to contact the police directly, let the community know what the police hope to achieve, locate offenders, conduct voluntary searches of private premises, look for evidence in plain view, etc.)
- Searching vehicles and interviewing drivers at roadblocks or checkpoints
- Seeking enhanced penalties (for example, by filing cases typically prosecuted under state laws or under federal laws) (p. 4)

Scott (2003) continues:

> ... carefully planned crackdowns, well supported by prior problem analysis, implemented with other responses to ensure longer-term gains, and conducted in a way that maintains public support and safeguards civil rights, can be an important and effective part of police strategies regarding a range of crime and disorder problems. (p. 30)

A specific illustration is a "crackdown" that took place in Richmond, Virginia. Seven high-crime areas received a massive thirty-day police intervention carried out in one area at a time beginning in April 1999. The police intervention was coupled with increased efforts by other city agencies to address quality-of-life and urban-decay problems in and around the targeted areas (Smith, 2001). An evaluation of this "Blitz to Bloom" initiative was conducted in the first of the seven neighborhoods. A 92 percent reduction in reported crime occurred in the target area during the month-long crackdown period. Significant reductions in reported crime persisted in some parts of the neighborhood surrounding the area up to six months after the crackdown ended (p. 60). A discouraging note is that six months after the blitz period ended, crime had returned almost to its pre-intervention levels within the target area.

Learning Objective

This fact illustrates, however, another contentious issue with the SARA model. The model implies permanent resolution of issues. Problem-oriented policing's success is defined as the problem completely and permanently resolved. In the real world "complete and permanent" seldom occurs. This is particularly true when dealing with disadvantaged, high-disorder, high-crime neighborhoods. The conditions that engender such neighborhoods are not going to be permanently resolved by crackdowns—even if the crackdown includes multiple city agencies and an array of quality-of-life initiatives. Problem-oriented policing is being set up to fail if complete and permanent resolution is the definition of success.

There is no inherent conflict between enforcement tactics and problem-oriented policing. Indeed, among flexible police managers and open-minded academics, there are innumerable situations where they are complementary—the strengths of problem-oriented policing compensating for the weaknesses of enforcement, and vice versa.

Finally, there are enforcement issues for which a perpetual string of arrests just makes no sense. Liquor establishments with frequent instances of disorderly conduct and assaults (fights) are an illustration. Rather than arrests every Saturday night, the seventeen problem-oriented policing interventions suggested by Scott and Dedel (2006) should be the preferred course of action, including:

- Formally regulating and enforcing relevant liquor-licensing laws
- Establishing responsible beverage service programs
  - Monitoring drinking to prevent drunkenness
  - Promoting slower drinking rates
  - Prohibiting underage drinking
  - Providing reduced-alcohol or nonalcoholic beverages
  - Requiring or encouraging food service with alcohol service
  - Discouraging alcohol price discounts
- Establishing and enforcing server liability laws

- Training staff to handle patrons nonviolently
- Establishing and enforcing clear rules of conduct for bar patrons
- Banning known troublemakers from bars

For some circumstances, problem-oriented policing rather than enforcement is appropriate, whereas for others problem-oriented policing with enforcement will be appropriate. The first requisite for success with problem-oriented policing is flexibility; the second is appropriate expectations.

IMPLICATIONS FOR STRATEGY

Debate about the character of community policing has become a perennial issue in policing. What can be said, however, is that the concept, defined as structured community contact, has evolved to a specialist function. Take your pick as to whether that represents its success or failure. Similarly, problem-oriented approaches are evolving. Where community policing specialists are used, the officers occasionally take on a problem-oriented project, but almost never using the SARA model. Further, POP frequently "comingles" with enforcement-based efforts. An important observation is that generalist patrol officers are not performing either function—structured community contact or problem-oriented approaches.

There is a new and redeeming trend with regard to both approaches, however. When agencies are asked whether the implementation of Compstat caused them to reconsider the utility of maintaining full-time community policing specialists, most sincerely responded that it did not. Indeed, departments frequently comment that they feel Compstat has reinforced and strengthened the role of their community policing specialists. More specifically, comments are made to the effect that Compstat has caused them to refocus their community policing specialists on core police issues, scaling back or abandoning altogether efforts that are characterized as community quality-of-life concerns. And their redirected effort is frequently coordinating a problem-oriented component to enforcement endeavors. Observations of this author during Compstat meetings confirm these comments. Community policing specialists are often employed as part of a specific Compstat response. Quite often the role of the community policing specialist is to develop a problem-oriented component to the response, but it is not confined to such a role.

Learning Objective

The degree of integration of community policing specialists into Compstat response varies by department, of course. In some departments, the community policing specialists are almost wholly engaged in Compstat response. To the extent that community policing specialists' roles have experienced "drift" into broad-based, nondirected community contact and quality-of life-issues, Compstat brings them back to a focus upon the core police mission—crime control.

SUMMARY

- To focus upon crime control does not mean that neighborhood-centered efforts should be eliminated. Criticism of community policing is directed at the "reinvention-of-policing" model, not citizen engagement.
- It is nearly impossible to link community-oriented policing to crime reduction. Nonetheless, the evidence that does exist does not indicate that community policing impacts strongly on crime or disorder. That does not imply that structured community contact should be abandoned. Neighborhood visibility and positive interaction with citizens is an integral part of democratic policing.

- There are three broad models of neighborhood deployment: the overlay, the "every officer is a community policing officer" model, and the "beat-team concept." Conceptual issues exist with each of the three models, challenging their efficacy. The primary issue with the specialist model is productivity, and more specifically linking activities to crime control. The primary issue for the every-officer model is whether community policing really occurs under this model, or whether it is simply political rhetoric. The beat-team approach presents problems of basic service efficiency and affordability.
- One must establish clear definitions of community policing and problem-oriented policing in order to engage in fruitful discussion of their efficacy. In practice, citizen engagement and problem solving frequently complement one another and are used concurrently. Nevertheless, community policing and problem-oriented policing are distinct approaches with their own sets of dynamics and issues.
- The most common form of structured citizen contact is the Three Citizens' Model: citizen advisory groups, citizens on patrol, and citizens' police academies. All three are widely employed, in the largest police agencies to some that are very small. Indeed, it is likely that about 90 percent of structured community contact conducted by agencies consists of a combination of programs in the Three Citizens' Model.
- Total restructuring of patrol deployment to maximize citizen engagement failed. However, a substantial number of agencies (and nearly all large agencies) maintain community policing specialist roles to coordinate both structured citizens' contact and problem-oriented efforts. These are patrol officer assignments, not civilian roles. A significant problem with the creation of specialist roles has been the tendency of assigned officers to drift into taking responsibility for broad community quality-of-life issues that might better be the responsibility of parks and recreation, schools, and other governmental entities. Recent years, however, have seen a reversal of that trend with a return of a focus upon crime interdiction. Indeed, agencies fully committed to Compstat report that community policing specialists have been fully integrated into the effort.
- The long-term role of problem-oriented policing in law enforcement is still in flux. Many agencies report difficulty with sustaining POP efforts. Among departments that report POP effort, in almost every instance the efforts are conducted by community policing specialists. Regular patrol officers or detectives are almost never engaged.
- A significant problem is unrealistic expectations for the long-term effect of problem-oriented interventions. Partial or short-term impact is too often regarded as failure.
- Whereas the success of nontraditional interventions suggested as an integral part of POP receives outsized attention, the numerous similar efforts that fail are ignored. The phenomenon is characterized as a "success bias."
- Ideally problem-oriented policing is implemented using the SARA model—scanning, analysis, response, assessment. The model has intrinsic appeal to academics because it parallels the scientific method. Among police agencies, however, the SARA approach is widely regarded as too complex, too cumbersome, and too time-consuming.
- It is extremely difficult to construct experimental designs to test the efficacy of problem-oriented interventions. First, the problem situations tend to be idiosyncratic. Likewise, the interventions are typically idiosyncratic to particular situations. Hence, the vast majority of problem-oriented policing projects do not lend themselves to inclusion of comparison groups—whether geographic areas, specific locations, or "problematic" people/groups.
- Research that has been conducted regarding the impact of problem-oriented policing on crime and disorder reports mixed results. A meta-analysis that included only POP evaluations that included a comparison (control) group identified only ten such assessments. Although the evaluations were overwhelmingly positive, a sobering note is that a hot spot approach to using problem-oriented policing was almost universal among the success stories—suggesting that problem-oriented policing may be particularly effective only when used in concert with hot spot policing. Research in Jacksonville, Florida, reinforced this finding.

- A comparison of problem-solving and enforcement-focused efforts finds considerable congruence. On the other hand, there is conflict between the two approaches.
- Enforcement "crackdowns" have proven effective, at least in terms of short range crime reduction. Crackdown components typically include conducting field interviews, traffic stops, conducting highly visible patrols, serving arrest warrants, and interviewing drivers at roadblocks or checkpoints.
- A contentious issue with the SARA model is that it implies permanent resolution of issues. Problem-oriented policing success is too often defined as complete and permanent resolution of the issue addressed. In the real world, "complete and permanent" seldom occurs. POP will never be judged successful if unrealistic expectations are set for its employment.
- When agencies are asked whether the implementation of Compstat caused them to reconsider maintaining community policing specialist roles, most sincerely respond that it did not. Indeed, community policing specialists have been tightly integrated into Compstat response by most departments.

REVIEW QUESTIONS

1. Three models of neighborhood deployment are described. Define each. What problematic issues are associated with each?
2. It is suggested that although community-oriented policing and problem-oriented policing frequently "comingle" in the real world, they are nevertheless distinct approaches. Cite the primary characteristics of each that distinguish it from the other.
3. It is suggested that 90 percent of positive structured community contact/engagement occurs under the aegis of the "Three Citizens' model. What constitutes the "Three C's" model? What is the relative prevalence of each of these components?
4. In what ways is the role of community policing specialist evolving? What factors are driving changes in the role?
5. The variation in approach between enforcement-focused crime interdiction efforts and nontraditional endeavors undertaken to eliminate underlying conditions of crime and disorder, that is, problem solving, conflict on several dimensions. What are the seven underlying elements of the conflict?

REAL-WORLD SCENARIOS

1. As director of planning and research, the chief of police has indicated to you that she intends to eliminate the role of community policing specialist. Nevertheless, she wants to maintain four critical community engagement programs: citizens' advisory groups, the agency's citizens on patrol program, a citizens' police academy, and, of course, the longstanding neighborhood watch program. Prepare a briefing document outlining how these programs are to be administered by the agency, lacking the role of community policing specialists.
2. Associated with the elimination of community policing specialist roles just described, the chief has also asked you to prepare a list of suggestions for encouraging problem solving among generalist patrol officers. However, the first step is to identify the probable obstacles to such engagement. List and describe several obstacles that you recognize as inherent in involving generalist patrol officers in problem-oriented endeavors.
3. You are the chief of police of a suburban agency with 50,000 residents. Twenty years ago—before you had even joined the department as a patrol officer—the previous chief had created four community policing specialist positions. He divided the city into quadrants, assigning a specialist to each. The police department, city manager, city council, and citizens in general have been satisfied with the contribution of the community

policing specialist roles, and strongly desire to continue those roles. However, a disturbing trend has developed since the last election, which saw a two-thirds turnover in city council seats. New council members have taken to directly calling the respective community policing specialists as a problem arises in their ward. Although this has led to quick resolution of some problems, issues have arisen with regard to some requests. You are aware that most police chiefs require all requests from city council members to come through their office. List the pros and cons of allowing city council members to directly contact "their" community policing specialists. Identify briefly the policy alternatives available to you as chief of police.

APPLICATION ACTIVITIES

1. Go to the website for the Center for Problem-Oriented Policing at the University of Wisconsin (http://www.popcenter.org/). Click on the link entitled POP Guides. Close to 100 problem-specific guides are available for download. Select any one of the guides that deals with a specific type of crime interdiction, for example, number 8, *Robbery at Automated Teller Machines;* number 34, *Robbery of Taxi Drivers,* or number 43; *Burglary at Single-Family House Construction Sites.* Write a synopsis of the nontraditional interventions suggested in the guide.
2. Find a resource that describes in detail the scanning, analysis, response, assessment (SARA) process. Descriptions are available at the website of the Center for Problem-Oriented Policing and in almost all community policing texts, for example, *Community Policing: Partnerships for Problem Solving* by Miller, Hess, and Orthmann. Provide a one-paragraph explanation for each of the four steps in the SARA process.
3. In this chapter, locate the inset entitled "The Problem with Problem Solving from the Private Sector" by R. Fritz. For each of the six issues, indicate whether you feel the assertion is germane to problem-oriented policing and, in a sentence or two, explain why or why not.

COURSEMATE

This available CourseMate has an interactive eBook and interactive learning tools, including flash cards, quizzes, and more. To learn more about this resource and access free demo CourseMate resources, go to **www.cengagebrain.com**, and search for this book. To access CourseMate materials that you have purchased, go to **login.cengagebrain.com**.

ENDNOTES

1. No, on second thought it is not open to debate. It is an inefficient use of public funds appropriated for crime control.

REFERENCES

Cordner, G. W., & Biebel, E. P. (2004). *Problem-oriented policing in practice.* Washington, DC: National Criminal Justice Reference Service.

deGuzman, M. C. (2002). The changing roles and strategies of the police in a time of terror. *ACJS Today, 22*(3), 8–13.

DeSimone, D. C. (2003). Federal budget: A mixed bag for state and local governments. *Government Finance Review, 19*(2), 66–69.

Eck, J. E., & Spelman, W. (1987). *Problem-solving: Problem-oriented policing in Newport News.* Washington, DC: Police Executive Research Forum.

Fritz, R. (1996). *Corporate tides: The inescapable laws of organizational structure.* San Francisco: Berrett-Koehler Publishers.

Goldstein, H. (2003). On further developing problem-oriented policing: The most critical need, the major impediments, and a proposal. *Crime Prevention Studies, 15,* 13–47.

Gurwitt, R. (2007). Bratton's Brigade. Governing.com. Retrieved from http://www.governing.com/print/article/brattons-brigade.

Innes, M. (2005). What's your problem? Signal crimes and citizen-focused problem solving. *Criminology & Public Policy, 4*(2), 187–200.

Pate, A. M., & Annan, S. O. (1989). *The Baltimore Community Policing Experiment: Technical report.* Washington, DC: Police Foundation.

Rosenbaum, D. (1989). Community crime prevention: A review and synthesis of the literature. *Justice Quarterly, 5*(3), 323–395.

Schmerler, K. (2005). *Disorder at budget motels. Problem oriented guides for police.* Problem-Specific Guides Series, No. 30. Washington, DC: U.S. Department of Justice, Office of Community Oriented Policing Services.

Scott, M. S. (2003). *The benefits and consequences of police crackdowns.* Problem-Oriented Guides for Police Response Guides Series, No. 1. Washington, DC: U.S. Department of Justice, Office of Community Oriented Policing Services.

Scott, M. S., & Dedel, K. (2006). *Assaults in and around bars—2nd edition.* Problem-Oriented Guides for Police Problem-Specific Guides Series, No. 1. Washington, DC: U.S. Department of Justice, Office of Community Oriented Policing Services.

Skogan, W. G. (1990). *Disorder and decline.* New York: Free Press.

Smith, M. R. (2001). Police-led crackdowns and cleanups: An evaluation of a crime control initiative in Richmond, Virginia. *Crime and Delinquency, 47*(1), 60–83.

Taylor, B., Koper, C. S., & Woods, D. J. (2011). A randomized controlled trial of different policing strategies at hot spots of violent crime. *Journal of Experimental Criminology, 7*, 149–181.

Uchida, C., Forst, B., & Annan, S. O. (1992). *Modern policing and the control of illegal drugs: Testing new strategies in two American cities.* Washington, DC: National Institute of Justice.

Weisburd, D., & Eck, J. E. (2004). What can police do to reduce crime, disorder, and fear? *Annals of the American Academy of Political & Social Science, 593*(5), 42–65.

Weisburd, D., Telep, C. W., Hinkle, J. C., & Eck, J. E. (2008). *The effects of problem-oriented policing on crime and disorder.* Manassas, VA: Campbell Systematic Reviews, George Mason University.

Willis, J. J. (2011). *First-line supervision under Compstat and community policing.* Washington, DC: U.S. Department of Justice, Office of Community Oriented Policing Services.

Wycoff, M. A., & Skogan, W. G. (1986). Storefront police offices: The Houston field test. In D. Rosenbaum (Ed.), *Community crime prevention: Does it work?* Beverly Hills, CA: Sage.

CHAPTER 5

A Typology of Crime Reduction Strategies

© iStockPhoto/Tim McCaig

The Compstat approach is certainly a dominant crime reduction strategy in the United States that serves as a framework for police efforts to control crime. However, police efforts to control crime and Compstat are not synonymous terms. In addition, there are other crime reduction programs, such as Crime Prevention Through Environmental Design (CPTED), which has been an articulated approach for over fifty years. Developed during the 1970s, two of the enduring programs of the Law Enforcement Assistance Administration (LEAA) were Managing Patrol Operations (Cawley & Miron, 1977) and Managing Criminal Investigations (Bloch & Weidman, 1975); both clearly were focused upon crime control. O. W. Wilson (1950), in his landmark book *Police Administration*, addressed the multiple purposes of law enforcement, but certainly focused upon crime control. Indeed, Robert Trojanowicz began his presentations on community policing by noting that community policing's primary purpose was to "take the predators off the streets" (Trojanowicz & Bucqueroux, 1990).

KEY TERMS

Advocacy books
Aggressive patrol
Geographic targeting
Offender targeting
Offense targeting
Philosophical approach
Policy
Program
Strategy
Tactic
Typology

LEARNING OBJECTIVES

After completing this chapter, you should be able to:

- Describe briefly the history of crime control as an element of the police role.
- Cite the five elements of a crime reduction approach that make it a strategy.
- Identify the five critical components necessary to make a strategic approach effective.
- List three types of crime intervention targeting.
- List six enforcement approaches commonly employed by police agencies.
- Identify ten intervention approaches derived from the combination of targeting and enforcement tactics.

Learning Objective

Some of the **"advocacy" books** that address Compstat, for example *The Compstat Paradigm* (Henry, 2002), imply that a focus upon crime control originated in New York City in the 1990s. That is a bit like asserting that teaching reading, writing, and arithmetic is a brand new function for K–12 education. Educational approaches may vary over time, and ancillary efforts of school systems outside the "3 R's" may receive temporary increased emphasis, but schools never stop teaching first graders how to read. Similarly, no police department has ever stopped investigating armed robbery in order to cultivate quality-of-life endeavors.

advocacy books
Publications that promote a particular concept or approach. Used herein to describe a series of books describing New York City's implementation of Compstat.

Required Attributes for Effective Crime Strategies

Learning Objective

To be effective, any crime control strategy must be: (1) contemplative, (2) proactive, (3) planned, (4) monitored, and (5) continuously modified. For crime reduction interventions to be effective, they must first be contemplative. That is, alternatives need to be considered and a reasonable match made between resources available and specific interventions selected. "Shooting from the hip" is irresponsible public administration.

Second, such actions must be proactive. Random routine patrol is neither contemplative nor proactive; repeating the phrase coined in New York City, "random patrol produces random results." Likewise, reactive investigations are neither contemplative nor proactive. Arrests made as a result of careful follow-up investigations should not be discounted. An efficient investigative unit will generate more arrests, and have a larger impact upon crime, than an inept unit. But efficiency in reactive investigations does not substitute for proactive efforts.

Third, effective crime control efforts need to be planned. Planned, used in this context, means specificity. The police do not simply try to "reduce burglaries," but rather make an effort to reduce residential burglaries in a particular neighborhood committed by school truants during daytime hours.

Fourth, effective crime control strategies require constant monitoring. There is some evidence that the impact wanes very quickly after imposition of an intervention. Stated differently, an intervention is most effective for the first few weeks it is in place, then the phenomenon of diminishing returns sets in (Sherman, 1990). Further, with or without police intervention, offenders rapidly change patterns and targets. Crime is constantly on the move. Only the most inept offenders continue to commit robberies at the same ATM machine at the same time of day, the same day of the week, week after week. Monitoring certainly means real-time crime analysis. But monitoring also means employing approaches best characterized as "qualitative" or "subjective" in order to constantly "keep one's finger on the pulse of crime." The computer cannot provide all of the answers. Information must be shared, discussed, and analyzed. Human brains must collaborate. The format certainly might take on the characteristics of a Compstat accountability meeting, but not necessarily so. As noted in Chapter 10, large police departments using a Compstat model that includes both agency-wide and precinct meetings all report that the "real" Compstat occurs at the precinct meetings. A precinct meeting does not entail anyone in a "hot seat," and accountability is not on the agenda. Rather, these are information-sharing meetings, and are specific to individual offenses or offense series.

Fifth, and finally, an effective crime reduction strategy must constantly be modified. Again, the fact that crime patterns are constantly changing requires that effective reduction strategies also constantly change.

Learning Objective

Given these five attributes, there are an additional five critical components to structured, offense-specific crime control approaches:

1. An agency must "free up" some form of discretionary quick deployment capability. Focused crime reduction requires resources. An agency does not have to be staffed at New York and Chicago levels (4.5 officers per thousand citizens), but must create a minimal ability for targeted deployment.
2. Multiple units are typically employed for response. Crime-specific deployment goes beyond "increased attention by patrol." Also engaged should be general investigations, tactical units, specialized investigative units, gang units, and community policing specialists.
3. Targeted enforcement is central. Specificity, specificity, specificity: Specific offenses committed at specific times, at specific locations, by specific offender types.
4. Proactive crime reduction is as much about values and motivation as it is strategic or tactical approaches. Although patrol should not be the only targeted enforcement response, patrol officers should be fully engaged.

5. Strategy should drive process, not the other way around.

Success requires that all, or substantially all, of these components be in place.

Deriving Enforcement Strategies

Crime rates in Dallas, Texas, are among the highest in major American cities. Southeast Dallas is particularly "crime ridden." Crime in some of the southeast neighborhoods occurs with many times the frequency of crime in the city of Dallas as a whole. Members of the Southeast Division of the Dallas Police Department identified the approaches enumerated in Table 5.1 to reduce crime in their precinct.

The approach taken by the southeast Dallas command staff is typical of plans to mount a concentrated effort to reduce crime. The focus upon gangs, guns, and drugs is mirrored elsewhere in the country. But the ten efforts listed in Table 5.1 are, in fact, a mixture of broad strategy and specific tactics. There is nothing wrong with the mix as an action plan for a police department division. But conceptually we need a frame of reference—a typology of strategies that subsumes an array of tactics within a given strategic approach. The use of various **philosophical approaches**, such as community engagement, problem solving, or focused enforcement, may be appropriate depending on circumstance. Within the context of broad approaches, various **strategies** may be appropriate; any given strategy might subsume more

philosophical approach
A set of assumptions about the role and function of the police that undergirds strategic decision making.

strategy
A broad set of interventions related to and complementing one another.

TABLE 5.1 Crime Reduction Strategies Employed by the Southeast Patrol Division of the Dallas Police Department

1. Apply resources to criminal intelligence/trends on a real-time basis.
2. Optimize use of our surveillance units by focusing on specific problems and having a strategic plan going into each target area.
3. Give watch commanders 24/7 responsibility for a defined geographic area.
4. Set up sting operations, in particular reversals, to deal with cargo thefts from truck stops.
5. Provide increased emphasis for the Project Safe Neighborhoods program and tracking of firearms used in/recovered from offenses/suspects. Work with ATF and ICE.
6. Address the unlicensed bars/clubs/dancehalls/strip joints and the crime associated with them by conducting bar sweeps and prostitution sweeps.
7. Deal with drug houses and open-air drug sales through undercover operations with narcotics.
8. Develop effective responses to shots-fired disturbances, realizing that these types of calls can be an indicator of future aggravated assaults and homicide locations. Track shots-fired disturbances.
9. Identify individuals with active warrants and work with fugitive and tactical sections on executing those warrants. Also look at parolees in our high-crime areas and work with fugitives on parolee-apprehension efforts.
10. Focus on gang-related activity.

 Data source: Southeast Division of the Dallas Police Department

tactic
A specific type of focused intervention.

Learning Objective

policy
A formal directive specifying either what employees of an agency are to do and/or how they are to do it.

program
A structured intervention with defined participants, characteristics, and goals.

geographic targeting
Focusing crime intervention efforts on a defined area with inordinately high crime rates, ranging from a specific problematic address to three or four square miles. Hot spot concentrated deployment is the most frequent form.

Learning Objective

offense targeting
Focusing interdiction efforts on a particular type of crime, for example, auto theft.

offender targeting
Focusing repression and/or apprehension efforts upon a given type of offender, for example, gang members.

aggressive patrol
Patrol activities designed to proactively intervene in the commission of offenses, or preparation for commission. Components include high visibility, frequent stops of suspicious vehicles or persons, and blanket warrant checks.

than one **tactic**. In turn, approaches, strategies, and tactics are operationalized by **policies** and **programs**.

A viable, sustainable, widely applicable crime reduction effort involves deriving criminal enforcement strategies from a combination of target selection and proactive tactics. Target selection, or specificity, takes three forms. The first and most prevalent is **geographic targeting**, a focus upon a particular area of a jurisdiction. Commonly receiving the most attention is high crime residential neighborhoods. But there are high crime commercial clusters or corridors that are just as problematic. A variant of geographic targeting is problem locations, or hot spots (Weisburd & Braga, 2006).

A second form is **offense targeting**. This sometimes entails targeting a very specific offense category, such as daytime residential burglaries. Just as frequently, however, the police end up targeting offense clusters, such as crimes against vehicles—theft from autos and theft of autos.

The third form of focus is **offender targeting**. Chicago's efforts focused, for example, upon gangs and gang violence in that city (Chicago Police Department, 2007). Prostitution is both a symptom of social tragedy, notably drug abuse, and a precipitating factor for other crime, and hence is often targeted by big-city police agencies. Drug dealers, and/or users, constitute a third common target of enforcement efforts. Persons under correctional supervision, usually parole rather than probation, have become the focus of efforts of a few agencies. Finally, those with outstanding warrants are a particular "offender group" and often the emphasis of enforcement targeting.

Targeting by a combination of geography, offense, and offender type constitutes half of the basis for deriving a criminal enforcement strategy. The other half is enforcement approaches. There are six options commonly employed by law enforcement agencies:

1. The first and most commonly employed is **aggressive patrol**. Aggressive patrol consists of regularly assigned patrol officers using uncommitted patrol time, time not spent on calls-for-service, to engage in frequent checks of persons and places.
2. Crime response teams are the second most common approach. For purposes of discussion herein, a crime response team is defined as uniformed officers in marked patrol units assigned full-time to crime reduction efforts. In general, such units will use the same approach as regular units operating in an aggressive patrol mode—that is, frequent checks of persons and places.
3. Surveillance in real time is occasionally employed. Surveillance techniques range from shallow to deep. Shallow surveillance can be nearly visible, with uniformed officers using unmarked patrol cars. Deep surveillance includes an unkempt appearance and the use of nondescript vehicles. (Deep surveillance for purposes of discussion herein does not involve the special case of undercover narcotics enforcement.)
4. Targeted proactive investigation of offenders, offenses, or stolen property markets engages detectives in direct intervention efforts. Parolee monitoring fits this category, as do sting operations.
5. Community engagement should always be considered. There are numerous circumstances that make community engagement cost effective for crime

control (Fridell & Wycoff, 2004). There is variation in "community"—from residents of a crime-ridden low-cost housing complex to business owners on a commercial thoroughfare.

6. Finally, there is problem-oriented policing (POP). POP is distinguished herein from community policing.

The typologies employed for the sake of discussion of law enforcement crime control strategy frequently meld in the real world. That is the case with community engagement and POP. As noted in Chapter 4, a high proportion of POP efforts involve some form of community engagement, for example, cooperation with a security company or collaboration with neighborhood watches (Braga, 2002). But not all POP efforts engage the community. Community engagement and problem-oriented approaches are distinguishable concepts even if they frequently meld in operation.

The combination of three types of targeting—geographic, offense, and offender—and six types of enforcement approaches—aggressive patrol, tactical patrol, surveillance, targeted investigation, community engagement, and problem-oriented approaches—on a **typology** graphic yields eighteen potential "cells." However, in reality, police agencies do not use every potential combination of targeting and enforcement approach. Instead, ten distinguishable enforcement strategies are employed (see Table 5.2).

Learning Objective

The ten strategies listed in Table 5.2 are intended to reflect the real world of law enforcement, not an artificially constructed model. In the real world of law enforcement, the first four strategies listed are forms of targeting—high crime residential area, high crime commercial locations, targeted offenses, and targeted offense clusters. Multiple enforcement approaches are almost always employed. The last six strategies are variations of enforcement approaches. Police agencies use combinations of the six approaches listed, depending on circumstance. At times the enforcement approach may be employed against geographic or offender targets, at other times the approaches are used throughout a jurisdiction and for an array of offenses or offenders.

One strategy listed might be viewed as a tactic: intense field interviews. The majority of the time, the tactic is geographically concentrated, but some agencies use it simply as a strategy in its own right. These agencies engage in frequent vehicle and pedestrian stops as a form of crime control, sometimes geographically

typology
A categorization scheme premised upon conceptual attributes of a phenomenon. In contrast, a taxonomy is a categorization scheme premised upon natural attributes—flora and fauna are categorized into taxonomies; organizational patterns typically are typologies.

TABLE 5.2 Crime Control Strategy Typology

1. High-crime residential areas
2. High-crime commercial locations
3. Targeted offenses
4. Offense clusters
5. Intense field interviews
6. Drug crackdowns
7. Gang violence reduction
8. Broken windows enforcement
9. Surveillance apprehension enforcement
10. Probation/parole/alias-capias enforcement

targeted and sometimes not, sometimes targeted on particular offenses or offense clusters and sometimes not. Hence, it is listed as a strategy in its own right. The sixth approach listed, drug crackdowns, is so frequently employed that it merits its own category. The various approaches to drug crackdowns are discussed in the next chapter. Likewise, the seventh strategy listed, gang violence reduction, merits inclusion as its own strategy. Clearly, gang violence reduction frequently overlaps with other strategic approaches, such as high crime residential area enforcement, or drug crackdowns. However, almost all major cities possess independent gang enforcement units. Sustained effort is dedicated to reduction of gang-related crime and particularly gang-related violence.

The next two strategies listed, broken windows enforcement and surveillance apprehension, represent polar extremes of the use of arrests as a means to deter offenders from committing additional offenses. Broken windows enforcement entails numerous arrests for relatively trivial offenses (Kelling & Coles, 1996), whereas surveillance apprehension is intended to focus upon making the "big bust"—a felony arrest of a serious offender. Finally, American police increasingly recognize the value of careful tracking of parolees and, to some extent, probationers (LaVigne, Solomon, Beckman, & Dedel, 2006). Everyone regrets that recidivism rates are 70 percent or higher, but given the fact that they are 70 percent or higher, targeting convicted offenders makes good "economic sense."

IMPLICATIONS FOR STRATEGY

Among the strategic approaches to crime control enumerated, there is no single superior approach. Indeed, there is not even a given superior approach to any particular situation. Rather, there is an optimal approach that balances resources required against probability of repression/interdiction/apprehension. Many offense clusters are best addressed by a mixture of the strategic approaches listed. Whatever approach is selected, it is important that the response be contemplative, proactive, planned, monitored, and modified regularly. These characteristics in turn imply that targeting and strategy choice is a top command staff decision.

SUMMARY

- Crime control has always been the central police role. O. W. Wilson, in his 1950 landmark book *Police Administration*, focused upon crime control as the primary police purpose. Two of the enduring programs of the Law Enforcement Assistance Administration, developed during the 1960s, were Managing Patrol Operations and Managing Criminal Investigations, both clearly focused upon crime control. Community policing was seen by many as deflecting the police from the focus on crime control, but Robert Trojanowicz, founder of the concept of community policing, noted that community policing's primary purpose was to "take the predators off the streets."
- To be classified as a strategy, a crime reduction approach needs to be contemplative, proactive, planned, monitored, and modified regularly.
- The critical components of a strategic approach's effectiveness include discretionary quick deployment capability, use of multiple units for response (patrol, detectives, tactical units, special-duty assignments), and targeted enforcement that focuses on specific offenses at specific times at specific locations

committed by specific offender groups. It should be noted that any intervention that includes these elements will incorporate components of Compstat.

- A crime-specific strategy entails a combination of a match between targeting and tactics. The three types of crime intervention targeting are geographic, by offense, or by offender type.
- The six enforcement tactics commonly employed are aggressive patrol, tactical patrol, surveillance apprehension, targeted investigations, community engagement, and problem-oriented approaches.
- A typology of ten intervention approaches is derived from the combination of targeting and enforcement tactics: high crime residential areas, high-crime commercial locations, targeted offenses, offense clusters, intense field interviews, drug crackdowns, gang violence reduction, broken windows enforcement, surveillance apprehension, and probation/parole/alias-capias enforcement. Each of the ten strategic approaches subsumes a potential range of tactics. For example, a high crime residential area might be approached by use of neighborhood engagement by community policing specialists, problem-oriented approaches, nuisance abatement, and public order enforcement. A range of options is available for targeting a particular offense, depending upon the nature of that offense. Auto theft interdiction is an illustration, which might include debriefing of apprehended offenders, surveillance of decoy vehicles, "stolen-parts-receiving" sting operations, "stolen-parts-selling" reverse sting operations, aggressive patrol programs, reactive follow-up of reports with leads, and enhanced prosecution.

The next three chapters review in detail how each of the six types of enforcement approaches is typically employed in the context of each of the three types of targeting—geographic, offense, and offender.

REVIEW QUESTIONS

1. Although crime control is certainly the central police role, the police indeed have other functions. What are some of those functions, and why are they the responsibility of law enforcement agencies?
2. Crime intervention targeting is characterized as being either geographic, by offense, or by offender type. What characteristics of offenses might be related to the type of targeting that is selected?
3. Why is community engagement used far more frequently in conjunction with geographic targeting than it is when targeting offense type or offender type?
4. Police targeting of parolees is suggested as having substantial potential for crime reduction. What ethical issues are raised? What safeguards must be in place to assure that monitoring of parolees does not degenerate to harassment of parolees?
5. What factors limit the utility of police sting and reverse sting operations?

REAL-WORLD SCENARIOS

1. You are the commander of a district with substantial commercial development—retail stores, office buildings, medical facilities, and the like. Thefts from vehicles in commercial-area parking lots are becoming increasingly frequent. Identify the range of alternative tactics for intervening. For each alternative, identify the number of personnel you would estimate as necessary to implement an intervention. If you had to select just one intervention from among those listed, identify which one it might be and why.
2. You are a lieutenant in charge of the night shift at a patrol substation. You recognize the probable truth of the axiom "random patrol produces random results." What activities that are suitable for the night shift might you consider to better employ the uncommitted patrol time of regular patrol units?

3. As the commander of a major agency investigative division, you have personally enjoyed some success in obtaining valuable information by debriefing arrestees. You note that few of your detectives bother to do so. Upon inquiry you are told by your staff that debriefing is not regarded as worthwhile because it infrequently results in actionable intelligence. Describe how information obtained through debriefing might be made more useful.

APPLICATION ACTIVITIES

1. Locate a book that is dedicated to community policing, for example, *Community Policing: Partnerships for Problem Solving,* by Miller, Hess, and Orthmann. Drawing from the text, describe several situations that successfully employed community engagement to combat crime in a neighborhood or apartment complex.
2. Construct a diagram to illustrate a frame of reference for crime intervention. At the top should be a designated philosophical approach. That approach should subsume two to three strategies; in turn each strategy should subsume more than one tactic. Describe how your diagram might be operationalized for a particular crime pattern or trend.
3. Access the website http://www.crimemapping.com, or Google "crime mapping police departments." Select a particular police agency from the listed returns, preferably from a city with which you are familiar. Zoom in on a manageable area, one that depicts twenty to thirty offenses. List the types of offenses by frequency of occurrence within your sample crime map. Discuss what else you might need to know about the characteristics of the most frequently occurring offense in order to plan an intervention strategy.

COURSEMATE

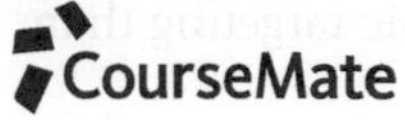

This available CourseMate has an interactive eBook and interactive learning tools, including flash cards, quizzes, and more. To learn more about this resource and access free demo CourseMate resources, go to **www.cengagebrain.com**, and search for this book. To access CourseMate materials that you have purchased, go to **login.cengagebrain.com**.

REFERENCES

Bloch, P. B., & Weidman, D. R. (1975). *Managing criminal investigations.* Washington, DC: U.S. Department of Justice.

Braga, A. A. (2002). *Problem-oriented policing and crime prevention.* Monsey, NY: Criminal Justice Press.

Cawley, D. F., & Miron, H. J. (1977). *Managing patrol operations—manual.* Washington, DC: U.S. Department of Justice, National Institute of Justice.

Chicago Police Department. (2007). *Making Chicago the safest big city in America, Chicago Police Department crime reduction initiatives: 2003–2007.* Chicago, IL: Chicago Police Department.

Fridell, L., & Wycoff, M. A. (2004). *Community policing: The past, present, and future*. Washington, DC: Police Executive Research Forum.

Henry, V. E. (2002). *The Compstat paradigm: Management accountability in policing, business and the public sector*. Flushing, NY: Looseleaf Law Publications, Inc.

Kelling, G. L., & Coles, C. M. (1996). *Fixing broken windows: Restoring order and reducing crime in our communities*. New York: Free Press.

LaVigne, N. G., Solomon, A. L., Beckman, K. A., & Dedel, K. (2006). *Prisoner reentry and community policing: Strategies for enhancing public safety*. Washington, DC: U.S. Department of Justice, Urban Institute Justice Policy Center, Office of Community Oriented Policing Services.

Sherman, L. W. (1990). Police crackdowns: Initial and residual deterrence. In M. Tonry & N. Morris (Eds.), *Crime and justice: An annual review of research* (Vol. 12). Chicago, IL: University of Chicago Press.

Trojanowicz, R., & Bucqueroux, B. (1990). *Community policing: A contemporary perspective*. Cincinnati, OH: Anderson Publishing Co.

Weisburd, D., & Braga, A. A. (2006). Hot spots policing as a model for police innovation. In *Police innovation: Contrasting perspectives* (pp. 225–244). New York: Cambridge University Press.

Wilson, O. W. (1950). *Police administration*. New York: McGraw-Hill.

CHAPTER 6

Geographic Targeting Strategies

© vdbvsl/Alamy

KEY TERMS

Diffusion
Displacement
Focused patrol
Foot patrol
Geographic targeting
Interactive programs
Police-operated surveillance cameras
Routine activities theory
Saturation patrol
Simple visibility
Strip-center corridors
Surgical zero tolerance
Vice-oriented business clusters
Victimizing the victims
Zero-tolerance crackdowns

LEARNING OBJECTIVES

After completing this chapter, you should be able to:

- Define a crime hot spot.
- Link the routine activities theory to the effectiveness of hot spot concentrated intervention.
- Characterize the research evidence for the effectiveness of hot spot concentrated deployment.
- Contrast recommended police interventions among four types of residential entities: stable single-family neighborhoods, stressed single-family neighborhoods, stable apartment complexes, and stressed apartment complexes.
- Describe why zero-tolerance crackdowns are a risk for a police agency.
- Distinguish enforcement efforts in commercial areas: malls and their environs, downtowns, commercial strip corridors, problem businesses, and vice-oriented commercial clusters.
- Identify where the use of police-operated surveillance cameras was initiated internationally, and in the United States.
- Characterize historically the extent of use of foot patrol in American policing.

Learning Objective

The core of geographically focused efforts is so called "hot spot" concentrations—locations where the prevalence of crime is substantially higher than the jurisdiction norm. There is no universal definition of the dimensions of a hot spot, but they are usually defined as areas of one to two square miles. Considerable variation exists, however. In both Minneapolis (Sherman & Weisburd, 1995) and Philadelphia (Lawton, Taylor, & Luongo, 2005), the definition of a hot spot was confined to a grouping of addresses or a bounded intersection. Larger geographic areas are more commonly employed: a combination of city blocks (Koper, 1995; Novak, Hartman, Holsinger, & Turner, 1999; Nunn, Quintet, Rowe, & Christ, 2006; Sherman & Rogan, 1995; Smith, 2001), census block groups (Weisburd, Morris, & Ready, 2008), and police beats (McGarrell, Chermak, Weiss, & Wilson, 2001).

Learning Objective

Although there is a "famine" of criminal justice experimentation, and concurrently widespread failure of randomized experiments to move into the mainstream of criminal justice evaluation, experiments in hot spot policing have played a critical role in policy and program development in this area (Weisburd, 2005). Weisburd traces the theoretical context of hot spot policing all the way back to Edward Southerland's classic work in 1947 (Sutherland, 1947). It is noted that a more definitive theoretical context exists in the **routine activities theory** or criminological perspective, which incorporates the well-known crime triangle of a motivated offender, a suitable target, and the absence of a capable guardian (Cohen & Felson, 1979). Obviously, hot spot policing assumes a

routine activities theory
A criminological perspective for which the core concept is the crime triangle of a motivated offender, suitable target, and lack of guardianship.

motivated offender, but attempts intervention aimed at a combination of the suitable target and capable guardian elements of the crime triangle.

geographic targeting Focusing crime intervention efforts on a defined area with inordinately high crime rates, ranging from a specific problematic address to three or four square miles. Hot-spot concentrated deployment is the most frequent form.

This chapter reviews the efficacy of **geographic targeting** interventions. An initial premise is that crime indeed clusters in some locations, commonly referred to as "hot spots." The most common hot spot intervention is concentrated deployment of patrol vehicles. Variation in tactics is required, however, by the nature of the hot spot. Different tactics are required for a high-crime neighborhood consisting dominantly of single-family residences as opposed to stressed apartment complexes. Similar variation exists for commercial strips versus malls versus downtowns.

In addition to concentrated patrol vehicle deployment, agencies increasingly are installing surveillance cameras at high-crime locations, such as street corners routinely used for drug sales. At the extreme is "live" surveillance—foot patrol. Originally police patrol was foot patrol. The popularity of foot patrol has waxed and waned over the decades, but it has remained a fixture of major city deployment.

Crime Concentration

In drawing conclusions from their analysis of fourteen years of Seattle data, Weisburd, Bushway, Lum, and Yang (2004) conclude that crime is tightly clustered in specific places in urban areas, and most places have little or no crime. They note, however, that there is a high degree of stability of crime at micro places—the majority of Seattle's high-crime street segments stayed high-crime street segments over a fourteen-year period. But not all. The crime drop in Seattle in the 1990s was not an overall drop, but rather confined to specific groups of street segments with decreasing crime trajectories over time. Weisburd et al. (2004, p. 310) note, "If the trends in Seattle are common to other cities, the crime drop (crime drop in the U.S. since 1991) should be seen not as a general phenomenon across a city but rather as focused at specific places. Such places in our study are also street segments where crime rates are relatively high. This reinforces a public policy approach that would focus crime prevention resources on hot spots of crime."

Additional data from Seattle confirm the tight clustering phenomenon. A focused review of juvenile crime found that, "Fifty percent of all juvenile crime incidents occurred at less than 1 percent of street segments—an area that includes the addresses on both sides of a street between two intersections. All juvenile crime incidents occurred at less than 5 percent of street segments" (Weisburd, Groff, & Morris, 2011). These findings are consistent with those from Jersey City, New Jersey, wherein 20 percent of robbery, assault, and weapons arrests and 40 percent of arrests for public morals offenses were concentrated in 4.4 percent of street segments and intersections (Weisburd & Green, 1995). Likewise, Spelman (1995) found that the worst 10 percent of locations in Boston accounted for about 50 percent of all calls-for-service. Reflecting the 10 percent figure, Eck, Gersh, and Taylor (2000) found that 10 percent of the places in the Bronx (New York City) accounted for 32 percent of a combination of robberies, assaults, burglaries, grand larcenies, and auto theft. Finally, as noted in Chapter 2, Sherman reported in the Minneapolis RECAP evaluation that 3 percent of the addresses accounted for 50 percent of calls-for-service;

5 percent accounted for 64 percent of the calls (Sherman, 1990). The combination of findings from these assessments suggests that hot spot policing is a reasoned, rational, thoughtful approach to crime reduction, not a sidebar artifact of the Compstat approach.

One might also argue that crime concentration suggests the validity of problem-oriented approaches. The stability of crime among certain street segments over a fourteen-year period in Seattle certainly argues for a strategy that transcends quick-fix saturation patrol. However, problem-oriented policing is not a guaranteed antidote to every social poison. The social, economic, and political issues that create long-term crime-ridden neighborhoods may not be amendable to any police intervention. That is, because the police might make a difference in some situations does not mean they can make a difference in every situation. We must be careful with the assertion that "the police can make a difference." In some places, under some circumstances, definitely, yes, police can make a difference. Perhaps even in most places under most circumstances. But not necessarily in all places under all circumstances. Conversely, this does not suggest that as a public policy police agencies give up on certain neighborhoods. Although there may be no legal mandate to attempt to reduce crime in every high-crime neighborhood, there certainly is an ethical obligation to do so. But we can set too high of an expectation either for simple saturation patrol or deep-drilling problem solving.

Efficacy of Hot Spot Strategies

Sherman (1990) noted that most crime prevention strategies do, in fact, initially deter crime. Sherman examined studies related to police crackdowns and found that there was an initial deterrence effect in fifteen out of eighteen crackdowns. Crackdowns are almost always focused upon small, high-crime geographic areas. Several assessments support the efficacy of the hot spot strategy (Braga, 2001; Braga et al., 1999; Koper, 1995; Sherman & Rogan, 1995; Sherman & Weisburd, 1995).

Empirical findings from two decades of research related to place-oriented policing strategies have indicated that focused intervention at hot spot places is associated with crime reduction. An early assessment was the carefully evaluated Minneapolis Hot Spot Experiment conducted in 1989. Sherman and Weisburd (1995, p. 627) note:

> A one-year randomized trial in Minneapolis of increases in patrol dosage at 55 of 110 crime "hot spots" was monitored by 7,542 hours of systematic observations. The experimental group received, on average, twice as much observed patrol presence, although the ratio displayed wide seasonal fluctuation. Reductions in total crime calls ranged from 6 percent to 13 percent. Observed disorder was only half as prevalent in experimental as in control hot spots. We conclude that substantial increases in police patrol presence can indeed cause modest reductions in crime and more impressive reductions in disorder within high crime locations.

Studies done recently confirm the historical conclusions. In 2011 an experimental design in Sacramento, California, focused upon very geographically focused "hot spots," testing the effect of extra patrol presence at high-crime street corners. In a ninety-day period, Sacramento patrol units were instructed during their shift to stop and park at a randomized rotation of three or four of forty-two street corners for twelve to sixteen minutes each. This translates to each hot spot being "visited" about every two hours. Evaluation by George Mason University's Center for Evidence-Based Policing indicated that Part I offenses dropped by 25 percent during the experimental period, and calls-for-service from the locations declined by 8 percent (Stroud, 2011).

Braga (2001, 2005, 2007) conducted a series of systematic reviews regarding the deterrent effect of law enforcement interventions on crime hot spots. At the core is a methodological assessment of nine hot spot evaluation studies based on four criteria: (a) type of research design, (b) definition(s) of hot spots, (c) nature of intervention(s), and (d) outcome measurements. Braga (2001) indicated that hot spot policing is an effective strategy in preventing crime; in seven out of the nine studies, a significant reduction in crime and disorder was attributed to hot spot policing efforts, whereas the remaining two studies failed to find a meaningful outcome due to "methodological problems in the research and evaluation designs" (p. 121).

displacement
The possibility that enforcement focused on a particular area will simply drive crime to surrounding areas.

Learning Objective

diffusion
The possibility that geographically focused police intervention efforts will have an effect beyond the boundaries of the area targeted; the opposite phenomenon of displacement.

Noted hot spot evaluations since 2000 are summarized in Table 6.1. There are several trends. First and foremost, crime reduction, regardless of the specifics of the intervention, generally occurred. Although the drops were usually not "astounding," they were significant. Second, although there is variation in the effects, in totality all crime types were impacted. Third, the fear of **displacement** is unfounded—it does not occur. Fourth, reinforcing this encouraging outcome is the fact that, conversely, **diffusion** of benefit frequently does occur. Crime goes down not only in the targeted area, but surrounding areas as well. In sum, nearly all assessments of hot spot concentrated patrol reinforce the efficacy of the approach. This is examined further in Chapter 15.

Residential Neighborhoods

There are four distinct approaches to residential area enforcement, best depicted by the matrix in Table 6.2. Along the horizontal axis is stressed versus non-stressed or, stated differently, high crime versus little to no crime. Along the vertical axis is single-family residence versus apartment complex. Each "cell" requires a different approach.

Table 6.2 is a typology, not a taxonomy. It provides a springboard for discussion, recognizing that four clean, neat categories seldom exist in the real world. Neighborhood stress is a continuum; a residential neighborhood may be only marginally stressed. Further, neighborhoods do not fall neatly into single-family residences and apartment complexes—multiple-family dwellings frequently commingle with single-family residences.

STRESSED SINGLE-FAMILY RESIDENTIAL NEIGHBORHOODS

There is no accepted definition of what constitutes a high-crime neighborhood. Certainly in the public image such neighborhoods are typically in the inner-city areas of major metropolitan areas, populated predominately by members of minority groups, infected with drug houses, terrorized by street gangs, and impervious to law enforcement efforts to reduce crime. It is precisely this type of

TABLE 6.1 Noted Hot spot Evaluations—Post 2000

Study	Intervention	Crime reduction	Other effects
Philadelphia Foot Patrol Experiment (Ratcliffe et al., 2010)	• Sixty 1.3-mile road segments assigned foot patrol, matched pairs used as control.	• Violent crime decreased by 22 percent and vehicle-related crime by 12 percent, while drug discovery increased by 28 percent.	• One violent crime reduced for every four arrests, 63 pedestrian stops, and 25 traffic stops.
Displacement and Diffusion of Crime Control in Jersey City, New Jersey (Weisburd et al., 2006)	• Two hot spot areas, one for drugs and one for prostitution, were selected based on high levels of activities measured by crime incident data, calls-for-service, and observations. • Each area consisted of five to eight city blocks. • Two surrounding areas for each target area were observed for the effects of displacement and diffusion.	• Target areas: statistically significant impacts for both drug and prostitution events. • Surrounding areas significant impacts for prostitution but no significant impacts for drugs because of the lower base rate of activities. • Diffusion of crime control benefits rather than displacement occurred.	• Incidents of social disorder significantly decreased in all of the areas.
The Effect of Arrest Interdiction on Drug and Serious Crime in Indianapolis (Nunn et al., 2006)	• A drug hot spot neighborhood covered about two and a half square miles, characterized by a high level of violence, drug trafficking, and street-corner drug sales. Surveillance and subsequent mass arrest of 21 drug dealers.	• Target area showed significant drops in CFS for gun violation, interpersonal violence, and robbery, while CFS drug complaints increased during the first year after the raid.	• No displacement effect.
Operation Safe Streets in Philadelphia (Lawton et al., 2005)	• 214 highest drug activity locations (34 street segments and 180 single addresses) were assigned saturation foot patrol 24/7. Effect 18 weeks later were measured.	• Citywide: nonsignificant reduction of homicide, violent crimes, and drug crimes. • Localized: significant reduction of violent and drug crimes.	• Diffusion of benefit for violent crime extending to within .1 mile of intervention site.
Evaluation of Police-Led Crack-downs and Cleanups in Richmond, VA (Smith, 2001)	• A 5-by-10-square-block hot spot area for homicides, violent crime, and drug markets was identified.	• Total Part I offenses and violent crime showed a significant drop in the target area. • No effect on calls-for-service. • No residual effect of the intervention after six months.	• No displacement effect in adjacent three zones.
Quality-of-Life Policing in Chandler, AZ (Katz et al., 2001)	• Four zones ranging in size from 1 to 1.5 square miles in a redevelopment district were identified.	• Nonsignificant reduction of calls-for-service for personal and property crimes.	• Reduced calls-for-service for public morale and physical disorder.
Problem-Solving in Public Housing in Jersey City, New Jersey (Mazerolle et al., 2000)	• Six public housing sites suffering drug-related and violent crime were identified. The number of households in each site varied from 230 to 645.	• Frequency of problem-oriented policing activities reduced total number of calls-for-service. • Found effects on calls-for-service regarding interpersonal violent crime (robbery, assault, and domestic assault), burglary, and auto theft.	n/a

TABLE 6.2 Approaches to Residential Area Enforcement

Condition of Neighborhood	Single-Family Residence	Apartments
Stressed Neighborhood	Stressed Single Family	Stressed Apartments
Stable Neighborhood	Stable Single Family	Stable Apartments

neighborhood that was envisioned as the target of community policing efforts. In reality, of course, police agencies had much more success with community policing programs in middle-income neighborhoods that needed little law enforcement effort. Be that as it may, we have recognized the need for extraordinary intervention efforts for decades. Despite such recognition, the phenomenon of inner-city crime-ridden neighborhoods remains an unfortunate part of the American landscape.

A comprehensive approach to neighborhood degradation was tried in the Phoenix, Arizona, suburb of Chandler. A "civilian" neighborhood service unit was responsible for enforcing city code violations pertaining to weeds, debris, inoperable vehicles, and graffiti. The unit also conducted a seven-point "house check" on private residences to ensure that properties met city zoning standards. A neighborhood response team consisting of six sworn officers and one sergeant engaged in **focused patrol**. The officers patrolled neighborhoods on bicycles, conducting field interviews, making traffic stops, and aggressively enforcing all municipal codes and county laws (Katz, Webb, & Schaefer, 2001). The evaluation notes:

focused patrol
Directing marked patrol units to proactively intervene in problematic situations; focused patrol may be geographically based, offense based, offender based, or a mixture.

> Neighborhood response team officers used both unmarked vehicles and bicycles to patrol zones. Unmarked vehicles were used for the surveillance of street-level drug trafficking, prostitution, gang activity, and suspicious persons. Bicycles were used to conduct field interrogations, issue summonses for traffic offenses, and enforce disorder crimes aggressively. Bike patrol also was used to make officers more accessible to neighborhood residents. Neighborhood response team officers were not dispatched to calls-for-service; thus they were free to police crime and disorder aggressively in the target area. (p. 841)

Analysis indicated that the number of calls-for-service for public moral offenses declined significantly from .46 to .30 per day (or, annually from 168 to about 110). The number of calls-for-service for physical disorder increased significantly from .86 to 1.10 per day (annually, from 314 to 402), and the number of calls-for-service for nuisances increased significantly from 3.88 to 4.38 per day (for an annual change from 1,416 to 1,598). Increases in these two categories, however, can be interpreted as a positive response to the neighborhood service unit's code enforcement initiative. The initiative made the clearest and strongest impact on two categories of crime and disorder: public morals and physical disorder (Katz et al., 2001). Public morals crimes (e.g., prostitution and public drinking) are often the most visible forms of disorder and crime in a neighborhood, and as such are perhaps the most suppressible by the police. At the same time, the program had a far less substantial effect on serious crime. This result argues, of course, against the broken windows strategy as a means to reduce serious crime, discussed more thoroughly in Chapter 8.

In contrast to the results in Chandler are the findings from a problem-oriented approach to high-crime public housing conducted in Jersey City. Efforts there led to reductions in assaults, domestic assaults, auto theft, burglary, and robbery—while having no effect upon drugs, morale and nuisance offenses, and suspicious persons (Mazerolle, Ready, Terrill, & Waring, 2000).

As in the Chandler study, multiple approaches were employed in Jersey City by teams that included one police lieutenant, who served as the project commander; two community service officers; one site-based police officer from the police department's public housing unit; one civilian site manager; one social service liaison officer; and one or more tenant representatives. Problem solving included efforts such as changing the public telephones to allow outgoing calls only, installing floodlights in dimly lit parking lots, and more traditional tactics such as setting up surveillance and enforcing open warrants to control drugs and incivilities. In addition, individual households were selected for problem-oriented policing intervention based on their recorded history. Why these efforts decreased serious crime but not "nuisance and disorder" offenses is an open question.

The Jersey City results may be due to the fact that in truly distressed neighborhoods, broken windows enforcement may be inconsequential. One does not spend public funds stomping on ants when the elephants are out of the pen. When gangs rule the streets and open-air drug sales occur on every other street corner, police agencies must strike in full force. When offenders commit offenses in plain view on a street corner, the public expects the police to respond. The first step in reconstructing quality of life in such neighborhoods is to clear the streets of predators.

In an ideal world there would be a concentrated governmental effort to rebuild such neighborhoods. At the core of that effort would be physical reconstruction. Abandoned and dilapidated buildings would be torn down, replaced with either new construction or pocket parks. In an ideal world, social service agencies would intervene to moderate drug use. In an ideal world, funds would flow to the neighborhood schools to provide layers of enhanced compensatory opportunities for students deprived of support systems at home. The list obviously goes on. But in the real world, one assumes the role of chief of police with a mandate to reduce crime, and physically rebuilding crime-ridden neighborhoods is not going to occur anytime soon. Indeed, until crime is reduced, it is unlikely that private investment will flow into an area.

Former Dallas Police Chief David Kunkle reported that efforts to organize neighborhood associations in south Dallas met with limited success. In the most stressed neighborhoods, the only citizens showing up for meetings were grandmothers. The term "grandmothers" is not used here symbolically or allegorically, but literally. Only grandmothers showed up. Just what is it we expect these grandmothers to do to take back their neighborhood from the Bloods, Crips, and Latin Kings?

No one can expect residents living in these circumstances to "take back" their neighborhood. Gang drug distribution in such neighborhoods is a highly organized criminal enterprise, the new form of organized crime. This new form of organized crime is even more violent, more ruthless, than its predecessors. If criminal gangs will routinely kill to maintain control of drug distribution at a

Learning Objective

saturation patrol
Assignment of extra patrol units to a small geographic area; the concentration of multiple marked patrol units in crime hot spots.

particular street intersection, they will certainly kill to maintain their very existence as an enterprise. The only choice under these circumstances is to engage in a quasi-military "take back" of such neighborhoods. **Saturation patrol** is always one component. When streets are controlled by those who are willing to kill another human being at the drop of a hat, naïve suggestions to reclaim such neighborhoods by engaging in citizen meetings are laughable. What is required is aggressive action by agents of the government with full authority to control behavior in public places and armed with lethal force to do so. Only the police can be effective in these circumstances.

Learning Objective

zero-tolerance crackdowns
Saturation patrol in a given area marked by frequent stops of vehicles and pedestrians; stops are made for the most trivial of violations or appearance of suspicious behavior. Most frequently used in areas with concentrated drug trafficking.

victimizing the victims
A product of zero-tolerance crackdowns whereby law-abiding residents of a neighborhood are stopped as frequently as offenders; in effect, inadvertent harassment of neighborhood residents innocently caught up in crackdowns.

surgical zero tolerance
Saturation patrol with frequent stops of vehicles and pedestrians, but done with care to avoid the inadvertent stopping of law-abiding residents.

At the same time, one must note that such quasi-military tactics, commonly referred to as **zero-tolerance crackdowns**, on the part of a law enforcement agency carry inherent risk. The primary risk is **victimizing the victims**. When the police saturate a residential area with a mandate to take back the streets, the tactic chosen is almost always zero-tolerance enforcement. Arresting a resident grandmother with an outstanding parking ticket is counterproductive. George Gascón, former assistant chief for operations of the Los Angeles Police Department, noted that efforts must reflect **surgical zero tolerance**. Although at first blush zero tolerance and surgical strikes may seem an oxymoron, this is not necessarily the case. Given some level of familiarity with the neighborhood, police agencies can reasonably target drug dealers, prostitutes, and supporting gang members.

A stressed single-family neighborhood thus requires a combination of engagement and proactive enforcement. In extreme situations, such as south Dallas, engagement must be measured against reasonable expectations. While the grandmothers mentioned earlier are not going to, on their own, rid the neighborhood of criminal activity, they can be organized to assist a police department. Engagement can make some difference in ridding a neighborhood of physical blight. Engagement can certainly make a difference in providing a police agency with up-to-the-minute information on criminal street activity. Neighborhood residents can be engaged in efforts by the police department to impose nuisance abatement foreclosure processes. What is primarily required, however, is vigorous enforcement. Because no agency is sufficiently staffed to saturate every stressed neighborhood all the time, a common approach is to maintain a rotation or roving system of saturation enforcement. What is important in this respect is that a police agency returns multiple times to stressed neighborhoods. A one-week saturation effort, followed by withdrawal—the police department never to be seen again—will not make a lasting difference. Indeed, one-time shots are counterproductive.

STRESSED APARTMENT COMPLEXES

The second cell, stressed apartment complexes, calls for a different approach. Stressed apartment complexes are the most common source of hot spot problems for police agencies. Analyses of call-for-service data indicate that a dramatically disproportionate number of conflict calls involving interpersonal violence emanates from such complexes, much less regular criminal offenses. The worst complexes become havens for open-air drug dealing and prostitution. The very worst are so bad that their names have achieved national recognition—Cabrini Green in Chicago, for example. That particular complex was demolished; it literally was beyond repair. It is not unheard of for calls to the worst apartment complexes to be routinely responded to by two police units with two officers in each unit. While two officers respond to the particular apartment generating the call, the other two stay in the parking lot to protect the patrol cars.

In these situations, police intervention must be extensive and dramatic. The beginning point is **interactive programs**, which include apartment management and ownership. Frequently, police agencies discover that stressed apartment complexes are not owned by local investors, but rather simply managed locally with the owners hundreds of miles, or even a continent, away. If engagement of apartment ownership requires threats or intimidation in the form of vigorous code enforcement, so be it. Working with managers is a related but separate issue. Managers in these situations may or may not be willing to cooperate with a police agency. Problematic apartment managers in these situations fall into three categories: (1) apathetic, (2) fearful of criminal residents and therefore paralyzed, or (3) participants themselves in the criminal activity (paid off with cash or drugs). Those apathetic or fearful must have confidence that the police will stay engaged. Those participating in criminal activity need to either be arrested or sufficiently threatened that they leave. Regardless, engagement of apartment managers will not be sufficient without the support of apartment ownership. Commitment from ownership must be obtained, either by friendly persuasion or otherwise. With the commitment of apartment ownership, and engagement of management, several common steps are then taken.

Learning Objective

interactive programs
Police interventions that require the engagement of residents or businesses to address problems of crime and disorder.

First, screening of current and potential tenants needs to occur. Those with a record of problems are either evicted or not rented to in the first place. Second, external blight has to be cleaned up. It is unrealistic to think that a police department can cause every apartment interior to be remodeled, but parking lots, lawns, and play areas can be made decent and even attractive. Third, the apartment complex should provide some level of formal security. Such security takes the form both of classic crime prevention through environmental design (CPTED) and, in larger complexes, the hiring of security guards. A police agency may choose to temporarily provide regular on-site presence, but cannot afford to do so in the long term. Further, provision of such security in the long term is arguably an inequitable distribution of public resources. Public housing is, of course, a different situation. Nevertheless, few agencies can afford to provide ongoing security even for public housing complexes.

The New Briarfield public housing project in Newport News, Virginia, achieved national notoriety with the publication of Eck and Spelman's (1987) *Problem-Solving* monograph. As discussed briefly in Chapter 2, New Briarfield was a classic case of public housing gone amiss. The complex was in disrepair. Residents who were on welfare complained to social workers that they were afraid to take a job that would take them away from their apartment for any period of time, as they would return to find that it had been burglarized. Former Chief Darrel Stephens decided to attempt a longer term, problem-oriented intervention. Two officers were assigned to the project to engage primarily in a structured CPTED effort. Stephens described the situation pointedly when he said, "I knew we were in trouble when I stopped by one morning to see how things were going. As I walked up to our store front (an apartment taken over by the police department) the assigned officers were directing maintenance personnel to the projects they were to work on that day. I realized at that moment that the Newport News Police Department was now running New Briarfield" (Stephens, 2000).

Stephens recognized that typical police responses were not going to work; a sustained commitment was necessary. But he also realized that police agencies have no business running public housing projects. The efforts by the police department from the outset were to develop a situation where the agency could "withdraw." Eventually like Cabrini Green, a decision was made that the best solution was demolition.

Most agencies do not face the challenge of a Cabrini Green or a New Briarfield. But most agencies do have within their jurisdiction blighted and/or stressed apartment complexes. Although such complexes are not necessarily public housing, in effect they function that way because a high proportion of residents are receiving public assistance. The goal of a police agency in such situations parallels in some ways American political goals in Afghanistan. Afghanistan served as a sanctuary for terrorists, and allowed the development of an organizational system sophisticated enough to engineer the 9/11attack. The sanctuary has by and large been eliminated, and although Al Qaeda has not been eliminated, it is far weaker than it once was. Similarly, a police agency will not eliminate an offending population from a jurisdiction by eliminating the sanctuary of a blighted housing project. However, a police agency will weaken that element considerably with the elimination of such sanctuaries.

STABLE SINGLE-FAMILY NEIGHBORHOODS

The third cell in the matrix is nonstressed, stable single-family neighborhoods. High-income, high-home-value neighborhoods experience almost no crime. That which does occur is largely nuisance offenses—kids causing problems, petty vandalism, and occasional theft from a garage. Additionally, the United States is blessed with innumerable lower-income neighborhoods that are likewise relatively crime free. They remain so because of a combination of social, economic, and cultural dynamics. Whether a stable neighborhood is high or low income, the same approach is generally employed by a police agency. That approach is best described by the term "**simple visibility**." Residents really do want to see a police cruiser occasionally drive past their front door. Special programs with clever acronyms are not necessary to meet this law enforcement objective. It is necessary, however, for police managers to remind officers that part of the agency role is to maintain such visibility. This requires officers to occasionally leave thoroughfares to simply drive through residential neighborhoods.

Learning Objective

simple visibility
The process of systematically driving throughout a patrol beat as a form of reassurance to residents that the police are present.

In some cases a neighborhood watch program might be deemed appropriate. There is no evidence that neighborhood watches actually reduce crime (San Miguel, 2005). Driving down a crime-free residential street does not reduce crime either. But part of the responsiveness that citizens want for their tax dollar is police stewardship of neighborhood watch programs. One must remember that such programs do not necessarily have to address only serious crime. Safety and traffic issues can also be included in police agency interaction with watch groups.

STABLE APARTMENT COMPLEXES

Learning Objective

The final category of residential enforcement is nonstressed apartment complexes. Police department responsiveness to such areas parallels the response to low-crime single-family neighborhoods. But drive-by visibility is usually not viable, and sometimes, such as with gated parking lots, literally impossible. Prevention of victimization is the primary goal in such apartment complexes.

That can be achieved through interactive programs, as well as with maintenance of communication with apartment complex managers. Many departments have found sponsorship of apartment managers' associations a worthwhile investment. Sponsorship entails either monthly or quarterly meetings that include updates by the police agency, discussion of crime prevention efforts, and related law enforcement concerns. Moreover, agencies have found that participation remains strong if the meeting also includes presentations relevant to routine management concerns—apartment management software, for example.

High-Crime Commercial Locations

Neither high-crime residential neighborhoods nor high-crime commercial locations come in neatly packaged categories. From the perspective of crime impact, both exist on a continuum from low stress to high stress. Commercial locations are even more difficult to place in categories than are residential areas. This is because whereas property values and crime are strongly inversely correlated in residential areas, the same is not necessarily true for commercial locations. High-value commercial locations, such as regional malls, attract criminal predation. There may in fact be more criminal events at high-value commercial locations than there are at median-value commercial locations. Stated in plain language, if one wishes to steal from cars, it pays to go where the cars are, and the cars are parked in the thousands at large regional malls and big-box retail outlets. Further, if one is intent on stealing designer jeans, he or she would be more likely to target a high-end retail store than the discount retailer down the street.

Despite the reality of a continuum of problems in commercial locations, it is useful to discuss police response in terms of categories of such locations, albeit with blurred lines between the categories:

1. Major shopping malls and their immediate environs
2. Downtowns
3. Strip-center corridors
4. Vice-orientated clusters
5. Isolated individual private business

Learning Objective

In general, police response to crime committed in commercial locations involves three dominant approaches:

1. Targeting offense clusters by tactical patrol units coupled with directed responsive patrol.
2. Surveillance, if appropriate, of the offense problem.
3. Engagement with businesses and private security providers.

Some mix of these approaches characterizes all efforts at commercial location crime control. But there is certainly variation in emphasis, depending upon which of the five location types is being addressed.

MAJOR SHOPPING MALLS AND THEIR IMMEDIATE ENVIRONS

What distinguishes enforcement at major retail malls, whether enclosed or in "town center" configuration, is the dilemma of enforcement on private property. Malls are certainly open to public access, and indeed are designed to be accessible. Importantly, "that is where the people are." Given these two premises—full public access and concentration of people—it can be argued that this is where the police should be. If owners attempted to deny police access to such a location, they would find themselves under arrest very quickly for interfering with a peace officer. Public police have a full right to be present at those locations when and where they choose. But with rare exception, public law enforcement chooses not to be there. Obviously this is an economic decision. We force ownership of malls to provide security for their patrons. But it can be argued that in so doing, public police agencies abdicate their responsibility to provide the safest possible environment for the citizens they serve. If the well-being of a jurisdiction's citizens depends upon the proclivities of a minimum-wage moonlight security officer, is the public police agency providing taxpayers the protection they deserve? And a police administrator who responds "Well, there is no crime at that mall" might be cautioned to more accurately state "Well, there is never any crime *reported* from that mall."

Beyond this philosophical problem there is the issue of responding to crime that is reported from such malls. Frequently thefts from these areas, either in the form of shoplifting or from automobiles, constitute a large portion of an agency's reported thefts. Curtailing shoplifting at a major department store may not be in the immediate public interest, but such offenses do consume public resources in the form of police reports and prosecutor efforts. And, of course, it can be argued that tolerance of any type of crime in a jurisdiction emboldens offenders, encouraging other crime at other locations.

Learning Objective

It is not argued here that public police agencies should routinely station officers in malls. On balance, public resources are better expended on more serious crime problems (assuming few serious offenses occur at large retail malls). But cooperative efforts with mall management and mall security are appropriate. An illustration is the Arlington, Texas, Police Department in relationship with The Parks at Arlington mall management and security. The city of Arlington decided some years ago that The Parks mall, a classic mega indoor shopping complex with several anchor department stores, was a major economic and social asset to the city. The mall draws tens of thousands of people to the city. Texas has a city sales tax, and the revenue to Arlington from The Parks mall is not trivial. Where tens of thousands of people cluster, predatory offenders will follow. Particularly problematic has been thefts from autos. The agency reached an agreement with the mall that prime enforcement of the parking lots belonged to the Arlington Police Department, while law enforcement presence inside the mall would be maintained by a private security firm. Crime at The Parks mall, even petty crime, is now very low. We cannot say whether the low crime rate is a product of the partnership between the police department and mall security—that would require a controlled experimental design—but the arrangement illustrates a compromise on the dilemma of the expenditure of public resources for policing private property balanced against policing where the people are.

DOWNTOWNS

The second category of commercial locations is downtowns. Downtowns are far more problematic for police agencies than malls and their environs. Because malls are private property, officials can legally control behavior, and to some extent even presence, on that property. Stated differently, problem people can simply be expelled from malls. Mall management does not tolerate, and indeed has a legal right not to tolerate, persons who engage in behavior that will drive paying customers away. Hence "undesirable" individuals are escorted from the property, including teenagers being loud and obnoxious, a homeless person who reeks of body odor, panhandlers, and even someone who behaves in subtle threatening ways. The police cannot do the same in downtowns.

Obnoxious or threatening persons cluster in downtowns not because downtowns are a more attractive environment to them than malls; it is that they cannot engage in their behaviors in malls. Frequently, their behaviors are consciously and deliberatively threatening. In order for obnoxious persons to "role play," they need the presence of large numbers of "regular citizens" as an audience. Panhandlers must be in a location with large numbers of potential donors; teenage "look-at-me" behaviors require the presence of "shocked" adults; power displays by gang members require the presence of individuals who will feel threatened. Downtowns are heavily populated, at least from 6:00 a.m. to 6:00 p.m. With no other convenient population clusters to prey upon, the obnoxious and threatening gravitate to downtowns.

American cities have fought the depravation of downtown districts since the development of the first retail centers following World War II. Billions of dollars have been spent, and whole city departments exist to attempt to maintain the viability of downtown districts. A full discussion of the dynamics of this phenomenon is far beyond our purposes here. What needs to be noted, however, is that downtown districts are frequently a resource sponge for police agencies—they will soak up whatever personnel are assigned. A strong police presence is indeed a critical component of maintaining the viability of a downtown. Downtown Chicago is a success story in this respect. It is anything but blighted; it is strong, vibrant, and growing. It has become a mecca for urban living. It has a strong retail business component in addition to business offices. And the Chicago Police Department maintains a strong and visible presence. But that is not the case in every American city. All too often downtowns find themselves in a downward spiral. Crime creates fear. Fear drives out business. Business retail outlets close and the downtown becomes an abandoned hollow core of an otherwise healthy community.

Learning Objective

Police intervention in downtowns requires broken windows enforcement. Obnoxious behaviors, and even obnoxious people themselves, must be controlled for downtowns to remain a viable part of a community. Tolerance of aggressive begging, sleeping on sidewalks, boom boxes, threatening behaviors, graffiti, and other signs of disorder requires aggressive police action. There will be challenges. Some of the challenges emanate from inappropriate self-interest, some from well-meaning individuals who see themselves as protecting the rights of the disadvantaged, and some from publicity seekers. A police agency must be prepared for a sustained public relations battle comingled with litigation if it is to control obnoxious behavior in downtown districts.

COMMERCIAL STRIP CORRIDORS

The third category of commercial location enforcement is **strip-center corridors**. These are arterial streets that contain a mix of retail and office buildings. Typically there will be numerous gas stations/convenience stores, fast food outlets, home improvement and home furnishing specialty stores, insurance

strip-center corridors Street segments dominated by small businesses and/or offices.

offices, and a scattering of multistory office buildings. Commingled apartment complexes are typical. Anybody who has driven through any American city can visualize exactly what is being described. For a police department, the primary problem in such corridors is usually traffic, not crime. Criminal offenses that do occur tend to be property-oriented and associated with vehicles—theft of and theft from automobiles. The enforcement approach in these areas is best described by the term "more presence." Such areas typically do not require aggressive enforcement and certainly do not require saturation patrol. Surveillance is out of the question. To the extent that the criminal offenses that do occur can be abated, it would be through focused patrol, usually conducted in conjunction with individual businesses.

Learning Objective

PROBLEM BUSINESSES

This leads to the fourth category of commercial locations—individual problematic businesses. Such businesses are frequently located in strip-center corridors, but not always. The single most frequent offense with which the police deal in this respect is gas station drive-offs—failure to pay for pumped gasoline. The second most frequent problem is grab-and-run thefts from convenience stores—so called "beer runs" because so often the merchandise stolen is a six pack of beer stacked in the store right at the doorway to engender impulse buying. To control the volume of such offenses, it is essential that a police department have the capability in its information system to identify frequent problem addresses. That identification should be done both by all calls-for-service and specific call or offense categories. It should be noted that a police information system may need to be modified to easily identify problematic locations. If, for example, all that can be retrieved from the information system is the broad category "theft," then it is extremely difficult to identify gas station drive-offs. One must search within the theft report for the word "gasoline" and even then there will be a number of misses. Similarly, a single classification of shoplifting does not distinguish $1,000 television thefts at Wal-Mart from beer runs. The first level of intervention is to counsel the owner/manager. If that does not work, then escalation of intervention is in order.

Learning Objective

By far the most effective intervention for many such problems is "prevention-oriented" city ordinances. For example, ordinances that require "pay before you pump" virtually eliminate the drive-off problem. Individual businesses may fight such an ordinance. But the premise is that such ordinances level the playing field—if motorists have to pay before they pump everywhere, then no particular service station has an advantage. Without such an ordinance, there is, of course a strong disincentive for service stations to impose such a requirement on their own. Numerous motorists will indeed choose to take their business to a service station that does not require you to pay before you pump.

Not every issue with problem-oriented businesses can be resolved by ordinances, of course. In most instances police agencies can maintain a positive relationship with such businesses to reduce the number of offenses. At other times, however, businesses have made a conscious decision to exploit public resources for their own profitability. A particular notorious practice is a loose policy on acceptance of payment by check. Some businesses choose not to pay for check clearance services, or, even more egregious, do not perform a decent identification check. A representative of one regional grocery chain had a bad reputation for walking into a police investigation unit with, literally, a cardboard box full of bounced checks. Several agencies that dealt with that grocery chain simply started refusing to take them. One detective captain from such an agency stated, "I think if a customer asked a clerk for a blank sheet of paper, and wrote on the sheet of paper pay to the order of ABC Grocery, entered the amount and signed it; the store manager would take it." The grocery chain obviously made a decision that a loose policy on taking checks would generate more profit than the cost of the checks that do not clear. Under such circumstances a police manager, responsible for the expenditure of public resources, can legitimately say this is the store's problem, not the public's. From one perspective it can indeed be argued that it is a civil matter, and not necessarily a criminal one. Granted, a professional thief can write a lot of bad checks. More frequently it is irresponsible behavior—failure to balance the checkbook—on the part of the customer. Irresponsible behavior is not necessarily criminal behavior.

vice-oriented business clusters
Business groupings dominated by adult book stores, strip clubs, liquor stores, low-level bars, and marginal businesses.

VICE CLUSTERS

The final category of crime control in commercial locations is **vice-oriented business clusters**. The core of such clusters is sexually oriented businesses—adult book stores and topless bars. Liquor stores are present as well. Additionally there will be run-of-the-mill taverns and, frequently, "private clubs"—whether one agrees with the right of such businesses to exist or not. Such clusters are problematic for police agencies. They attract what is clearly illegal behavior—prostitution and drug distribution; they are the favorite meeting places of chronic offenders; they attract the full range of "street people." In such settings otherwise law-abiding citizens who choose to "take a walk on the wild side" are particularly prone to predation. Complicating the situation are conjoined offenses, for example, customers of prostitutes who end up being "rolled." (The offense usually comes to the attention of the police as an "I lost my wallet" complaint.) Crime control in this environment requires resources. A single approach seldom produces substantive outcomes. Hot spot saturation, broken windows enforcement, neighborhood restoration led by nuisance-abatement efforts, and problem-oriented endeavors are all required.

police-operated surveillance cameras
Cameras placed outdoors in areas of public access, such as street corners, to monitor problematic behaviors; surveillance cameras are most frequently placed at intersections plagued by persistent drug dealing and/or curbside prostitution.

Learning Objective

Camera Surveillance

The deployment of **police-operated surveillance cameras** at drug distribution, high-crime, or problematic public locations is exploding. Agencies throughout the nation have acquired surveillance cameras, frequently termed police observation devices, or PODs. Extensive deployment of PODs began in the United Kingdom, Great Britain. The British are not as sensitive about privacy issues as are Americans, and not as fearful that police use of such technology will result in infringement of basic liberties. The deployment of public surveillance cameras in Britain dates back to the planting of explosive devices by the Irish Republican Army. With that kind of threat, the concern about the intrusiveness of the police was brushed aside.

Learning Objective

In the United States in 2004, the Chicago Police Department under the administration of then Superintendent Phillip J. Cline led the way in the deployment of PODs. Experimentally, twenty PODs were deployed at intersections plagued by chronic open drug sales and prostitution solicitation. Initial

Learning Objective

deployment was not without controversy, but the PODs were generally supported by residents of the experimental neighborhoods, who saw them as preferable to control of the streets by drug distribution gangs. Lukewarm public support intensified overnight into red-hot public support. Once deployed in selective neighborhoods, there was an outcry from innumerable citizen groups for a POD in "my neighborhood." The initial concern of the Chicago Police Department about public rejection of the devices quickly morphed into concern about how rapidly additional devices could be purchased and deployed. By 2009 there were over 1,500 PODs deployed in Chicago, and the number is climbing (Bulkeley, 2009). The city links the cameras that police have placed in trouble spots with thousands more that have been installed by other government agencies and the private sector in city buses, businesses, public schools, subway stations, housing projects, and elsewhere. There may be as many as 15,000 private cameras linked to "Operation Virtual Shield," Chicago's fiber-optic video-network loop.

The cost of the initial PODs deployed was over $9,000 each. The cost was driven by the fact that it was assumed that drug dealers would attempt to sabotage the devices by shooting at them; hence they were armor plated. Such an incident never occurred, and now PODs are purchased at a much more reasonable $3,000 each. They are monitored by the police department. There have only been a handful of instances of offenses in progress being observed, and interrupted. There is, however, one compelling video of one drug dealer murdering another. For the most part, however, the PODs function as a deterrent on one hand and investigative tool on the other, with the occasional dispatch of a patrol vehicle to investigate suspicious behavior. LaVigne, Lowry, Dwyer, and Markman (2011, p. 22) note that ". . . law enforcement may choose among overt, semi-overt and covert camera options . . . Police typically employ highly visible cameras for their deterrent effect and the fact that they symbolize the city's commitment to the safety and security of the public."

An evaluation of the effect of Philadelphia's deployment of eighteen cameras in eight surveillance areas indicated an overall reduction of 13 percent in suppressible street crime and disorder offenses (Ratcliffe, Taniguchi, & Taylor, 2009). An evaluation of Baltimore's installation of 500 cameras downtown and in high-crime neighborhoods in 2005 indicated that crime dropped by more than thirty incidents per month on average (La Vigne, Lowry, Markman, & Dwyer, 2011). By 2008, the lower numbers were holding steady, with thirty fewer incidents of crime in March 2008 than in March 2007, and half the number in April 2008 than the year before. However, the cameras' effects on crime were mixed in other Baltimore neighborhoods. One area experienced no reduction in crime after the cameras were installed. Similar mixed results occurred in other cities. In Chicago, although analysis indicated cameras alone in some areas were likely responsible for a nearly 12 percent drop in the crime rate, an evaluation of cameras in the West Garfield Park neighborhood found no change in the crime rate. Likewise, cameras had a mixed effect on crime in Washington, D.C. At surveillance intersections the number of violent crimes and assaults with a deadly weapon fell, but theft went up (La Vigne, Lowry, Markman, & Dwyer, 2011).

Critics of police camera surveillance raise the issue of "big brother is watching." While we should not be dismissive of concerns regarding the intrusiveness of emergent technology into our lives, the use of any technology, and digital technology in particular, entails some loss of privacy. Any credit card company can easily trail an individual's movement across a city or the country through charges at gas stations, fast food restaurants, and coffee shops. Automatic billing systems on toll ways store our driving location and time. The use of a smartphone provides close monitoring of movement, a fact not lost to the police, who routinely obtain mobile phone records for such purposes. Further, we are on camera far more than we realize already through the use of monitoring video in commercial establishments. At every convenience store, every hotel lobby, every Wal-Mart, and most private parking areas, we are being "watched" constantly. Finally, there is the issue of "Does big brother really care?" The police are looking for drug dealing and solicitation for prostitution. They have neither the time, the resources, nor the concern with scanning untold hours of video tape to note: "Hey, there's Mary getting her third Starbucks' grande latte of the day, and she told us she was on a diet."

Foot Patrol

A variant of geographic deployment is **foot patrol**. Much of the imagery of policing "in the good ole days" is based upon romantic visions of officers *walking* their beats. A recruit graduating from an academy today likely has no idea what a "call box" is—but there are still a few old timers who recall them.[1] Foot patrol has experienced variation in popularity, but has never disappeared. Indeed, survey data compiled by the Bureau of Justice Statistics indicate that in 2007, regularly scheduled foot patrol was employed by nine out of ten departments serving a population of 1 million or more, and by about eight out of ten departments serving a population of 250,000 to 999,999. Some 32 percent employed bicycle patrol (Reaves, 2010, p. 15).

Learning Objective

foot patrol
Assignment of officers to walking beats; foot patrol beats are employed predominantly in downtowns and problematic strip-center corridors.

Indeed, two of the most employed deployment strategies discussed extensively in this book—community policing and broken windows enforcement—both have their origins in assessments of foot patrol. Robert Trojanowicz conceptualized community policing as a derivative of his evaluation of foot patrol in Flint, Michigan (Trojanowicz, 1982). The broken windows conceptual framework was formulated from the qualitative elements of an evaluation of the Newark, New Jersey, Foot Patrol Experiment (Wilson & Kelling, 1982).

The use of foot patrol is concentrated in large, "vertical" East Coast and Midwest cities. Foot patrol is all but nonexistent in suburban settings. The closest may be a patrol car "park-and-walk" effort—having officers occasionally stroll "town center" shopping areas. West of the Mississippi, foot patrol is seldom employed even in downtown areas of central cities. When employed in the West, it is limited to business hours. However, foot patrol is still very much part of the American policing landscape, and is extensively used in other parts of the world. Most police officers in developed Asian nations, such as China and Japan, are, in fact, foot patrol officers.

The effect of foot patrol on crime is unclear. Foot patrol in Flint only impacted burglary, and then only marginally (Trojanowicz, 1982). Likewise, in Newark there was no substantive reduction in crime (Wilson & Kelling, 1982). Citizen support for foot patrol was nonetheless overwhelmingly strong in both Flint and Newark. Additionally, there was less tangible but important reductions in citizens' fear of crime and incidents of disruptive or threatening public behavior.

A more recent collaborative effort between Temple University and the Philadelphia Police Department has produced encouraging results. The Philadelphia Foot Patrol Experiment was a randomized controlled trial, using about 250 officers to patrol 60 violent crime locations during the summer of 2009. Beats were chosen based upon classic hot spot analysis. In 2008 the top 5 percent of corners accounted for 39 percent of robberies, 42 percent of aggravated assaults, and 33 percent of homicides.

> Commanders identified 129 potential foot beats, and from these 120 were selected for the experiment. Each area contained about 15 street intersections and 1.3 miles of roads. The foot beats were ranked by the weighted volume of violent crime and paired with a foot beat of similar crime rate. One from each pair was randomly selected to be a target beat, while the other became a control (or comparison) area. (Ratcliffe et al., 2010)

The authors (2010) note that after twelve weeks in the target areas and relative to the comparison areas:

- Violent crime decreased 22 percent.
- Vehicle-related crime decreased 12 percent.
- Drug-related incident detections increased 28 percent.
- Pedestrian stops conducted by police increased 51 percent.
- Vehicle stops and traffic enforcement increased 33 percent.
- Arrests increased 13 percent.

With the increased police activity, the authors estimate that in the target areas, one violent crime was reduced for every additional four arrests, sixty-three pedestrian stops, and twenty-five traffic stops (Ratcliffe et al., 2010).

Whether reported crime reductions will be sustained is, of course, as yet unanswered. Research from other geographic targeting efforts indicated rapid decay. The issue is sustainability of "treatment." Indeed, one of the goals of the evaluation was to provide productivity information—is the reduction in crime worth the investment of resources on a permanent basis? Foot patrol is expensive. And when calls-for-service start accumulating in queue, foot patrol officers are nearly always pulled from their walking beats and placed in patrol cars.

IMPLICATIONS FOR STRATEGY

Geographically focused interventions are currently the most popular of the three "focusing" strategies—the other two being offender and offense foci. Relatively speaking, the efficacy of geographically based intervention is supported by far more research than any other approach. But research also indicates that a geographic focus does not always produce crime reduction. Usually it does, but not always.

Variation in specific tactics is demanded by different problematic areas. The approach for a stressed single-family residence neighborhood varies from that of a stressed apartment complex. Likewise, interventions aimed at reducing crime along commercial strips will differ from those routinely employed for crime prevention at malls and their environs. Downtowns remain problematic, despite an array of various efforts to make them more inviting.

Camera surveillance of chronically problematic public places by police departments has grown explosively over the past few years. Nearly all major city agencies now employ some level of camera surveillance. Cameras are seldom monitored in real time; for the most part they are employed for post-event review.

The most intense form of geographic focus is foot patrol. Although the Flint and Newark evaluations did not indicate an appreciable crime impact, the more recent assessment of the effectiveness of foot patrol in Philadelphia indicates substantial reductions in crime on foot patrol beats. Nonetheless, foot patrol is expensive, and hence limited to densely populated areas.

SUMMARY

- A crime hot spot is defined as a stipulated area of a jurisdiction with inordinately high rates of crime, particularly suppressible street crime. Geographically, hot spots vary in size from a single address to a city block to a square mile to the four or five square miles that constitute a typical police beat. There is no "correct" definition of a hot spot area—it depends on circumstances and the nature of police intervention.
- Theoretical support for hot spot concentrated patrol can be found in a primary tenant of the routine activities theory, which stipulates that for a crime to occur there must be a motivated offender, suitable targets, and lack of guardianship of suitable targets.
- Research to date indicates that hot spot saturation deployment is effective. Definitively it reduces the incidents of so-called "nuisance or disorderly" behaviors, such as street-corner prostitution, open drug sale or use, aggressive begging, and obnoxious or threatening actions. Evidence is less definitive on the effectiveness of hot spot concentration on more serious crime, but research tends to indicate that both nuisance behaviors and serious crime are affected.
- The nature of sustained interventions among varying types of residential entities varies dramatically. Citizens residing in stable single-family neighborhoods primarily desire simple visibility—an occasional drive-by of a police patrol unit. Complaints in such neighborhoods tend to concern relatively minor issues, such as teenagers hot-rodding and barking dogs. The situation in stressed single-family residence neighborhoods is very different. Police response to these areas should definitely be more aggressive, but would certainly vary by the extent of deterioration. Citizen engagement and focused problem-oriented efforts might suffice for neighborhoods still basically under control. Neighborhoods where the streets are ruled by gangs, drug dealers, and prostitutes require the full weight of aggressive intervention led by saturation patrol with intense field interrogations. For stable apartment complexes, visibility is often not an option, as access to even the apartment's parking facility is frequently gate controlled. Classic community policing engagement is most relevant, such as crime prevention orientation programs. Stressed apartment complexes, like stressed neighborhoods, require far more aggressive intervention. Agencies have enjoyed success by assigning officers full-time, working out of a designated apartment in the complex, and working cooperatively with complex management in comprehensive efforts to improve the complex.
- An extreme version of hot spot saturation patrol is zero-tolerance crackdowns. The hallmark of zero-tolerance crackdowns is pedestrian and vehicle stops for either suspicious behavior or commission of the most trivial of offenses—for example, failure to signal a lane change. The primary risk for a

police agency is harm done to law-abiding residents of such areas. If they are subjected to constant police stops and questioning, their support for the police crackdown will wane quickly. The term to describe this phenomenon is "victimization of the victims." If a neighborhood is so deteriorated that a zero-tolerance crackdown is the only option left for a police agency, then certainly the agency should make an effort to assure that targeting is "surgical," focused upon offenders, not legitimate residents.

- As in residential areas, enforcement efforts in commercial areas vary depending upon the nature of a commercial zone. Criminal offenses in healthy commercial strip areas, arterial streets with a rich mix of businesses and occasional apartment complexes, generally involve motor vehicles—theft from and theft of cars. Enforcement in such areas is most effective if an agency partners with targeted businesses to increase security and surveillance. Likewise, malls, big-box stores, and their environs require business cooperation for effective crime-prevention efforts. Downtowns present a different set of challenges; for most downtown problems business partnerships are irrelevant. Downtowns attract the homeless, aggressive beggars, disorderly behavior, and individuals intent on asserting a visible presence. If obnoxious behaviors by so-called "street people" are not controlled, there is high risk of a downward spiral of downtown deterioration. Effective police response includes assertive regulation and classic broken windows enforcement. Crime in vice-oriented commercial clusters presents yet a different set of challenges. Routine patrol is insufficient to address the conditions that breed serious crime in these areas. A range of interventions may be necessary depending upon individual circumstances, but generally what we refer to as problem-oriented efforts are most effective.
- A relatively new phenomenon is the use of police-operated surveillance cameras placed in problematic public locations. Such cameras have been used effectively for years by the police in the United Kingdom. The widespread employment in the United States was initiated by the Chicago Police Department. Initial concerns by the Chicago police that there would be vocal public objection to such surveillance evaporated rapidly as residents of stressed neighborhoods clamored for installation of cameras on their block. Their use has spread across the United States, and continues to grow substantially.
- From one perspective, the most intense form of police saturation is foot patrol. Although the extent of foot patrol has waxed and waned over the years, it is a sustained part of American policing. However, foot patrol is largely limited to major cities, and in particular the downtown areas of major cities.

REVIEW QUESTIONS

1. It has been suggested that the relatively frequent evaluative studies of hot spot deployment in comparison to other strategic approaches to crime control are due to the ease of assessment. What makes hot spot deployment easier to evaluate than other approaches, such as community engagement or problem solving?
2. Consistent results have been obtained from numerous analyses of crime and call-for-service concentrations at particular locations/addresses. What policy implications flow from these analyses?
3. The catchphrase "victimizing the victims" refers to what enforcement approach? Why does such an approach frequently victimize the victims? What can be done to prevent the outcome?
4. Low-crime, stable neighborhoods and stable apartment complexes should engender what types of police crime control approaches? How does this contrast with approaches used in high-crime stressed neighborhoods and apartment complexes?
5. Why are downtown commercial districts so frequently problematic for the police? What approaches to the problems appear to be most effective?

REAL-WORLD SCENARIOS

1. Your crime analysis unit reports a surge in theft reports at a particular multiple-building apartment complex. Most of the thefts are from parked vehicles, but items have also been stolen from porches. The complex is otherwise problem-free. It is a quality facility with responsible management, spacious and well-maintained grounds, and gated access to parking that requires a code number for entry. What alternatives should be considered for a police response?
2. Residents of a neighborhood plagued by gangs and open-air drug use and sale approach you as Police Chief to help them restore the area as a desirable place to live. Among their requests is that the police department install a surveillance camera at a particularly dangerous intersection. They have heard about the successful use of cameras in other jurisdictions. You agree; a camera is purchased and installed. News media coverage of the "new crime-fighting tool" engenders a blistering attack on the police department from a political group, accusing the department of "big brother" intrusion that will evolve into constant tracking of the movements of every citizen. Respond to the criticism that camera surveillance of a high-crime location carries too much risk of evolving to dangerous privacy invasion.
3. You are the commander of the Downtown Division of a major municipal department. Anchoring the west end of the downtown area is an entertainment district with several conference hotels, restaurants, gift shops, night clubs, theaters, and so forth. A strong association of businesses in the area maintains a constant presence at city council meetings. The viability of the area is considered essential to attract national conferences and tourists. A church recently opened a food bank in a building adjoining the entertainment district. Since then, the presence of the homeless has become common in the entertainment district, accompanied by aggressive begging. The business association asserts that this is alienating delegates considering the city as a future conference site. The police department also has received numerous complaints from tourists regarding obnoxious behavior and intrusive panhandling. Develop an action plan for dealing with the emergent problem.

APPLICATION ACTIVITIES

1. It is noted that concentrated patrol at hot spots is consistent with the criminological theory termed "routine activities theory." Research the routine activities theoretical perspective. Describe its major tenets, and contrast those tenets with those of another criminological perspective, such as social disorganization theory.
2. The circumstances of homelessness are tragic, particularly when a homeless person is suffering from mental illness. Aggressive police tactics that merely keep the homeless invisible are not an ultimate solution. Yet the problem seems at times to be intractable. Find in the literature descriptions of both successful and less-than-successful efforts to address the issue of homelessness.
3. Is foot patrol worth the cost? Review either two of the sources cited in the References section of this chapter (Ratcliffe, 2011, and Wilson & Kelling, 1982) or other literature on the topic. (Note: The Trojanowicz publication in the References on the Flint Foot Patrol evaluation is not widely available.) Summarize what the authors observe regarding the cost-effectiveness of foot patrol. Distinguish hypothetical benefit from benefits confirmed by evaluative research.

ENDNOTES

1. A call box is a dedicated telephone placed in what was always a blue box at each end of a foot patrol beat. An officer called in on a schedule—first from one end of the beat, then from the other. Call boxes were both a welfare check and a means to assure that officers were diligently walking their beat. Call boxes were replaced by handheld radios.

COURSEMATE

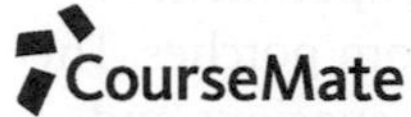

This available CourseMate has an interactive eBook and interactive learning tools, including flash cards, quizzes, and more. To learn more about this resource and access free demo CourseMate resources, go to **www.cengagebrain.com**, and search for this book. To access CourseMate materials that you have purchased, go to **login.cengagebrain.com**.

REFERENCES

Braga, A. A. (2001). The effects of hot spots policing on crime. *Annals of the American Academy of Political and Social Science, 578*, 104–125.

Braga, A. A. (2005). Hot spots policing and crime prevention: A systematic review of randomized controlled trials. *Journal of Experimental Criminology, 1*, 317–342.

Braga, A. A. (2007). The effects of hot spots policing on crime, a Campbell Collaboration systematic review. Available at http://www.aic.gov.au/campbellcj/reviews/titles.html.

Braga, A. A., Weisburd, D., Waring, E. J., Mazerolle, L. G., Spelman, W., & Gajewski, F. (1999). Problem-oriented policing in violent crime places: A randomized controlled experiment. *Criminology, 37*(3), 541–580.

Bulkeley, W. M. (2009, November 17). Chicago's camera network is everywhere. *The Wall Street Journal*. Available at WSJ .com/article/.

Cohen, L. E., & Felson, M. (1979). Social change and crime rate trends: A routine activity approach. *American Sociological Review, 44*, 588–605.

Eck, J. E., Gersh, J., & Taylor, C. (2000). Finding crime hot spots through repeat address mapping. In V. Goldsmith, P. McGuire, J. Mollenkopf, & T. Ross (Eds.), *Analyzing crime patterns: Frontiers of practice*. Thousand Oaks, CA: Sage.

Eck, J. E., & Spelman, W. (1987). *Problem-solving: Problem-oriented policing in Newport News*. Washington, DC: Police Executive Research Forum.

Katz, C. M., Webb, V. J., & Schaefer, D. R. (2001). An assessment of the impact of quality-of-life policing on crime and disorder. *Justice Quarterly, 18*(4), 825–876.

Koper, C. S. (1995). Just enough police presence: Reducing crime and disorderly behavior by optimizing patrol time in crime hot spots. *Justice Quarterly, 12*(4), 649–671.

La Vigne, N. G., Lowry, S. S., Dwyer, A. M., & Markman, J. A. (2011). *Using public surveillance systems for crime control and prevention: A practical guide for law enforcement and their municipal partners*. Washington, DC: U.S. Department of Justice, Urban Institute Justice Policy Center, Office of Community Oriented Policing Services.

La Vigne, N. G., Lowry, S. S., Markman, J. A., & Dwyer, A. M. (2011). *Evaluating the use of public surveillance cameras for crime control and prevention—a summary*. Washington, DC: Urban Institute, Justice Policy Center.

Lawton, B. A., Taylor, R. B., & Luongo, A. J. (2005). Police officers on drug corners in Philadelphia, drug crime, and violent crime: Intended, diffusion, and displacement impacts. *Justice Quarterly, 22*(4), 427–451.

Mazerolle, L. G., Ready, J., Terrill, W., & Waring, E. J. (2000). Problem-oriented policing in public housing: The Jersey City evaluation. *Justice Quarterly, 17*(1), 129–158.

McGarrell, E. F., Chermak, S., Weiss, A., & Wilson, J. M. (2001). Reducing firearms violence through directed police patrol. *Criminology & Public Policy, 1*(1), 119–148.

Novak, K. J., Hartman, J. L., Holsinger, A. M., & Turner, M. G. (1999). The effects of aggressive policing of disorder on serious crime. *Policing: An International Journal of Police Strategies and Management, 22*(2), 171–190.

Nunn, S., Quintet, K., Rowe, K., & Christ, D. (2006). Interdiction day: Covert surveillance operations, drugs, and serious crime in an inner-city neighborhood. *Police Quarterly, 9*(1), 73–99.

Ratcliffe, J. H., Groff, E., Wood, J., Taniguchi, T., Johnson, L., McGuire-Taylor, C., et al. (2010). *The Philadelphia Foot Patrol experiment: Research brief*. Philadelphia, PA: Temple University and Philadelphia Police Department.

Ratcliffe, J. H., Taniguchi, T., & Taylor, R. B. (2009). The crime reduction effects of public CCTV cameras: A multi-method spatial approach. *Justice Quarterly, 26*, 746–770.

Reaves, B. A. (2010). *Local police departments, 2007*. Washington, DC: U.S. Department of Justice, Office of Justice Programs, Bureau of Justice Statistics.

San Miguel, C. (2005). *An analysis of neighborhood watch programs in Texas*. Huntsville, TX: Sam Houston State University.

Sherman, L. W. (1990). Police crackdowns: Initial and residual deterrence. In M. Tonry & N. Morris (Eds.), *Crime and justice: An annual review of research* (Vol. 12). Chicago: University of Chicago Press.

Sherman, L. W., & Rogan, D. P. (1995). Effects of gun seizures on gun violence: "Hot spots" patrol in Kansas City. *Justice Quarterly, 12*, 673–694.

Sherman, L. W., & Weisburd, D. (1995). General deterrent effects of police patrol in crime "hot spots": A randomized, controlled trial. *Justice Quarterly, 12*(4), 625–648.

Smith, M. R. (2001). Police-led crackdowns and cleanups: An evaluation of a crime control initiative in Richmond, Virginia. *Crime and Delinquency, 47*(1), 60–83.

Spelman, W. (1995). Criminal careers of public places. In J. E. Eck & D. Weisburd (Eds.), *Crime and place: Crime prevention studies 4*. Monsey, New Jersey: Willow Tree Press.

Stephens, D. (2000). Personal interview.

Stroud, M. (2011). Fighting crime in an era of belt-tightening. *Journal*. Available at http://www.theatlanticcities.com/neighborhoods/2011/09/fighting-crime-era-belt-tightening/112/.

Sutherland, E. (1947). *Principals of criminology*. Chicago: J. B. Lippincott Co.

Trojanowicz, R. J. (1982). *An evaluation of the Neighborhood Foot Patrol Program in Flint, Michigan*. East Lansing: Michigan State University.

Weisburd, D. (2005). Hot spots policing experiments and criminal justice research: Lessons from the field. *Annals of the American Academy of Political and Social Science, 599*(5), 220–245.

Weisburd, D., Bushway, S., Lum, C., & Yang, S. M. (2004). Trajectories of crime at places: A longitudinal study of street segments in the city of Seattle. *Criminology, 42*(2), 283–320.

Weisburd, D., & Green, L. (1995). Policing drug hot spots: The Jersey City drug market analysis experiment. *Justice Quarterly, 12*(4), 711–734.

Weisburd, D., Groff, E., & Morris, N. (2011). *Hot spots of Juvenile crime: Findings from Seattle.* Washington, DC: U.S. Department of Justice, Office of Justice Programs, Office of Juvenile Justice and Delinquency Prevention.

Weisburd, D., Morris, N. A., & Ready, J. (2008). Risk-focused policing at places: An experimental evaluation. *Justice Quarterly, 25*(1), 163–200.

Weisburd, D., Wyckoff, L. A., Ready, J., Eck, J. E., Hinkle, J. C., & Gajewski, F. (2006). Does crime just move around the corner? A controlled study of spatial displacement and diffusion of crime control benefits. *Criminology, 44*(3), 549–591.

Wilson, J. Q., & Kelling, G. L. (1982). Broken windows: The police and neighborhood safety. *Atlantic Monthly, 249*(March), 29–38.

CHAPTER 7

Offense Targeting Strategies

© Juice Images/Alamy

KEY TERMS

Bait vehicles
Buy and bust
Buy and walk
Buy and warrant
Consent searches
Crime analysis
Crime response team
Field interviews
Malum prohibitum
Malum in se
Offense clusters
Pawn shop records submission
Racial profiling
Racial proportionality
Reverse sting operations
Salvage yard inspections
Tactical patrol

LEARNING OBJECTIVES

After completing this chapter, you should be able to:

- List the offenses generally regarded as constituting suppressible street crime.
- Characterize the value of bait vehicles in combatting auto theft.
- Define tactical patrol, also known as a crime response team.
- Describe what the range of approaches to auto-theft suppression illustrates about strategic approaches to theft.
- Identify how many common types of robbery exist and what variation among the types implies.
- Define offense clusters.
- Identify in legal terminology what best describes the "evil" associated with drug distribution.
- Identify the "macro" approaches to controlling drug distribution enterprises.
- Describe why the use of intensive field interviews is considered a strategy in its own right.
- Explain why the police should avoid indiscriminate use of efforts to obtain consent search authorization.
- Characterize what data indicate regarding the racial/ethnic makeup of citizens subjected to either traffic or pedestrian stops.
- Distinguish explanations for widespread disproportionality in the racial/ethnic makeup of citizens stopped by the police.

More than any other approach, targeting a particular offense requires the engagement of multiple units in a police agency. Typically employed are tactical uniform patrols, forms of surveillance, directed response patrol, and specialized investigative units. Additionally, effective efforts to target an offense require very heavy support from crime analysis/deployment operations.

Learning Objective

The offenses that become the focus of targeting usually, but not always, fall into the classification commonly termed "suppressible street crime." Suppressible street crime includes auto theft, larceny from a motor vehicle, robbery committed in public places, burglary, street theft, vandalism, and gang-related shootings/homicide. Open-air drug market and prostitution enforcement is its own category, typically classified as disorder enforcement rather than suppressible street crime. Occasionally agencies do select other offenses for targeting. For example, some agencies have been successful in working with businesses to curb passing of false checks, or systematic deliberative writing of checks with insufficient funds. Theft offenses associated with problematic business locations, such as gas station drive-offs, also fall into the category of criminal behavior that the police may be able to affect, but not through patrol tactics. However, these efforts are typically not sustained over long periods of time.

From this perspective, suppressible crimes are those offenses susceptible to repression or intervention by patrol. Not all crime is subject to suppression by patrol. Forms of intervention beyond patrol are likewise important. Domestic violence, for example, requires atypical forms of intervention. Whereas assertive social intervention programs may reduce the occurrence of an offense such as domestic violence, police patrol will not. Fraud schemes require proactive investigative initiatives. This chapter reviews the most common offense-specific intervention tactics. Some are conducted by patrol, some by investigative units, and some by special units, whereas others require a combination of agency divisions.

Bait Property

VEHICLES

bait vehicles
Vehicles placed by the police in opportune locations for theft; starting the vehicle triggers a geographic positioning system (GPS) device, allowing the police to trace its location.

In recent years, the use of **bait vehicles** by police agencies has become particularly popular. Desirable vehicles from a thief's perspective are acquired by an agency. A desirable vehicle is then left parked in an area with a high prevalence of auto thefts. Typically the keys are left in the ignition, and the doors are unlocked. A radio transmitter and global positioning system (GPS) device are planted in the vehicle. When the vehicle is started, an alarm signal is generated and GPS tracking is initiated. Marked units are then dispatched to intercept the vehicle. When a marked vehicle has the bait car in sight, a radio signal is broadcast back to the bait vehicle that shuts down the engine and concurrently locks all doors so they cannot be opened from the inside.

If the truth be known, one of the primary attractions of bait vehicles is the satisfaction of being able to symbolically say to an offender: "Surprise!" In addition to the other electronics, most bait vehicles have a tape recorder planted inside the passenger compartment to record any conversation between multiple offenders, or if the offender makes a cell phone call to report to a handler. (Cell phone records have become, by the way, an excellent resource for identifying the associates of an offender.) Such recordings frequently are humorous, particularly when the "surprise" occurs.

Learning Objective

There are two significant caveats that must be offered with regard to bait vehicles. First, as a percentage of all arrests for theft of or theft from automobiles, the use of bait vehicles counts for only minuscule amounts. Second is the opportunistic thief issue. Certainly a portion of the apprehensions made is of individuals who are not professional auto thieves and who do not routinely steal cars. For example, a teenager walks by a late-model sports car with the keys dangling, the temptation is too much, and the teen decides to take it for a classic joy ride. Certainly, this is not entrapment from a legal perspective; the teen was not induced or persuaded to steal the vehicle. But if the goal is breaking up organized auto theft rings, use of a bait vehicle under these circumstances is not very productive.

GPS TRACKING

As the size of GPS transmitting units and their costs have shrunk, their use to track other types of attractive items for theft has grown. One agency experienced a rash of thefts of lawn-care equipment from trailers parked on the street by landscaping firms while the workers were in the backyard. Working with the landscaping firms, the agency attached GPS tracking devices to the equipment. Two separate rings of thieves were arrested within two weeks.

Directive Responsive Patrol

Directive responsive patrol is defined as the use of patrol units assigned to be responsible for calls-for-service response, but focused during uncommitted patrol time to crime reduction. As noted in Chapter 2, following the Kansas City Preventive Patrol Experiment (Kelling, Pate, Dieckman, & Brown, 1974), several jurisdictions experimented with so-called directed patrol. Directed patrol assumes that police management through crime analysis has identified problematic locations, and when officers clear from a call they are directed to a specific location to patrol against a specific offense or set of offenses. Such efforts were widely tried. Although there appeared to be some effect, cities abandoned the effort.

The current approach to employment of responsive patrol officers (units with routine call-for-service response as their prime responsibility) for crime reduction does not depend on mandates from dispatchers. The current approach is to provide patrol officers with available **crime analysis** information—crime patterns and trends on their beats. It is then left to the individual officers' discretion as to how to focus their uncommitted patrol time for intervention purposes. Agencies employing variants of Compstat may provide "suggested areas of emphasis," but patrol officers are generally not doggedly monitored. This approach represents an enhancement of the professional status of patrol officers. It engages them in the endeavor most thought they were signing on for when recruited—crime control.

crime analysis
Plotting of crime patterns and trends, usually employing geographic information systems (GIS).

Tactical Patrol

Learning Objective

Tactical patrol is defined here as marked or semi-marked patrol units freed from call-for-service responsibility and assigned full-time (or nearly full-time) responsibility for crime interdiction. In larger agencies, such patrol is usually done by teams of officers. Terminology varies; probably the most frequent used term is simply *tactical patrol* or *tactical officers*, but the terms **crime response team** and *targeted response team* are also frequently employed. The Chicago Police Department had, for example, three "companies" of eighty officers each that were assigned saturation and aggressive patrol responsibilities. Simple visibility is part of this tactic. Primarily, however, such units engage in numerous traffic and pedestrian stops, conducting field interviews.

tactical patrol
Marked patrol units freed from normal call-for-service responsibility; typically assigned to concentrated patrol at hot spots.

crime response team
Another term for tactical patrol; patrol units freed from normal call-for-service responsibility and charged with concentrated patrol at hot spots.

Multiple Concurrent Approaches

The use of multiple approaches to target a suppressible offense is illustrated by approaches to auto theft, which might include any or all of the following:

- Salvage yard/accessory dealer inspections
- Surveillance of known habitual offenders
- Surveillance of decoy (bait) vehicles
- Stolen-parts-receiving sting operations
- Stolen-parts-sales reverse sting operations

- Reactive follow-up of reports with leads
- Aggressive patrol programs
- Enhanced prosecution

Direct interdiction of an auto theft in progress is a relatively rare event. Although one frequently hears news reports of high-speed pursuits that involved a stolen vehicle, the vast majority of these were initiated as a routine traffic stop, and the offender attempted to evade officers, not realizing that the police were unaware the car was stolen. The approaches to auto theft suppression illustrates an important point regarding approaches to theft cases in general: It is frequently more effective to attack the market for stolen goods than it is to attempt to interdict the theft in progress. Market interdiction does not have the appeal of more clever and glamorous interventions, such as the use of bait cars or reverse stings. But it is likely that far more auto thefts are prevented by simple **salvage yard inspections** than any other intervention. The problem for many police managers is that they encounter passive resistance to such efforts. What self-respecting crime fighter wants to spend her or his eight-hour day scanning salvage yard part numbers?

Learning Objective

salvage yard inspections
Inspections of businesses engaged in recycling auto parts, typically from inoperable vehicles involved in collisions; police inspections are designed to intercept parts stripped from stolen vehicles for resale.

Burglary is another example of an offense requiring multiple approaches. The *Problem-Oriented Guide for Policing* addressing burglary of retail establishments published by the Center for Problem-Oriented Policing lists the following:

Police responses:
- Targeting repeat offenders
- Targeting repeatedly burglarized stores
- Disrupting markets for stolen goods
- Establishing business/shop watch programs

Retailer actions:
- Upgrading external security
- Installing burglar alarms
- Safeguarding cash and valuable stock
- Locking escape routes
- Screening and training shop staff
- Employing security guards after hours
- Using crime prevention through environmental design (CPTED)

City planning measures:
- Improving street surveillance through lighting and cameras
- Promoting "living over the shop"
- Promoting business-improved districts (Clarke, 2002)

Although domestic violence is not regarded as suppressible street crime, efforts to reduce its occurrence often use a multidimensional approach. In this case collaboration with prosecutors is essential. Beyond the prosecutor, effective domestic violence intervention also requires engaging social service providers. The point here is that a wide range of offenses can be optimally addressed using multiple approaches.

Problem-Oriented Guide for Policing
Problem-Specific Guide Series

An excellent resource for offense-specific approaches is the *Problem-Oriented Guides for Police*. Funded by the U.S. Department of Justice's Office of Community-oriented Policing Services, and edited by the Center for Problem-Oriented Policing at the University of Wisconsin at Madison, these guides provide insight into approaches to an array of law enforcement responsibilities. Among the guides not mentioned herein addressing specific offenses are:

- Auto Theft in Shopping Facilities
- Identity Theft
- Street Prostitution
- Robbery of ATMs

Numerous other issues are also addressed. For more information, go to www.popcenter.org.

Specification

Learning Objective

Specification is of particular importance in developing an offense-targeting strategy. Robbery illustrates the need for explicit, narrow definitions of offense types. Monk, Heinonen, and Eck (2010) identify nine forms of robbery. Taking license to modify their enumeration to provide even more distinction among robbery categories provides a derived list of twelve robbery types:

1. Street robbery, stranger
2. Street robbery, related to drug transactions
3. Street robbery, derived from prostitution luring
4. Street robbery, taxi drivers (its own category due to frequency)
5. Street robbery, delivery vehicles (frequently pizza)
6. Armored trucks (its own category due to sophistication necessary)
7. Acquaintances (usually linked to prior conflict over "loans")
8. Schoolyard bullying
9. Home invasion
10. Pickpocketing, degenerating to required use of force
11. Purse snatching, degenerating to required use of force
12. Carjacking

Each of these categories has its own distinct characteristics (place, time, victim attributes, offender attributes, modus operandi), and hence requires varying types of police intervention. Although all twelve are included in the single *Uniform Crime Reports* (UCR) category of robbery, an intervention designed to abate "rolling of johns" by prostitutes will bear little resemblance to efforts to interrupt a string of bank robberies. Indeed, even within any one of the twelve categories there is variation. Offenders preying upon ATM users may or may not ever prey upon passengers exiting public transportation.

The *Problem-Oriented Guide for Policing* on street robbery (Monk et al., 2010) suggests a wide range of potential responses (see Table 7.1). Some are traditional and obvious (e.g., deploying visible foot/vehicle-directed patrols), whereas others range to the esoteric (e.g., diverting potential offenders to legitimate activities). Although resources or public patience will almost never make the latter a feasible police response, responding to every one of the twelve robbery types with directed patrol is clearly both simplistic and ineffectual. As noted earlier in this chapter, offense-specific intervention requires multiple approaches.

TABLE 7.1 Responses to Street Robbery

Responses
Offender-Oriented Responses
1. Deploying visible foot/vehicle-directed patrols
2. Using covert directed patrols
3. Using intelligence to target repeat robbers
4. Disrupting stolen goods markets
5. Publishing photos of known robbers
6. Improving robber identification methods
7. Diverting potential offenders to legitimate activities
8. Using probation and parole information to target repeat offenders
9. Removing robbery "tools"
Victim-Oriented Responses
10. Launching a robbery awareness campaign
11. Providing safe transportation
12. Improving how victims report robberies
13. Reducing target attractiveness
14. Reducing intoxication in high-risk areas
15. Rewarding awareness and safety
16. Redesigning certain "craved" items
17. Making senior citizens less vulnerable
18. Making immigrants less vulnerable
Location-Oriented Responses
19. Removing hiding spots
20. Increasing lighting at high-risk sites
21. Installing closed-circuit television (CCTV)
22. Increasing pedestrian density near risky places
23. Removing escape routes
24. Increasing site-specific robbery awareness
25. Installing emergency call stations
Routine-Oriented Responses
26. Improving special event planning
27. Planning for holiday shopping
28. Notifying parents just before the school year starts
29. Providing safe routes during construction
30. Encouraging businesses to use alternative payment methods
Responses with Limited Effectiveness
31. Using police decoys
32. Arming potential victims

Source: Monk, K. M., Heinonen, J. A., & Eck, J. E. (2010). Street Robbery. Problem-Oriented Guides for Police Problem-Specific Guides Series, No. 59. Washington, D.C.: U. S. Department of Justice, Office of Community Oriented Policing Services.

Pawn Shop Monitoring

Every state has a set of statutes that govern the operation of pawn shops. The right of the police to access pawn shop records is universal in those statutes. The devil is in the details. Monitoring paper copy pawn shop records is time consuming and hence very expensive. In major metropolitan areas, the amount of information is simply overwhelming—no process can reasonably be put in place that adequately will monitor paper records. Recognizing the need to provide electronic copies of records, some states have supplemented their statutes in recent years with a requirement that **pawn shop records submission** be done electronically. Indeed, the majority of pawn shops, 90 percent plus, now employ electronic records themselves. Although the majority of pawn shop companies are cooperative in this respect, some even supportive, a vocal minority lobbies state legislatures to not require electronic submission. The list of half-baked excuses is almost laughable. For example, pawn shops claiming they cannot computerize their records have twenty computers sitting on their shelves for sale. Regrettably, these lobbying efforts have been successful in many states, and so electronic submission is not universal.

pawn shop records submission
The process of police compilation of information from pawn shops to identify items being pawned that have been stolen; police also monitor pawn shop records to identify frequent pawners likely disposing of stolen merchandise.

One must realize, however, that even with electronic submission, identification of stolen property that is being pawned is not that simple. Despite crime-prevention efforts encouraging homeowners to engrave property and/or maintain records of serial numbers, only a small minority of households do so. Thus, in a burglary where electronic equipment is taken from a house, the television, for example, typically is listed in the police report as "late model, Sony, color television set, 30-inch screen." In a large urban area, there are Sony televisions being legitimately pawned every week. Given this limitation, police agencies have found it more useful to identify frequent pawners rather than attempt to locate specific items of stolen property. About the time someone comes in with the fourth Sony color television in a month, suspicion certainly ought to be raised.

Again, however, there are limitations. Thieves with any street savvy at all frequently work with false IDs and provide different identification every time they pawn an item. They move from store to store, making matching of records more difficult. Further, they move from jurisdiction to jurisdiction to pawn, requiring effective control techniques to be regional—problematic anywhere in the United States. One also encounters, of course, legitimate frequent pawners. A segment of our population employs pawn shops as "payday loans." Generally, it is simple to sort such individuals from thieves. Payday loan pawners almost always retrieve the item they pawn once they have some cash, and reuse the same item again the next time they need a payday loan.

Other Stolen Goods Markets

Pawn shops are not the only otherwise legitimate businesses sometimes used as a conduit to convert stolen goods to cash. The list also includes secondhand outlets, garage sales, flea markets, and antique and collectable businesses. Sometimes there are even door-to-door sales of items such as furniture. Thieves typically tell customers that they represent a distributor or manufacturer overstocked due to a store refusing delivery of an order. They are driving a legitimate-appearing delivery truck, with a legitimate-sounding name such as "Smith's Furniture Distributing" appropriately painted on the side, and offer the furniture or other goods at bargain prices.

Behind all of these apparent "direct-to-customer" delivery systems are fencing operations. Fencing exists on a continuum from amateur to organized professional (Sutton, 2010). The following typology was constructed by Lewis (2006) to outline the dynamics of different types of commercial fencing operations:

- Level-1 fence: A thief sells directly to a level-1 fence (often a storeowner such as a pawnbroker or jeweler).
- Level-2 (wholesale) fence: A level-2 fence buys from a level-1 fence and then often cleans up and/or repackages the goods.
- Level-3 fence: A level-3 fence takes repackaged goods from level-2 wholesale fences and diverts the goods to retailers.

A professional fence is thus more than a drop-off point for stolen goods. Professional fences are the core of a ring of thieves, coaching and even directing the thefts of specific types of goods. At the other end of the transaction process, the professional fence is part of a network of stolen goods distribution (Sutton, 2010). Illegal or "careless" fencing is often combated by sting and **reverse sting operations**.

reverse sting operations
An undercover technique entailing the sale of stolen goods or drugs; a sting involves the police posing as customers to purchase stolen goods or drugs, whereas a reverse sting involves the police posing as illegitimate goods sellers to arrest those who knowingly are buying illegal or stolen goods.

Offense Clusters

Police interventions, particularly patrol interventions, although focused on a given offense, may well have impact upon multiple problems. Indeed, frequently tactical patrol deployment is designed to attack clusters of related offenses rather than a single offense. For example, essentially the same tactics that are designed to reduce theft will also reduce theft of autos (carjacking is a separate offense category, of course). If one is conducting a surveillance of targeted parking lots for theft of automobile parts or contents, it certainly would not be unheard of to witness an attempted theft of the auto itself. On a more mundane level, salvage yard inspections will reduce both thefts of parts and thefts of entire autos for stripping purposes.

Learning Objective

There are other less obvious forms of offense clustering. Alcohol is the root of much evil, the failure of prohibition notwithstanding. Alcohol-related enforcement might target problematic bars, driving while intoxicated, disorderly conduct associated with drunkenness, and fights (assaults) associated with alcohol consumption.

Prostitution represents another form of offense clustering. Despite the quaint depiction of prostitution in the play and subsequent movie *The Best Little Whorehouse in Texas*, prostitution is not quaint. Most prostitutes did not choose the oldest profession as a way of life independent of other personal problems, most frequently alcohol and drug abuse. Indeed, one encounters disproportionate childhood sexual abuse among prostitutes. The prostitutes themselves are routinely victimized by would-be customers, often subjected to physically abusive behavior. The *Pretty Woman* scenario, marrying the charming and wealthy customer, is pure Hollywood. Conversely, the customers of prostitutes are frequently the target of robbery or theft. Thus, targeting prostitution is in reality targeting a multitude of sins, both literally and figuratively.

Gun offenses follow a parallel pattern of associated clustered offenses. Illegal transport, exchange, and distribution of firearms are frequently associated with other offenses, usually very serious offenses. At the very least gun trafficking is part of both gang violence and drug distribution. Gun enforcement is a tactic employed by many agencies to reduce the cluster of associated offenses, particularly homicides. The Kansas City Gun Experiment, described in Chapter 2, for example, linked gun seizures to homicide reduction. A major part of Chicago's gang violence reduction effort was focused upon interdiction of firearms. The 33 percent reduction in homicides in Chicago was undoubtedly due to multiple efforts aimed at the trilogy of gangs, guns, and drugs. But Chicago attributed at least part of the drop in homicides to the middle segment of the intervention trilogy, gun seizures.

Drug Market Crackdowns

We will not win the "war" on drugs. The use and therefore distribution of mind-altering chemicals is a classical intractable problem. Prostitution may be the oldest profession, but drug distribution is a close second. The use of hallucinogenic or trance-inducing substances is as old as human civilization. Mind-altering drug use is neither a recent problem nor one associated only with industrial society. What is prohibited behavior on the streets of American cities is fodder for anthropological analysis if the setting is an isolated and "primitive" tribe. An Amazonian shaman's induced trance is called drug abuse in New York City. Indeed, it is harmful to even characterize efforts to control and inhibit mind-altering drug use as a "war." The goal of any police agency ought to be reasonably set at control and containment. Eradication is impossible.

That having been said, there is no other activity more destructive to the social and economic fabric of a neighborhood than drug distribution. When the situation deteriorates to so-called open-air, or curbside, selling, a neighborhood is lost. Although drug distribution per se is, from the perspective of the previous paragraph, ***malum prohibitum*** (not harmful in and of itself), it is associated with numerous ***malum in se*** (inherently harmful or evil) offenses. Organized crime on several levels derives its income from drug distribution. We need only consider the murder of Mexican government and police officials to understand how profoundly drug distribution "attacks" all societies.

The "macro" approaches to control of drug distribution include interdiction internationally by intervening in the growth of plant sources of illegal drugs, interruption of international transport, and long-term investigations focused upon conviction of high-level so-called drug kingpins. Such efforts are the purview of the U.S. Drug Enforcement Administration. For the typical municipal American police agency, control of drug distribution takes the form of undercover drug purchases with subsequent arrests of the sellers. There are four primary forms of intervention. In a **buy-and-bust** situation, a buy or closely knit series of buys of illegal drugs are made, culminating in arrests temporally immediate to the buy. A second variant is a **buy-and-walk** operation. Arrests are deferred in favor of gaining more information about the distribution enterprise and its leadership. **Buy and warrant** is a subset of buy and walk—a series of buys is made with audio and/or video recording, and a warrant is obtained premised upon that evidence. Under these circumstances, the identity of undercover police officers is

malum prohibitum
Term used to describe offenses that involve behaviors that in and of themselves are not harmful; drinking of alcohol is not inherently harmful to others, but may be so if the individual drinks excessively and then drives a vehicle.

malum in se
Term used to describe behavior that is inherently evil or harmful to others.

buy and bust
The process of undercover officers purchasing drugs and immediately arresting the seller.

Learning Objective

buy and walk
A drug enforcement technique whereby undercover officers purchase drugs but do not immediately make an arrest in favor of either identifying a pattern of sales and/or obtaining search warrants to allow a broadening of the investigation.

Learning Objective

buy and warrant
A form of buy-and-walk strategy where the goal is focused on obtainment of a search warrant for vehicles or residences.

better protected, as the arrest is not proximate to the buy. Officers other than the ones involved directly in the buy actually make the arrest. The fourth form of direct intervention is surveillance of either open-air drug markets or drug houses, again with video recording. Once sufficient evidence has been gathered, a search warrant is sought as the follow-up. Execution of the search warrant entails the seizure of illegal substances and arrests of those controlling the substances.

There are obvious limitations to all four approaches. Both buy-and-bust and buy-and-warrant operations often result in revealing the identity of undercover officers. The advantage of surveillance with search warrant follow-up is elimination of the need for the use of undercover officers. However, the investment of time in conducting an effective surveillance operation is enormous. Additionally, enforcement does not necessarily resolve the problem. Sherman et al. (1995) carefully measured the effect of crack house raids:

> We tested the block-level deterrent effects on crime of uniformed police raids of crack houses. Court-authorized raids were legally possible on 207 blocks with at least five calls for police service in the preceding 30 days. Raids were assigned randomly to 104 locations and were conducted at 98 of those sites; the other 109 were left alone. Experimental blocks, in relation to controls, showed reductions in both calls-for-service and offense reports, but effects were quite small and decayed in two weeks. Raids in which arrests were made (23 of 104 assigned) had no consistently different impact from raids in which no arrests were made. . . . Alternative police methods may be far more cost-effective than raids in "harm reduction" for crack houses. (p. 755)

One must note that what was measured was neighborhood effects in terms of disorder and crime—not the interruption or cessation of drug distribution from the raided locations. The finding, simply stated, is that a crack house raid is not going to in and of itself clean up a neighborhood. As is stated frequently herein, expectations need to be realistic.

An evaluation of a drug distribution crackdown in Indianapolis (Nunn, Quintet, Rowe, & Christ, 2006) illustrates this point. The effort targeted a group of more than two dozen chronic offenders with long arrest records who were living and operating within the Brightwood neighborhood—using it as a site for drug trafficking. "Ultimately, all of them were convicted to long federal prison terms, thus taken from the streets of Brightwood" (p. 74). The authors note, however, that residents actually protected the drug dealers because of the extra money they brought in, consistent with discussion of why deteriorated neighborhoods in Philadelphia tolerated and sometimes protected drug dealers—because the illegal drug market offered a source of "employment" (though illegitimate) and income-generating activities where there were almost no legitimate alternatives.

In 2002, the Philadelphia Police Department launched Operation Safe Streets, stationing officers at 213 of the highest-drug-activity locations in the city twenty-four hours a day, seven days a week. Geographically focused analyses showed significant localized intervention impacts for both violent and drug crimes. Operation Safe Streets had a significant negative impact on violent crime within 0.1 mile of the intervention site. Here, the intervention prevented on average one violent crime a week per km^2. The program resulted in significantly less drug crime, the targeted offense, about three per week per km^2, in the target areas (Lawton, Taylor, & Luongo, 2005). A caveat is the exorbitant expenditure required. Stationing officers 24/7 on 213 street corners could not be financially sustained for long.

Weisburd and Green (1995) examined a multifaceted interdiction as part of the National Institute of Justice's Drug Market Analysis Program (DMAP). In Jersey City, New Jersey, fifty-six hot spots of drug activity were randomized to experimental control conditions. Drug hot spots were generally composed of either one or a group of two to four street segments. The intervention strategy included problem-oriented approaches, including engagement of business owners and citizens in crime control efforts, police crackdowns, and a maintenance program once drug activity had abated. The control areas received traditional unsystematic arrest-oriented narcotics enforcement based on ad hoc target selection. Comparing seven-month pre-intervention and post-intervention periods, there were consistent and strong effects of experimental strategy upon drug-related 911 calls. Interestingly, there was little evidence of displacement to areas near the experimental hot spots; indeed, the opposite, diffusion, appeared to be the case.

Agencies have had some success with less costly simple disruption. Disruption takes several forms. Interference sometimes involves numerous field interrogations of both distributors and potential customers. A common approach is simply having a marked patrol unit stay in the distribution area, parked, for example, in front of a known drug house. What is important to recognize is the need for "aggressive" intervention. Depending upon community policing/neighborhood engagement to control entrenched drug distribution is not feasible because (1) frequently a high proportion of the neighborhood has been integrated into the drug distribution economy (e.g., paid to stash drugs in their homes, children employed as lookouts), or (2) citizens are afraid to inform because they might be killed (Brennan, 2005). Proactive field intervention is required, including intense field interviews.

INTENSIVE FIELD INTERVIEWS

Learning Objective

The use of field interviews has been mentioned in the preceding descriptions of crime intervention strategies. Field interviews constitute a tactic for several of the strategic approaches. However, it is appropriate to address the intensive field interview as a strategy in its own right. In this context, the purpose of intensive field interviews is to reduce an entire constellation of crime and disorder problems in a geographic area—be it downtown, a vice-oriented commercial cluster, a residential neighborhood, or a high-crime apartment complex. Indeed, if a police manager were to implement one change in an agency otherwise relatively passive and reactive with regard to crime control, it would be to implement a program of intensive field interview in the patrol division.

No police crime control strategy is potentially more effective, or more controversial, than intensive field interviews. **Field interviews** are defined herein as patrol stops of vehicles or pedestrians for inquisitory purposes. In that sense, traffic enforcement may or may not be a field interview technique. Conducted in some settings, traffic enforcement is just traffic enforcement, and nothing more. In other settings, monitoring for traffic violations serves as a pretext for a stop to conduct a field interview. So it is the purpose of the stop, not the technique, that defines a field interview.

field interviews
Stopping of vehicles or pedestrians triggered by suspicious behavior or unexplained presence in high-crime areas; the primary purposes of field interviews are to run warrant checks on the individuals stopped and/or deter criminal behavior.

Courts have always granted American police enormous latitude in conducting investigations in general, and field interviews in particular. The general position has been that as long as the police actions do not interfere with individual liberty, or become a form of harassment, the police may investigate at will. In the context of field interviews, courts have held that police may, for example, set up sobriety checkpoints. The police actions are permissible as long as the vehicles are stopped in a nondiscriminatory manner, for example, every tenth vehicle.

No other experiment in policing conducted during the golden era of the police foundation produced more dramatic or definitive results than the San Diego Field Interrogation Experiment. As noted in Chapter 2, after a short period of time crime rose substantially in the beats for which the field interrogations set up in this study had been withdrawn. Suppressible street crime rose from a monthly average of 75 offenses to 104. A 33 percent increase in suppressible crime is hardly trivial. That is dramatic and pronounced. Random routine patrol may not make a difference, but stopping and questioning suspicious persons while on patrol does make a difference.

There are limits to the use of field interrogations, or if one prefers a more politically correct term, field interviews, in a democracy. One of the unwritten rights of the U.S. Constitution is freedom of movement. Citizens have a right to move about their community without being harassed or harangued by the police. If stopped by the police on mere suspicion, at the very least the demeanor of the officer should be courteous and detention should be of short duration.

Learning Objective

consent searches
A search of a person, vehicle, or residence with the permission of an authorized agent or owner.

A problematic element of field interrogation is **consent searches**. Citizens are prone to consent to a search, whether they want to or not. Without question there is an element of intimidation when a uniformed officer asks if it is okay to look through a vehicle. If law enforcement agencies expect that a process of rummaging through a vehicle on a random search for contraband will leave a warm and fuzzy feeling with the consenting citizen, they are deluding themselves. Blanket fishing expeditions should not be part of an intensive field interview program. What we are trying to achieve is not apprehension, but deterrence. Deterrence is largely achieved through the mere process of making a stop and asking pointed questions. It is not necessary to tear out the back seat for purposes of deterrence.

It is legitimate to run a warrant check as part of such stops. And in a surprising number of instances a warrant check will be a hit. Apprehension of fugitives is a legitimate purpose of field interviews. Moreover, a high proportion of the time vehicles that are carrying persons with outstanding warrants are also carrying contraband. Because an arrest on an outstanding warrant justifies an inventory search of the vehicle, consent searches under these circumstances are irrelevant. In instances where there is no warrant, police purposes will be better served by wishing the driver and occupants well, rather than turning the car upside down, even with consent.

Field interviews can alienate citizens. Perhaps better said, field interviews will alienate at least some citizens. No matter how courteous the officer's demeanor, being stopped and questioned by the police is not a pleasant experience. Intensive field interviews implemented under the auspices of zero tolerance target the innocent as well as the guilty. Indeed, as noted earlier, a descriptive phrase for the phenomenon exists—victimizing the victims. Then there is the racial profiling issue.

FIELD INTERVIEWS AND RACIAL PROFILING

Numerous police agencies have gathered data regarding the racial/ethnic makeup of persons subjected to either traffic or pedestrian stops. Their experience is almost universal: Data indicate that racial/ethnic minorities are stopped more frequently than whites. Numbers vary substantially, but it is not unusual to find that, proportionately, members of racial/ethnic minorities are stopped twice as frequently as their numbers in the population would predict. The issue is, of course, why?

When police managers or law enforcement labor groups voice opposition to collecting data on the race of drivers involved in traffic stops, many persons assume that "there must be something to hide." The knee-jerk reaction to allegations of even the remote possibility of racial profiling most frequently is "let's gather data." But the limitations and misinterpretations are numerous.

Crime is not evenly distributed across American society. Aristotle said over 2,000 years ago that poverty is the root of crime and revolution. It is still true. Wealth is not proportionally distributed in the United States by race. Minorities are disproportionately poor. Poverty breeds crime. The police deploy to where crime occurs. And where the police are deployed, more traffic stops will occur.

Further, deployment by crime rates is reinforced by deployment by demand for service. The number of 911 calls received by a police department varies dramatically by neighborhood. The poor call upon the police far more often than the rich. The poor disproportionately live in circumstances breeding greater conflict. Dilapidated apartment dwellings with thin walls bring complaints of disturbing noise from neighbors. Crowded parking lots lead to conflict. Insufficient or inadequate play areas bring other problems. Thus, not only is crime disproportionately clustered in poor areas, but also calls for police service to manage conflict are disproportionately clustered in poor areas. Because minorities are disproportionately poor, we inevitably find increased police presence in minority neighborhoods.

Because police officers are deployed proportional to demand, more officers are placed in neighborhoods that generate a higher proportion of calls-for-service. If this approach were not followed, the police would be unavailable to respond to such calls, or response would be substantially delayed. Indeed, there is no other defensible way to deploy the police other than proportional to demand for service. But placing more police officers in economically disadvantaged neighborhoods, that is, minority neighborhoods, means there will be more traffic stops made in those neighborhoods. For a jurisdiction as a whole, this factor alone will cause the statistics to reflect substantial disproportionate stops of minorities.

Recent efforts at more effective police procedures have even included rapid redeployment by crime pattern every day, or at least every week. With its genesis in New York City's Compstat program, the practice of "deployment by analysis" is now widespread. Modern information systems have allowed real-time analysis of crime patterns and trends, and law enforcement agencies have capitalized upon this capability by virtually instantaneous redeployment of resources to problem areas. This only exacerbates the problem.

Learning Objective

Hard evidence exists to support the assertion that deployment patterns significantly impact the racial proportion of traffic stops. In Richmond, Virginia, the average Part I crime rate is 45 percent higher in majority-African American census tracts compared with majority-White census tracks (Smith & Petrocelli, 2001). And, indeed, analysis indicated that Richmond officers proportionately stop more Black citizens. In an analysis of traffic stops in San Jose, California, the fact that Hispanics and Blacks were stopped at rates higher than their population representation (43 percent of stops vs. 31 percent population for Hispanics; 7 percent vs. 4.5 percent for Blacks) was attributed by the agency to concentrated deployment in minority neighborhoods to handle greater per capita volume of calls-for-service (San Jose Police Department, 1999). The disparity in proportionality in Lansing, Michigan, 27 percent versus 22 percent, was also attributed by researchers at Michigan State University to deployment variation (Carter, Katz-Bannister, & Schafer, 2001).

No one would argue that the police should do anything but attempt to make every neighborhood in which they are deployed as safe as they can make it. And proactive police interventions are an established way to do so. The "broken windows" concept emerging out of the Newark Foot Patrol Experiment underscored the value of vigorous enforcement of all statutes, and controlling in particular petty incivilities, as a valuable technique to reduce crime (Kelling & Coles, 1996). Vigorous enforcement means numerous field interrogations and numerous traffic stops. If the police are disproportionately deployed in minority neighborhoods, minorities will disproportionately be the targets of such tactics.

Police agencies have long recognized the deleterious effects of this pattern. They have made special efforts to establish structured community relations programs in minority neighborhoods, at least partially to offset the negative effect of well-intentioned vigorous enforcement efforts. It is widely recognized that minority youth are more likely to have been picked up for petty misbehavior than White youth, simply because more police were present to catch them. Police recruitment efforts aimed at attracting minorities into the police service have recognized this phenomenon, and even incorporated expanded tolerance limits for petty misbehavior for youth from such neighborhoods. But all of these efforts do not eliminate the problem.

Learning Objective

Deploying the police proportional to crime or call-for-service demand does not constitute racial discrimination. Indeed, the opposite would be the case. If we deployed the police absolutely proportionately across a jurisdiction, ignoring crime rates and demand for service, the quality of police service in minority neighborhoods would plummet, and criminal victimization would increase. In effect, efforts to provide the highest possible quality of police services to minority communities, and to make those communities as safe for the residents as possible, results in statistics indicating that the police are doing the opposite—insidiously discriminating against minorities.

This author conducted a study of the genesis of disproportionate stops of minorities by the Houston Police Department (Hoover, 2002). An expected number of stops was calculated, corrected for deployment density. That is, citizens of the city of Houston do not have an equal probability of being stopped by police. Officers will make traffic stops in the beat to which they are assigned. If the overwhelming majority of residents of that beat are minority, then the overwhelming majority of stops will be of minorities. It is, of course, the case that not everyone stopped in a given beat will be a resident of that beat. Residents of Houston driving across just a portion of the city will drive through several police beats. Nevertheless, a statistical probability corrected for deployment density is a more realistic predictor of the chances of being stopped by police than one based solely on the overall racial composition of the city.

Although Whites and Blacks were stopped more than expected, Hispanics and other racial groups were stopped less than expected. Houston's population composition at that time was 35 percent White, 24 percent Black, 34 percent Hispanic, and 7 percent other. Females, regardless of their race, were stopped proportionately less, indeed considerably less. Of all the race and gender compositions, Black males were most prone to police stops—exactly twice what their population proportion would "predict"—12 percent of the population versus 24 percent of stops. Controlling for police deployment density accounted for most of the disproportion found.

For the analysis, the study went one step further and examined complaints regarding drug trafficking. The goal was to determine whether the higher proportion of stops in predominantly Black beats, particularly "investigative" stops, could be explained by the amount of drug enforcement.

Data were obtained from Houston Police Department records indicating the number of complaints received regarding drug trafficking, categorized by beat. Sources of complaints include both calls to 911 and calls to the agency's drug "hotline." There were a total of 17,551 complaints of narcotics-related activity received via the 911 system, and 2,142 received via the drug hotline. A linear regression showed a significant relationship between the number of complaints about drug-related crime given to the police and the proportion of Black residents in a beat. The higher the proportion of Black residents, the more complaints of drug-related offenses were received by police. We should emphasize that these are not officer-initiated events—they are complaints received from citizens residing in the beat in question.

These results provided additional explanation for the variance in the police stops. The more complaints from citizens that were received with regard to narcotics in a particular beat, the more officers were deployed to that beat, and therefore more police stops were conducted. Subsequent narcotics arrests were also highly correlated. Given that drug-related complaints from citizens were generally concentrated in the beats where the majority of the racial composition is Black, the correlation may explain the racial disproportion in the number of police stops. Indeed it can be argued that the practice is the opposite of racial profiling. That is, stops were disproportionately made in beats where citizens—Black citizens—called the Houston Police Department to complain of drug trafficking. This is police responsiveness to citizen demand, not police discrimination.

There is no magic bullet for deflecting criticism of racial bias. But one thing is absolutely clear: Do not expect the data to show exact **racial proportionality** to a residential population. It goes without saying that if data do indicate bias by race—**racial profiling**—police managers are expected to forcefully intervene. But disproportionate data may well be a product of legitimate deployment practices and/or citizen demand for street-level drug enforcement. Analysis of data from several cities indicates that disparity in traffic stops in urban environments is simply another measure of racial, social, and economic disparity—with parallel social disorganization in Black neighborhoods. It should also be noted that residents of areas where aggressive traffic enforcement is employed to reduce

racial proportionality
The relative proportion of minorities arrested, stopped, cited, or searched in comparison to their population proportion.

racial profiling
The illegal practice of using race as criteria for vehicle or pedestrian probative stops.

crime do not necessarily think that the police are harassing them (Chermak, McGarrell, & Weiss, 2001).

However, it should also be noted that regardless of the reasons, Black residents, and youthful Black males in particular, are still subject to more police stops than their White counterparts. The fact that the reasons are not necessarily bigotry and profiling does not change the reality of being pulled over twice as often. We should not expect youthful Black males to be happy about the situation. Extra effort to enforce equitably, explain the reasons for stops, and show great restraint in requesting permission to search is good police policy. Cessation of enforcement is not.

IMPLICATIONS FOR STRATEGY

Although efforts to reduce suppressible street crime—auto theft, larceny from a motor vehicle, robbery committed in public places, burglary, street theft, vandalism, and gang-related shootings/homicide—always include patrol, other agency divisions are usually also engaged. Auto theft is an illustration, involving patrol intervention, use of bait vehicles, salvage yard inspections, and proactive investigations based upon intelligence. Likewise, there are at least twelve forms of robbery, and thus interventions relevant to one form (e.g., robbery of taxi drivers) are irrelevant to other forms (e.g., prostitutes "rolling" customers). For burglary and theft, interventions aimed at stolen goods markets are likely more effective than direct interdiction efforts.

Control of drug distribution is its own category of offense-specific strategy. Control of drug distribution requires multiple forms of intervention. Efforts must be sustained. Research indicates that the effect of crackdowns is very short lived. Intensive field interviews are frequently the strategy of choice to control open-air distribution that has reached the point of causing neighborhood decimation. Agencies must be very careful, however, not to victimize the victims by engaging in random intrusive stops. Additionally, stressed neighborhoods tend to be minority neighborhoods, and intensive field interviews carry the liability of racial disparity and perceptions of racial profiling.

SUMMARY

- Offense targeting frequently takes the form of efforts to reduce a grouping of offenses commonly called "suppressible street crime." Suppressible street crime includes auto theft, larceny from a motor vehicle, robbery committed in public places, burglary, street theft, vandalism, and sometimes gang-related shootings/homicide. These offenses are typically addressed by tactical patrol, also known as a crime response team. Tactical patrol units are freed from normal response to call-for-service responsibility, and are directed to engage full time in crime reduction efforts, most frequently saturation patrol accompanied by intensive field interviews. However, this is far from the only approach employed to reduce suppressible street crime.
- Street-level interdiction is often more glamorous than effective, as illustrated by the use of bait vehicles. Bait vehicles are prewired with global positioning system (GPS) locators and mechanisms to stop the car on police command and concurrently lock all the doors so that they cannot be opened from the inside. Although colorful, use of bait vehicles makes only a minor dent in the rate of auto theft.

- ➤ The range of approaches to auto theft suppression illustrates that, for property crime, targeting stolen goods markets is often far more effective than street-level interdiction.
- ➤ As a guide to interdiction efforts, the legal definition for various offenses may not be relevant. For example, there are twelve common types of robbery ranging from a youth using some degree of force to snatch a purse to a group of professionals attacking an armored truck. Variation among the types clearly implies variation in police interdiction approaches.
- ➤ Enforcement approaches sometimes address related clusters of offenses. For example, alcohol-related enforcement might target problematic bars, driving while intoxicated, disorderly conduct associated with drunkenness, and fights (assaults) associated with alcohol consumption. Similarly, essentially the same tactics that are designed to reduce theft from autos will also reduce theft of autos. Although some approaches may be common throughout particular offense clusters, more typically the intervention must be focused upon the peculiar dynamics of the offense.
- ➤ Interference with drug distribution is one of the most common offense-specific forms of police targeting. Although the use of mind-altering drugs is not inherently "evil," usually regarded as falling in the classification of *malum prohibitum* rather than *malum in se*, behaviors that are inherently evil are intrinsically linked to drug distribution.
- ➤ Macro approaches to control of drug distribution include international interdiction by intervening in the growth of plant sources of illegal drugs, interruption of international transport, and long-term investigations focused on conviction of so-called drug kingpins. Such efforts are the purview of the U.S. Drug Enforcement Administration. For the typical municipal American police agency, control of distribution takes the form of undercover drug purchases with subsequent arrests of the sellers.
- ➤ The use of intensive field interviews to target various offenses is considered a strategy in its own right because of the commonality of its use, and its concurrent employment to target several offenses. The downside of intensive field interviews is the potential to harass law-abiding citizens. Field interviews should be focused, sometimes called surgical.
- ➤ In addition to careful use of field interviews, police must avoid indiscriminate use of efforts to obtain consent search authorization—a practice that frequently alienates innocent citizens.
- ➤ A particular form of citizen alienation engendered by intensive field interviews is the accusation of racial profiling. The racial/ethnic makeup of citizens subjected to traffic or pedestrian stops in almost every jurisdiction is disproportionate to their population within the community. Data overwhelmingly support the assertion that racial and ethnic minorities, particularly Black citizens, are disproportionately stopped by the police.
- ➤ Although some attribute the disproportionality to police bigotry, other explanations exist. In particular, it is noted that for complex historical reasons, minorities disproportionately constitute the residents of stressed neighborhoods with high crime rates. As part of legitimate efforts to limit victimization of innocent citizens of such neighborhoods, the police deploy disproportionately more patrol units to these areas. Where there are more patrol units there will be more stops. Disproportionate deployment is further reinforced by field interview efforts to better control crime in these neighborhoods, particularly drug distribution.

REVIEW QUESTIONS

1. What offenses are generally included in the definition of suppressible street crime? What characteristics make these crimes potentially suppressible—that is, what distinguishes suppressible crime from non-suppressible crime?
2. The effectiveness of bait vehicles to apprehend professional vehicle thieves has been characterized as "questionable at best." Why might bait vehicles be ineffective at disrupting organized car-theft rings? What alternatives exist?

3. What is implied in terms of interdiction approaches by the substantial variation among the forms and circumstances of robbery?
4. Residents of stressed, crime-ridden neighborhoods most frequently welcome drug distribution crackdowns. But not always. Why might residents fail to support drug distribution control efforts?
5. Racial disproportionality of traffic stops in major cities is the rule, not the exception. What might explain the disproportionality, other than institutionalized police bigotry?

REAL-WORLD SCENARIOS

1. While other UCR Part I offenses have been declining in your jurisdiction, robbery has been increasing. The increase has been so substantial that it has resulted in an overall increase in violent crime, despite reasonable decreases in murder, rape, and aggravated assault. You have been assigned as the commander of a task force charged with developing a "plan of attack." Describe how you would approach analyzing the issue, focusing on development of insight relevant to the selection of effective interventions.
2. Recent efforts by your agency to shut down open-air drug sales in a particular neighborhood appear to have been successful. However, although the neighborhood is certainly the better for it, you soon learn that the drug dealers from that area have all relocated their enterprises to a rundown "no-tell" motel on a nearby thoroughfare. The operation is so well organized that "security guards" check vehicles as they enter the parking lot to be sure the customers are not the police. As the captain in charge of the agency's drug enforcement unit, how do you approach enforcement in such a situation?
3. You are the police chief of a jurisdiction in a state that recently passed a law in response to concerns about possible racial profiling that requires police agencies to document the race and/or ethnicity of both pedestrians and vehicle occupants stopped for any reason. You know from the experience of other police agencies that the data will almost certainly indicate disproportionate stops of minorities. Prepare a press release that explains why you expect disproportionality in the data, and what you intend to do to distinguish inappropriate discrimination from disproportionality expected from legitimate deployment practices.

APPLICATION ACTIVITIES

1. Auto theft is motivated by several factors—joy riding, resale of the vehicle itself, resale in foreign countries (particularly Mexico), stripping for parts to be sold, and occasionally with the intent to use the vehicle in the commission of another crime, usually robbery. Use an Internet search engine to locate the websites of several state auto-theft-prevention authorities (among them: Florida, Illinois, Michigan, Texas). Develop an outline of the range of efforts discussed on each authority's website, identifying in particular those aimed at a particular type of theft.
2. To combat property-theft offenses, police agencies occasionally employ both stings and reverse stings. Details of such efforts are discussed in most criminal investigation texts. Locate two or three criminal investigations texts and summarize the observations regarding the dynamics of stings.
3. A broad strategic approach to combating property crime is disruption of stolen goods markets. Locate the *Problem Oriented Guide for Police, No. 57, Stolen Goods Markets* by Michael Sutton. Go to www.popcenter.org/guides/, the website for the Center for Problem Oriented Policing at the University of Wisconsin. Outline the approaches to disruption discussed in the guide.

COURSEMATE

This available CourseMate has an interactive eBook and interactive learning tools, including flash cards, quizzes, and more. To learn more about this resource and access free demo CourseMate resources, go to **www.cengagebrain.com**, and search for this book. To access CourseMate materials that you have purchased, go to **login.cengagebrain.com**.

REFERENCES

Brennan, C. (2005). Compstat in Philadelphia. Presentation to the Law Enforcement Management Institute of Texas (Major Cities Chiefs Program), Austin, TX.

Carter, D. L., Katz-Bannister, A. J., & Schafer, J. (2001). *Lansing Police Department MATS data: Six month analysis*. Lansing, MI.

Chermak, S., McGarrell, E., & Weiss, A. (2001). Citizens' perceptions of aggressive traffic enforcement strategies. *Justice Quarterly, 18*(21), 365–391.

Clarke, R. V. (2002). *Burglary of retail establishments. Problem-oriented guides for police, problem-specific guides series, no. 15*. Washington, DC: U.S. Department of Justice, Office of Community Oriented Policing Services.

Hoover, L. T. (2002). *Racial profiling data analysis: Final report*. Huntsville, TX: Sam Houston State University.

Kelling, G. L., & Coles, C. M. (1996). *Fixing broken windows: Restoring order and reducing crime in our communities*. New York: Free Press.

Kelling, G. L., Pate, T., Dieckman, D., & Brown, C. E. (1974). *The Kansas City Preventive Patrol Experiment: A summary report*. Washington, DC: Police Foundation.

Lawton, B. A., Taylor, R. B., & Luongo, A. J. (2005). Police officers on drug corners in Philadelphia, drug crime, and violent crime: Intended, diffusion, and displacement impacts. *Justice Quarterly, 22*(4), 427–451.

Lewis, L. (2006, April). Organized retail crime: Retail's no. 1 security issue. *California Grocer*, 2–11.

Monk, K. M., Heinonen, J. A., & Eck, J. E. (2010). *Street robbery. Problem-oriented guides for police, problem-specific guides series, no. 59*. Washington, DC: U.S. Department of Justice, Office of Community Oriented Policing Services.

Nunn, S., Quintet, K., Rowe, K., & Christ, D. (2006). Interdiction day: Covert surveillance operations, drugs, and serious crime in an inner-city neighborhood. *Police Quarterly, 9*(1), 73–99.

San Jose Police Department. (1999). *Vehicle stops demographic study*. San Jose, CA: San Jose Police Department.

Sherman, L. W., Rogan, D. P., Edwards, T., Whipple, R., Shreve, D., et al. (1995). Deterrent effects of police raids on crack houses: A randomized controlled experiment. *Justice Quarterly, 12*(4), 755–781.

Smith, M. R., & Petrocelli, M. (2001). Racial profiling? A multivariate analysis of police traffic stop data. *Police Quarterly, 4*(1), 4–27.

Sutton, M. (2010). *Stolen goods markets. Problem-oriented guides for police, problem-specific guides series, no. 57*. Washington, DC: U.S. Department of Justice, Office of Community Oriented Policing Services.

Weisburd, D., & Green, L. (1995). Policing drug hot spots: The Jersey City drug market analysis experiment. *Justice Quarterly, 12*(4), 711–734.

CHAPTER 8

Offender Targeting Strategies

KEY TERMS

COPS
Demographic setting
Fare jumping
Networked adult street gangs
Open-air drug dealing
Pulling-levers strategy
Squeegee men
The Godfather
Undercover surveillance

LEARNING OBJECTIVES

After completing this chapter, you should be able to:

- List four categories of individuals frequently the focus of offender based targeting.
- Describe the range of behaviors associated with individuals creating public disorder.
- Characterize the results of research testing the effectiveness of "broken windows" enforcement.
- Explain why interference in disorderly behaviors may be more cost-effective than arrest.
- Explain why undercover surveillance is seldom effective.
- Explain the rationale for a police focus on probationers and parolees.
- Contrast the illegal activities of today's adult street gangs with those of the mafia.
- Define "lever pulling."
- Describe the role of specialized gang units.

In the classic 1942 film *Casablanca* the French police captain Louis Renault (Claude Rains) utters the famous phrase, "Round up the usual suspects." Policing in the twenty-first century still deals with "the usual suspects." Four categories of usual suspects are addressed in this chapter: offenders creating disorder, known repeat offenders, parolees, and gang members.

Learning Objective

The broadest category of the four is offenders creating disorder. The range of disorder begins with simply obnoxious behavior—carrying a blaring boom box, obtrusive panhandling, and threatening stares. The next level includes escalation to behaviors such as using loud and grossly profane language in public places, cat calling, and aggressive panhandling. An extreme level of disorderly behavior crosses the line to illegal activities, including soliciting behaviors for drug transactions and prostitution. Although an array of approaches might be employed, broken windows enforcement is the most frequently used.

Learning Objective

Known repeat offenders is a second category of offender-specific targeting. Surveillance might initially appear to be the most efficient approach to apprehension, but it has serious limitations. The last two categories of offenders are actually subcategories of known repeat offenders—parolees and active gang members. It is a given that parolees have paid their debt to society and deserve every opportunity to reintegrate into society and live useful and law-abiding lives. But parolee status does not grant one the right to anonymity. Parole is a privilege, not a right. It is perfectly legitimate for police agencies to monitor a parolee's behavior.

Participation in gangs does not automatically elevate one to offender status. In theory one might be a gang member and not engage in unlawful behavior, or at least not engage in serious unlawful behavior. But that is in theory. In reality a substantial majority of gang members become engaged in criminal enterprises. Beyond the criminal behavior, existence of gangs is destructive to neighborhood quality of life. And inter-gang rivalry inevitably leads to violence.

Broken Windows Enforcement

The most common form of offender targeting is broken windows enforcement. Again, recall that "broken windows enforcement" is a metaphor referring to the phenomenon that if all windows in an abandoned building are intact, all will tend to remain intact, but if one broken window is left unrepaired, soon every window will be broken. The linkage to crime is that if we tolerate so-called nuisance offenses—drunkenness, vandalism, prostitution, open drug use—or even incivilities such as loud or obnoxious behavior, aggressive begging, cat calls, and threatening displays, then serious crime will follow.

The broken windows model was tested by Wesley Skogan (1990). He surveyed 13,000 residents of forty neighborhoods in six major cities to examine the relationship between neighborhood disorder and perceptions of neighborhood crime problems, fear of crime, and experience of robbery victimization. Skogan found that perception of neighborhood crime problems, fear of crime, and experience of robbery victimization were positively related to actual neighborhood social and physical disorder. They were better explained by neighborhood disorder than other predictor variables such as ethnicity, poverty, and residential instability. This empirical finding supported Wilson and Kelling's broken windows model and provided justification for the police to arrest offenders for petty offenses in order to prevent serious crime (Kelling & Coles, 1996).

Using New York City's monthly crime and arrest data and socioeconomic data collected between 1974 and 1999, Corman and Mocan (2005) also tested the effectiveness of broken windows policing. Seven index crimes and misdemeanor arrests were used as dependent variables of broken windows policing. The time-series analysis reported that as the growth rate of misdemeanor arrests increased, the growth rate for robbery, motor vehicle theft, and grand larceny declined after controlling for other independent variables (i.e., each crime category's arrest rate, size of the police force, and prison population).

Braga and Bond (2008) evaluated the effects of policing disorder within a problem-oriented policing framework in Lowell, Massachusetts. Thirty-four hot spots were matched into seventeen pairs, and for one member of each pair officers engaged in "shallow" problem solving, implementing a strategy that more closely resembled a "policing disorder" strategy rather than carefully designed problem-oriented responses. Misdemeanor arrests increased by 29.4 percent. The impact evaluation revealed significant reductions in crime and disorder calls-for-service, with no evidence of significant crime displacement. The authors note: "The results of this randomized controlled experiment contribute to the growing body of evidence that the more focused and specific the strategies of the police are and the more tailored the strategies are to the problems the police seek to address, the more effective the police will be in controlling crime and disorder. . . . These results do lend considerable creditability to Wilson and Kelling's (1982) perspective that policing disorder can generate crime-prevention gains" (p. 597).

Taylor (2001) conducted a comprehensive study examining incivilities and crime in sixty-six neighborhoods in Baltimore, Maryland, focusing on the relationship between social and physical incivilities and neighborhood crimes. His findings partially supported the broken windows model; whereas certain types of incivilities were related to certain serious crimes, others were not.

The Baltimore findings imply a larger issue—it is debatable whether broken windows enforcement works in every **demographic setting**. Without question, it had an enormous impact in the New York City subway system. Individuals who raise doubt about that are desperately grasping at straws to discredit the validity of the effectiveness of saying "you're under arrest." Almost as certainly, broken windows enforcement was effective when transferred to the surface streets in New York City. Anyone who has been victimized by the **squeegee men** will attest that at least with regard to the pleasantness of visiting Manhattan, broken windows enforcement worked.

demographic setting
An area or neighborhood with given population, housing, and economic characteristics.

Learning Objective

Whether broken windows enforcement is effective in the horizontal cities west of the Mississippi and certainly whether it is effective in suburban and rural areas, is, however, open to debate. First of all, in many such areas, the kinds of offenses that broken windows enforcement targets are simply not prevalent. If broken windows enforcement is defined as saturation patrol with high arrest rates for disorderly conduct, illegal solicitation (begging), vandalism, public intoxication, and littering, then a broken windows approach is simply not relevant in middle-class suburbia. Further, a few problematic public inebriants do not merit a wholesale broken windows enforcement effort. Youth congregating in public places and being obnoxious may merit intervention, but not necessarily in the form of broken windows enforcement. Stated simply, when citizens are overwhelmingly in vehicles rather than on foot, the relevance of broken windows enforcement rapidly wanes. George Gascón, former assistant chief of operations (patrol and investigations) in Los Angeles under the Bratton administration, reported that for most areas of Los Angeles, broken windows enforcement simply was not relevant. There was no **fare jumping**, there were no squeegee men, and there were no aggressive beggars. Sections of downtown Los Angeles are a different story, but even there the relevance of such enforcement was limited to particular areas.

squeegee men
Aggressive panhandlers who approach vehicles stopped at an intersection and without permission "wash" the windshield. If demands for a donation are not met, the usual response is to curse the driver.

fare jumping
Leaping over a fare turnstile in subway systems to avoid having to pay the fee.

In the evaluation of the successful Compstat effort in Fort Worth, Texas, Jang, Hoover, and Joo (2010) noted that in totality broken windows enforcement was a minor component of Fort Worth's effort. Indeed, after the implementation of Compstat there were *decreases* in arrests for prostitution, vandalism, and vagrancy. When broken windows enforcement was employed in Fort Worth, it was in the form of drunkenness arrests, concentrated in hot spots, at particularly problematic liquor establishments.

This phenomenon underscores the need for specificity in police strategy. One size does not fit all. Nonetheless, because broken windows arrests are not relevant in every setting does not mean that the underlying premise of broken windows is not relevant. Threatening, disruptive, and even uncivil behaviors will cause "regular" citizens to abstain from going to an area. Thus, aggressive homeless panhandlers in an entertainment district of a downtown have the potential for causing the collapse of that entertainment district. A couple from the suburbs celebrating their anniversary with dinner at an upscale steakhouse do not feel like being accosted by panhandlers while going in and out of the restaurant. The process of being accosted is inherently threatening. It does not take much to throw cold water on what would otherwise have been an enjoyable evening.

As long as panhandling does not cross certain aggressive barriers, it may not be illegal. But police interference with such behavior is not illegal either.

Learning Objective

open-air drug dealing Engaging in the sale of illegal drugs in outdoor, public places—street corners, parking lots, and so forth.

Panhandling, street prostitution, and **open-air drug dealing** are all behaviors that have an economic base. If they were not profitable, people would not engage in them. Interference in such activities, short of arrest, disrupts the economic equation; that is, it reduces the hourly rate of pay. Reduce the hourly rate of pay enough, and the enterprise is no longer attractive. In some settings, interference may indeed be more cost-effective for the police than arrest. An arrest removes an officer from the street for one to four hours, depending on the jurisdiction and individual circumstances of the arrest. Sidewalk panhandling, street-side prostitution, and open-air drug sales are almost always multiple-person enterprises. One seldom finds a single prostitute in a pick-up area; one finds a dozen. Arresting a single entrepreneur in these circumstances, then leaving the scene for four hours, may be less productive than simply staying visible in the area. Individuals engaged in these enterprises do not avoid arrest because they fear having their reputation tarnished; they do not avoid arrest because spending the night in jail is a traumatic and dreadful experience for them; they do not avoid arrest because they will have to spend the next ten years in the state penitentiary (it is more likely that they will spend ten hours in confinement). They avoid arrest because it disrupts their economic enterprise. If the economic balance sheet can be tilted with mere interference, it may be cost-effective to interfere and nothing more.

Undercover Surveillance

Learning Objective

Surveillance is expensive, very expensive. Beyond the expense, it is tedious, and potentially demoralizing to officers. Even high-rate offenders do not commit offenses at such a high rate that short-term surveillance is likely to produce immediate results. Indeed, surveillance duration is never measured in hours, and frequently requires weeks for success, if there is ever success.

Nevertheless, undercover surveillance is alluring from two perspectives. First, it has an element of "police glamour" associated with it. It is super-sleuth work. And there are legendary successes involving high-profile offenders. Second, it intuitively makes sense. If you virtually know that an individual is a chronic offender, then it seems logical to set up a surveillance routine to apprehend the individual actually in the act—assuring conviction and hopefully a lengthy imprisonment. In a mid-size or small jurisdiction, taking one chronic high-rate offender off the street will actually show up in the agency's *Uniform Crime Report* statistics, published annually by the Federal Bureau of Investigation. So the temptation to use undercover surveillance for apprehension is strong. Unfortunately, it is of questionable cost-effectiveness.

Effective 24/7 surveillance requires as many as ten officers. Yes, it is not always necessary to conduct a surveillance 24/7, but the type of individuals put under surveillance are as likely to be active in the middle of the night as the middle of the morning. Even sustained surveillance over an eight-hour segment of the day will require four officers. So it is expensive. Second, it is not as easy to maintain the secrecy of surveillance as television or movie renditions would lead you to believe. Surveillance of a fixed location, an offender's residence, requires some observation point not immediately obvious to everyone in the neighborhood. Maintenance of a moving surveillance, following a subject while he is driving his car, for example, is even more difficult. Using just a single surveillance tailing car increases the risk of detection substantially. But whether one tailing vehicle or two are used, just maintaining visual contact in an urban area can be a challenge. If surveillance is used to any extent by an agency, offenders will be alert—aware that it is used through communication with other offenders. Agencies that routinely conduct known offender surveillance report that offenders have become adept at both detecting and/or losing a tail. They double back, they make illegal left turns, they wait until a green light is about to turn red to proceed through an intersection, and so forth.

By employing crime analysis information regarding the likelihood of the next theft location, surveillance of crime targets can be effective. For example, agencies have used this technique when they feel a particular convenience store may be targeted for robbery or theft. The downside is that it is easy to trigger a shoot-out in such circumstances. At the same time, it is argued that an occasional target surveillance apprehension has a substantial deterrent effect—that offenders cannot be guaranteed that the absence of uniform police officers means that the police are not present.

Surveillance is obviously focused upon apprehension, not prevention. A play upon words might be: *an ounce of arrest is worth a pound of visibility*. However, there is no research, experimental or otherwise, that sheds any light on the effectiveness of surveillance for either apprehension or deterrence. Surveillance rarely begets big busts; the preponderance of arrests are for relatively petty offenses. But the deterrent effect may be substantial. Of course the most difficult outcome in the world to measure is deterrence.

Given the limitations, real-time surveillance should be used sparingly. It may well be worth the expense for certain offenses—for instance, armed robbery and sexual assault—or for individuals such as gang leaders. But it does not appear to be cost-effective to apprehend a car burglar, as chronic an offender as that car burglar may be.

Probation/Parole Partnerships

Partnerships between law enforcement and correctional agencies have been slow to develop. There are only a handful of sustained cooperative arrangements across the country. That is not to say that law enforcement agencies and probation/parole departments do not ever communicate with each other. There is indeed occasional focused communication with regard to a specific offender. But there are few instances of structured, sustained cooperative endeavors aimed at apprehending reoffending probationers/parolees. This is disconcerting because the potential for more effective crime control is enormous. For most crime categories, two-thirds of released prisoners are rearrested within three years of release; nearly half of all releasees return to prison within that same period, either for a new crime or for a technical violation of the conditions of their release. It is well documented that the majority of released prisoners will reoffend and contribute to a substantial share of crime (LaVigne, Solomon, Beckman, & Dedel, 2006, p. 8). It is also noted in a federal Community-Oriented Policing Service Office (**COPS**) monograph that "arrest frequencies for returning prisoners are 30 to 45 times higher than for the general population" (LaVigne et al., 2006, p. 16).

There are both philosophical and practical reasons for the paucity of sustained cooperative programs. First, philosophically, probation and parole

Learning Objective

COPS
The Community-Oriented Policing Services Office, a federal agency in the U.S. Department of Justice.

officers are dedicated to successful reintegration of offenders. Apprehension and return to jail or the penitentiary is not typically counted as a success. Understaffed and overworked, probation and parole officers may in fact be able to do little to help offenders successfully reintegrate—but that does not negate the fact that reintegration remains their primary goal.

Second, there are practical bureaucratic obstacles. First, the majority of criminal enforcement occurs in municipalities; that is, the police agencies that would benefit the most from such a partnership are part of city government. Probation agencies are either part of county or state government. Parole agencies are always part of state government. So not only is one dealing with separate bureaucracies, one is dealing with separate bureaucracies at separate layers of government.

Further, within the separate and distinct bureaucracies, no one is sitting at a desk looking for something to do. Caseloads are notoriously high for probation and parole officers. Offense caseloads are notoriously high for police investigative units. For a sustained structured program to exist, busy professionals in both bureaucracies must set aside other things they are doing, and those other things they are doing are not perceived as trivial.

Notwithstanding the obstacles just enumerated, there are instances of probation/parole and law enforcement working cooperatively in sustained programs. Again, an excellent illustration of this is by the Chicago Police Department. Working cooperatively with the Illinois Department of Corrections, the Chicago Police Department created the Parole Restriction Program, entailing several cooperative initiatives (Chicago Police Department, 2007). The effort included police officers accompanying parole officers on home visits to the residences of selected parolees. Parole officers have the right to make such visits to assure compliance with parole conditions—keep in mind that parole is a privilege, not a right; the alternative for the offender is to remain in the penitentiary for the duration of his or her sentence. Further, parole officers have a right to take a police officer with them if they have concern for their safety. The types of offenders visited under the auspices of the Parole Restriction Program presented a *prima facie* safety risk. The stated goal of the Chicago Police Department with this program is not the ability to conduct a warrantless search. The goal is deterrence. It delivers a no-nonsense message that "we know who you are, and we know where you live." It removes any illusion of anonymity that an offender in a city of 5 million might have.

A second element of the cooperative arrangement between the Illinois Department of Corrections and the Chicago Police Department is a release notification program. The Chicago Police Department is notified whenever high-risk offenders are being released from the penitentiary system. Of particular concern are gang leaders. Remember that gang leadership does not end with a sentence to a penitentiary. Offenders are sophisticated enough to maintain communication, and often control, from inside a penitentiary. Using undercover surveillance, the Chicago Police Department videotaped one notorious gang leader walking out of the Joliet Penitentiary with his cardboard box of possessions, getting in a vehicle, and immediately violating parole by driving across the state line into Indiana for a meeting with gang affiliates. Upon his return to Illinois, the Chicago Police Department and the Illinois State Police pulled the vehicle over and arrested him for violation of parole conditions. The individual enjoyed five hours of freedom (Chicago Police Department, 2007). Obviously, you cannot do that very often—word travels fast in criminal networks. But it delivers a message.

Yet a third component of the partnership entails cooperation between the police department and the parole board in setting parole restrictions. In Chicago, the most effective restriction was prohibition against being in designated portions of the city—gang leaders were prohibited from returning to their home gang's territory.

The message to be delivered by the success of the partnership between the Chicago Police Department and the Illinois Department of Corrections is that such endeavors can work. However, it requires that correctional personnel recognize that for some offenders, rehabilitation and reintegration is all but an unachievable goal. Hardened, violent, manipulative gang leaders in charge of drug distribution networks are not going to be responsive to vocational training preparing them for the job of bricklayer. The goal in these situations is reapprehension for reoffending or simply deterrence. At the very least, cooperative programs make it more difficult for gang leaders to run their drug distribution operations than it was before incarceration and parole supervision. Weisburd and Eck (2004, p. 55) note: "Two randomized trials suggest that covert investigation of high-risk, previously convicted offenders has a high yield in arrests and incarceration per officer per hour, relative to other investments of police resources" (citing Abrahamse & Ebener [1991]; Martin & Sherman [1986]).

Gang Disruption

Learning Objective

Networked adult street gangs are far more destructive than the mafia ever thought of being. Today's gangs contribute to higher violent crime rates; induce community deterioration through behaviors such as vandalism, graffiti, and drug dealing; and increase public fear of victimization (Langton, 2010). Whereas the core enterprise of the mafia was vice—gambling, liquor during prohibition, and prostitution—the core enterprise of today's organized crime is drug distribution. Like the mafia, today's form of organized crime demonstrates flexibility and will pursue other enterprises, but drug dealing constitutes 90 percent of the economic flow. Like the mafia, the new form of organized crime is attempting to move some of its ill-gotten money into legitimate enterprises, for example, by purchasing real-estate. Traditional organized crime was nationality based; today's organized crime is overwhelmingly racially based, but with occasional nationalistic overlay. Traditional organized crime routinely engaged in turf wars; so do today's gangs. Traditional organized crime was networked, but loosely so, as is today's version of organized crime.

However, there are very important distinctions between traditional organized crime and today's version. The mafia operated quietly and behind closed doors; think ***The Godfather***. The mafia never engaged in inherently aggressive offenses, such as burglary and robbery. Today's street gang members do. The mafia did routinely engage in extortion, collecting protection money from, in particular, the transportation and distribution industries. In contrast, systemic, structured extortion is almost never an enterprise of today's street gangs (gangs typically do not demand money from food distributors to operate in their neighborhoods). Traditional organized crime infiltrated and corrupted numerous labor unions. Today's organized crime does not know what a labor union is. For traditional

networked adult street gangs
Professionally operated criminal enterprises, almost always engaged in drug sales. Such gangs are usually affiliated with other gangs that control drug sales in other neighborhoods. Linkages exist to international drug distribution networks.

The Godfather
A 1972 film that depicts the criminal enterprises of the Italian-American Corleone family. Stars Marlon Brando as the family patriarch.

organized crime, you were either a member of the family or you were not; there was no "affiliated" but not quite on the inside. In today's organized gangs, there is a gradation of association. At one extreme are the core gang leaders operating at least citywide if not statewide. At the other extreme are curbside drug sellers who have no idea how the distribution network is structured.

This leads to an important distinction. Although gang affiliation and lifestyle should properly be thought of on a continuum, there is a real distinction between high-school-age street gangs and networked criminal-enterprise adult gangs. Almost every adult gang hoodlum got his or her start in a youth gang. But not every youth gang member ends up a criminal adult hoodlum. That is not to say that most entrenched youth gang members find their way to honorable adult professions as accountants, physicians, and ministers. But they do not necessarily all gravitate to sustained careers in criminal enterprises. Given the layered complexity of the gang phenomenon, it is hardly surprising that law enforcement is challenged to find a cohesive, effective response to gang crime.

The effectiveness of the approach is dependent upon the characteristics of the gang being targeted. The Dallas Police Department focused on five target areas that were home to seven of the city's most violent gangs. The strategies included saturation patrol and aggressive curfew and truancy enforcement. Control areas were selected, and pre-intervention and post-intervention measures of gang violence and offenses were analyzed. Analysis indicated that aggressive curfew and truancy enforcement led to significant reductions in gang violence, whereas simple saturation patrol did not. However, curfew and truancy enforcement are obviously irrelevant to adult gang violence (Fritsch, Caeti, & Taylor, 1999).

Learning Objective

pulling-levers strategy
An approach to controlling inter-gang violence initiated by the Boston Police Department. Tactics include direct communication with gangs, which if unsuccessful results in "pulling every available lever" to prosecute.

A more "offender-focused" approach has come to be called "lever pulling." The strategy's origin is Boston's Operation Ceasefire. Focusing attention on a small number of chronically offending gang-involved youth responsible for much of Boston's youth homicide problem, the **"pulling-levers" strategy** involved deterring violent behavior by reaching out directly to gangs, saying explicitly that violence would no longer be tolerated, and backing that message by "pulling every lever" legally available when violence occurred. The strategy was not designed to eliminate gangs or stop every aspect of gang activity but to control and deter serious violence (Braga, Kennedy, Waring, & Piehl, 2001).

Boston averaged forty-four youth homicides per year between 1991 and 1995. In 1996, after the Ceasefire program, the number of youth homicides decreased to twenty-six and then further decreased to fifteen in 1997. The intervention was also associated with a 25 percent decrease in the monthly number of citywide gun assault incidents, a 32 percent decrease in the monthly number of citywide shots-fired calls-for-service, and a 44 percent decrease in the monthly number of youth gun assaults in district B-2. The authors (2001) note:

> Although some cities may have experienced a similar decrease, these analyses suggest that Boston's significant youth homicide reduction associated with Operation Ceasefire was distinct when compared to youth homicide trends in most major U.S. and New England cities. (p. 215)

The pulling-levers approach is dramatically different than hot spots concentrated patrol, broken windows enforcement, and offense targeting.

Minneapolis also experienced sharp reductions in its homicide rate after having implemented the pulling-levers strategy (Kennedy, 1998; Kennedy & Braga, 1998). The Indianapolis Violence Reduction Partnership employed a similar approach, using both state and federal sanctions to deter illegal gun carrying and use, to communicate this strategy through as many venues as possible to those individuals believed to be most at risk for involvement in violence, and to link potential offenders to legitimate opportunities and services. A time-series analysis indicated that monthly homicides were reduced by 34.3 percent following the April 1999 intervention (McGarrell, Chermak, Wilson, & Corsaro, 2006). The authors observed that:

> Combining Boston, Minneapolis and Indianapolis, we see evidence from three cities experiencing group-related firearms violence that a lever-pulling strategy involving face-to-face communication of a deterrence message and a Federal crackdown on a violent gang resulted in immediate and significant reductions in homicide. All three cities experienced what Kennedy has referred to as a "light-switch" impact on homicide. (p. 227)

An evaluation of the approach in a smaller, less violent city, Lowell, Massachusetts, saw a reduction in gang-related homicides from an average of 3.1 per year from the 1996–2002 pre-test period to one homicide per year post-intervention, 2003–2005 (Braga, Pierce, McDevitt, Bond, & Cronin, 2008).

Because street-level drug distribution is central to the economic vitality of gangs, police response to gangs is often synonymous with police response to open-air drug markets. That is, the drug dealers and gang members are one and the same time. This was the assumption, and the approach, employed by Chicago starting in 2004. At the same time, the destructive influence of visible street gangs upon the sanctity of the neighborhood was so extreme that law enforcement response was often gang focused, not narcotics focused. Drive-by shootings, for example, were as frequently motivated by "tribal" gang rivalry as they were by disputes over drug distribution territorial claims.

In 2007, 365 of 1,084 of the nation's large (>100 sworn officers) police departments and sheriffs' offices had specialized gang units, with 35 percent of these units established between 2004 and 2007, suggesting a recent heightened interest in using specialized units to address gang issues (Langton, 2010). An unresolved debate is the effectiveness of specialized gang units. Gang units tend to be "decoupled," both organizationally and strategically, from the rest of their departments; they also lack adequate performance measures and, as a consequence, any documentation of effectiveness (Katz & Webb, 2006). Katz and Webb go on to note: "This seems consistent with evidence that indicates that the 'dosage' of gang enforcement is relatively low, and it may not be realistic to expect much of an impact on gang crime" (p. 273).

Learning Objective

A second unresolved debate is whether the prevalence and/or criminal enterprise influence of gangs is growing, receding, or stable. Katz and Webb (2006) reported a growing lack of consensus about the magnitude and nature of local gang problems. Quite obviously there is indeed variation across the country. And because the problem may not be getting worse does not mean it is inconsequential. If it had been "really bad," it is still bad—even given some diminishment.

IMPLICATIONS FOR STRATEGY

Intuitively it would appear to be cost-effective for police agencies to implement interventions that focus upon chronic repeat offenders. Indeed, there is considerable evidence that the classic 80/20 rule applies here—at least 80 percent of offenses are committed by only 20 percent of offenders. Unfortunately, however, a classic homily also applies to this situation—"the devil is in the details." Sorting high-rate offenders from normal-rate offenders is more difficult than one might think. Then, even if high-rate offenders are accurately identified, catching them in the act of committing a crime has proven extremely difficult. Undercover surveillance is extremely expensive, usually detected, and hence very seldom productive.

Nonetheless, some approaches to offender-based strategy have shown promise. These include enhanced prosecution efforts once repeat offenders are apprehended—essentially efforts to be sure that such offenders are vigorously prosecuted and not allowed to plea bargain a short sentence. Second, embryonic efforts to cooperate with parole agencies to increase parolee monitoring have shown great promise. Finally, intervention to halt gang-related violence has proven beneficial in some jurisdictions, particularly the approach termed "lever pulling."

A wholly different set of issues pertains to dealing with persons routinely engaging in behaviors that are obnoxious, threatening, or skirt on being illegal. Enforcement in the broken windows style is most frequently employed. For combating behaviors that are dominantly economically driven—aggressive panhandling and drug or prostitution solicitation, for example—simple interference in the enterprise may be more cost-effective than arrest.

SUMMARY

- The four categories of individuals typically focused on in offender-based targeting are individuals creating public disorder, known repeat offenders, parolees, and active gang members.
- Disruptive public behavior encompasses many types of activities. Some of the behaviors are irritating but technically not illegal—for instance, a panhandler uttering a loud "God bless you" to everyone who walks by. Other behaviors fall into the illegal activity gray zone—such as panhandlers blocking entranceways unless a donation is provided.
- Assertive broken windows enforcement is the most common police response to disruptive public behavior. As noted previously, broken windows is a metaphor referring to the phenomenon that if all windows in an abandoned building are intact, all will tend to remain intact, but if one broken window is left unrepaired, soon every window will be broken. The linkage to crime is that tolerating incivilities and nuisance offenses leads to serious offenses. There have only been a few tests of the efficacy of the broken windows model. Those that have been conducted generally support its utility. However, broken windows enforcement in the horizontal cities west of the Mississippi River, as well as in suburban and rural areas, is seldom cost-effective. In most such areas the kinds of offenses targeted simply are not prevalent.
- Interference with disorderly behaviors may be more cost-effective than arrest. Effecting an arrest removes an officer from the streets for one to four hours. Some types of disorderly behavior are best regarded simply as economic enterprises, including sidewalk panhandling, street-side prostitution, and open-air drug sales. Perpetrators avoid arrest because it disrupts their economic enterprise. It is frequently more cost-effective for the police to interfere with engagement in the economic enterprise and nothing more.

- Arresting known repeat offenders is more difficult than one might initially envision. Undercover surveillance of such offenders is rarely successful. Surveillance frequently requires weeks for success, if there is ever success, and is hence both expensive and tedious. Effective 24/7 surveillance requires as many as ten officers. Surveillance of an offender's residence requires some observation point not immediately obvious to everyone in the neighborhood. Maintenance of a moving surveillance is even more difficult. An offender with any street savvy will quickly recognize that he or she is being followed. Agencies that have attempted extensive surveillance programs have found it to be demoralizing to engaged officers, given the tedium and infrequent reward.
- A special category of known repeat offenders includes probationers and parolees. Partnerships with corrections agencies have been slow to develop. This is disconcerting because the potential for more effective crime control is enormous. Philosophically, we all want probationers and parolees to succeed—to find employment and successfully reintegrate into society. Nonetheless, as noted by the Community-Oriented Policing Services Office, "arrest frequencies of returning prisoners are 30 to 45 times higher than for the general population." The Chicago Police Department has been particularly successful in a partnership arrangement with the Parole Division of the Illinois Department of Corrections. The police department is notified whenever high-risk offenders are being released. Further, parole restrictions are imposed for gang leaders, prohibiting them from returning to their home gang's territory.
- This leads to the next category of offender targeting—gang disruption. Today's networked adult street gangs are far more violent than the mafia ever thought of being. Further, whereas the core enterprise of the mafia was vice, the core enterprise of today's organized crime is drug distribution. The most aggressive mafia actions involved extortion from selected business enterprises; mafia members never engaged in inherently aggressive offenses, such as burglary and robbery. Today's versions of organized crime, adult street gangs, literally take over entire neighborhoods. "Brute-force enforcement" is necessary to combat organized adult street gangs.
- A more nuanced approach has resulted in some success in combating violent youth gangs. Initiated in Boston, the approach called "lever pulling" has been replicated successfully in Minneapolis, Indianapolis, and several other jurisdictions. The approach involves targeting violent gang leaders and "pulling every lever" to stop inter-gang violence.
- The cost-effectiveness of specialized gang units is an unanswered question. The primary problem with such units is that they become focused solely on gang intelligence—knowing who is doing what—and never translate that intelligence to intervention. At the same time, it should be acknowledged that the ultimate effect of possessing intelligence is difficult to document.

REVIEW QUESTIONS

1. How tolerant should we be of deliberative behaviors in public places that make others uncomfortable or are irritating? Does the constitutional mandate of freedom of speech (expression) protect individuals who consciously engage in such behavior?
2. Some types of disorderly behavior are best regarded as economic enterprises, including sidewalk panhandling, street-side prostitution, and open-air drug sales. It is suggested that it is frequently more cost-effective for the police to interfere with engagement in the economic enterprise than to attempt to effect arrests. What forms might such interference take? Is it ethical for the police to choose interference because it is more cost-effective when an arrest can be justified?
3. Why is sustained undercover surveillance of known repeat offenders seldom successful?
4. Describe the differences between the illegal operations of the mafia and that of today's adult street gangs. Why do many police officials perceive that today's adult street gangs a greater threat to society than the mafia ever was?
5. What range of interventions exists under the auspices of the approach to reducing youth gang violence called "lever pulling"?

REAL-WORLD SCENARIOS

1. You are the commander of the downtown division of a major municipal department. Obnoxious, rude, and even aggressive behavior on the part of panhandlers has become a political issue. For the past two months officers in your command have made innumerable arrests of particularly problematic individuals. This tactic has been ineffectual—first, because the panhandlers are back out on the street within hours, and second, because your officers are out of service for hours in transporting subjects to the jail and booking them. You decide that interference with their "economic enterprise" might be more cost-effective. How might you operationalize the word "interference"?
2. With virtual certainty you know the identity of the perpetrator of a string of convenience store robberies. You lack, however, probable cause to effect an arrest. As the commander of the crimes against persons investigation unit, you decide that it is worth the expenditure of resources to initiate twenty-four-hour surveillance of the suspect. What resources will you require to successfully implement such surveillance?
3. As commander of the gang unit, you are responsible for intervening in a cycle of escalating violence among five prevalent youth gangs in your jurisdiction. You have heard about the "lever-pulling" strategy employed successfully in Boston and elsewhere. You decide to employ the technique. What levers are available for you to pull to successfully stop the escalation of inter-gang violence?

APPLICATION ACTIVITIES

1. Wilson and Kelling postulated that tolerance of incivilities and nuisance offenses in stressed neighborhoods would degenerate to the prevalence of serious crime. They suggested a metaphor to describe this phenomenon—*broken windows*. The use of a metaphor can be a powerful communication technique. Discuss why the metaphor *broken windows* is so appropriate for the approach suggested by Wilson and Kelling.
2. Assume you are a career criminal committed to your lifestyle; that is, you have no intention of ceasing your criminal activity. You suspect that you are under surveillance by the police. Imagine that you have devised a list of surveillance detection techniques to be employed while driving your vehicle. Describe at least five techniques that will allow you to detect and/or evade any undercover police vehicles tailing you. (Techniques should actually be demonstrated only by professional criminals; do not try this in your hometown. ☺)
3. The 1972 epic film *The Godfather* chronicles the Italian-American Corleone family. Sequels were produced in 1974 and 1990. Watch the original film, listing the criminal enterprises alluded to in the script. Additionally, describe the dynamics of membership in the "family," and contrast them with membership requisites in today's adult street gangs.

COURSEMATE

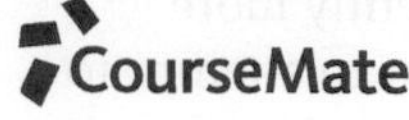

This available CourseMate has an interactive eBook and interactive learning tools, including flash cards, quizzes, and more. To learn more about this resource and access free demo CourseMate resources, go to **www.cengagebrain.com**, and search for this book. To access CourseMate materials that you have purchased, go to **login.cengagebrain.com**.

REFERENCES

Abrahamse, A. F., & Ebener, P. A. (1991). An experimental evaluation of the Phoenix repeat offender program. *Justice Quarterly, 8*(2), 141–168.

Braga, A. A., & Bond, B. J. (2008). Policing crime and disorder hot spots: A randomized controlled trial. *Criminology, 46*(3), 577–607.

Braga, A. A., Kennedy, D. M., Waring, E. J., & Piehl, A. M. (2001). Problem-oriented policing, deterrence, and youth violence: An evaluation of Boston's Operation Ceasefire. *Journal of Research in Crime and Delinquency, 38*, 195–226.

Braga, A. A., Pierce, G. L., McDevitt, J., Bond, B. J., & Cronin, S. (2008). The strategic prevention of gun violence among gang-involved offenders. *Justice Quarterly, 25*(1), 132–162.

Chicago Police Department. (2007). *Making Chicago the safest big city in America, Chicago Police Department crime reduction initiatives: 2003–2007*. Chicago, IL: Chicago Police Department.

Corman, H., & Mocan, N. (2005). Carrots, sticks and broken windows. *Journal of Law and Economics, 48*, 235–266.

Federal Bureau of Investigation. (Annually). *Crime in the United States, Uniform Crime Reports*. Washington, DC: U.S. Department of Justice.

Fritsch, E., Caeti, T., & Taylor, R. (1999). Gang suppression through saturation patrol, aggressive curfew, and truancy enforcement: A quasi-experimental test of the Dallas anti-gang initiative. *Crime and Delinquency, 45*(1), 122–139.

Jang, H. S., Hoover, L. T., & Joo, H. J. (2010). An evaluation of Compstat's effect upon crime: The Fort Worth experience. *Police Quarterly, 13*(4).

Katz, C. M., & Webb, V. J. (2006). *Police gangs in America*. New York: Cambridge University Press.

Kelling, G. L., & Coles, C. M. (1996). *Fixing broken windows: Restoring order and reducing crime in our communities*. New York: Free Press.

Kennedy, D. M. (1998). Pulling levers: Getting deterrence right. *National Institute of Justice Journal 7*, 2–8.

Kennedy, D. M., & Braga, A. A. (1998). Homicide in Minneapolis: Research for problem solving. *Homicide Studies, 2*, 263–290.

Langton, L. (2010). *Gang units in large local law enforcement agencies, 2007*. Washington, DC: Bureau of Justice Statistics.

LaVigne, N. G., Solomon, A. L., Beckman, K. A., & Dedel, K. (2006). *Prisoner reentry and community policing: Strategies for enhancing public safety*. Washington, DC: U.S. Department of Justice, Urban Institute Justice Policy Center, Office of Community Oriented Policing Services.

Martin, S. E., & Sherman, L. W. (1986). Selective apprehension: A police strategy for repeat offenders. *Criminology, 24*(1), 155–173.

McGarrell, E. F., Chermak, S., Wilson, J. M., & Corsaro, N. (2006). Reducing homicide through a "level-pulling" strategy. *Justice Quarterly, 23*(2), 214–231.

Skogan, W. G. (1990). *Disorder and decline*. New York: Free Press.

Taylor, R. B. (2001). *Breaking away from broken windows: Baltimore neighborhoods and nationwide fight against crime, grime, fear and decline*. Boulder, CO: Westview Press.

Weisburd, D., & Eck, J. E. (2004). What can police do to reduce crime, disorder, and fear? *Annals of the American Academy of Political & Social Science, 593*(5), 42–65.

Wilson, J. Q., & Kelling, G. L. (1982). Broken windows: The police and neighborhood safety. *Atlantic Monthly, 249*(March), 29–38.

CHAPTER 9

Compstat and Crime Control

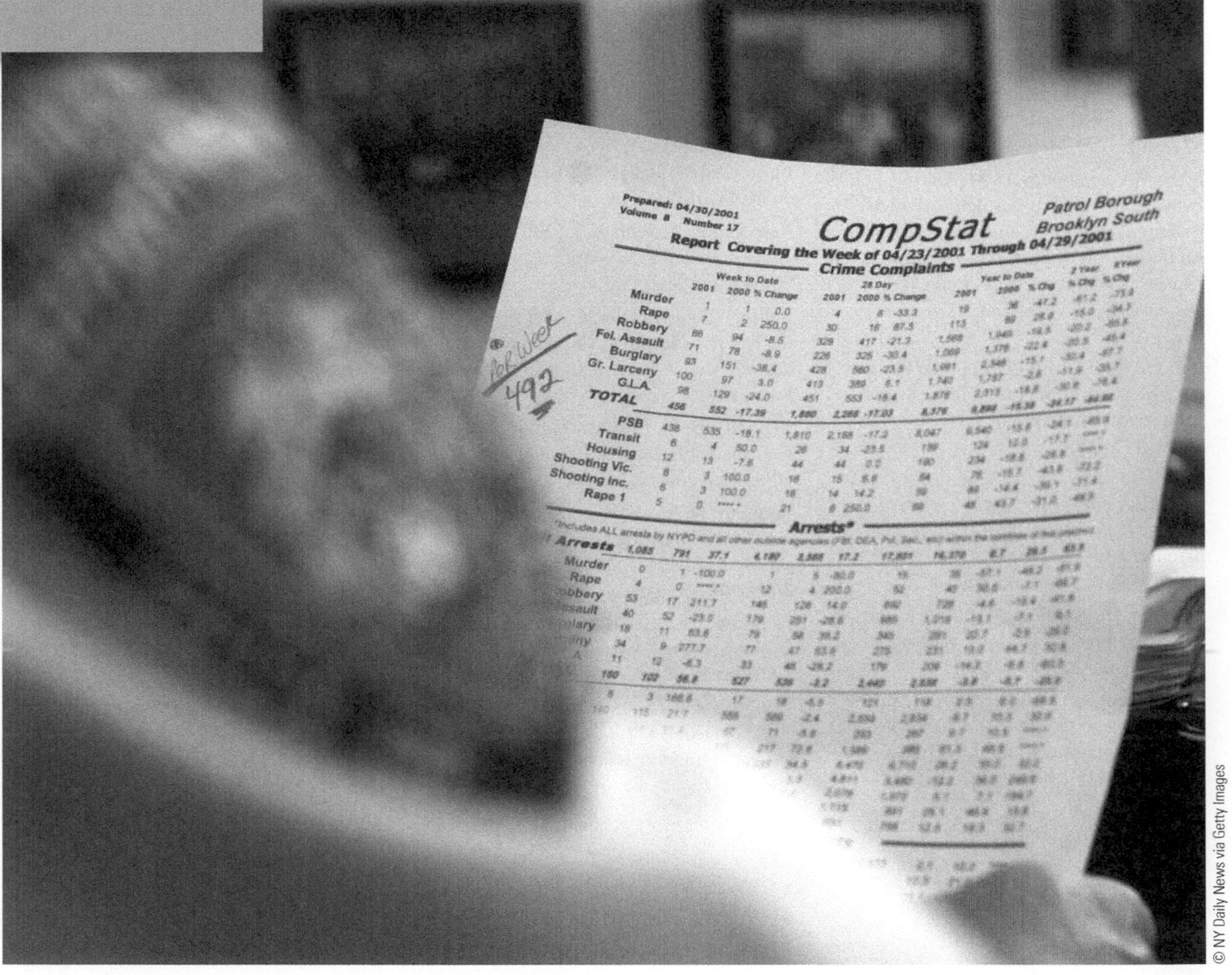

© NY Daily News via Getty Images

KEY TERMS

Occam's razor

Paradigm

Real-time crime analysis

Reinventing an organization

LEARNING OBJECTIVES

After completing this chapter, you should be able to:

- ➤ List the usual components of Compstat as a broad approach to crime control.
- ➤ Describe the origins of Compstat.
- ➤ Characterize the relationship between Compstat and community policing approaches, as well as problem-oriented interventions.
- ➤ Characterize evidence for the effectiveness of Compstat.
- ➤ Identify Compstat's core element.
- ➤ Explain why Compstat might best be regarded as the infusion of positive elements of corporate culture into policing.
- ➤ Define "focusing" as it pertains to Compstat.

Learning Objective

A new and very different approach to structured crime control effort materialized in the 1990s—Compstat. The primary characteristics of Compstat include:

1. **Real-time crime analysis**
2. Targeting specific locations, crimes, and offenders
3. An overlay of broken windows enforcement
4. Crime response teams
5. Unit commander accountability
6. Periodic meetings, frequently weekly, to review progress and assess interdictions
7. A police application of organization development
8. A reorientation of community policing to crime-specific strategies

Although the origins of Compstat are with the New York City Transit Police under the tutelage of William C. Bratton, the integration of the elements listed above manifested themselves as a strategic approach during his administration of the New York City Police Department (NYPD). Compstat was brought to New Orleans and Miami with promises of invigorating those agencies. In 2003 the city of Los Angeles hired William Bratton as chief of police with the sole purpose of bringing the NYPD Compstat model to that embattled organization. Chicago also implemented Compstat. By 2003, Weisburd et al. reported widespread dissemination of the Compstat approach (Weisburd, Mastrofski, McNally, Greenspan, & Willis, 2003).

Vincent Henry (2002) characterized Compstat as a "**paradigm**." It is a bit early to judge whether Compstat is actually a paradigm shift in law enforcement. In any case, it certainly offers agencies an alternative conceptual framework to structuring crime control efforts.

real-time crime analysis
Data regarding crime trends and patterns that are current. Because offense reports must be proofread and approved by a supervisor, "real-time" is generally within three days of the present.

paradigm
A broad conceptual model or approach that serves as a framework for development.

Defining Compstat

Compstat is a combination of a strategy and a management style. As a strategy, Compstat might be called crime-specific policing. Crime-specific policing is targeted enforcement aimed at specific offenses committed by specific offenders at specific times and at specific places. As a management style, the core of Compstat is strict management accountability for achieving crime reduction goals. The hallmark of Compstat accountability is periodic meetings, weekly or monthly, during which patrol command staff make presentations about crime patterns and trends in their area of responsibility and field "tough" questions about what they are specifically doing to counter those patterns and trends. Indeed, Compstat is perceived by many as synonymous with Compstat meetings.

It is the organizational hostility of those meetings as initially conducted in the NYPD in the 1990s that have become legend. Precinct commanders were literally asked to retire on the spot. The degree of turnover among the command staff at NYPD immediately following Compstat's implementation was astounding. Henry (2002) reported that within one year more than two-thirds of the agency's seventy-six precinct commanders had been replaced. With this legacy it is a small wonder that some police managers rejected Compstat as a potential approach for their agency. However, Compstat's practice nationally does not follow the "hard, cold, and cruel" model initially employed in New York City. Indeed, even New York's style has mollified.

Development of the Compstat Model

Learning Objective

Whereas the origins of both problem-oriented and community policing are attributed to academics—Herman Goldstein and Robert Trojanowicz, respectively—Compstat's origins are attributed to a practitioner, William Bratton. Bratton's career began in the Boston police department. In 1991, he was hired by the New York City Transit Authority to head the 3,500 officers of the New York Transit Police, then a separate agency, now a division of NYPD. Bratton was given one year to "clean up the subways" or lose his job. He did not lose his job. Bratton implemented a combination of a demanding and unforgiving management accountability program with an equally demanding and unforgiving broken-windows-style enforcement approach. The homeless were expelled from the subway system, beggars and fare jumpers were arrested, and an aggressive program of graffiti clean-up was initiated. Crime in the subway system plummeted. Robbery dropped by an astounding 64 percent; all felonies dropped by 75 percent (Kelling & Coles, 1996).

The success of Bratton in the New York City subways did not go unnoticed. Newly elected Mayor Rudolph Giuliani hired Bratton to head the NYPD with the same singular goal—reduce crime. Bratton implemented in "the big department" the same approaches he had used with the transit police—but added the Compstat meeting to the repertoire. Crime began to drop on the street level as it had below ground. Furthermore, New Yorkers were immensely gratified by the heavy-handed enforcement of nuisance laws—in particular, Bratton's aggressive stance toward the notorious "squeegee men."

Compstat became institutionalized in the NYPD. Bratton left New York for the Los Angeles Police Department and has since retired from that agency, but left a vigorous Compstat program behind in both agencies. NYPD has had several commissioners since Bratton, and all of them have remained strongly committed to Compstat. Further, the program has been copied by almost all other major municipal agencies.

Components of the Compstat Process

The fundamental definition of Compstat was provided earlier—a combination of crime-focused operational strategies and management accountability. But that definition is an inadequate description. Compstat is, in fact, an amalgam of several law enforcement operational and management approaches, including:

Real-time crime analysis. Compstat requires up-to-the-minute crime trends and pattern data. The employment of geographic information systems (GIS) for visual display of such patterns and trends is generally regarded as an essential component. Crime analysis in this context consists of more than a simple summary of *Uniform Crime Reports* (UCR) data and includes drilling down to very specific offense types.

Targeted enforcement. Compstat incorporates crime-specific strategic approaches—specific, defined interventions that are targeted at specific offenses committed by specific offenders at specific times at specific places. Compstat in this sense exceeds a mere "get-tough-on-crime" philosophy.

Broken windows enforcement. The 65 percent decrease in robberies in the New York City subway system in the early 1990s is not attributed to arrests for the crime of robbery. Rather, the drop is attributed to vigorous nuisance offense enforcement for transgressions such as fare jumping, aggressive begging, and trespassing. It is a classic illustration, perhaps *the* classic illustration, of the broken windows approach—when you clean up a neighborhood of incivility, deterioration, and nuisance offenses, serious crime goes away as well.

Crime response teams. Although the Compstat process is designed to fully integrate regular patrol, an important component is crime response teams. Crime response teams, or tactical units, have been around in law enforcement for a long time. O. W. Wilson used them in Chicago in the 1950s. The difference under the Compstat approach is focus—their efforts are directed by upper command and monitored daily.

Command accountability. The Compstat meetings are a means, not an end. They are designed to engender unit accountability. As initially conducted, accountability was focused upon precinct commanders in the NYPD. Compstat as currently practiced in New York and elsewhere broadens the accountability model to investigative and even support command as well.

A police application of organization development. The Compstat approach could be described as a police version of management by objectives—agency goals with increasingly specific objectives delineated as one goes down the hierarchy and measured on a very short time frame—monthly or even weekly. Compstat might alternatively be seen as a police version of total quality management (TQM). TQM incorporates proactive and vigorous monitoring approaches and the principle of continuous improvement. Another perspective is Compstat as results-oriented management.

Yet another perspective is Compstat as a law enforcement variation of the knowledge management approach currently being employed in the corporate world. The important point is that Compstat transcends a street-level strategic approach; it is concurrently a management style. It is intended as organizational invigoration.

Compstat Conflict with Community Policing

Among the issues raised is the question, "Does Compstat conflict with community policing?" The answer is "Yes, no, and maybe." It all depends upon one's definition of community policing. As noted in Chapter 3, the question of "What is community policing?" has never really been answered.

Learning Objective

If community policing is defined very broadly as a philosophical framework under which law enforcement agencies should be responsive to the communities they serve, then the answer is "No, Compstat does not conflict." On the other hand, such a definition of community policing is really simply a definition of democratic policing. So that is not very helpful. If community policing is defined as programmatic structured citizen contact under what is commonly referred to as the Three Citizens' model (Three C's model)—citizen advisory groups, citizens' police academies, and citizens on patrol—then the answer is probably "No, there is no conflict." Implementation of a Compstat program does not require that the Three C's model be eliminated. On the other hand, if community policing is defined as a total and sweeping structural and strategic approach to policing, then the answer is "Absolutely, there is head-on conflict." If under the Compstat paradigm there is a choice between resources directed at a specific crime pattern or resources directed at generic quality-of-life issues, crime wins every time (quality of life here is not being defined as broken windows enforcement, but broader community structural, social, and economic interventions). So the unfortunately vague answer to the question has to be "Maybe."

Nonetheless, one thing needs to be made clear. Compstat is not community policing nor is it any variant of community policing. Compstat is an alternative to community policing. Resources previously dedicated to extensive structured community contact and quality-of-life problem solving are redirected to targeted enforcement. Compstat proponents do not reject community policing as a philosophical ideal, but they are very clear that if there is a choice between quality of life and crime, crime comes first.

The issue of limited law enforcement resources and the necessity to make hard choices among competing programs is addressed in Chapter 12. Law enforcement managers do not have the resources to be all things to all people. If on a Tuesday morning a police manager has to make a choice between assigning an officer to meeting with the community book club to discuss policing philosophy in Middleburg or assigning that same officer to surveillance of a robbery suspect, under Compstat it is surveillance.

Using "meeting with the community book club" as the illustration of a community policing activity is unfair, and even cynical. However, the point being made here is that election of a Compstat approach will inevitably require that some broader quality-of-life initiatives be eliminated. Any police manager—sheriff, Police Chief, or unit commander—has a limited amount of discretionary resources. Hard choices are inevitable. Yes, it is a good idea to attend numerous community group meetings. Yes, it is a good idea to engage in a wide range of crime-prevention efforts. Yes, it is a good idea to have very strong programs in the Three C's model—citizen advisory groups, citizens' police academies, and citizens on patrol. Yes, it is a good idea to have contact with youth via some combination of programs (e.g., school resource officers, police athletic leagues). But at some point some choices must be made. Implementation of Compstat does not require that an agency with a strong citizens on patrol program eliminate that program. Indeed, the citizens on patrol program might be an integral part of a Compstat approach. But an agency administrator committed to making Compstat more than another buzzword needs to face the reality of choice among approaches.

Does an agency contemplating implementation of Compstat have to eliminate every one of its community-contact, problem-solving, and/or crime-prevention programs? Clearly not. But if one is going to have the resources available for a crime response team, then a police manager might well have to red-line other programs in order to gain those resources.

Evaluation of Compstat Effectiveness

Compstat has been featured on the cover of *Time* magazine (Pooley, 1996). Yet, almost incredibly, objective evaluations of the Compstat process are limited. The "nonobjective" assessments that do exist are limited to the New York City experience. They consist entirely of books written by persons deeply involved in the NYPD Compstat effort, including William Bratton with Peter Knobler (1998: *The Turnaround: How America's Top Cop Reversed the Crime Epidemic*), Jack Maple and C. Mitchell (1999: *The Crime Fighter*), Phyllis McDonald (2002: *Managing Police Operations: Implementing the New York Crime Control Model—Compstat*), and Vincent Henry (2002: *The Compstat Paradigm: Management Accountability in Policing, Business and the Public Sector*). As noted in Chapter 5, all of these books are essentially "advocacy" works, premised upon the assumption that Compstat is a dramatic and successful innovation in policing.

The closest to a results evaluation of the impact in New York City is the work by Kelling and Sousa (2001) that focused upon the "broken windows" component of Compstat by correlating the number of misdemeanor arrests and extent of violent crime in two matched areas of New York City (Greenwich Village and Flatbush). Broken windows enforcement was defined, however, exclusively as misdemeanor arrests. That is not to imply criticism of the authors—that was the only measure that was available to them. However, it is a very limited assessment in a single atypical circumstance. While the results indicate a correlation, more misdemeanor arrests = less violent crime, this research offers little in the way of strong evidence as to whether the Compstat process itself is effective. Broken windows enforcement does not equal Compstat. Indeed, the debate still rages over whether NYPD "cooked the books" to minimize reported crime (e.g., "Retired Officers Raise Questions on Crime Data," *New York Times*, 2010; "Mugging Compstat: Assault on NYPD Crime-Tracking Program is Wrongheaded," *New York Daily News*, 2010).

An objective study was conducted with National Institute of Justice (NIJ) funding by the Police Foundation in 1999. The report published from this effort was *Compstat and Organizational Change in the Lowell Police Department* (Willis, Mastrofski, Weisburd, & Greenspan, 2003). The authors do not attempt to pronounce Compstat either a success or failure, but rather note its strengths and weaknesses. There is a series of articles that appeared in the journal *Criminology and Public Policy*. The core article, "Reforming to Preserve: Compstat and Strategic Problem Solving in American Policing" (Weisburd et al., 2003), describes a survey of major departments regarding which had implemented variants of the NYPD Compstat model. Two "reaction" articles appeared in conjunction with the Weisburd piece—Firman (2003) "Deconstructing Compstat to Clarify Its Intent" and Moore (2003) "Sizing Up Compstat: An Important Administrative Innovation in Policing." Neither of the reaction articles, however, was based upon more than intellectual analysis.

This author, together with Hyunseok Jang and Hee-Jong Joo, assessed the impact of Compstat in the Fort Worth (Texas) Police Department. We concluded:

> Using monthly time series arrest and crime data over a multi-year period, the study examines whether Compstat engendered a significant increase in "broken windows" arrests (minor nuisance offenses) and, using multivariate time-series analysis, the role of the Compstat strategy in explaining changes in violent, property and total index crimes. Findings indicate that the implementation of Compstat significantly increased some types of broken windows arrests in the Fort Worth Police Department, while others decreased. Analysis indicates significant decreases in property and total index crime rates after controlling for rival factors, but fails to show a significant change in violent crime rates . . . The primary component of the Compstat model is focusing, not broken windows enforcement, and the primary impact is upon property crime. (Jang, Hoover, & Joo, 2010)

The Compstat program of Queensland (Australia) Police Services (QPS) also was evaluated (Mazerolle, Rombouts, & McBroom, 2007). Following NYPD's Compstat model in 2001, the QPS implemented Compstat-style meetings, termed "Operational Performance Reviews" (OPRs). However, the approach in Queensland did not include an increase in broken windows enforcement. Instead, the OPRs focused on problem-oriented approaches to a wide range of offenses, not simply the classic suppressible street crimes. Using time-series analysis, Mazerolle et al. (2007) examined monthly counts of offenses for 295 police divisions in the QPS. The results showed that the introduction of OPRs was significantly related to a decrease in the total number of reported offenses and a decrease of unlawful entry offenses. In addition, the OPRs were cost-effective by saving more than a million dollars (Mazerolle et al., 2007).

PRIMA FACIE SUPPORT FOR COMPSTAT EFFECTIVENESS

Learning Objective

The evidence, regardless of the reason, that Compstat accomplishes crime reduction is very strong. Table 9.1 is a summary of the crime decrease between 1992 and 1999 in New York City compared to other U.S. cities with populations over 1,000,000 (Federal Bureau of Investigation, 2012).

The time frame 1992 to 1999 is used because Compstat was being employed in New York City during this period, but had not yet significantly diffused. Crime was dropping everywhere in the 1990s, but the drop in New York City was profoundly more dramatic. Further, it is difficult to accuse Bratton of simply "cooking the books" when murder fell in New York City by 67 percent compared

TABLE 9.1 Comparative Crime Drop in New York City versus Other Cities >1,000,000 (Crime Decrease Between 1992 and 1999)

	New York City	Other >1,000,000
Murder	67%	42%
Robbery	61%	44%
Auto Theft	69%	35%
Burglary	61%	38%
Index Total	53%	27%

to 42 percent in the nine other cities over 1,000,000. It is difficult to distort UCR statistics, to hide bodies, with regard to homicide. Zimring (2011, p. 77) notes confirmatory evidence from both public health records and auto insurance claims:

> Over the 19 years when the police reported the dramatic decline in most crimes, the agreement between the health and police reports each year was practically perfect *(referring to homicide statistics)*. In the second case, auto theft (which went down by a spectacular 94 percent), insurance companies record claims by victims. The most complete statistics of insurance claims indicated a decline in theft rates of slightly more than 90 percent.

The evidence is overwhelming that NYPD did not "cook the books."

Occam's razor—the idea that the simple explanation is usually correct—is relevant here. As noted by Berman (2009),

> So when astronomers at NASA's Jet Propulsion Laboratory in Pasadena, Calif., first observed straight lines on the surface of the Jovian moon Europa in 1979, their initial hunch wasn't "runways built by aliens for their mother ships." No, they started with: "Looks like cracks in ice."

Occam's razor
One of the core principles of science—the simple explanation is usually correct. Stated differently, all other things being equal, the least complex causative theory is most likely to be true.

When crime plummets in a matter of months concurrent to the NYPD launching a major crime reduction effort, we do not look for a miraculous instantaneous confluence of an array of criminological root causes. We start with "Looks like Compstat works."

The NYPD as a Unique Setting. The real question about what happened in New York City is whether it was the Compstat process *per se* that reduced crime or merely the invigoration of the NYPD. Many would assert that by the time William Bratton took the helm in New York City, the organization bordered on dysfunctional. Certainly those who worked closely with the NYPD, including this author, would never have held it up as exemplary of quality policing. Indeed, it is fair to characterize the NYPD in 1993 as the epitome of "blue-collar policing." This author was even struck by the fact that NYPD officers referred to calls-for-service as "jobs"—reflecting a mind-set about their role and the tasks they perform. What is clear from the detailed descriptions of the implementation of Compstat in New York City is that it was a multifaceted program. On the one hand, it was a precinct commander accountability program. On the other hand, it was a real-time crime analysis program. Another perspective is that it was a strategic quick-response program. It was also broken windows enforcement where there had been none before. It was uttering the words "You are under arrest" with the same frequency as other professional police departments. Finally, it was a classic program of "**reinventing an organization**."

reinventing an organization
An approach to organizational growth and renewal that emphasizes comprehensive analysis of purpose, product, and process—amidst a changing environment. Also referred to as reengineering the organization.

Indeed, given the circumstances in New York City in 1993, given the fact the agency underwent a radical organizational transformation, and given the fact that New York City is not typical of American cities, it is impossible to assess whether Compstat is an effective program from analysis of data from the NYPD. Likewise, one would experience similar difficulty in assessing the impact of the various elements of Compstat in cities to which it was transported from New York City as a "reform" effort. Thus, for example, the reported success of Compstat in New Orleans must be assessed with caution. New Orleans had a genuinely dysfunctional police agency before Superintendent Pennington and Compstat. Its national reputation was dismal—the agency was reportedly inefficient and plagued with corruption allegations. The question that must be raised is not whether Pennington's reforms had a dramatic impact—even after its mixed response to Hurricane Katrina, hardly anyone would argue that they did not—but whether those reforms were inherently political in nature or related to Compstat strategy. It is possible that one might have brought accountability to the New Orleans police department by means other than Compstat and accomplished the same thing.

Compstat as a Management Approach

The notion that Compstat is a management approach instead of a strategy or even a set of strategies should not be quickly dismissed. Indeed, it should be noted that Compstat is strikingly similar to the generic principles of organizational success articulated by Peters and Waterman (1982) in their classic work *In Search of Excellence*:

- *A bias for action* (immediate and definitive response to crime trends);
- *Close to the customer* (responsive to citizen complaints of crime problems);
- *Autonomy and entrepreneurship* (delegation to precinct commanders with innovation expected);
- *Productivity through people* (tough-minded accountability);
- *Hands-on, value-driven* (the police can control crime, and we are here to do so);
- *Stick to the knitting* (crime control, not quality of life);
- *Simple form; lean staff* (back in uniform, back to patrol); and
- *Simultaneous loose–tight properties* (monitored at headquarters, but implemented at the precinct level, with precinct-to-precinct variation).

An evaluation of Compstat must begin with careful definition of the operational variables. It is possible—if Compstat's reported success is actually due to implementation of Peters and Waterman's principles—that strategy does not matter much. On the other hand, strategy may be everything. We do not know what the cause-and-effect relationship is, or even if there is one. Proactive strategy implementation may cause implementation of new forms of management—or new forms of management may engender innovative strategies. Finally, Compstat may simply be a reorientation of the resources dedicated to a vague and nebulous concept called community policing to crime-specific interventions.

Indeed, Compstat runs the same risk as community policing of suffering from a lack of a clear definition. Compstat may be different things to different people. Before declaring it either successful or unsuccessful, one must first define what is being measured.

However, it is extremely difficult to "measure" management approaches. Indeed, one of the criticisms of Peters and Waterman's (1982) *In Search of Excellence* is methodological. They consciously visited only successful corporations. On the basis of those visits and related analyses, they proclaimed the famous eight characteristics of successful business enterprises. (Tom Peters did follow-up work that is said to establish that the same principles apply to government agencies.) What is a real possibility, however, is that decidedly unsuccessful businesses employ (or employed) the same principles. There is no comparison or control group. Every assessment done of total quality management approaches suffers from the same limitation. No one can walk into a corporation's CEO office and say "We want to study why you are failing." The same certainly holds true for interviewing a Police Chief who is under duress.

It makes better sense to start with strategy than management style. Not only is strategy inherently more measurable, it is inherently more transferable. In the Compstat context, strategy can be viewed as the extent and nature of the engagement of the following organizational units in crime reduction efforts:

- *Patrol* (enhanced information and directed effort);
- *Divisional detectives* (focused investigations, proactive approaches such as stings);
- *Community policing officers* (prevention, neighborhood engagement, problem solving);
- *Structured tactical units* (crime response teams);
- *Patrol special-duty assignments* (saturation patrol, surveillance); and
- *Specialized investigations* (gang units, auto theft, narcotics)

Jang et al. (2010) concluded that the central strategic element of Compstat may be simply "focusing." However, focusing is not as simplistic an approach as one might initially assume. One division commander in Fort Worth described the role of Compstat as the *"headlight in the middle of night."* That kind of superlative is not generated by a mere "we are going to pay more attention to crime." Observations and interviews by the authors indicate that Fort Worth's intervention approaches were (1) contemplative, (2) proactive, (3) planned, (4) monitored, and (5) modified. Within this context specific interventions entailed the deployment of various combinations of several organizational units—patrol, divisional detectives, tactical (Zero-Tolerance Units), patrol special-duty assignments, gang units, centralized/specialized investigative units, and community policing officers.

Learning Objective

IMPLICATIONS FOR STRATEGY

Without question crime dropped far more precipitously in New York City during the 1990s than in other major jurisdictions. Although there are still a few who refuse to attribute the phenomenon to the implementation of Compstat, the vast majority of both scholars and police administrators believe that the difference was indeed Compstat. However, we have noted that as implemented in

New York City, Compstat was an amalgam of several strategies, programs, and policies—with an overlay of organizational invigoration. It is impossible to separate the individual effect of each. What we do know from research in Fort Worth, Texas, and Queensland, Australia, is that broken windows enforcement is not an essential component of a successful Compstat endeavor.

It is asserted by some that there is inherent conflict between Compstat and community policing. However, comments from Police Chiefs from major agencies that have implemented Compstat suggest otherwise. Agencies have found that community engagement is effective in some circumstances—not all circumstances, but some. Among agencies that have created specialist positions in community policing, the effect of Compstat has been to refocus the specialist's role upon crime control as opposed to broader quality-of-life issues.

Compstat is widely seen as one of the key programs that has impacted the strategic thinking of policing. See Table 9.2 for sample observations of Police Chiefs attending a Police Executive Research Forum conference on the status of Compstat (Wexler, 2011, pp. 9–11). It is important to note that Compstat is an evolving process. Even in New York City, the process is in constant flux. Los Angeles now practices what the agency refers to as Compstat II.

TABLE 9.2 Strengths and Directions for Compstat

Montgomery County, MD **Assistant Chief Wayne Jerman** "One key is relentless follow-up. Once a crime trend is identified, what is the commander doing about that trend?"
Salt Lake City, UT **Deputy Chief Mike Brown** "The numbers are not as important as having a strategy for dealing with the problems."
St. Louis, MO **Lt. Colonel Antoinette Filla** "Compstat is all about sharing information."
Milwaukee, WI **Captain Terrence Gordon** "Compstat needs to be more than just a snapshot of crime and performance measures for a period of time. We need to take that information and drive the department's future strategies from that."
Dallas, TX **Assistant Chief Vincent Golbeck** "What we've done now is decentralize. . . . So you have the gang unit and narcotics and vice now meeting on a weekly basis, talking intel. You have property crimes meeting weekly. We couldn't do all of that within a two-hour period."
Arlington, TX **Assistant Chief Will Johnson** "We need technology to push the tactical intelligence out to us automatically, so a sector commander gets a message on his Blackberry® saying, 'You just had three robberies within six blocks of each other.'"
Houston, TX **Captain Charles Dunn** "So if you've got a string of robberies that just happened in your area, I provide you with the wanted suspects in that area who may have a history of robbery, along with parolees, probationers, and the gang-bangers. The important thing is not just to give patrol commanders the crime data, but also the other tools they need to target a response."

(continues)

TABLE 9.2 (Continued)

Tampa, FL **Assistant Chief John Bennett** "We have a strategy called "Focus on Four." We look at robbery, burglary, B&E auto, and grand theft auto as having a "halo effect" on other offenses."
Las Vegas, NV **Deputy Chief Joseph Lombardo** "And sometimes people in the meeting are just looking to get past the meeting and hope they don't get called on."
Arlington County, VA **Deputy Chief Daniel Murray** "We have some pretty elaborate records management systems, but if you look at them, much of the data that has been inputted is in pretty bad shape."
Louisville, KY **Colonel Yvette Gentry** "One thing we do that's a little different is map officer activity. We map their self-initiated activity and compare it to where our crime is occurring."

SUMMARY

- Compstat is a broad approach to crime control characterized by incorporation of real-time crime analysis, targeted enforcement, public order and broken windows enforcement, directed and aggressive patrol, and unit commander accountability.
- Compstat (an abbreviation for *computerized statistics*) was initiated in the New York City Transit Police Department in 1991 under Chief William Bratton. Its success in the transit system led to Bratton's appointment as the Commissioner of the New York City Police Department in 1993. Compstat matured and evolved to an encompassing crime control approach in the NYPD. The element of "unit commander accountability" is operationalized in the form of crime control strategy meetings during which unit commanders make presentations regarding their proactive efforts to reduce crime in their area of responsibility.
- Every police agency has limited resources, and difficult decisions must be made regarding the expenditure of those resources among various crime control approaches. There is inevitable conflict among alternative strategic approaches—an agency does not have the resources to implement every approach. In that sense, Compstat does conflict with community policing efforts, particularly when community policing efforts are diffuse and emphasize quality-of-life issues. Nonetheless, most police agencies have found that community engagement remains an important component of crime intervention in the Compstat model. The role of community policing specialists in a crime-focused agency is refocused upon neighborhood or business-area engagement as a tactic. Likewise, problem-oriented policing "properly applied" focuses on crime and disorder—not taking over the responsibilities of parks and recreation or the school district. Infusion of problem-oriented policing into Compstat crime strategy meetings is a counter to the short-term bias and limited response mode of Compstat.
- While crime was dropping everywhere in the 1990s, it dropped far more precipitously in New York City after implementation of Compstat. A few argue that Compstat has never proven its effectiveness, but most scholars and administrators in the field believe that it is worthwhile. Two evaluations of Compstat outside of New York City have occurred, one in Fort Worth, Texas, and another in Queensland, Australia. Both evaluations supported the effectiveness of Compstat, although it should be noted that broken windows enforcement was not a component in either Fort Worth or Queensland.
- If one were to characterize the core element of Compstat it would be crime-specific strategy. Compstat focuses enforcement attention on specific offenses committed in specific locations at specific times by specific categories of offenders. Proactive action is taken to intervene in crime patterns and trends, including

enhanced information and directed effort to patrol, patrol special-duty assignments, engagement of divisional detectives, expanded use of tactical units (crime response teams), and engagement of specialized units such as gang, auto theft, and narcotics. A problem-oriented approach to persons or locations is often incorporated.

- Another perspective on Compstat is that it is a method to infuse positive elements of corporate culture into policing. Indeed, Compstat may exemplify the attributes of successful corporations identified in Peters and Waterman's classic book *In Search of Excellence*: a bias for action, staying close to the customer, autonomy and entrepreneurship, productivity through people, hands-on and value-driven, stick to the knitting, simple form and lean staff, and simultaneous loose–tight properties. For a moribund police agency, Compstat may represent a form of reinventing the organization. For an already proactive police agency, it may be implementation of "learning organization" initiatives.
- The Fort Worth evaluation characterized the most important component of Compstat as simple "focusing." However, focusing is not as simplistic an approach as one might initially assume. It requires intervention approaches that are (1) contemplative, (2) proactive, (3) planned, (4) monitored, and (5) modified.
- The next chapter will examine Compstat in practice—both in terms of management style and strategy, but primarily in terms of strategy.

REVIEW QUESTIONS

1. What evidence exists for the success of Compstat in New York City during the 1990s? Why is there nevertheless doubt regarding its effectiveness?
2. Should the broken windows enforcement strategy be regarded as an essential or critical component of Compstat? What environmental factors affect the utility of the broken windows approach?
3. What is meant by a crime-specific strategy? Of the types of specificity that are suggested, which might have the greatest import?
4. What is the role of community policing specialists in a Compstat approach to crime control? Should the role include leadership in initiating problem-oriented interventions?
5. In their classic book *In Search of Excellence*, Peters and Waterman identified eight characteristics of successful corporations. Link each of the eight to the characteristics of a Compstat approach to crime control.

REAL-WORLD SCENARIOS

1. You are in charge of a twenty-officer crime response team responsible for "aggressive" interdiction. Among the three types of targeting—geographic, offense, offender—you decide to focus on geographic. What criteria might you employ to identify geographic areas for which aggressive uniform patrol interdiction (high visibility, frequent stops of suspicious vehicles and persons, frequent warrant checks, broken-windows-style interventions) will be most effectual?
2. You are the commander of a community- and problem-oriented policing unit in a major municipal agency. What criteria do you employ to decide when community engagement is an appropriate component of a specific crime intervention effort? Conversely, when is it likely that community engagement will have little relevance or effect on a particular intervention?
3. You are the chief of police of a city of 500,000. You have been alerted by the city manager that there is discussion among city council members of saving budget dollars by eliminating your ten-officer crime response team. The perception is that the role of the crime response team can be adequately fulfilled by regular patrol units during intervals between handling calls-for-service. Prepare a briefing document for the city council enumerating five reasons why regular patrol units responsible for handling calls-for-service cannot fulfill the role of a crime response team.

APPLICATION ACTIVITIES

1. Several books are available that describe the implementation of Compstat in New York City. The chapter References list includes those authored by Bratton and Knobler, Henry, Maple and Mitchell, and McDonald. Based on a perusal of any one of these books, identify the primary evidence offered by the author that Compstat was effective. In contrast, also identify any segment of the book that might be characterized as either neutral analysis or skepticism regarding Compstat's impact.
2. Using the same source as in the previous activity, describe both the substance and tone of crime strategy meetings in the early days of Compstat in New York City. From the description you read, were the meetings tilted toward unit commander accountability or crime intervention tactics? Did the author have an opinion on the appropriateness of the confrontational nature of the early Compstat effort?
3. Locate the article by Jang, Hoover, and Joo published in *Police Quarterly*, "An Evaluation of Compstat's Effect upon Crime: The Fort Worth Experience" (2010). Explain why the authors felt that the relatively simplistic term "focusing" is nonetheless the best descriptor of what makes Compstat successful.

COURSEMATE

REFERENCES

Berman, B. (2009). Applying Occam's razor. *Astronomy Magazine*, 14.

Bratton, W., & Knobler, P. (1998). *The turnaround: How America's top cop reversed the crime epidemic*. New York: Random House.

Federal Bureau of Investigation. (2000). *Crime in the United States, Uniform Crime Reports*. Washington, DC: U.S. Department of Justice.

Firman, J. R. (2003). Deconstructing Compstat to clarify its intent. *Criminology & Public Policy*, *2*(3), 457–460.

Henry, V. E. (2002). *The Compstat paradigm: Management accountability in policing, business and the public sector*. Flushing, NY: Looseleaf Law Publications, Inc.

Jang, H. S., Hoover, L. T., & Joo, H. J. (2010). An evaluation of Compstat's effect upon crime: The Fort Worth experience. *Police Quarterly, 13*(4).

Kelling, G. L., & Coles, C. M. (1996). *Fixing broken windows: Restoring order and reducing crime in our communities*. New York: Free Press.

Kelling, G. L., & Sousa Jr., W. H. (2001). Do police matter? An analysis of the impact of New York City's police reforms. In *Civic report* (Vol. 22). New York: Manhattan Institute for Policy Research.

Maple, J., & Mitchell, C. (1999). *The crime fighter*. New York: Doubleday.

Mazerolle, L. G., Rombouts, S., & McBroom, J. (2007). The impact of Compstat on reported crime in Queensland. *Policing: An International Journal of Police Strategies and Management*, *30*, 237–256.

McDonald, P. P. (2002). *Managing police operations: Implementing the New York crime control model—Compstat*. Australia: Wadsworth Thomson Learning.

Moore, M. H. (2003). Sizing up Compstat: An important administrative innovation in policing. *Criminology & Public Policy*, *2*(3), 469–494.

Mugging Compstat: Assault on NYPD crime-tracking program is wrongheaded. (2010, February 11). *New York Daily News*. Available at http://www.nydailynews.com/fdcp?1265997016418.

Peters, T., & Waterman, R. (1982). *In search of excellence*. New York: Harper and Row.

Pooley, E. (1996, January). One good apple. *Time*, 55–56.

Retired officers raise questions on crime data. (2010, February 7). *New York Times*.

Weisburd, D., Mastrofski, S. D., McNally, A. M., Greenspan, R., & Willis, J. J. (2003). Reforming to preserve: Compstat and the strategic problem solving in American policing. *Criminology & Public Policy*, *2*(3), 421–456.

Wexler, C. (2011). Police leaders at PERF/BJA meeting discuss Compstat: Best practices and future outlook. In C. Fischer (Ed.), *Subject to debate* (Vol. 25, No. 2). Washington, DC: Police Executive Research Forum.

Willis, J. J., Mastrofski, S. D., Weisburd, D., & Greenspan, R. (2003). *Compstat and organizational change in the Lowell Police Department*. Washington, DC: Police Foundation.

Zimring, F. E. (2011). How New York beat crime: With its judicious use of cops and innovative methods, the Big Apple is a model for how to stem homicides, muggings and other ills. *Scientific American*, *305*(2), 75–79.

CHAPTER 10

Conducting Crime Strategy Meetings

This chapter was adapted with permission from "Conducting an Effective Compstat Meeting," Law Enforcement Executive Forum, Vol. 7, No. 2, March 2007.

The primary characteristics of a crime-specific strategy or approach include instant and detailed crime analysis, immediate responsive deployment of resources, active enforcement, concentration of several diverse organizational units and approaches on emerging crime patterns, and a strict management accountability program centered on crime control. These characteristics come together in the famous—or if you choose, infamous—Compstat meeting. The core of Compstat is crime strategy meetings where district commanders are expected to know the major problems in their beats and to have initiated remedial interventions. According to Compstat doctrine, such a forum promotes brainstorming and creative problem solving, but research on how Compstat works in practice suggests significant slippage from this ideal (Willis, 2011).

KEY TERMS

Challenging questioning
Chop shops
Division-level meetings
Geographic information systems (GIS) analysis
Geospatial crime analysis
Moribund
Patrol as the backbone of law enforcement

LEARNING OBJECTIVES

After completing this chapter, you should be able to:

- Describe the primary components of a crime strategy meeting under the Compstat umbrella.
- Identify measurement errors that frequently occur in crime strategy meetings.
- Describe how geographic information systems should be employed during a crime strategy meeting.
- Characterize appropriate implementation of unit commander accountability as a component of crime strategy meetings.
- Explain the import of data presentation format.
- Identify the primary issues pertaining to implementation of tactical interventions.

Characteristics of Crime Strategy Meetings

The perception of every citizen west of the Appalachian Mountains is that Americans on the East Coast speak relatively abruptly. Those who live on the East Coast would respond, of course, that they are forthright and forthcoming; that the pace of life in East Coast big cities does not allow for routine exchange of "how's the family doing" niceties. In that context, the assertion is often made that the degree of confrontation in the New York Police Department (NYPD) model would only be tolerable in the New York City culture. Another perspective is that the program as implemented by Bratton was designed to jumpstart a **moribund** organization, and the confrontation had nothing to do with the local culture but rather was a necessary evil to rid the organization of complacency. Both factors probably played a role.

moribund
Stagnant and unresponsive to change.

Whether a confrontational character was required in NYPD to make Compstat work in that setting is certainly debatable. Regardless, the style is not a necessary component of a crime strategy meeting implemented in an otherwise healthy department policing a community where crime is perhaps not as low as one would like, but not out of control. The vast majority of police agencies that have implemented crime strategy meetings argue vehemently that confrontation is unnecessary. In fact, they all suggest that confrontation would be counterproductive to the effectiveness of the program. Indeed, observers of the NYPD have noted that, although still stressful, Compstat is not the confrontational model that it was in the 1990s (O'Keefe, 2004). Nevertheless, a crime strategy meeting is not run like a family reunion. They are "no-nonsense" business meetings. On numerous occasions, what the U.S. State Department would call "frank and forthright" conversations occur. For an effective meeting, six characteristics must be present:

Learning Objective

1. Accountability and tactical planning balance
2. Crime pattern specificity

3. Geographic information systems (GIS) integration
4. Challenging questioning
5. Appropriate presenting entities
6. A base of divisional meetings

Each is discussed in this section.

ACCOUNTABILITY AND TACTICAL PLANNING BALANCE

If one were to conceive a continuum anchored at a "1" with a crime strategy meeting as a pure accountability program and a "10" with a crime strategy meeting as a pure tactical planning program, an effective meeting would be an 8 or 9—that is, leaning heavily toward tactical planning. A key to discerning whether that balance exists is the currency of the data used at a crime strategy meeting. If the data being presented are a month old, then the meeting is likely an accountability check, not a tactical planning session. The use of monthly data is appropriate if the goal is indeed an accountability program—with division commanders reporting on patterns, trends, and related interdictions already implemented. If, on the other hand, a crime strategy meeting is regarded as a tactical planning session, then one would argue that the most recent data possible are employed—weekly not monthly. Many agency reporting systems are not "up to the minute," but the system should certainly be current within two or three days. Tactical planning is premised upon evolving crime patterns and trend information, not patterns a month old.

CRIME PATTERN SPECIFICITY

Critical to the success of a crime-specific approach is that very specific crime interdiction tactics be discussed. It is not enough to simply review crime patterns and trends. It is interdiction that makes a difference, and if this is not included in the meeting format, the meetings are doomed to degenerate into staff briefings.

The key to a crime-specific approach is depth, not breath. Although a portion of a crime strategy meeting might legitimately be dedicated to broad trends in crime rates, the purpose of the meeting is to develop tactics to interdict specific offense patterns. The fact that burglary is up or down 5 percent year-to-date compared to last year-to-date can be communicated in a brief memo. The purpose of a crime strategy meeting is to examine what types of burglaries are now occurring, where and when they are occurring, and develop interdiction tactics.

Several related points are worth noting. First, seasonal variation in crime statistics requires that the analysis used include not only patterns and trends in the last several months, but a comparison to "this month last year" and "year-to-date this year compared to year-to-date last year." Second, *Uniform Crime Report* (UCR; published annually by the Federal Bureau of Investigation) offense categories are insufficient for crime-specific approach analysis. For example, agencies emphasizing tactics break theft into categories that made sense from an interdiction perspective—rather than theft in the UCR aggregated format, the offense is disaggregated into, for example, theft from a

TABLE 10.1 Classic Compstat Measurement Errors

Lack of linkage between measurement and strategy:
• Using gross UCR categories, e.g., theft should be subdivided—gas station drive-offs, "beer runs," shoplifting, from vehicles, of vending machines.
• Measuring all arrests, whether officer initiated or product of a call-for-service.
• Inability to link arrests to specific assignments and/or units.
• Inability to measure field interviews and/or to link to specific assignments and/or units.
• Inability to track debriefings of arrestees.

vending machine, gasoline drive-offs, so-called "beer runs" (snatch and grab merchandise at the doorway of convenience stores), shoplifting—overlaid against short-term patterns or targets. Similarly, burglaries are broken down not only by commercial and residential, but within residential by apartment and single-family dwelling. See Table 10.1, listing common errors. The key is the need for targeted enforcement, and targeted enforcement requires delineation of specific offenses, at specific locations, at specific times, by a specific offender type.

Learning Objective

GEOGRAPHIC INFORMATION SYSTEMS INTEGRATION

Since the mid-1990s, the use of **geographic information systems (GIS) analysis** of crime patterns, allocation of resources, focused deployment, and strategic planning has been widespread. Cities such as Chicago, New York, and Los Angeles employ sophisticated GIS to support their Compstat programs. In addition, regional centers have been created to facilitate the application of **geospatial crime analysis**, such as the Baltimore County Police Department's Regional Crime Analysis GIS (RCAGIS), San Diego's Automated Regional Justice Information System (ARJIS), the Illinois Criminal Justice Authority's Spatial and Temporal Analysis of Crime (STAC), the Regional Crime Analysis Program in Virginia (LaVigne & Wartell, 2001), and the Delaware real-time crime reporting system (Leipnik & Albert, 2003). By 2001, 62 percent of departments with 100 or more officers had adopted some form of GIS (Weisburd & Lum, 2005). That number now approaches 100 percent.

geographic information systems (GIS) analysis
Use of computerized mapping programs for crime analysis. Most frequently used in policing to depict the locations of given offenses over stipulated time periods.

geospatial crime analysis
The use of sophisticated GIS analysis to identify linkages among crime patterns or trends. Merged databases are often a component, such as known offender addresses.

Successful cases of the implementation of GIS has been reported in police departments such as Lincoln, Nebraska (Casady, 2003); Knoxville, Tennessee (Hubbs, 2003); Phoenix, Arizona (Hill, 2003); and Spokane, Washington (Leipnik & Albert, 2003). Collectively in these reports, GIS technology is credited with reducing officially reported crime, depressing residential burglaries, tracking parolees and serious habitual offenders, and identifying hot spots.

GIS crime mapping is employed not only to understand the geographical distribution of crime, but also to identify hot spots and facilitate intervention deployment decisions. Examples of the impact of GIS include the contribution to Compstat tactical planning (Chilvers & Weatherburn, 2004; Eck & Maguire, 2000; Mazerolle, Rombouts, & McBroom, 2007), GIS-assisted hot spot identification (Braga & Bond, 2008; Sherman et al., 1995; Weisburd & Green, 1995), the impact of crime maps on citizens' perception of crime (Groff et al., 2005;

Paulsen, 2004), and the effects of geographic offender profiling on criminal investigation (Canter, Coffey, Huntley, & Missen, 2000; Paulsen, 2006; Rossmo, 2000). The Philadelphia Police Department has employed GIS in several innovative ways:

- A circle is placed around the addresses where a burglary apprehension occurs, with subsequent *modus operandi* review of nearby burglaries possibly committed by the same offender.
- The most recent twenty-eight-day offense cycle is shown on a map, with the previous twenty-eight-day cycle shown in a different color.
- Robbery maps distinguish "gun used" by displaying a dot in the middle of a circle.
- Recovered vehicle locations are mapped to identify likely locations of **chop shops**.
- Plots list addresses of all Pennsylvania Department of Corrections releasees by offense type. (Brennan, 2005)

chop shops
Locations where stolen vehicles are "disassembled" to recover and then market expensive parts.

The application of GIS analysis to hot spot deployment has attracted the most interest. For example, in their study of problem-oriented policing in Lowell, Massachusetts, Braga and Bond (2008) applied mapping technology to identify hot spots for intervention. Similarly, Potchak, McGloin, and Zgoba (2002) geographically identified the location of 201 offenders who were arrested for auto theft in Newark, New Jersey, in 2000. They overlaid layers of the opportunity structure such as land use, public housing, and major roadways, creating a comprehensive map of auto-theft patterns.

Learning Objective

In strategy meetings there are typically two computer projectors and two screens in the room. Projected on one screen are the types of data that are being discussed, presented in table and graph format. Projected on a second screen are GIS crime occurrence maps. In the best circumstances, the GIS projection is not of static slides transferred to PowerPoint®, but rather is drawn from a live interactive GIS database. If a good GIS operator is available, the second projection can be modified on the fly for such purposes as rapid zoom into a high-density crime location. Additionally, a good GIS technician can immediately apply filters to the data, such that auto thefts can be projected first in totality, and if a query is made regarding time of day, immediately filtered to reflect only those occurring during evening hours or taking place in commercial parking lots. It should be emphasized that for this type of system to be functional, a highly skilled GIS analyst is necessary. Considerable skill is necessary to employ GIS in real time. An agency contemplating employment of GIS should expect to spend far more on thorough training of analysts/operators than it will spend on the software itself.

Participants in crime-specific approach meetings indicate that although GIS is useful, it usually does not meet original expectations. It does not obviate much in the way of aggregate crime patterns that could not otherwise be observed in a table of addresses. It certainly does not solve crime. For some issues, it simply is not relevant. See Table 10.2. No one suggests that GIS is not worth the investment of effort, just that expectations have to be set realistically. The most cited problem is that a GIS display is too often a blur of scores if not hundreds of dots on a jurisdictional map. When there are too many dots on the map, nothing is obvious. When such intensely populated maps do illustrate a pattern, it is frequently a pattern known to everyone in the

TABLE 10.2 Illustrative Compstat Activity Summary

Field Stops	This Month Current Year	This Month Last Year	YTD Current Year	YTD Last Year	YTD% Change
Total Field Stops	18,000	21,300	162,000	158,000	3%
Number of Citations	16,700	20,500	172,300	166,900	3%
Hazardous	7,700	9,800	78,500	74,000	6%
Nonhazardous	8,000	9,500	83,000	81,000	2%
Warning Citations	1,000	1,200	10,800	11,900	−10%
Driving While Intoxicated Arrests	400	370	3,300	3,800	−15%

room—for example, dots representing thefts from autos cluster around commercial shopping areas.

CHALLENGING QUESTIONING

Learning Objective

Nonconfrontational does not mean comfortable. Commanders who are in the "hot seat" are frequently challenged—"Have you tried this technique? Have you employed this approach? Should you talk to this or that unit?" There may be congenial conversation, with coffee served before the meeting and lunch together after the meeting. But during the meeting, the interactions are characterized better by the term "civility" than "congeniality." On the other hand, the interactions involve **challenging questioning**, not "confrontation."

challenging questioning
The practice during crime strategy meetings of aggressively quizzing unit commanders regarding whether they have done everything reasonably possible to interrupt a crime pattern or trend.

For example, when asked about the management in a specific problem apartment complex, division captains are expected to know the manager's name. It is expected that patterns will be pointed out by the commander in the hot seat, not pointed out to her or him. An illustration of inadequate questioning occurred during one observation by this author. During a presentation by the detective division, there was a slide regarding financial fraud incidents. The number of such instances had dropped from 132 in April to 28 in May. Yet, this slide was passed by with no comment or question regarding what is clearly an issue that should be discussed. The fact that it was a drop and not an increase is irrelevant—an 80 percent change in the rate of any offense merits discussion.

A critical issue is "Who does the questioning?" In most agencies questioning is led by an assistant chief (second in command). First, this acknowledges that questioning should be from the highest levels of the agency. However, the preparation time necessary to effectively challenge argues against the questioner being the chief of police (except perhaps in agencies with fewer than 100 sworn officers, and even then it is debatable). Additionally, the line between tough challenge and confrontation can be thin. A chief may want to leave "challenging" interaction to an assistant chief in order to assure sound relations with command staff. That being said, it is regarded as absolutely critical to the success of a crime-specific approach that the chief of police be present. The absence of the chief conveys a clear message that this is not a priority. The chief should ask him- or herself the same question that should be asked of commanders requesting excessive absences, "What in your job description is more important than crime?"

APPROPRIATE PRESENTING ENTITIES

patrol as the backbone of law enforcement
A metaphor conveying the premise that the patrol division has been and remains the "core" of a police organization.

In 1950, O. W. Wilson characterized **patrol as the backbone of law enforcement**. A half a century later there is nearly universal agreement that it still is. Crime-specific approach interdictions are dominated by patrol. However, numerous other police units and programs are also involved. Crime-specific approach interdiction tactics frequently draw upon ancillary police agency programs. In some instances, they are prevention-oriented, for example, having a law enforcement explorer scout group go door-to-door urging residents to close their garage doors. Community policing specialists are often called upon. A few police departments include discussion of working cooperatively with probation or parole; a very few even have probation and parole representatives attend the Compstat meeting. Because a particular crime problem is frequently addressed using multiple tactics and employing multiple units, there is usually breadth of reporting. Another purpose of having all divisions report is to maintain communication throughout an agency.

That being said, the nature of the presentations changes dramatically when the meeting moves from patrol divisions to special and ancillary units. The format of the patrol division reports focuses on crime incidents and control tactics. Once the meeting moves to the ancillary divisions, the character of the presentations too often changes to that of a staff briefing. If police command staff perceives that there is sufficient value to include presentations by all divisions, then the character of the presentations by the ancillary divisions needs to parallel that of the patrol divisions. More specifically, the data presented by the ancillary divisions is usually in the format of rates, not raw numbers. Further, rates are depicted in trend or pattern format—not in the form of "this month we processed 3,000 incident reports." For a number of ancillary divisions it is possible to include productivity information, for example, response time trends from a communications division.

An option is to rotate presentations at crime-specific approach meetings, with the geographic patrol divisions always presenting but a rotational schedule for other divisions. Some agencies employ this technique. Another option is for the ancillary divisions to produce written reports but either eliminate or substantially abbreviate their oral presentations.

A BASE OF DIVISIONAL MEETINGS

division-level meetings
Crime strategy meetings conducted at substation (precinct) facilities. These meetings focus only on crime within the division boundaries, and are much more specific than agency-wide sessions.

Division-level meetings are a critical element of a crime-specific approach in agencies large enough to have substations (precincts). Many agencies will attest that "where Compstat really occurs" is at the precinct meetings. Precinct-level meetings are particularly effective when they reach all the way down to patrol officers. Yes, this creates logistics and overtime issues. However, engagement of regular patrol is critical to crime interdiction. During substation Compstat meetings, former Los Angeles Assistant Chief George Gascón would ask a particular officer about crime problems on her or his beat (Gascón, 2005). It is stressed that the division-level meetings employ data that are as current as possible, as it is clearly a meeting designed to develop tactical response.

Data Analysis Format

Learning Objective

A crime-specific approach meeting is only as good as the data presented. Effective presentation exceeds a mass of individual numbers, but rather emphasizes patterns and trends. The best format is usually easy-to-understand graphical figures. At the same time, a crime-specific approach meeting cannot be allowed to degenerate into a "dog and pony show." When a "PowerPoint® of the Month" prize starts to be informally awarded, it is time to pull back. Several principles apply.

First, most analytic comparisons are very recent—the last four weeks. However, data providing a longer-term perspective are also needed. For example, employing "this month this year" compared to "this month last year" is appropriate. Crime rates fluctuate considerably by month of the year—related to weather effects, school schedules, and holiday seasons. Thus, such comparisons are maintained. It is also useful for some of the trend data to include a line graph that illustrates patterns in the last several months—at least the last three months. Although it is important to know whether theft from automobiles is up or down compared to this month last year, it is also important to know the recent trend. See Table 10.3. This does not contradict the assertion made earlier that the focus is tactical deployment premised upon recent (weekly) trends. Annual or quarterly trends are not usually the focus of discussion, but they do provide a quick review to maintain the "big-picture" perspective.

Analysis of rates by telescoping from large to small reporting areas is important. Part of a crime-specific approach is the comparison of rates by reporting area for analysis and targeting purposes. Second, it is useful to incorporate information regarding problematic addresses, for example, the most frequent locations for gas station drive-offs. Third, actionable information requires delineation of crime type by victim or target. For example, many agencies have found it useful to distinguish thefts from autos from thefts of auto parts (which tend to be perpetrated by a different type of offender). Robbery of an individual is distinguished from robbery of a convenience store. As noted earlier, the crime categories used for analysis reflect the type of targeted intervention that is possible for the department to initiate.

Role of Crime Analysts

Talented crime analysts are critical. Effective crime analysis does not equate to pretty electronic pin maps. As noted, specificity, or targeted enforcement, is an essential component of a crime-specific approach. Even in a large department's agency-wide meeting, discussion frequently zeros in on a specific offense, or offense series. Crime analysis is not the production of simple trend-line graphs. An effective crime analysis unit routinely "drills down" in an effort to link offenses and offenders.

Additionally, target selection for concentrated effort month to month is typically guided by recommendations from crime analysis. In effect, target "nomination" comes from the crime analysis unit. There is then almost always a meeting with division commanders to review the nominations and settle on specified target issues/locations. Nominations from crime analysis are

TABLE 10.3 Illustrative Compstat Offense Trend Summary

City Hometown, USA	Population 100,000		
CRIMINAL INCIDENTS	Jan	Feb	Mar
Criminal Homicide	2	0	1
Rape	5	3	3
Robbery	7	8	5
Aggravated Assault	12	9	14
TOTAL VIOLENT CRIME OFFENSES	**26**	**20**	**23**
Annualized Violent Crime Rate Per 1,000 Population	3.12	2.40	2.76
Burglary	18	27	19
Residential	10	12	8
Building	8	15	11
Theft from Motor Vehicle	20	14	18
Other Thefts	43	29	17
Burg. Coin Op. Mach.	12	14	4
Larceny	31	15	13
Auto Theft	3	5	1
Arson	0	1	0
TOTAL PROPERTY CRIME OFFENSES	**84**	**76**	**55**
Annualized Property Crime Rate Per 1,000 Population	10.08	9.12	6.60
TOTAL PART-I OFFENSES	**110**	**96**	**78**
Annualized Part 1 Crime Rate per 1,000 Population	13.20	11.52	9.36
Part 1 Offenses Cleared	24	18	13
Part 1 Percent Offenses Cleared	**22%**	**24%**	**24%**
Stolen Property	**$125,000**	**$115,000**	**$130,000**
Recovered Property	**$12,500**	**$15,000**	**$9,000**
% Of Property Value Recovered	10.0%	13.0%	6.9%

not rubber stamped. One model is to have the crime analysis unit document three to five issues/areas for consideration by each division, and the division commanders then select two to three of the five. Occasionally division commanders would even be expected to substitute a different target at their own discretion.

Efficiency Improvement

An unexpected observation is the frequency with which generic efficiency issues are addressed during crime strategy meetings. Discussion of specific intervention tactics frequently engenders recognition of needed operational or management improvements. These are issues that do not necessarily relate directly to tactics or directly to a specific crime series, but rather to overall agency operations. An example might be the time required to complete the booking of an arrestee. As in any other organization, the process of focusing a police agency upon a particular problem often results in more generic operational improvements.

Tactics

Division-level discretion and flexibility are essential for a crime-specific approach to operate successfully. If everything is controlled from headquarters, program effectiveness is severely hampered. Division commanders need to be provided the discretion to develop not only their own targeting but their own tactics as well. But discretion does not translate into no guidance at all. From an analysis of Compstat implementation among six agencies, Willis suggests that sergeants were likely to receive guidance from their superiors and crime analysts on serious crime issues. Guidance did not, however, include detailed instructions on how best to respond to these crime problems. What was most important was that sergeants were doing something—thus speed took precedence over quality of response (Willis, 2011).

The most important tactical consideration is the availability of discretionary resources to focus and concentrate upon a problem issue/area. Some kind of discretionary quick-deployment resource must be available if a crime-specific approach is to work. One approach is to staff patrol at a sufficient level that a few officers can be pulled from call-for-service response and assigned to ad hoc tactical response. Alternatively, a quick-response discretionary "pool" might be the use of community policing specialists. It could also be the temporary reassignment of divisional detectives, gang officers, auto-theft detectives, or other investigative personnel. It might be a standing full-time tactical unit. But if some kind of discretionary resource is not available, an agency might as well save its time and resources. Focused interdiction, not sophisticated crime analysis or a monthly meeting, is the key to crime-specific approach success.

Agencies employ a variety of interdiction tactics. Some are very innovative, such as use of a civil injunction to prohibit a particular gang from congregating in the central business district. The interdiction tactics employed are, of course, an issue of "it depends on the problem." Typical is theft from motor vehicles. The interdiction tactics might include crime prevention (urging people to lock their cars and keep valuables out of open view), suppression efforts using uncommitted time by regular patrol units, repression efforts by ad hoc tactical patrol, and focused follow-up investigations on offenses that have already occurred.

Interestingly, the classic SARA model—scanning, analysis, response, adjustment—problem solving approach is seldom observed in crime strategy meetings. One agency notes that over the years of its Compstat program, the emphasis has shifted from "chasing dots on a map to chasing identified perpetrators." Some smaller jurisdictions target either one premise and/or one person each month. One observed crime-specific approach includes presentations by the detectives in the agency, not patrol commanders. Investigations are described and information disseminated that is useful throughout the agency.

A crime-specific approach is not necessarily just a large agency program. By modifying the scope, it can also be effectively employed by departments responsible for small communities.

IMPLICATIONS FOR STRATEGY

Crime strategy meetings have been institutionalized in nearly all major municipal police agencies in the United States. Indeed, the practice has defused internationally. There are three primary implications for strategy. First, it is not necessary that crime strategy meetings be confrontational. They are definitely business meetings, but they can be cordial. Second, the meeting's focus should remain on discussion of potential tactical intervention targeting a specific crime trend or pattern. Unit commander accountability still exists, but is secondary. Third, the highest level of the agency should attend—the chief of police or sheriff.

SUMMARY

- The primary characteristics of a crime-specific approach include instant and detailed crime analysis, responsive deployment, active enforcement tactics, concentration of diverse organizational units on particular interventions, and a strict management accountability program. Effective crime strategy meetings incorporate examination of these elements through a balance between accountability and tactical planning. The primary purpose of a crime strategy meeting is to examine trends now occurring, concurrently identifying tactical intervention, not review of patterns that are months old. Broad offense categories are subdivided into subgroups. For example, theft is broken down into theft from vending machines, gasoline drive-offs, snatch-and-run merchandise theft, and shoplifting. The categories used are flexible. The level of specificity depends on the interventions considered—a given intervention might address one or some combination of subcategories.
- There are several measurement errors that frequently occur in crime strategy meetings. Primary among them is the lack of linkage between measurement and strategy. This includes using aggregate UCR offense categories rather than actionable subgroups, measuring all arrests rather than only those officer initiated, the inability to link arrests to specific assignments and/or units, an inability to measure field interviews and/or to link to specific assignments and/or units, and an inability to track the utility of intelligence information. Additional errors include a rigid adherence to format—format driving strategy rather than vice versa; meaningless statistical review—too many trend statistics; GIS maps that are a blur of dots; and, once again, lack of specificity—including a standardized response to every crime problem, "Let's increase patrol."
- GIS is an integral part of a crime strategy meeting. Properly employed, GIS will identify fluid crime patterns by time of day, day of week, type of target, and even probable offender type.
- Although unit commander accountability may be one of the purposes of crime strategy meetings, that issue is secondary to assisting unit commanders in planning and organizing tactical interventions. Questioning of unit commanders is challenging without being hostile: "Have you tried this technique?"; "Have you employed this approach?"; "Should you talk to this or that unit?" The presenting commanders always include patrol, but other unit commanders are frequently called upon as well. Additionally, in large agencies with substations (precincts) there are division-level meetings as well. Indeed, the division-level meetings are frequently characterized as "where Compstat really occurs."
- A crime strategy meeting is only as good as the data presented. The format should be in easy to understand graphical figures, and not degenerate to a "PowerPoint® of the month contest." Although the focus

should be on current trends, annual or quarterly trends might be included to provide the big picture. Data telescopes from large to small reporting areas, and includes comparison of rates by reporting area, problematic addresses, and crime type by victim or target. Talented crime analysts are critical; analytic reports extend beyond the production of trend-line graphs and GIS dot maps. Effective crime analysis drills down—the criteria is always specificity at a level that is actionable.

- Division commanders need to be provided the discretion to develop not only their own targeting but their own tactics as well. But discretion does not translate into no guidance at all. The most important tactical consideration is the availability of discretionary resources to focus and concentrate upon a problem issue/area. Some kind of discretionary quick-deployment resource must be available if a crime-specific approach is to work. Focused interdiction, not sophisticated crime analysis or a monthly meeting, is the key to crime-specific approach success. A crime-specific approach is not necessarily just a large agency program. By modifying the scope, it can also be effectively employed by departments responsible for small communities.

REVIEW QUESTIONS

1. What are some illustrations of broad crime categories that must be delineated into subgroups in order for interventions to be viably focused?
2. At its most simplistic level, GIS is simply a computer version of traditional crime pin maps. But properly employed GIS offers far more crime analysis capability. Describe some of the "sort" features of GIS that make it an invaluable resource for identifying crime patterns and trends.
3. In the early days of Compstat at NYPD, the grilling of unit commanders was described as brutal. That model was never adopted outside of the NYPD. How is unit commander accountability operationalized today in a crime strategy meeting, both at the NYPD and elsewhere?
4. Conversion of incident numerical data to rates is considered an essential element of crime analysis. Rates are particularly important in the process of geographic targeting. However, using residential population as the denominator is usually inadequate and indeed frequently misleading. What is the range of elements that might be employed as denominators in the calculation of offense rates?
5. Describe several measurement errors that frequently occur in crime strategy meetings.

REAL-WORLD SCENARIOS

1. You are the crime analyst at a mid-sized city (population is 200,000) responsible for data compilation and presentation at crime strategy meetings. The presentation includes the use of GIS. What principles would guide your selection of format? More particularly, how do you employ GIS to accomplish more than the projection of static pin maps?
2. You are the chief of police of a major municipal police department. In the process of implementing Compstat, the question arises as to who should do the "tough questioning" of unit commanders during crime strategy meetings. Discuss why you might choose an assistant chief of police to perform this role rather than do it yourself.
3. Although crime is certainly the focus of crime intervention strategy meetings, other police responsibilities are frequently discussed as well. One of those is traffic enforcement. Assume you are the commander of the traffic unit of a major municipal jurisdiction. Prepare a PowerPoint® presentation (or similar program) consisting of a minimum of five slides to convey traffic activity and police response.

APPLICATION ACTIVITIES

1. Data display of long-term crime trends usually includes not just recent months but "this month last year." This is to account for the fact, of course, that crime rates vary seasonally. Discuss why the month of December might have a pronounced effect in this respect. (We all know that the core is that it is the holiday season; be more specific.)
2. It is noted in this chapter that effective crime analysis employs subcategories of broad offense classifications such as theft. The issue was also discussed in Chapter 7 with regard to robbery subtypes. Identify subcategories for the offense of assault/aggravated assault (in some states called assault and battery). For each subcategory you identify, list at least one potentially effective police intervention approach.
3. Police agencies frequently find that a high proportion of thefts is gas station drive-offs (failure to pay after filling the tank). As a pattern, a small number of gas station/convenience stores typically accounts for a very high proportion of this offense; the worst locations might have drive-off rates ten times the average. List the alternatives to combat gas station drive-offs at a chronic high-rate station/store.

COURSEMATE

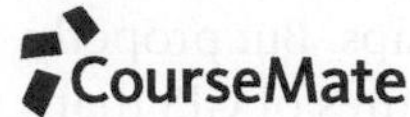

This available CourseMate has an interactive eBook and interactive learning tools, including flash cards, quizzes, and more. To learn more about this resource and access free demo CourseMate resources, go to **www.cengagebrain.com**, and search for this book. To access CourseMate materials that you have purchased, go to **login.cengagebrain.com**.

REFERENCES

Braga, A. A., & Bond, B. J. (2008). Policing crime and disorder hot spots: A randomized controlled trial. *Criminology, 46*(3), 577–607.

Brennan, C. (2005). Compstat in Philadelphia. Presentation to the Law Enforcement Management Institute of Texas (Major Cities Chiefs Program), Austin, TX.

Canter, D. V., Coffey, T., Huntley, J., & Missen, C. (2000). Predicting serial killers' home base using a decision support system. *Journal of Quantitative Criminology, 16*, 457–478.

Casady, T. (2003). Lincoln police department—specific examples of GIS successes. In M. Leipnik & D. P. Albert (Eds.), *GIS in law enforcement: Implementation issues and case studies*. London: Taylor & Francis.

Chilvers, M., & Weatherburn, D. (2004). The New South Wales Compstat process: Its impact on crime. *Australian and New Zealand Journal of Criminology, 37*(1), 22–48.

Eck, J. E., & Maguire, E. (2000). Have changes in policing reduced violent crime?: An assessment of the evidence. In A. Blumstein & J. Wallman (Eds.), *The crime drop in America*. Cambridge, England; New York: Cambridge University Press.

Federal Bureau of Investigation. (Annually). *Crime in the United States, Uniform Crime Reports*. Washington, DC: U.S. Department of Justice.

Gascón, G. (2005). Compstat in Los Angeles. Presentation to the Law Enforcement Management Institute of Texas (Major Cities Chiefs Program), Austin, TX.

Groff, E., Kearley, B., et al. (2005). A randomized experimental study of sharing crime data with citizens: Do maps produce more fear? *Journal of Experimental Criminology, 1*(1), 87–115.

Hill, B. (2003). Operationalizing GIS to investigate serial robberies in Phoenix, Arizona. In M. Leipnik & D. P. Albert (Eds.), *GIS in law enforcement: Implementation issues and case studies*. London: Taylor & Francis.

Hubbs, R. (2003). Mapping crime and community problems in Knoxville, Tennessee. In M. Leipnik & D. P. Albert (Eds.), *GIS in law enforcement: Implementation issues and case studies*. London: Taylor & Francis.

LaVigne, N., & Wartell, J. (2001). *Mapping across boundaries: Regional crime analysis*. Washington, DC: Police Executive Research Forum.

Leipnik, M., & Albert, D. (2003). *GIS in law enforcement: Implementation issues and case studies*. London: Taylor & Francis.

Mazerolle, L. G., Rombouts, S., & McBroom, J. (2007). The impact of Compstat on reported crime in Queensland. *Policing: An International Journal of Police Strategies and Management, 30*, 237–256.

O'Keefe, J. (2004). Personal interview with the former director of the NYPD Academy, now on the faculty at St. John's University in New York City.

Paulsen, D. J. (2004). Map or not to map: Assessing the impact of crime maps on police officer perceptions of crime. *International Journal of Police Science & Management, 6*(4), 234–246.

Paulsen, D. J. (2006). Human versus machine: A comparison of the accuracy of geographic profiling methods. *Journal of Investigative Psychology and Offender Profiling, 3*, 77–89.

Potchak, M. C., McGloin, J. M., & Zgoba, K. M. (2002). A spatial analysis of criminal effort: Auto theft in Newark, New Jersey. *Criminal Justice Policy Review, 13*, 257–285.

Rossmo, D. K. (2000). *Geographic profiling*. New York: CRC Press.

Sherman, L. W., Rogan, D. P., Edwards, T., Whipple, R., Shreve, D., et al. (1995). Deterrent effects of police raids on crack houses: A randomized controlled experiment. *Justice Quarterly, 12*(4), 755–781.

Weisburd, D., & Green, L. (1995). Policing drug hot spots: The Jersey City drug market analysis experiment. *Justice Quarterly, 12*(4), 711–734.

Weisburd, D., & Lum, C. (2005). The diffusion of computerized crime mapping in policing: Linking research and practice. *Police Practice and Research, 6*(5), 419–434.

Willis, J. J. (2011). *First-line supervision under Compstat and community policing*. Washington, DC: U.S. Department of Justice, Office of Community Oriented Policing Services.

CHAPTER 11

The Resurrection of Sherlock Holmes

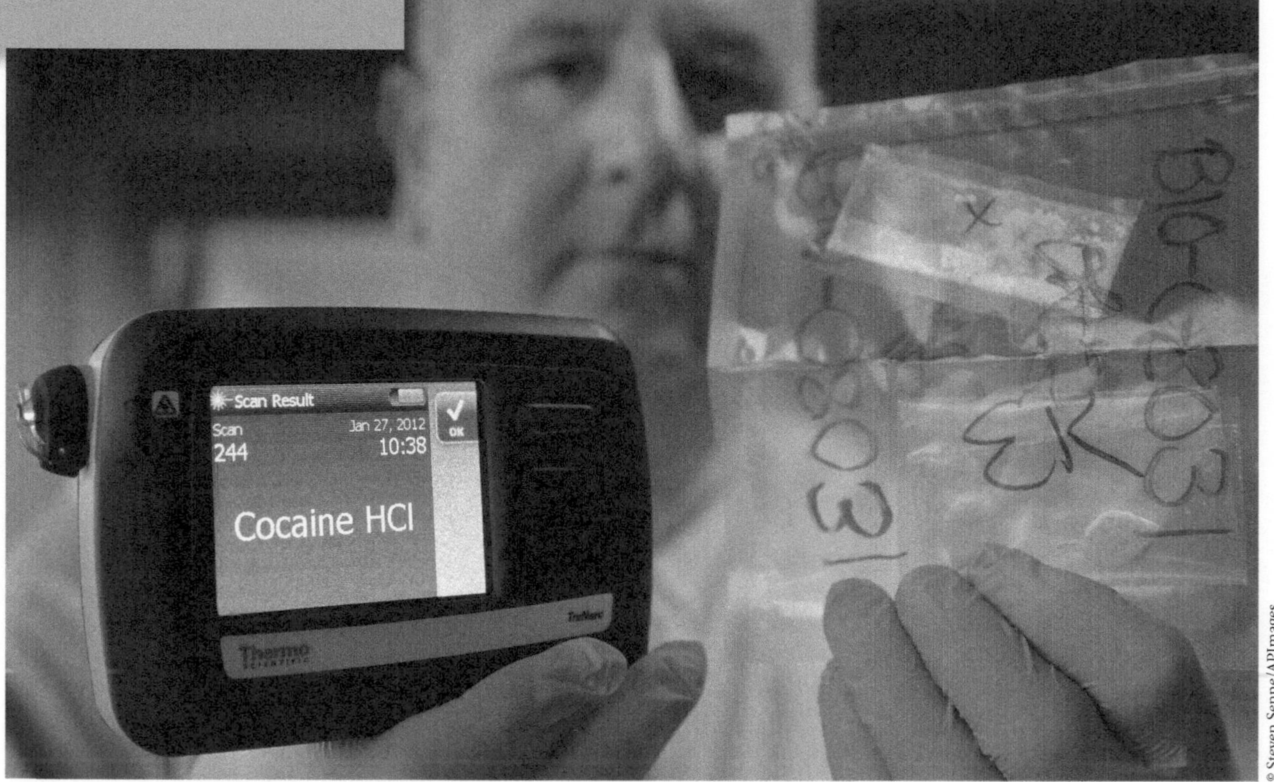

© Steven Senne/APImages

At the turn of the century, the year 2000, the mystique of the police detective was all but a thing of the past. The halcyon days of a detective as an incredible super sleuth appeared to be over. For better or for worse, uniformed patrol officers were at the center of policing. No one in Washington, D.C., talked of putting more detectives on the street. When a police officer was invited to sit in the gallery next to the first lady during a state of the union address, it was a beat officer, not a detective. The *Dragnet* TV series (the original ran from 1951 to 1959—"The story you are about to hear is true; only the names have been changed to protect the innocent," and perhaps even more remembered, "Just the facts, ma'am") is as antiquated to today's generation as its contemporary, *I Love Lucy.* In the early 2000s, network TV's programming chronicled the excitement of high-action uniformed patrol. Even the detective novel, for decades a mainstay of light fiction, had all but disappeared.

KEY TERMS

Clearance by arrest
Clearance by exception
DNA
Investigative caseload
Prosecutor acceptance rates

LEARNING OBJECTIVES

After completing this chapter, you should be able to:

- Contrast the evolving status of detectives among the general public to that within the policing profession.
- Explain why the true role of detectives varies substantially from the glamorized version.
- Explain why targeting known repeat offenders has seldom been successful.
- Identify six varying styles of investigation.
- Explain why measuring the productivity of investigators is problematic.
- Explain why the "real" work of detectives should be recognized for what it is.
- Characterize the state of research intended to guide deployment of investigative resources.
- Describe how technology is playing a larger role in investigations.

The effects of several nationally prominent crimes upon the image of detectives had been devastating. The O. J. Simpson case tarnished the image of investigators everywhere, fairly or unfairly. The JonBenét Ramsey case was ceaselessly the basis for late-night comedian jokes about the competence of the Boulder Police Department. Those within the profession know that the characterizations derived from both of those cases are grossly unfair and even blatantly false. But the cases indeed formed public perception in the 1990s and into the early 2000s regarding the competence of police detectives.

But times have changed yet again. **DNA** has resurrected the mystic of detective work. Television programming is now saturated with *CSI* (*Crime Scene Investigation*) and its copycats. At some time slots, all mainstream networks (ABC, CBS, NBC) concurrently broadcast mythical "forensic investigators" solving the most difficult of crimes, and all within an hour. The effect of the forensic investigation craze is indeed so strong that prosecutors report juries being swayed by the lack of incriminating physical evidence even in cases where there was no possibility of such evidence existing.

DNA
Abbreviation for deoxyribonucleic acid, the core of a cell that encodes functional instructions for the living organism. DNA fingerprinting is the process of identifying the unique combination of molecules in every person's genetic makeup.

Expectations Within the Profession

Learning Objective

There is an element of irony in the turnaround in public perception, because even within the profession of law enforcement itself, the status of investigations has been waning for three decades. While the diminution has leveled off, there will be no return to the mystic imagery. The trend nationally is toward an investigative role as an assignment, not a promotable rank. The phenomenon can be visualized as a continuum, starting on the left as merely an assignment phasing to a permanent, "promotable" rank on the right. See Figure 11.1. Investigations have increasingly become decentralized in major agencies, with investigators reporting to a patrol commander, not a separate investigative hierarchy. This phenomenon can likewise be visualized as a continuum, starting on the left with investigations fully integrated into patrol units, phasing as we shift right to a separate investigative hierarchy with investigative lieutenants, captains, and so forth. See Figure 11.2. The trend is clearly movement to the left side of the continuum. The CSI craze has not reversed this trend.

Patrol is indeed "first" in many agencies, with investigators assigned to neighborhood patrol districts, and even drawing patrol shifts. Police chiefs are now typically wearing a uniform instead of a suit. Both Compstat and community policing focus upon crime repression and/or prevention, not follow-up solution. At the core of the debate regarding the value of investigators to the mission of crime control is our inability to reliably measure detective productivity.

The Productivity Issue

The opening salvo on the status of investigations was the RAND Criminal Investigation Study (Greenwood & Petersilia, 1975; Greenwood, Petersilia, & Chaiken, 1977). The study sought to determine if differences in training, staffing, workload, or procedures had an effect on arrest or clearance rates. The research was a form of natural variation analysis, not an experimental design.

FIGURE 11.1 Investigative Staffing Issues Continuum of Position Prestige

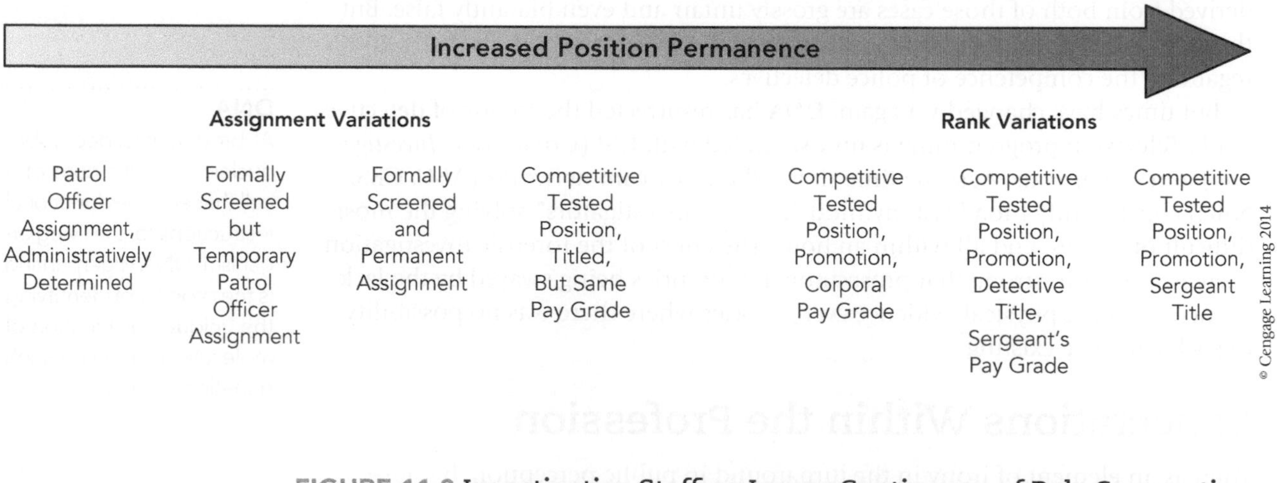

FIGURE 11.2 Investigative Staffing Issues Continuum of Role Segregation

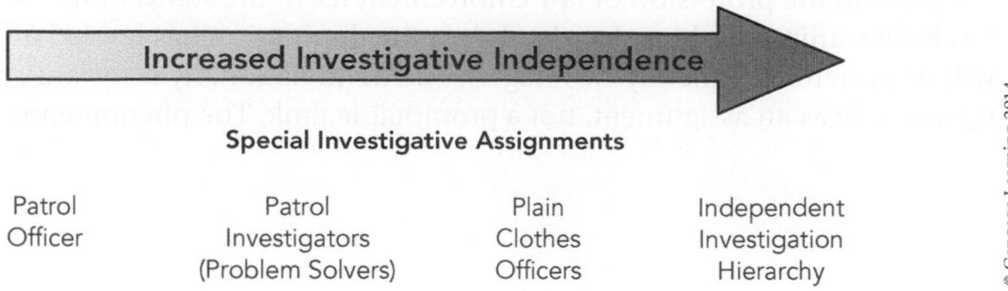

The finding that received all the attention was that rather than the embodiment of Sherlock Holmes, detectives were "glorified clerks for the district attorney." The researchers could find no linkage between investigative effort and clearance rates. Subsequent analysis and several evaluative settings have by and large confirmed the RAND results—there is no clear relationship between investigative staffing or technique and clearance rates. The question that is then raised is, "How can investigative productivity be measured?"

At the core of the productivity issue is the difficulty of isolating "productive" investigative effort versus "nonproductive" investigative effort. The reality is that there is a lot of mundane, routine, unglamorous work involved in investigations. Super sleuthing is indeed rare. Instead, enormous amounts of time are spent (1) just finding someone, (2) preparing a file for the prosecutor, (3) waiting in court, (4) driving from point A to point B, (5) telephoning victims, and, last but not least, (6) filing meaningless supplemental reports. Police agency efforts to engender better public relations by keeping victims informed of progress on a case have only compounded the problem. The reality is that the vast majority of cases in an investigator's caseload in a given month have seen no progress. Investigators who are assigned offenses that have already occurred (reactive investigators) spend a substantial majority of their time on activities that cannot be tangibly and directly linked to solving a crime.

Learning Objective

To the extent that the efforts of reactive investigators are difficult to link directly to crime solution, proactive components, such as drug, vice, and gang units, are even more notorious for failing to document the linkage between effort and outcome. Narcotics units spend months getting ready to make "the big bust." But the big bust never seems to come. Gang units spend an enormous amount of time gathering information about who is associated with whom, what the gang colors are, and what the gang signs are, all without any tangible linkage to solving a particular offense. Intelligence units are notorious, of course, for keeping all the intelligence to themselves. The impact of preventive regulatory functions cannot be quantified; it is difficult to point to the direct impact of a detective in an auto-theft unit spending time on salvage yard inspections.

As an innovative form of proactive investigations, repeat-offender units were the rage in the early 1990s, but have now all but disappeared. Agencies universally point to a lack of arrest productivity as the reason. As discussed in Chapter 8, targeting known repeat offenders appears intrinsically to make sense. However, the creation of specialized investigative units to target such offenders was universally unsuccessful. In most jurisdictions repeat offender units evolved to warrant apprehension units. Other units simply focused their attention on enhancing prosecution efforts for repeat offenders. There were several specific problems: screening criteria to identify target offenders were problematic; the per-arrest cost was extremely high; offenders identified by repeat offender units were generally already known by relevant specialized units (burglary, auto theft, robbery, narcotics)—thus it was more cost-effective for these units to link the offender to an existing open case; and, finally, diversion of resources was inevitable—to major case investigations, warrants, or narcotics.

Learning Objective

Detective work varies substantially in nature and hence activity. There are six identified styles of investigation.[1] First is reinforcing patrol—a citizen complains, patrol initially responds, and then an investigator is subsequently assigned to the matter. Domestic assaults are an illustration. Second is standard

Learning Objective

reactive—robbery and burglary are illustrations. These cases require some level of response, but follow-up is a little or a lot depending upon the particular case. Third are major cases—homicides and unknown-assailant sexual assaults are illustrations. All such incidents are investigated to the exhaustion of viable leads. Fourth are regulatory inspections—pawn shop and auto salvage yard inspections fall under this category. The activity is as much crime prevention as it is crime solution. Fifth is passive notation—routine stolen property reports and bad-check cases are illustrations. There is only very selective investigative effort extended in such cases. Sixth is discovery enforcement—proactive investigations where covert officers detect occurrence of crime and identify suspects. Narcotics units are the most frequently employed. Productivity measurement varies depending upon the "style" of investigative effort.

Beyond these inherent problems that are embedded in the very role that investigators are expected to play is the fact that in many agencies investigations is indeed a "place to hide." Our inability to effectively measure productivity makes it easy for someone who is seeking to ride out a few years until retirement to "slide to retirement" in these roles. Although this cannot be documented, the observations of many in the police profession are that agencies do indeed develop a tolerance for this pattern. It gets the older cops off the street, away from the stress, and rewards them for their years of loyal service. The practice of using the detective role as a slide into retirement may not be widespread, but it is prevalent enough to create cynicism about detective productivity.

clearance by arrest
Categorizing an offense as solved, with the perpetrator arrested specifically for the particular case in question.

PRODUCTIVITY MEASUREMENT OPTIONS

Learning Objective

clearance by exception
Categorizing an offense as resolved (not necessarily solved). Most frequently cases are cleared by exception because a suspect admits to committing the offense while being debriefed in the course of arrest for a different offense. The category also includes cases that are determined to be unfounded (although reported as such, an offense did not actually occur) and cases where an offender cannot be arrested because he or she has subsequently died.

Clearance rates are, of course, the primary means by which investigator productivity is measured. However, clearance rates are imbued with measurement difficulty. First of all, there are two basic types of clearance—**clearance by arrest** and **clearance by exception**. Although the clearance-by-arrest statistic is clearly preferable, it is widely accepted that clearance by exception counts as well. Making a bust that clears one burglary is not equivalent to making a bust that clears one hundred. The clearance-by-exception statistic is an important overlay to clearance by arrest as a proxy measure of the importance of the arrest. It is a way to sort an arrest of a sixteen-year-old stealing his first car for a joy ride from the arrest of members of a professional auto-theft ring stealing hundreds of cars a year. Unfounded cases also fall into this category, and it is certainly good detective work to ascertain that a crime indeed did not occur. That having been said, clearance by exception is the epitome of fuzzy math. The criteria for clearing a case by exception vary by jurisdiction, by investigative unit within a jurisdiction, and by individual investigators. The highest standards for clearance by exception requires some tangible independent evidence that an offender arrested for one offense indeed committed the other offenses that are being cleared by exception. At the other extreme are situations where an apprehended burglar at 2:00 a.m. is in the precinct station nodding "Yes I did it" to every address that is read to him.

Beyond definition issues, clearance varies enormously according to circumstance. It varies by the type of case—for example, domestic violence cases are virtually always cleared while theft of wheel covers is almost never cleared. Clearance varies by the type and size of jurisdiction. Crimes are more difficult to clear in large urban areas than they are in small towns where the list of "usual suspects" is reasonably short. Finally, clearance rates vary by the standards of proof required by agency custom and tradition. The issue was mentioned earlier with regard to standards for clearance by exception, but applies to clearance by arrest as well.

Given the problem with using clearance rates as a productivity measure, it is often suggested that **prosecutor acceptance rates** be used instead. But this statistic has its own set of shortcomings. First, it obviously varies by county. The standards for acceptance employed by one prosecutor's office may be dramatically different than the standards employed by another. This makes interjurisdictional comparison of the relative efficacy of investigations impossible. Second, even within the same county district attorney acceptance rates will vary over time. Changes in the personnel in the office or changes in the political climate will cause the rates to change. Rates can even vary by the individual assistant prosecutor reviewing the case. Shopping for a friendly assistant district attorney is common practice, and testimony to the phenomenon. Thus, various value sets, prosecutor workload, pressure from courts, reaction to the defense bar, reaction of political opponents, and the amount of pressure to win a high percentage of cases cause this statistic to fluctuate widely.

prosecutor acceptance rates
The proportion of all arrests by a police agency for which the accused perpetrator is actually charged by a prosecuting attorney.

INAPPROPRIATE EXPECTATIONS

Learning Objective

It is not merely the public that struggles with the detective mystique. Within the profession of policing there is as much reluctance to accept the fact that the real role of detectives does not mimic that of Sherlock Holmes, and it is thus inappropriate to use cold case clearance as a measure of investigative productivity. The characterization of detectives as "glorified clerks for the district attorney" is unfair. Investigation is more than simple clerking. Granted, there is a great deal of mundane work embedded in criminal investigations. But it is not all mundane. Moving a case from a standard of proof of *probable cause* to *beyond reasonable doubt*—that is, preparing a case with a known offender for court presentation—is a sophisticated and respected role. This investigative function comes much closer to representing "real detective work" than cold case clearance. Sanders (1977) argued that detective work is best analyzed as a craft. Like a craft, there is a body of knowledge that is difficult to transmit in a classroom setting, a long apprenticeship is necessary to become proficient, and intangible personality attributes have as much to do with success as any acquired body of knowledge. And like the definition of quality craftsmanship, most police managers have difficulty defining good detective work, but know it when they see it.

Difficulty in defining productivity is compounded even further by the deterrence argument. It may be true that follow-up investigation on unknown-suspect cases seldom results in an arrest. But the deterrent effect of an occasional arrest may be substantial. Offenders communicate with one another. A single case where an offender was tracked down by super-sleuth detectives removes the aura of invincibility from burglars, auto thieves, and armed robbers. We cannot, of course, quantify that effect. But it is perfectly legitimate to argue that the time invested in twenty cases for follow-up may be worthwhile if even one results in an arrest.

CASELOAD ISSUES

The difficulty in ascertaining productivity creates serious problems in ascertaining what an appropriate **investigative caseload** might be. There is enormous variation in the time dedicated per case by the type of offense. In many

investigative caseload
The number of individual cases assigned to a given detective (or occasionally an investigative unit). The most common accepted way to express caseload is in "new cases assigned per month." Typically that number is about thirty per month for investigators assigned crimes against persons, and thirty-five per month for property crime.

jurisdictions, for example, the domestic violence caseload is four times the standard crimes-against-person caseload. For a domestic violence incident, the offender's identity is always known, and case preparation seldom involves physical evidence—consisting almost entirely of statements from victims (with the exception of an occasional photograph of victim bruises).

Caseload within even a given offense category might vary by the impact of the specific subcategory of offending behavior upon victims. We are not as likely to pursue vigorously bad-check cases against grocery stores that are sloppy about verifying the validity of the check as we are against check writers who victimize individual people. There is additional variation depending upon the political import of an offense. Political import in this context is not necessarily used with a negative connotation but rather refers to the relative social impact of certain offending behaviors. A computer virus, for example, may not be inherently an offense that strikes us as heinous. However, the enormous impact upon society is such that vigorous pursuit in prosecution of those who plant viruses is called for. Finally, caseload might vary legitimately by the probability of a successful solution for a type of case. Solution of thefts from automobile cases has such a low probability of occurring that, almost universally, reactive investigation of such offenses does not exist. Caseload in this instance consists of report filing, primarily for insurance purposes. If the offense is to be addressed, it will be by proactive efforts, usually focused upon the secondary parts market.

In John Eck's work *Solving Crimes: The Investigation of Burglary and Robbery* (1983), he observed that quantification of the probability of solvability was nearly impossible. He suggested instead that cases be triaged into: (1) those cases that cannot be solved with a reasonable amount of effort; (2) those cases that have already been solved by circumstance, and only require the suspect to be apprehended; and, (3) those cases that with a reasonable amount of effort might be solved, but certainly will not be solved without such effort. It is, of course, the last category that we typically think of as "real detective work." No one has made any effort to firmly calculate the percentage of cases that fall into the third category, but it is certainly safe to say that it is very low—no more than 5 percent. Managing caseloads under this model consists of dedicating some time to screening out the cases in the first category (those that cannot be solved), dedicating a fair amount of time to preparing solved cases for court (the second category), while saving as much time as possible to be dedicated to the 5 percent of cases where some effort might make a difference in clearance.

Learning Objective

Little carefully structured research exists on average time spent investigating offenses. Brandl and Frank (1994) compiled data on mean time spent in hours on burglary and robbery investigations, sorted by strength of suspect information—categorized as weak, moderate, or strong. Their findings with suspect leads but no on-scene arrests are summarized in Table 11.1. There is surprisingly little variation in the hours spent—given that burglary is a property offense and robbery a violent crime. The implication is that the time to process a case does not correlate strongly with the seriousness of the offense—with the likely exception of homicide.

Interestingly, more time was spent on cases with moderate suspect information than those with weak or strong. This is consistent with the hypothesis that detectives use discretionary judgment to concentrate on cases that with more effort can be solved.

TABLE 11.1 Time Spent by Case Characteristics

Suspect Leads:	Weak	Moderate	Strong
Burglary	3.01	3.87	2.56
Robbery	3.32	4.63	3.40

Data Source: Brandl, S. G., & Frank, J. (1994). The relationship between evidence, detective effort, and the disposition of burglary and robbery investigations. *American Journal of Police, XIII*(3), 149–168, Tables Two and Three.

Efforts to guide decision making in this respect through "solvability models" have not worked. The Stanford Research Institute follow-up investigative decision model postulated decades ago (Greenberg, Yu, & Lang, 1972) is not employed anywhere. Agencies that attempted to employ a quantifiable follow-up model found that it failed miserably to sort "important" cases from "unimportant" cases. Use of the decision models resulted in all follow-up effort being dedicated to cases where the victim knew the offender. Although some cases of this nature certainly merit investigative effort (e.g., domestic violence), no investigative follow-up decision model should "screen out" all cases involving stranger-to-stranger armed robbery—which the models in effect did (this was not the intent, but nevertheless the result, as solvability is largely determined by the ability to immediately identify the perpetrator).

MEASURING PRODUCTIVITY—THE RESULT

Our inability to effectively measure outcome or even to establish reasonable workload parameters results in a focus on process rather than result. That is, the tendency is to substitute measurement of means for measurement of ends. Hence we assess investigator productivity by whether supplements are filed on time, the quality of writing in reports, whether victims are called back, the case filing rate—regardless of the quality of cases—and ultimately whether the investigator appears to stay busy. Horvath and Meesig (2002) found that the most commonly reported criteria for assessing investigator performance were, in rank order, success in a major investigation, report writing, clearance statistics, periodic caseload review, caseload statistics, and generic supervisor evaluation (p. 53). Achieving success on a major investigation may or may not be linked to either investigative effort or acumen. Luck certainly plays a role in any "one-time-shot" success criterion. The problems with employing clearance as a measure were discussed earlier. It is not that some of these measures are not legitimate, but ultimately they are not sufficient. They provide us no real insight into how time should best be spent by investigators.

Research on Investigative Effectiveness

In a typical municipal police department, 60 percent of personnel are assigned to patrol, 20 percent to investigative units, 15 percent to support services (traffic, records, custodial, planning and research), and 5 percent to administration. Although from one perspective there is little research on the effectiveness of various patrol strategies, compared with research on the effectiveness of investigations, the catalog of patrol research reports looks like the Library of Congress.

There is almost no research on the relative efficacy of the strategies used by 20 percent of the personnel in a typical urban police agency.

Like the patrol function, the criminal investigations function suffers from an early macro-analysis with overgeneralized results. As noted earlier, in 1975 the RAND Corporation study tried to ascertain if any broad approaches to criminal investigation worked better than others by analyzing approaches used in major urban police departments (Greenwood & Petersilia, 1975). A written questionnaire was sent to 300 agencies employing more than 150 personnel, inquiring about investigative training, staffing, workload, and procedures. RAND received 153 responses. Researchers then made site visits to twenty-five of the responding agencies to gather more detailed information.

RAND concluded that the investigative divisions' organization and staffing could not be significantly related to variations in arrest or clearance rates, as reported by participating police departments to the Federal Bureau of Investigation (FBI) for compilation in its *Uniform Crime Reports*. The ancillary conclusions the researchers drew were as important as the primary one. They noted that (1) 65 percent of all serious crimes received no more than superficial attention from investigators; (2) the single most important factor in whether a case will be solved is the information the victim supplies to the responding patrol officer; (3) in cases that are solved, the investigator spends more time on post-clearance processing than on identifying the perpetrator; and (4) of cases ultimately cleared in which a perpetrator was not identified during the initial police incident-reporting processes, almost all were solved as a result of "routine police procedures" (fingerprinting, obtaining tips from informants, etc.). For those inclined to believe that the police are by and large ineffective, the RAND report reinforced their view. While the preventive patrol experiment "demonstrated" that uniformed officers make no difference, the RAND study similarly "demonstrated" that plainclothes officers are equally useless.

The RAND study is a classic example of exploratory research inappropriately being used as the definitive answer. It was, first of all, the first real research ever conducted on the investigative function. Although the RAND researchers had done precursory work in New York City and Kansas City, the national survey was the first effort at using a quasi-experimental design (Eck, 1996). There were shortcomings in identifying independent and dependent variables. The researchers simply looked for naturally occurring variation in investigative structure and workload, then compared what variation might exist with a *very questionable* dependent variable—agency reports on arrest and clearance rates. As noted, both rates are subject to definitional ambiguity and manipulation. One would expect that a poorly run investigative unit would tend to inflate the numbers, whereas a well-run unit would be far more conservative in reporting arrests and clearances. To the extent that better-run investigative units would use more effective strategies, the use of conservative criteria for reporting arrest and clearance rates would conceal the efficacy of those efforts in any comparative analysis.

It is not that the RAND study was inherently flawed. Rather, we should not expect dramatic results from this type of research approach. At best, tentative conclusions might be reached—for example, specialization in investigations appears to, or does not appear to, result in higher clearance rates for the specific crimes. It is grossly inappropriate to assert that investigative units are useless.

Further, the study overdoes the issue of investigators as "clerks for the district attorney." As noted earlier, moving a case from a standard of probable cause to a standard of proof beyond a reasonable doubt is not a trivial task, and it certainly should not be characterized as the work of a clerk. Moreover, the fact that relatively few offenders are identified from super-sleuth techniques does not negate the importance of skilled investigative follow-up. Again, the deterrent effect of such an approach may be enormous.

The point is that police efforts must be analyzed in terms of focus. If all investigative follow-up is aggregated, it is impossible to tease out effective strategies. However, when we sort cases, a different picture emerges. In particular, when we rule out the majority of cases for which investigative follow-up is largely a waste of time, then analyze only the very small subset for which it is potentially fruitful, a *very different* picture emerges. Detectives do make a difference, indeed a dramatic difference, with regard to those cases. Given the fact that very few offenders commit only one crime, it is easy to understand why, if a detective makes a difference in only 5 percent of the cases, that 5 percent may be critical. An offender committing only one crime every three weeks, will, on average, be caught annually. A single "cleared by arrest" by a skilled investigator can prevent scores of crimes over a few years.

The Immediate Future: DNA and Surveillance Cameras

Learning Objective

The fantasy of the CSI television craze notwithstanding, DNA—and forensic evidence more generally—holds enormous potential. The first criminal conviction based on DNA evidence occurred in Florida in 1987, and in 1990, the FBI launched its Combined DNA Index System (CODIS) (Griswold & Murphy, 2010). There are two obstacles to substantially broadened use of DNA. First, laboratory facilities need to be expanded. The joint problems of backlog and expense for obtaining DNA analysis are amendable to political solution; there are no significant technological issues to resolve. Second, the value of DNA evidence is increased several fold if there is a prior-offender DNA database for comparative matching. There has been opposition to establishing DNA databases premised upon highly speculative misuse scenarios, such as use of DNA data by insurance companies in determining eligibility and rates for coverage. DNA "markers" indeed can indicate propensity for a number of diseases. Rather than limit the cataloging of arrestee DNA, we should impose restrictions and penalties—just as is done with computerized criminal histories or juvenile records. DNA evidence is important not only in the identification and prosecution of criminal offenders, but also in ruling out innocent persons and in some cases exonerating persons who have been falsely convicted (Griswold & Murphy, 2010). We have been taking the fingerprints of all arrestees for over a hundred years, and abuse has yet to occur. It is ironic that we roll a set of fingerprints for arrestees when we would have better tracing evidence just by swabbing their fingertips.

Less recognized is the expanding investigative utility of surveillance cameras. Chicago's extensive use of surveillance—both the police department's and that made available by the private sector—has already been mentioned. Cameras are now being deployed even in smaller agencies. Camera footage related to several recent homicides has found its way into the national news media. Rather than canvass for witnesses, in serious cases detectives now canvass for cameras. At times the actual offense is caught on tape. More often the camera images are broadcast with a "Does anyone recognize this person?" message. Once a suspect is identified, DNA can seal the case.

IMPLICATIONS FOR STRATEGY

The resurrection of Sherlock Holmes is in progress. The unexpected investigative techniques and clever logic of the super-sleuth may be missing, but the outcome is the same. The perfect crime is becoming increasingly difficult to commit—at least in public places with surveillance cameras, and/or requiring the offender to leave no DNA behind at the scene. And aerial drones that hover above, watching everything, are already deployed by a few American police agencies—fresh from remote Afghanistan, where the drones are even armed.

SUMMARY

- From 1970 to the year 2000 the status of detectives steadily declined among both the public and within the profession. Community policing focused upon the role of patrol, problem-oriented policing seldom involved investigative units, and Compstat was oriented toward enforcement by uniformed personnel. However, the CSI craze on television has swung the pendulum back once again among the public. Indeed the pendulum may have swung too far back, creating unrealistic expectations among citizens of the ability or resources of the investigative process.

  Likewise, within the profession the status of detectives had been steadily decreasing. But in the case of the policing profession, television programming did not reverse that trend. The trend has been and continues to be toward investigations as an assignment, not a rank. Decentralized investigators usually report to a patrol commander. A recent phenomenon is to have detectives draw periodic patrol shifts, ostensibly to keep them touch with the field.
- Indeed, the role of a detective does not reflect the glamor of media portrayals. There is a great deal of routine, tedious work: pursuing bad-check cases and gambling debt thefts, finding a suspect or witness, preparing a file for the district attorney, waiting in court, driving from point A to point B, telephoning victims, and, last but not least, filing meaningless supplements. Although the RAND criminal investigation study characterization of detectives as "not the embodiment of Sherlock Holmes, but glorified clerks for the district attorney," was unfair, nevertheless the report brought recognition that the majority of investigative effort is case preparation for court, not identification of otherwise unknown offenders.
- As discussed in Chapter 8, targeting known repeat offenders appears intrinsically to make sense. Efforts to do so by the establishment of repeat offender units proliferated in the 1990s. They were universally unsuccessful. In most jurisdictions repeat offender units evolved to warrant apprehension units. Other units simply focused their attention on enhancing prosecution efforts for repeat offenders. There were several specific problems: screening criteria to identify target offenders were problematic; the per-arrest cost was extremely high; offenders identified by repeat offender units were generally already known by relevant specialized units (burglary, auto theft, robbery, narcotics)—thus it was more cost-effective for these units to link the offender to an existing open case; and, finally, diversion of resources was inevitable—to major case investigation, warrants, or narcotics.
- Detective work varies substantially in nature and hence activity. There are six identified styles of investigation. First is reinforcing patrol—a citizen complains, patrol initially responds, and then an investigator is

subsequently assigned to the matter. Second is standard reactive—robbery and burglary are illustrations. These cases require some level of response, but follow-up is a little or a lot depending upon the particular case. Third are major cases—homicides and unknown-assailant sexual assaults are illustrations. All such incidents are investigated to the exhaustion of viable leads. Fourth are regulatory inspections—pawn shop and auto salvage yard inspections fall under this category. The activity is as much crime prevention as it is crime solution. Fifth is passive notation—routine stolen property reports and bad-check cases are illustrations. Sixth is discovery enforcement—proactive investigations where covert officers detect occurrence of crime and identify suspects. Narcotics units are the most frequently employed.

- Measuring productivity of investigators is problematic. The most frequently suggested measure is clearance rates. However, clearance rates vary by type of case, type and size of jurisdiction, and by the standards employed for clearance by exception (admissions by a suspect). Moreover, clearance does not equal conviction. Prosecutor (district attorney) acceptance rates are frequently suggested as alternative. However, these are also problematic—they vary by county, over time, and by the assistant district attorney reviewing the case, and are the product of various constituencies and value sets—the prosecutors, the courts, the reaction of the defense bar, the reaction of the district attorney's political opponents, and related pressure to win a high percentage of cases actually prosecuted.
- Detective work should be recognized for what it is. Indeed, even the mundane role of making victims feel better may be a laudable goal in its own right. Even if only one in twenty unknown suspect cases is resolved by proactive investigation, this may have a significant deterrent effect. Further, careful preparation for court of known-suspect cases is a laudable goal in its own right. Moving a case from a standard of probable cause to proof beyond reasonable doubt is not the role of a glorified clerk, but a skilled professional.
- There is little research to guide deployment of investigative resources. John Eck's study of robbery and burglary resulted only in a nonquantitative model for efficacy of follow-up investigation—the triage typology: those cases that cannot be solved with a reasonable amount of effort; those cases that have already been resolved by circumstance; and those cases that with a reasonable amount of effort may be solved, but certainly will not be solved without investigative effort. The last category includes fewer than 5 percent of all criminal events. The issue is that reliable identification of which cases fall into that 5 percent is problematic. Efforts to construct quantified solvability indices have been unsuccessful. A limitation is that useful suspect information is typically associated with a preexisting relationship between the victim and suspect. Thus, using solvability indices results in the crimes receiving attention being those between acquaintances, not the more feared stranger-to-stranger offenses.
- The exaggerated ability of crime scene analysis depicted on television aside, technology is indeed playing a larger role in investigations. However, technology demands sophisticated specialists. Cybercrime, identity theft in particular, is the most obvious example. Other illustrations include international and transnational crime, use of networked information sources, crime scene technicians, and skilled forensic scientists.

REVIEW QUESTIONS

1. It is suggested that the CSI television craze creates unrealistic expectations of investigative proficiency among members of the general public. Under what circumstances might these unrealistic expectations be harmful? What can be done to mitigate the effect of unrealistic expectations?
2. The RAND Criminal Investigation Study characterized detectives as glorified clerks for the district attorney rather than super-sleuths in the image of Sherlock Holmes. What is the basis for the RAND assertion? Why is the characterization unfair?
3. What are the six "styles" of investigation? Include an illustrative offense for each of the six.
4. Why are clearance rates an inadequate and/or inappropriate measure of investigator productivity?

5. John Eck suggests that offenses can be characterized by a triage typology: those cases that cannot be solved with a reasonable amount of effort, those cases that have already been solved by circumstance, and those cases that with a reasonable amount of detective effort may be solved, but certainly will not be solved without such effort. Briefly describe the circumstances of offenses that would fall into each of the three categories.

REAL-WORLD SCENARIOS

1. Clearance rates are reported to the FBI's *Uniform Crime Reports* in two broad categories—clearance by arrest and clearance by exception. Clearance by exception includes a range of circumstance, but consists primarily of admissions by offenders arrested for one offense to other crimes. As the detective commander, you have noted that the clearance-by-admission rates reported by your investigative units vary enormously. The greatest variation exists for the crime of burglary. Construct guidelines for the detectives in your agency that stipulate what evidence or knowledge concerning an offender of a particular burglarized location is necessary before the burglary may be cleared by admission.
2. You are the newly appointed commander of a five-person criminal intelligence unit in a major municipal department. The unit has been criticized by operational divisions for keeping all the intelligence to itself. The chief of police has instructed you to assure that intelligence reaches individuals who can translate the information to action. Drawing upon the literature base, describe how agencies have been successful in achieving this objective.
3. Solvability indices have been designed to screen cases for follow-up investigation, sorting those that with virtual certainty cannot be solved from those that might be solved with some reasonable level of detective effort. Universally, however, agencies have found it necessary to have a human being review the "computer sort," partially to assure that cases that offend public sensibility receive attention, whether it is likely they will be solved or not. A recent example is the theft of a money envelope from a group of Girl Scouts selling cookies at a grocery store entrance. One of the leaders who attempted to retrieve the envelope was assaulted by the offenders. The incident made national news. Although the case may have been thoroughly investigated anyway, given the public outrage, the investigating agency "pulled out all the stops" (and made an apprehension, using surveillance camera footage of the suspects). Identify at least three victim characteristics that would engender a similar reaction to the Girl Scout robbery. Construct a hypothetical victimization scenario for each that would likely lead to a public outcry for police action.

APPLICATION ACTIVITIES

1. Use the Internet to find information on the JonBenét Ramsey homicide, which occurred in Boulder, Colorado, in 1996. Wikipedia® has an excellent synopsis. From the review of several descriptive sources, discuss why this case was so problematic for the Boulder Police Department. Include discussion of the challenge of conducting an investigation in the glare of national/international media 24-hour coverage.
2. Numerous police agencies have created specialized units to handle domestic violence cases. Explain why a specialized unit is generally thought necessary. Describe the role of such units, particularly as that role transcends normal investigative response.
3. Although every arrestee of an American police department is routinely fingerprinted, statutes in many states limit concurrent gathering of a DNA swab. Contrast the arguments on both sides of the issue: one position arguing that a DNA sample should be taken from every arrestee, and the opposing position arguing that, if used at all, DNA sampling should be limited to arrestees for violent offenses.

COURSEMATE

This available CourseMate has an interactive eBook and interactive learning tools, including flash cards, quizzes, and more. To learn more about this resource and access free demo CourseMate resources, go to **www.cengagebrain.com,** and search for this book. To access CourseMate materials that you have purchased, go to **login.cengagebrain.com.**

ENDNOTES

1. A staffing analysis of investigative functions completed by Professor Jerry L. Dowling of Sam Houston State University. Unpublished.

REFERENCES

Brandl, S. G., & Frank, J. (1994). The relationship between evidence, detective effort, and the disposition of burglary and robbery investigations. *American Journal of Police, XIII*(3), 149–168.

Eck, J. E. (1983). *Solving crimes: The investigation of burglary and robbery*. Washington, DC: Police Executive Research Forum.

Eck, J. E. (1996). Rethinking detective management. In L. T. Hoover (Ed.), *Quantifying quality in policing*. Washington, DC. Police Executive Research Forum.

Greenberg, B., Yu, O., & Lang, K. (1972). *Enhancement of the investigative function: Volume 1—Analysis and conclusions.* Springfield, VA: National Technical Information Service.

Greenwood, P., & Petersilia, J. (1975). *The criminal investigation process—Volume I: Summary and policy implications*. Santa Monica, CA: RAND Corp.

Greenwood, P., Petersilia, J., & Chaiken, J. (1977). *The criminal investigation process*. Lexington, MA: D. C. Heath.

Griswold, M. E., & Murphy, G. R. (2010). *It's more complex than you think: A chief's guide to DNA*. Washington, DC: Police Executive Research Forum.

Horvath, F., & Meesig, R. T. (2002). *A national survey of police policies and practices regarding the criminal investigation process: Twenty-five years after RAND*. East Lansing, MI: Michigan State University, School of Criminal Justice.

Sanders, W. B. (1977). *Detective work: A study of criminal investigations*. New York: Free Press.

CHAPTER 12

Staffing for Crime Control

© Boston Globe via Getty Images

Learning Objective

Organizations such as the Police Executive Research Forum and the International Association of Chiefs of Police routinely receive inquiries that are a variant of "How many police officers do we need?" There is no "right" answer to the question. How many police officers are needed depends upon what level of police service is desired. There are no fixed standards in this respect. Some communities want a priority-one response time of four minutes; some are willing to tolerate seven or eight. It takes considerably more officers to provide a four-minute response than it does to provide an eight-minute response. Some communities want four hours per shift of proactive patrol; some are willing to get by on two. Some communities want extensive traffic law enforcement; some do not. Some communities want high patrol visibility in residential neighborhoods; for others, one drive through a neighborhood every two weeks is plenty. There is no "rule" requiring that at least one patrol unit always be available in a jurisdiction for a true 911 emergency, but most jurisdictions want there to be at least one unit free all, or nearly all, of the time. Other communities enjoy readily available back-up for true emergencies, such as contiguous jurisdictions or a university campus police department within the jurisdiction, and can therefore staff at lower levels. If citizens insist on follow-up investigation for every burglary, viable leads or not, more officers will be

KEY TERMS

D.A.R.E.®
Dynamic system
Global positioning system (GPS)
Police-to-citizen ratios

LEARNING OBJECTIVES

After completing this chapter, you should be able to:

- Identify the right answer to the question, "How many police officers are needed?"
- Describe the limitations of computer simulation staffing models.
- Identify the jurisdictional variables in a patrol simulation staffing model.
- Identify the policy variables in a patrol simulation staffing model.
- Characterize the "state of the art" in investigative simulation staffing models.
- Describe three different approaches to estimating desirable investigative staffing.
- Describe the recommended approach to specifying quantification of investigative effort.
- Characterize the effect of global positioning system (GPS) tracking of patrol units.
- Identify the typical allocation of staffing resources among core police agency functions, and identify the typical allocation of patrol resources among core patrol functions.
- Link the concurrent development and elimination of particular specialized units to the issue of limited resources.
- List three hypothetical reasons police-to-citizen ratios vary dramatically in major municipal jurisdictions.

required than if solvability screening occurs. The answer to these questions is, in reality, the answer to the question "How many police officers do we need?"

The Value of Patrol Models

Most of us have heard a recitation of the two contrasting ways to calculate the trajectory of an artillery shell. Version one is to employ complex mathematical calculations using trigonometry and calculus to account for the weight, launch velocity, drag coefficient, and effect of gravity. The second technique is to lob a shell out, see where it lands, and adjust the artillery piece accordingly. If one's mathematical models are not too accurate, or are too time consuming, and one has lots of shells available, the latter makes sense. But for innumerable human enterprises, simply lobbing out a shell to see where it lands does not work well. It would not do as a technique in our deterrent nuclear arsenal. Although the consequences of error are not quite as dramatic as a misdirected missile, police patrol services is one of those enterprises in which just lobbing out a shell is not feasible.

Our artillery shells, patrol units, are extraordinarily expensive to field. Patrol units require enormous investment in both personnel and equipment. A jurisdiction can ill-afford to deploy one hundred units this year instead of seventy-five just to see what difference it might make. Computer models now exist that provide agencies the ability to calculate the resources necessary to deliver stipulated levels of service. Such models are designed to provide a reasonable estimate to an agency, given a particular call load, of the number of patrol units necessary to maintain particular levels of deterrent patrol, visibility, response time, and immediate availability for emergency response.

However, it must be remembered that fielding patrol units is not comparable to firing an intercontinental ballistic missile. The path followed by a missile can be calculated with enormous accuracy because one is dealing only with physical properties of the environment. Patrol units are driven by human beings, and are multifunctional. They are concurrently responding to service demand, both critical and noncritical; maintaining spatial and time distribution to assure rapid response to emergency situations; providing reassuring visibility to a community; engaging in active crime deterrent efforts; and remaining on emergency standby for truly critical situations. A computer model can accurately calculate how many patrol units are necessary to drive by a given point on any residential street once every thirty-six hours—a visibility objective. Whether those units actually drive by that point is a different issue. Clearly, different officers will have different patrol patterns, and some spots on residential roadways will be driven by more frequently than others. All that we can say is that, on average, a patrol unit will drive by any given spot every x number of hours, given the accuracy of the variables entered into the model.

Learning Objective

dynamic system
Any system that alters response based on environmental changes; in policing, refers to the fact that patrol officers alter the time they spend on certain types of calls-for-service depending on the current call queue.

A related problem in using either technique to calculate needed police resources, lobbying a shell out or a mathematical model, is the fact that policing is a **dynamic system**. A dynamic system is one that adjusts in reaction to changes in the environment. In the case of the patrol function, officers will alter their behavior depending upon call load. On a shift with a light call load they will tend to spend more time on calls, not to mention breaks and administrative duties at the police station. On shifts where calls are in queue, and particularly when critical calls are backing up, officers will adjust their behavior. With the rare exception of dysfunctional agencies, officers under such circumstances will cut short their time at the police station, take fewer breaks, and even skip a lunch break. More important, they will reduce the amount of time spent on individual calls. Arguably, the quality of service may suffer when officers make such an adjustment, but at the same time they are being responsive to the need to get to other pending volatile situations quickly. Thus, any mathematical model that is designed as a simulation of such a system will be an estimate at best. We cannot mathematically predict with precision what the response times to priority-one calls will be with a given staffing level. We can provide a reasonable estimate based on our prior experience, but in the real world human beings are constantly adjusting their behaviors and thus changing the values of the input variables "on the fly." Once again, however, it should be reiterated that a mathematical model that provides a reasonable estimate of service levels given stipulated variation in staffing levels is far superior than mere guesswork.

Patrol Staffing

The number of patrol officers needed for a jurisdiction is dependent on both jurisdictional characteristics and a series of policy decisions regarding levels of service provided. The jurisdictional characteristics include the following:

Learning Objective

- *Number of calls-for-service.* Obviously, the number of calls-for-service a department receives impacts the allocation of officers to patrol. Typically, allocation models are based on one year of call-for-service data. However, these models can also be used to determine fluctuations in the need for officers assigned to patrol based on seasonal variations in crime and calls-for-service. The numbers of calls-for-service should also take into account back-ups as well. Administrative and self-initiated activities are typically excluded from calls-for-service numbers in allocation models because these activities are taken into account through policy decisions, as discussed later in this chapter.
- *Average service time.* Average time spent on calls-for-service impacts the number of officers that need to be assigned to patrol. It is calculated based on the elapsed time from when an officer is dispatched to when an officer clears the call.
- *Number of roadway miles.* Patrol visibility is a concern for police administrators. The public wants the police to be visible in their communities and in their neighborhoods. Travel time and level of visibility of officers impacts the number of officers that need to be assigned to patrol. Agencies with a commitment to high visibility in their community will need more officers assigned to patrol than agencies with less commitment to visibility of patrol officers.
- *Average patrol speed.* In order to determine the number of officers needed to meet the visibility standards set by agency administration, the average patrol speed on arterial and residential roadways is also needed. Average patrol speed by roadway type is used to calculate the number of officers needed to meet visibility standards. Basically, the previous two variables impact allocation because how visible officers can be varies by the number of roadway miles in a jurisdiction and how fast officers typically travel on these roadways.
- *Area (square miles).* The area, in square miles, of a jurisdiction is taken into account in allocation models when determining the number of officers needed to meet the response time goals set by the department.
- *Average response speed for emergency activities.* In addition to the area, in square miles, the average response speed for emergency (priority-one) activities is taken into account in allocation models in determining the number of officers needed to meet the response-time goals set by the department. Similar to average patrol speed, the average response speed for emergency activities is frequently not available within an agency. If the average response speed for emergency activities is not available, alternate stipulated values can be used. For example, the average response speed for emergency activities in jurisdictions that have used the Patrol Allocation Model (PAM) funded by the National Highway Traffic Safety Administration is 38.13 miles per hour. This may seem low; however, it takes into account the time in which the officer must slow down at stoplights, to make turns, and to maneuver through traffic.

- *Average response speed for nonemergency activities.* In determining the number of officers needed to meet the response time goals set by police administrators, the average response speed for nonemergency (priority-two) activities is also needed. This information is typically not available within an agency either. The average response speed for nonemergency activities for other jurisdictions that have implemented PAM is 18.9 miles per hour.
- *Leave rate.* The leave rate also has a significant impact on allocation decisions. Typically, each officer is contracted to work 2,086 hours per year (40 hours per week × 52.14 weeks per year). However, an officer does not actually work the entire 2,086 hours. There are numerous instances in which officers may not actually be on patrol during the 2,086 hours they are contracted to work. In order to accurately determine the net annual work hours per officer, all instances in which an officer is not available to work on patrol must be taken into consideration, including:
  - Vacation time
  - Use of compensatory time
  - Sick leave
  - Training
  - Holidays
  - Personal days
  - Military service
  - Provisions of the Family and Medical Leave Act
  - Light-duty assignments required for injured staff
  - Time away from the job while on special assignment
  - Jury duty
  - Worker's compensation time off
  - Administrative leave

The net annual work hours can then be used to calculate the leave rate by subtracting the net annual work hours from the number of hours officers are contracted to work each year.

Learning Objective

Jurisdictional characteristics are not the only set of variables affecting the number of patrol officers required by a jurisdiction. A critical point is that staffing of patrol requires a series of policy decisions. The following are the policy variables:

- *Visibility interval.* This performance objective is used to determine the number of officers needed for patrol visibility. The performance objective is based on the answer to the question, "How often should a patrol officer pass any given point on a roadway?" Basically, if a person was to stand at a given location, how often would he or she see a patrol unit? Typically, two performance objectives are set based on different types of roadways: arterial and residential. An arterial roadway includes freeways, highways, and other major thoroughfares. It is expected that officers will be more visible on arterial roadways in comparison to residential roadways; therefore a separate performance objective is set for each type.
- *Response time objective for priority-one and priority-two calls.* If response time goals are set fairly high, then fewer officers will need to be assigned to patrol to meet this objective in comparison to when response time goals are set fairly low. As with all the policy decisions, these values can be modified as changes

in policy occur. In other words, a department may have a six-minute response time goal for priority-one calls and patrol is staffed at a level to meet this goal. If the administration decides to lower this goal to five minutes, allocation models can be used to determine the number of officers that need to be assigned to patrol to meet the new response time goal of five minutes.

- *Percentage of priority-one calls for which there will be at least one officer available.* This performance objective is based on the issue of availability. It is necessary for agencies to have officers available on patrol who can immediately respond to an emergency. Because priority-one calls are potentially life-threatening emergencies, the percentage set for this objective is typically very high, but it can range from a low of 75 percent to a high of 99 percent. Typically, 98 percent is employed.
- *Percentage of patrol activities that cannot be preempted.* When allocation models determine the number of officers needed to provide an immediate response to a priority-one call, it is assumed that there are occasions when an officer who is on another call-for-service can clear that call and respond to the priority-one call. When the officer is finished responding to the priority-one call, then the officer can return to the previous call if another officer has not already covered it. Therefore, a certain percentage of calls-for-service can be preempted if an officer is needed to respond to a priority-one call-for-service. However, it is also argued that some calls-for-service cannot or should not be preempted because of the severity of the call-for-service or because of citizen satisfaction reasons. Therefore, the percentage of calls-for-service that cannot be preempted is a policy decision and its value impacts patrol allocation. The same is true for administrative activities and self-initiated/directed patrol activities; some of these activities can be preempted so that an officer can respond to a priority-one call. The percentage of time that calls can and cannot be preempted is a policy decision that must be made by administrators.
- *Administrative time.* Administrative time also impacts patrol allocation. Allocation models take into account the administrative time an on-duty officer spends in determining the number of officers that need to be assigned to patrol. Administrative time can include meal breaks, other breaks, vehicle maintenance, court time, as well as other administrative activities. Although this is a policy decision, it is certainly influenced by department-specific data. Data can be collected on the amount of time officers spend in court, the amount of time officers are allotted per shift for meal and other breaks, and the amount of time officers spend on vehicle maintenance (e.g., putting gas in the patrol vehicle).
- *Self-initiated/directed patrol time.* Agencies that expect patrol officers to conduct numerous traffic stops, stop suspicious individuals, target "hot spots," and perform other self-initiated activities per shift will require more officers assigned to patrol in comparison to agencies that do not place as much emphasis on self-initiated activities. This policy decision is based on the answer to the question, "How many minutes per hour should an officer spend on proactive self-initiated/directed patrol activities?"
- *Unrecoverable patrol time.* It is recognized that some patrol time is not used for any of the purposes just described and thus should be classified as unrecoverable. In other words, the time period is too short to increase visibility, to perform

a directed patrol activity, or to conduct an administrative activity. This includes short periods of time between the clearing of one call and the receiving of another, time when an officer is stuck in traffic, and other "interrupting" events.

- *Percentage of time patrol units are staffed with two officers*. Patrol allocation models also make adjustments for the percentage of time patrol units are staffed with two officers. Two-officer units do reduce the need for back-up units on certain calls-for-service, but two-officer units are not twice as capable as one-officer units of meeting the performance objectives. For example, a two-officer unit is not twice as visible as a one-officer unit. Likewise, a two-officer unit cannot respond twice as fast to a call-for-service as a one-officer unit. It is important to note that even in agencies that deploy 100 percent one-officer units, there will often be two-officer units deployed for field training of recruits, and this must be taken into consideration when making allocation decisions.

Taken together, the policy decisions regarding patrol performance objectives have a substantial impact on necessary patrol staffing.

Investigative Staffing

Learning Objective

Typically 16 percent to 20 percent of sworn personnel are assigned to investigations (Horvath & Meesig, 2002). Only patrol consumes more resources—typically 60 percent. However, unlike patrol allocation formulas, which have received a fair amount of attention over the last two decades, little empirical research has been conducted on the development of corresponding investigative staffing formulas. The research that has been done has been more theoretical than applied. Indeed, a major shortcoming in the development of investigative staffing models is the near total lack of reliable data regarding the actual tasks performed by investigators and, importantly, the time ranges necessary to perform such tasks. Likewise missing is information about the likelihood of case clearance relative to time spent and techniques utilized. As noted in Chapter 11, Brandl and Frank (1994) found that, on average, three to four hours are spent on burglary and robbery cases with some suspect information. The few studies that have been conducted, as well as anecdotal evidence, suggest that investigators actually spend most of their days either in the office doing paperwork or on the telephone, or traveling by automobile from one location to another. The time spent on the latter factor, of course, has the potential for wide variability depending on the size and nature of the jurisdiction as well as whether investigators are centralized or decentralized. (Centralized investigators in a major city would presumably have to drive further per trip than decentralized investigators.) Similarly, scant data exists on the relationship of investigative time spent and subsequent identification of criminal offenders.

What is known is that the single greatest contributor to a successful criminal investigation is the quality of information gathered by the responding patrol officer. Review of case clearance rates by investigators nationwide shows a very low number: Less than 10 percent of serious offenses are cleared by follow-up investigative work. Unfortunately, the low clearance rates in larceny/theft-type offenses, which make up the bulk of the Federal Bureau of Investigation (FBI) Part I *Uniform Crime Report* (UCR) offenses, published annually, are aggregated in this number and obscure whatever higher rate of success might have been attained by follow-up investigators in murder, rape, and robbery cases.

This is not to suggest that investigators do not serve an important police function. Indeed, arresting offenders is only one goal of investigators. For instance, the societal outrage at murders mandates that each receive follow-up investigative attention, even though homicides constitute a very small percentage of overall crime. Indeed, public expectations are that homicides will be investigated until an offender is identified and brought to justice. Unsolved cases often are carried on in an open status and continue to utilize some level of investigative resources months after their occurrence. Similar public policy concerns require that extensive resources be devoted to sexual assault investigations and robbery cases. Only in property crimes does a police department have some degree of latitude in deciding which cases to pursue further and the level of investigative effort to be expended.

Learning Objective

There are three different approaches in examining investigative staffing. For simplicity, these are summarized as follows:

1. *Benchmark comparison approach.* This strategy involves comparing investigative staffing levels in cities of comparable population to that of a given jurisdiction. It should be noted that this strategy, although displaying a fair level of face validity, is subject to criticism and results must be viewed cautiously. The underlying problem is why other cities have decided on their particular levels of staffing. Perhaps they are understaffed, or even overstaffed, with investigators. Accordingly, a comparison to these jurisdictions may simply establish that a given jurisdiction is no worse off than other police departments without actually determining whether any of the agencies is adequately staffed. This "keeping up with the Joneses" approach says little about whether staffing levels are adequate within the individual agency. Additionally, two key variables can greatly affect the conclusions drawn from such comparisons: the level of responsibility of the uniform patrol officer in the investigative process and case screening/assignment practices. An agency that empowers patrol officers to conduct complete preliminary investigations will likely need fewer follow-up investigators, whereas a department in which patrol officers simply hold the scene and notify detectives upon discovery of a felony will need proportionally more investigators. Likewise, agencies that assign every case for investigative follow-up will either need more investigators or to allot less time to each case than a department where cases are screened prior to assignment. Such screening for "solvability" or for other purposes will greatly influence caseload levels and the number of investigators needed. These caveats should be kept in mind when reviewing comparative data.
2. *Longitudinal time-comparison approach.* A longitudinal time study of a given jurisdiction's investigative staffing levels is desirable. Essentially, this strategy involves comparing current staffing levels with the staffing levels from some years earlier. Factored into this equation would be the presumed change in criminal events over the intervening time frame and a determination as to how well staffing levels have paralleled changing workload demands. Although this view does provide some guidance in establishing contemporary staffing needs, any judgments made should be made cautiously because of the underlying assumption that the base staffing levels were appropriate at the designated time in the past. Here, too, the base staffing levels against which current levels are compared may have been deficient or overly generous at the time.

3. *Workload projection approach.* In deciding on future investigative staffing levels, one may assume that each new investigator added will take, on average, about the same amount of time to process a case as the role incumbents. Thus, a reasonable estimate will be able to be made regarding the effect that each newly assigned investigator will likely have on case clearances, arrests, and other investigative outcomes.

Learning Objective

The third approach, workload projection, provides insight into expected results achieved by adding personnel. As noted earlier, new investigators can be expected to perform at approximately the same rate as incumbent detectives. Thus, one can reasonably hypothesize that if, on average, one investigator can process x cases and will make y arrests, two investigators will process $2x$ cases and make $2y$ arrests. However, this formula is nonlinear; research suggests that at some point the productivity rate of the *nth* investigator will drop because factors outside the investigator's control will prevent a case from reaching satisfactory conclusion. The ideal staffing formula would account for the fact that although every investigator would be working, on average, at the same level of investigative efficiency, at some point the clearance rate would begin dropping with the addition of one more investigator.

Typical burglary and theft data is illustrative. In many large municipal agencies only about 10 percent of burglary and theft cases are actually assigned to an investigator. From another perspective, 90 percent of the complaints never receive investigative attention due to lack of human resources and/or futility of assignment even if resources were available. In a staffing analysis of a major agency, while 12,693 cases were cleared, 22,773 were believed to have workable leads but were never followed up due to lack of personnel.[1] The 22,773 cases deemed workable but never followed up represented approximately 25 percent of the cases that came to the division.

A typical burglary and theft clearance rate is about 18 percent. Would one expect that 18 percent of the unworked 22,773 cases with leads might be cleared if additional personnel were added? The answer is likely "no." The cases worked are those with the greatest potential for clearance by arrest. Pursuing additional cases, although potentially worthwhile, is not likely to result in the same arrest rate. The foregoing discussion is made to present the complexity of the staffing issue, particularly in the high-volume category of "crimes against property." Research suggests that the overwhelming bulk of burglary and theft cases are "solved" by a patrol officer making an arrest at the scene, and that the investigator's responsibility is largely twofold: prepare the case for prosecution and interview the suspect in an effort to identify other offenses he or she may have committed.

One approach is to incrementally add investigators and concurrently monitor productivity rates. If each additional investigator, on average, processes and clears cases at the existing division rate, then the addition of the individual will add to the effectiveness of the division. When the division clearance rate begins dropping as additional personnel are added, one might rightly assume that the efficiency saturation point has been reached. At that point, it would be understood that further staffing will not likely produce as great a result as previously, and policy choices then come into play as to whether such additions are wise, given other demands for resources. But this option is never politically feasible.

QUANTIFICATION OF INVESTIGATIVE EFFORT

One existing model is designed to allow police management to quantify the additional investigative effort that will be attained with the addition of more detectives in meaningful metrics.[2] This model first categorizes cases into a typology that relates to required investigative effort, rather than to the criminal code or UCR classification of the offense. The typology can be conceptually thought of as a matrix. Across the top are four categories of case clearance status upon assignment to an investigator; down the left margin are twenty-seven offense categories.

The suspect categories of the 10×17 matrix produce 170 cells, plus the 10 investigative incidents without suspect categories, for a total of 190 cells. See Table 12.1. Investigative effort is specified in anticipated hours of follow-up, translated in the table to proportion of offenses and proportion of investigative time spent. Expectations can then be set for each of the 190 cells. For example, although larceny events with no suspect information represent 70% of all larcenies, but the proportion of investigative time dedicated to this category of larceny is only 50%. Larcenies with no suspect information will involve, at most, a pawn property check and a victim courtesy call-back. At the other extreme is a homicide investigation with some suspect identification present. The seriousness of the offense justifies an extensive investigation, and the fact that there is some suspect identification developed provides leads—something to investigate. If investigative units do not handle a particular case type, perhaps not handling lost/found property, for example, a zero is entered.

Public order offenses (e.g., prostitution) are listed, but data are entered only for assignments that are made on a case-by-case basis, such as response to citizen complaints or post-arrest case processing. If a separate proactive drug or vice investigation unit exists, productivity data for that unit is separately calculated. There is no means to calculate "time-required" data for proactive investigations. Staffing levels for proactive investigations remain a policy issue.

The key to employing the matrix as an investigative allocation tool is to understand that staffing will determine the extent to which each of the 190 cells receives what level of investigative effort. In an investigative division that is severely understaffed, even serious offenses with suspect identification developed will receive only nominal amounts (less than thirty minutes) of effort. If thirty minutes of investigation does not identify the suspect, then the case is filed. Further, even cases with known but at-large suspects, and cases with the suspect in custody, will receive only basic attention (thirty-one minutes to three hours). Pursuit of convincing and overwhelming evidence for a trial, or negotiated plea, could potentially be strengthened by more investigative effort, but will not be.

"Purchasing" Investigative Services. The model provides a tool for specifying what will be purchased with increased investigative staffing. Rather than generically, "we need more detectives," the model moves discussion to "we need to conduct extensive rather than basic investigations on robberies with identified or in-custody suspects (to assure conviction or an acceptable plea)." It also forces explicit policy on uncomfortable issues—"we are not going to investigate theft cases with unknown suspects beyond victim courtesy call-back (nominal = <30 minutes)."

TABLE 12.1 Typical Proportional Number of Cases/Percent of Time Spent

	Proportion of Cases					Proportion of Time Spent				
	Suspect Unknown	Possible Suspect ID	Known Suspect At-Large	Suspect in Custody	Prop. of All Cases	Suspect Unknown	Possible Suspect ID	Known Suspect At-Large	Suspect in Custody	Prop. of All Cases
Crimes Against Persons										
1. Murder/criminal homicide	5.0%	10.0%	50.0%	35.0%	0.25%	5.0%	10.0%	50.0%	35.0%	2.5%
2. Robbery	15.0%	70.0%	5.0%	10.0%	2.0%	5.0%	60.0%	5.0%	30.0%	5.0%
3. Aggravated assault	10.0%	10.0%	45.0%	35.0%	3.7%	5.0%	10.0%	50.0%	35.0%	6.0%
4. Other assaults	5.0%	10.0%	55.0%	30.0%	8.0%	5.0%	10.0%	55.0%	30.0%	7.6%
5. Forcible rape	5.0%	15.0%	60.0%	20.0%	0.25%	5.0%	15.0%	60.0%	20.0%	0.5%
6. Sex offenses	10.0%	10.0%	60.0%	20.0%	1.2%	5.0%	10.0%	65.0%	20.0%	5.0%
7. Offenses against family	0.0%	0.0%	70.0%	30.0%	0.8%	0.0%	0.0%	85.0%	15.0%	1.0%
Crimes Against Property										
8. Burglary	65.0%	20.0%	10.0%	5.0%	11.0%	30.0%	30.0%	20.0%	20.0%	10.5%
9. Larceny/theft	70.0%	10.0%	10.0%	10.0%	26.0%	50.0%	20.0%	15.0%	15.0%	20.0%
10. Motor vehicle theft	70.0%	5.0%	20.0%	5.0%	4.5%	40.0%	15.0%	35.0%	10.0%	4.0%
11. Fraud/forgery/counterfeiting	60.0%	10.0%	25.0%	5.0%	9.5%	40.0%	20.0%	35.0%	5.0%	8.7%
12. Vandalism/criminal mischief	70.0%	5.0%	20.0%	5.0%	7.0%	30.0%	15.0%	35.0%	20.0%	4.0%
13. Arson	20.0%	30.0%	40.0%	10.0%	0.25%	10.0%	40.0%	40.0%	10.0%	0.25%
Public Order Investigations										
14. Disorderly conduct	50.0%	5.0%	20.0%	15.0%	0.7%	20.0%	10.0%	50.0%	20.0%	0.7%
15. Weapons offenses	0.0%	0.0%	10.0%	90.0%	0.6%	0.0%	0.0%	20.0%	80.0%	0.8%
16. Traffic violation follow-up	45.0%	25.0%	10.0%	20.0%	5.0%	20.0%	50.0%	10.0%	20.0%	4.0%
17. Misc. criminal investigations	10.0%	10.0%	30.0%	50.0%	8.5%	5.0%	15.0%	40.0%	50.0%	9.5%

Noncriminal Incidents (no suspect categories)		
18. Death investigation (noncriminal)	1.0%	3.5%
19. Abandoned vehicle	1.0%	0.3%
20. Lost/found property	2.5%	1.0%
21. Missing person	0.6%	0.7%
22. Runaways	1.3%	0.6%
23. Other noncriminal	3.52%	2.0%
Discretionary Proactive/ Reactive (no suspect categories)		
24. Code enforcement/inspections	0.1%	0.5%
25. Drug/narcotics investigations	0.33%	0.75%
26. Prostitution/vice	0.2%	0.5%
27. Gambling	0.2%	0.1%

Further, one does not allocate resources based upon extreme and rare events. We cannot staff patrol to handle a major riot at any time 24/7. We call in other agencies and off-duty officers in such circumstances. Similarly, we cannot afford to staff investigations to handle a JonBenét Ramsey case. Should such a case arise, extra resources will have to be budgeted on an emergency basis.

The Effect of Global Positioning System Tracking

global positioning system (GPS) Satellite-based positioning system now ubiquitous in cell phones, vehicle navigation systems, and other applications.

Learning Objective

Global positioning system (GPS) installation in patrol cars can provide dispatchers with a view of available units in the entire jurisdiction. They provide a real-time display in the police communication room of the location of each patrol unit in the system. With recent adjustments to GPS, the accuracy is now within several meters virtually anywhere, and with enhanced GPS to within one meter. Clearly the system is accurate enough to select which patrol unit is closest to a given call-for-service. Hypothetically, this could allow more efficient use of patrol resources, and fewer units in the field. The effect of GPS has not, however, been dramatic. There are several reasons.

First, there are relatively few calls that justify overriding dispatch of the designated beat unit in order to obtain a more rapid response. Stated differently, the number of priority-one calls for which a unit other than the designated beat unit is closer is relatively small. Thus, even with GPS installation, in most cases the unit dispatched to a call-for-service is still the designated beat unit, assuming it is available. Second, GPS tends to be useful only to enhance response time. Agencies that employ GPS do not use it to guide other patrol functions. Thus, for example, one does not hear a dispatcher transmitting to a patrol unit, "Our GPS data indicates you have not maintained sufficient visibility in the southwest quadrant of your beat this evening; please drive to that sector to do so." In theory, we could use GPS this way, but are choosing not to. This is where the human factor overrides technology. If we are to treat patrol officers as professionals, then we have to trust their professional judgment with regard to the areas of a beat where they maintain visibility, engage in traffic law enforcement, or initiate proactive efforts to repress crime. Beyond this issue, administrators recognize that in a profession with a tradition for nearly a century of relative autonomy for officers deployed in a patrol car, one will immediately alienate them with efforts to control their every move. Thus, GPS in practice is nothing more than "who is closest to a call in a genuine emergency?" There are, of course, other useful functions. GPS locations will assist dispatching back-up to an officer in trouble. GPS is very useful to track the location of high-speed pursuits. But these issues have nothing to do with the allocation and deployment of patrol units.

Discretionary Police Resources

A crucial factor beyond the performance issues discussed earlier, however, is community demand for neighborhood deployment. A police manager has a finite amount of resources to do an infinite job. Given the nature of the police role, there is, for all practical purposes, no limit upon what a community might call upon the police to do. Many agencies, for example, operating with a community policing philosophy, have become immersed in innumerable quality-of-life issues—from rehabilitating playgrounds to demolishing abandoned structures. The first issue a police manager must face when making decisions about neighborhood responsiveness is "How much can I afford?" Quite obviously, every police agency has core responsibilities that must be met. Those core responsibilities consume the vast majority of the resources available.

Learning Objective

A typical allocation of police staffing resources is depicted in Figure 12.1. There is certainly variance, but as noted in Chapter 11 on average about 60 percent of the resources in a police agency are allocated to patrol, 20 percent to investigations (adding both reactive and proactive), 15 percent to support services, and 5 percent to administration. With the assumption that investigative resources are always stretched thin, and the other functions listed are, relatively speaking, minimally staffed, then we are left with patrol as a source of personnel to staff other endeavors. Figure 12.2 depicts the typical allocation of patrol resources. On average, about 40 percent of a patrol officer's time is committed to calls-for-service, 25 percent to administration and breaks, and 10 percent is essentially unrecoverable time spent traveling to and from a beat or in the short intervals between responses to calls-for-service, leaving 25 percent of the time available for proactive efforts. Given that patrol represents 60 percent of all police human resources, and the amount of time available for proactive activities in patrol averages 25 percent, simple arithmetic tells us that a police manager has, at best, only 15 percent of her or his resources available for proactive efforts (see Figure 12.3). Note that this does not mean that 15 percent of patrol personnel can be pulled for specialized assignments, whether to neighborhood responsiveness programs or other focused efforts. Agencies that have tried this technique have failed. Response times skyrocket, and agencies find themselves a high proportion of the time with no patrol unit free to respond to a genuine emergency call.

Learning Objective

There are a number of options that exist competing for the scarce proactive resources that are available. An agency might deploy community resource officers. There might be an organized structured effort at problem-oriented endeavors. Officers might be assigned to schools, either as school resource officers or

FIGURE 12.1 Percent of Typical Allocation of Police Staffing Resources

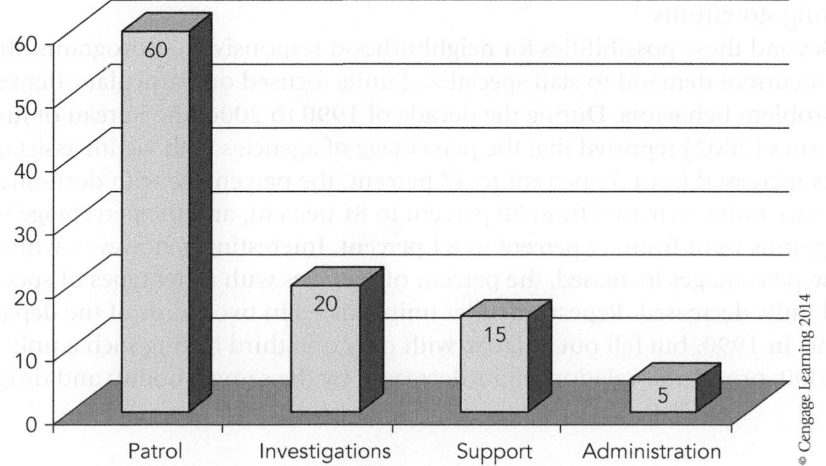

FIGURE 12.2 Percent of Typical Allocation of Patrol Resources

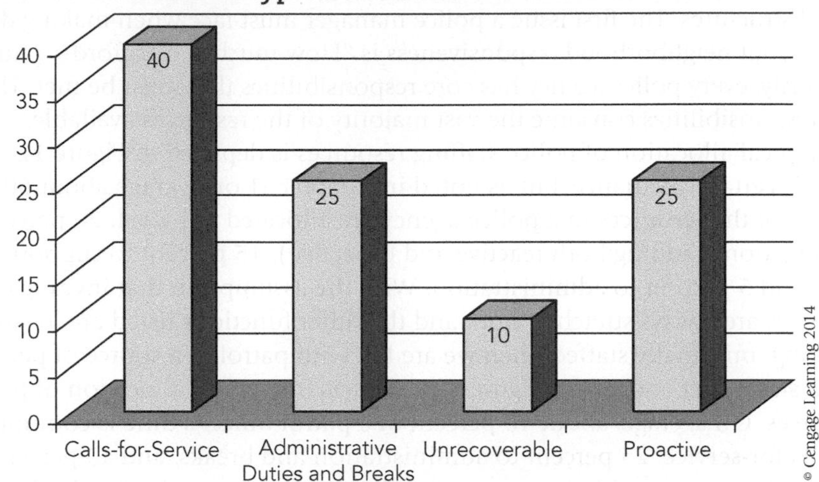

FIGURE 12.3 Percent of Resources Available for Proactive Patrol

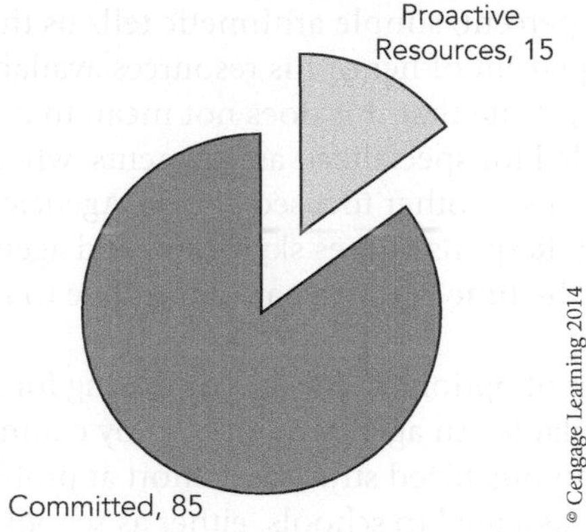

D.A.R.E.®
Registered trademark of Drug Abuse Resistance Education, Inc.; school-based program intended to inculcate an inherent negative attitude toward illegal drug use.

D.A.R.E.® officers. Regular patrol officers might spend a portion of their time on foot patrol or bicycle patrol, or even mounted patrol. Yet another alternative is staffing storefronts.

Beyond these possibilities for neighborhood responsiveness programs, there is concurrent demand to staff specialized units focused on particular offenses or problem behaviors. During the decade of 1990 to 2000, the Bureau of Justice Statistics (2002) reported that the percentage of agencies with victim assistance units increased from 32 percent to 47 percent, the percentage with domestic violence units increased from 50 percent to 81 percent, and the percentage with gang units went from 69 percent to 84 percent. Interestingly, however, while these percentages increased, the percent of agencies with other types of specialized units decreased. Repeat-offender units existed in two-thirds of the departments in 1990, but fell out of favor, with only one-third having such a unit in 2000; prosecutor relations units decreased by the same amount; and drug education programs were dropped by a large proportion of agencies, with the number decreasing from 90 percent to 73 percent. Even specialized DWI units lost ground, dropping from 56 percent to 40 percent. *The fact that some specialized units increased in number while others decreased underscores the point of limited resources.* Police managers cannot afford to concurrently address the full range of issues listed with the assignment of personnel on a full-time basis to specialized units. Difficult choices have to be made. If one is going to create a domestic violence unit, something else has to give, such as the elimination of a prosecutor relations unit.

Learning Objective

Difficult Choices

A police manager faces "difficult choices" in determining whether resources are more effectively spent on crime response teams, specialist investigative units, repeat-offender units, other crime-specific approaches, community engagement, problem solving—and the list goes on. Evaluative research to date contributes little to answering this question.

Efforts to control illegal drug trafficking illustrate the difficulty of the issue. It is postulated that both drug trafficking and drug use *per se* generate a community environment that is unsavory, unsafe, and potentially the source of a downward spiral in numerous quality-of-life measures, not the least of which is the crime rate. In that sense, investment in control of dangerous drugs is regarded as a form of crime prevention, not an expenditure of police resources as an alternative to crime control.

Stephen Lindbloom (1959) indicated in his seminal article "The Science of Muddling Through" that for public administrators goals are fairly clear, but objectives are not. Thus, for example, a local community might indicate through various mechanisms (and hopefully primarily through democratically elected city, county, or state representatives) that its police agency is expected to engage in illegal drug control efforts. But community "mandates" are seldom any more specific than that. After that, it is up to police managers as public administrators to decide whether or not that indicates that 1 percent of police resources will be dedicated to drug enforcement or 20 percent; whether the police agency will transfer 30 percent of its discretionary resources to a D.A.R.E.® program, or leave drug-prevention education to the local school district; whether the mandate implies that we simply address street-level drug dealing within our jurisdiction limits, or whether we send a cadre of officers to a regional interagency drug interdiction task force; and whether we treat drug cases like any other criminal offense, or whether we dedicate detectives to an enhanced prosecution effort. Across the country there is enormous variation in the proportion of police agency resources dedicated to drug control. It is certainly debatable whether that variation is a genuine reflection of variance in community mandates or a result of the personal predilections of individual police managers. This author would suggest that 90 percent of the variance is accounted for by the personal predilections of police managers, not variance in the strength of the community mandate. Police chiefs exercise more discretion as public administrators than is frequently recognized even by the chiefs themselves.

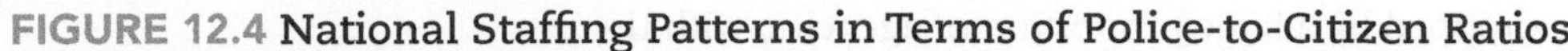

FIGURE 12.4 **National Staffing Patterns in Terms of Police-to-Citizen Ratios**

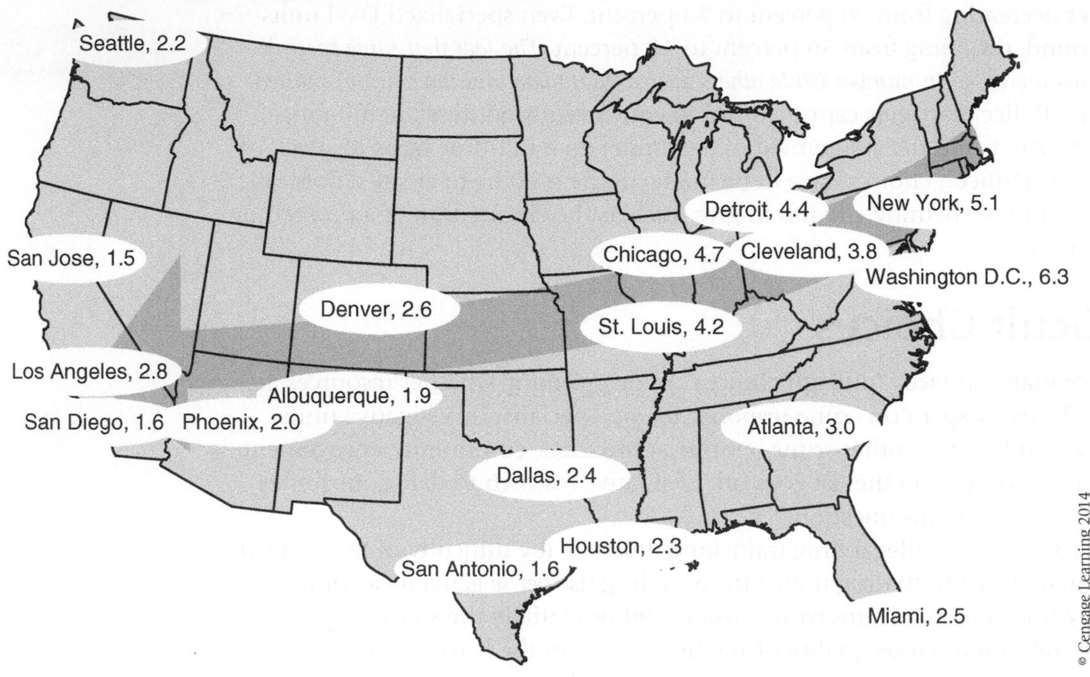

The Pervasive Comparative Statistic: Police-to-Citizen Ratios

police-to-citizen ratios
Proportion of officers to population; typically expressed as number of officers per 1,000 persons; ranges from 4.0 per 1,000 in large East Coast cities to 1.5 per 1,000 in cities west of the Mississippi.

Figure 12.4 depicts national staffing patterns in terms of **police-to-citizen ratios**. Overall, municipal and township police departments employ an average of 2.3 full-time officers per 1,000 residents (Reaves, 2010). However, there is enormous variation. If one draws a diagonal line from Bangor, Maine, to San Diego, California, one will find increasingly smaller police-to-citizen ratios in moving from the Northeast to the Southwest. Large cities in the Northeast typically have very high ratios. New York City has over five sworn officers per 1,000 residents. Chicago, Detroit, and St. Louis all have over four officers per 1,000 residents. As we move out of the Northeast and upper Midwest, however, the numbers begin to drop. Atlanta has 3.0 officers per 1,000, Miami 2.5, Houston 2.3, and Denver 2.6. By the time we reach the Southwest, the numbers for many jurisdictions drop below 2.0. Albuquerque has only 1.9 officers per 1,000, San Diego 1.6, and San Jose 1.5.

Interestingly, within weeks after William Bratton took the reins of the Los Angeles Police Department, he announced that "there simply are not enough officers to police this city." Los Angeles is now staffed at approximately 2.8 officers per 1,000. Bratton had come, of course, from Boston and New York, where he had over twice the relative number of officers available for deployment as he had in Los Angeles. Los Angeles is the second largest city in the nation; Chicago is the third. If Los Angeles had the same police-to-citizen ratio as Chicago with a ratio of 4.7 per 1,000, it would have 17,500 sworn officers instead of the approximate 9,700 it does have. If Los Angeles police commanders had twice as many officers as they currently do—that is, if they were staffed at the same ratio as Chicago—they could do a lot more responsiveness policing.

Learning Objective

The striking consistency of variation in staffing levels across the United States suggests underlying determinate environmental influences. It is empirically difficult to validate, but three factors are minimally involved:

1. Vertical cities require more officers than horizontal cities. Northwest and north central cities tend to be "vertical"—more densely populated, and containing even more densely built business districts. Cities west of the Mississippi are popularly referred to as horizontal cities—less dense both in population and structure. In a vertical city more regulation may be required as well as more traffic control (both literally and figuratively), and more "in each other's way" disputes to resolve may thus arise.
2. Jurisdictions in the East ask more of their police departments. This phenomenon relates to number 1, but is distinguishable. Social problems (e.g., "I have nowhere to stay") are brought to a New York precinct station more frequently than they are to a Los Angeles division station.
3. The use of two-person patrol cars in the East is more prevalent than in the West. Tradition is part of the reason. Additionally, the ability to get a backup unit to a scene is more difficult in the crowded and narrow streets in eastern vertical cities—arguing for two-officer units.

Other factors likely influence the variation in ratios. Their linkage, however, is more speculative. For example, police agencies in the East have a longer history of unionization, and the unions are more politically influential. Unionization may have some influence on staffing. Another possible influence is that more agencies in the East were created in the political spoils era, and part of that era was the use of police and firefighting positions as political patronage. It is possible that there is yet an enduring effect on "inflated" staffing levels.

IMPLICATIONS FOR STRATEGY

The answer to the question "How many police officers?" is not simple. Although comparable police-to-citizen ratios are relevant, they do not provide a definitive answer. A better approach is the use of performance based allocation tools. Even then, however, questions are left unanswered. Such tools call for the user to specify several "performance variables." These include the amount of time officers spend on proactive efforts. Proactive efforts include activities ranging from traffic law enforcement to undercover narcotics infiltration. These are policy decisions for which there is no "outside answer." It depends upon what a given community wants to "purchase" in policing services. Even then, however, police managers have enormous discretion in resource allocation.

SUMMARY

- There is no right answer to the question "How many police officers are needed in a jurisdiction?" Ultimately, the number of officers depends upon the level of police service desired. There are no fixed standards in this respect. The number of officers required depends on citizens' desire pertaining to service levels such as response time, proactive patrol, traffic law enforcement, patrol visibility in residential neighborhoods, and extent of follow-up investigation.
- Computer simulation models that stipulate the number of officers required to provide given levels of service have been developed. There are, however, serious limitations. The most important is the fact that police patrol is a dynamic system—officers modify their behavior depending on workload demand.
- Simulation models take into account both jurisdictional and policy characteristics. Jurisdictional variables include number of calls-for-service, average response time, number of roadway miles, average patrol speed, area of the jurisdiction, average response speed for both emergency and nonemergency activities, and the amount of leave provided to officers (vacation, sick, etc.).
- Policy variables affecting needed patrol staffing and used in simulation models include the amount of patrol visibility on both arterial and residential roadways, response-time objectives, the percentage of patrol activities that cannot be preempted, administrative time required, self-initiated/directed patrol time desired, unrecoverable patrol time, and the percentage of time patrol units are staffed with two officers.
- In contrast to patrol, we know even less about investigative workload. Indeed, a major shortcoming in the development of investigative staffing models is the near total lack of reliable data regarding the actual tasks performed by investigators and, importantly, the time ranges necessary to perform such tasks. Likewise missing is information about the likelihood of case clearance relative to time spent and techniques utilized.
- The three basic approaches to examining investigative staffing are benchmark comparison, longitudinal comparison, and workload projection. Workload projection is the most reliable. The best models in this respect account for differentiation of investigative effort by offense category subdivided into four levels of suspect status—no suspect identifying information, some suspect identifying information, suspect identified but not apprehended, and suspect under arrest.
- Simulation models are the best tool for quantifying investigative effort. Such models specify investigative effort by offense, further subdivided by suspect status. Rather than generically, "we need more detectives," the model moves discussion to "we need to allocate more resources to investigations of robberies with identified or in-custody suspects (to assure conviction or an acceptable plea)." It also forces explicit policy on uncomfortable issues—"we are not going to investigate theft cases with unknown suspects beyond victim courtesy call-back."
- Although useful, global positioning system (GPS) tracking of patrol units has proven to be of limited utility. It is not good policy to always dispatch the unit closest to a call-for-service request. The maintenance of "beat integrity" must also be considered.
- A typical allocation of police staffing resources is approximately 60 percent to patrol, 20 percent to investigations, 15 percent to support services, and 5 percent to administration. Within patrol, on average, about 40 percent of an officer's time is committed to calls-for-service, 25 percent to administration and breaks, and 25 percent to proactive or directive patrol, with 10 percent essentially unrecoverable time spent traveling to or from a beat or in the short intervals between other activities.

- Data compiled by the U.S. Department of Justice's Bureau of Justice Statistics indicate that as some specialized units are created, others are in turn eliminated. The fact that when some specialized units increase in number others concurrently decrease underscores the point of limited resources. Difficult choices have to be made regarding enforcement emphasis.
- Police-to-citizen ratios vary dramatically across the United States. Large cities in the Northeast typically have very high ratios, some exceeding four officers per 1,000 residents. As we follow a diagonal line from the Northeast to the Southwest, citizen ratios consistently decrease. Some major West Coast cities have ratios as low as 1.5 officers per 1,000 residents. Although some of this variation is idiosyncratic, in general differences are accounted for by three phenomena: (1) vertical cities require more officers than horizontal cities, (2) jurisdictions in the East ask more of their police departments, and (3) the use of two-person patrol cars is more prevalent in the East than in the West.

REVIEW QUESTIONS

1. What is the "right" answer to the question, "How many police officers does a jurisdiction need?"
2. What are the limitations of computer models intended to provide police agencies with the means to calculate resources necessary to deliver stipulated levels of patrol service?
3. Data enumerating the amount of time detectives spend investigating various types of offenses are very scarce. Worse yet, information is nonexistent about the likelihood of case clearance relative to time spent and investigative techniques utilized. Why is information about how detectives spend their time, and results thereby obtained, so difficult to collect?
4. Modern police communication centers include a GPS-generated display of the location of every patrol unit. However, agencies have found such displays to be of limited use. Why is this the case? Likewise, in what situations is GPS display very important?
5. Large municipal agencies on the East Coast typically have two to three times as many police officers as agencies on the West Coast serving comparable populations. It is suggested that one reason is that East Coast cities tend to be vertical, whereas those on the West Coast are horizontal. What does this mean, and why is it relevant to variation in police-to-citizen ratios?

REAL-WORLD SCENARIOS

1. You have been assigned by the chief of police to determine the optimal level of patrol staffing for your jurisdiction. Develop a descriptive list of the service-delivery variables that would be affected by the level of patrol staffing. Rank order the importance of the service-delivery variables you have identified, justifying the most and least important rankings assigned.
2. You are the investigations commander for a large police agency. Your division has been allocated one additional detective position. You have narrowed the possible assignment for that position to either the burglary and theft unit or the robbery unit. Discuss the factors that you would take into account in making the decision to assign the new detective to one unit or the other.
3. As the commander of support services, you are in charge of the communication/dispatch unit. Your agency has recently placed GPS units in each patrol vehicle, allowing display in the communication center of the location of each unit. Although you recognize that rapid response is important for some calls-for-service, it is also the case that the agency attempts to maintain beat integrity. Develop a policy statement that enumerates when the closest patrol unit should be dispatched, whether beat integrity is violated or not.

APPLICATION ACTIVITIES

1. An important data element in computer simulations of patrol staffing is average patrol speed. Average patrol speed is not as easy to calculate as one might initially assume. The most widely used data set was generated by the Northwestern Traffic Institute in the early 1990s with support from the National Highway Traffic Safety Administration. That data set indicates that average patrol speed is much slower than one might initially perceive. Working with a colleague, track the average speed between several points in your community. A device with stopwatch capability will be necessary. Log at a minimum three measurements at different times of the day. Display the variation in time on a spreadsheet.
2. To be reasonably accurate, a computer simulation staffing model for investigations must take into account not only the offense type, but the suspect status. Of necessity, suspect status is divided into categories, usually four: no suspect information, some suspect information, suspect identified but at large, and suspect apprehended. In reality, however, suspect information exists on a continuum, not in categories. Construct a continuum of suspect identification information, starting with illustrations of the most vague and ending with very specific identifying attributes. At a minimum include ten illustrations.
3. Go to the website for the *Uniform Crime Reports* published by the Federal Bureau of Investigation: http://www.fbi.gov/about-us/cjis/ucr/ucr. Link to the police employee data, then to city agencies, then the data for your state. Using the population data and total officers list (not the total law enforcement employees list), calculate the police-to-citizen ratio for ten agencies of varying sizes, expressed as officers per thousand residents. Is there a pattern? If so, what might explain that pattern?

COURSEMATE

This available CourseMate has an interactive eBook and interactive learning tools, including flash cards, quizzes, and more. To learn more about this resource and access free demo CourseMate resources, go to **www.cengagebrain.com,** and search for this book. To access CourseMate materials that you have purchased, go to **login.cengagebrain.com.**

ENDNOTES

1. A staffing analysis of the investigative functions completed by Professor Jerry L. Dowling of Sam Houston State University. Unpublished.
2. An investigative staffing simulation model developed by Justex Systems, Inc., the Allocation Model for Investigations©.

REFERENCES

Brandl, S. G., & Frank, J. (1994). The relationship between evidence, detective effort, and the disposition of burglary and robbery investigations. *American Journal of Police, XIII*(3), 149–168.

Bureau of Justice Statistics. (2002, May). *Special report: Police departments in large cities, 1990–2000*. Washington, DC: U.S. Department of Justice, Bureau of Justice Statistics.

Federal Bureau of Investigation. (Annually). *Crime in the United States, Uniform Crime Reports*. Washington, DC: U.S. Department of Justice.

Horvath, F., & Meesig, R. T. (2002). *A national survey of police policies and practices regarding the criminal investigation process: Twenty-five years after RAND*. East Lansing: Michigan State University, School of Criminal Justice.

Lindblom, C. E. (1959). The science of "muddling through." *Public Administration Review, XIX*(2), 79–88.

Reaves, B. A. (2010). *Local police departments, 2007*. Washington, DC: U.S. Department of Justice, Office of Justice Programs, Bureau of Justice Statistics.

CHAPTER 13

Deployment for Crime Control

© Ap Photo/Paul Beaty

Structured intervention strategies are clearly most effective if there are layers of discretionary resources. Various crime problems call for the immediate redeployment of resources. Some require that gang units be immediately focused on the issue. Some require that an auto theft unit be able to drop whatever else it is doing and give attention to a developing theft pattern. Some require that **generalist divisional investigators** be able to refocus their effort for at least a short period of time. Some require the narcotics unit to be involved. But if everyone is stretched so thin that there is not an extra minute available from any unit in the police department, an agency might as well abandon crime reduction as a goal.

Learning Objective

The Multiple Goals of Deployment

It is worth spending some time discussing Fort Worth, Texas, to reinforce this assertion. Fort Worth anchors the west end of the Dallas/Fort Worth (D/FW) metroplex. It is a city of 550,000, policed by an agency of 1,300 officers, for a ratio of 2.4 officers per thousand citizens. The agency deploys from four

KEY TERMS

Generalist divisional investigators
Ministerial alliance
M/O
Referendum

LEARNING OBJECTIVES

After completing this chapter, you should be able to:

- State the implication for crime control if an agency has no discretionary resources for deployment.
- Explain the import of the multiple demands for various police services in Fort Worth.
- Explain the ramifications of the fact that proactive patrol is still a critical component of police crime control efforts.
- Describe the rationale for the use of temporary assignment of patrol officers to tactical response.
- Explain the relationship between Compstat and community policing.
- Describe the new policing role emerging from the use of community policing specialists in Compstat environments.
- Explain the implications of the need for specialist units to inform generalist patrol of their activities.

substations to approximately eighty beats. The Fort Worth Police Department is a committed community policing agency. Among its programs are the following:

1. An overlay model of community policing specialists. The specialists are called Neighborhood Patrol Officers (NPOs). At one point there were 88 officers of the 1,300 sworn so deployed, one per beat plus a few in several special areas. That is a commitment of 7.5 percent of the sworn strength to full-time community resource officer roles—a percentage far higher than that of most major agencies. (In contrast, Seattle, with a similar size, has thirty-six officers so assigned.)
2. A citizens-on-patrol program that is one of the most well developed, largest, and most active in the country. The program is over twenty years old and going strong. Citizens on patrol units are out every evening in every sector of the city.
3. An active **ministerial alliance.**
4. Programs in the schools, including school security and drug abuse education.
5. A citizens' police academy.
6. Twelve "district stations" within the four substation structure designed to function as mini police stations. Officers actually deploy from some of the district stations.
7. Storefront sites over and above the district stations.

generalist divisional investigators
Detectives assigned to substations (precincts) with responsibility for investigating routine offenses such as assault, auto theft, burglary, theft, and sometimes sexual assault and robbery; range of responsibility depends on the extent of centralized specialty investigative units.

ministerial alliance
Volunteer group of ministers sponsored by a police agency as a special point of contact with citizens; employed for both routine community engagement efforts and as a communication medium when community relations problems occur.

referendum
A policy or program that is subject to a general election vote.

Many of these programs, although not all, were funded by a special tax that has been overwhelmingly renewed by **referendum**. (Texas tax law permits the creation of crime control districts, generally cities, with a surcharge on sales tax. A district must be renewed by popular vote every five years.) This is clearly not a department out of touch with its community. Quite the opposite. The agency cultivates sustained relations with virtually all community elements—from a downtown business group to minority neighborhood associations.

In 2002 this author was engaged to lead a team of consultants to conduct a comprehensive operations analysis of the agency (Hoover et al., 2002). Three core issues triggered the review of the police department: (1) immediate availability to respond to genuine emergencies, (2) reasonable response times even to nonemergencies, and, (3) some level of visibility to provide feelings of security. Neighborhood patrol officers, citizens on patrol, citizens' police academies, school programs, and an array of other community responsiveness efforts were strongly supported by the community. Interestingly, however, the primary issue among citizens was visibility in neighborhoods. Citizens simply wanted to see patrol units drive by. They did not want to give up their assigned NPOs for visibility, but they wanted visibility. This observation is reinforced by findings from a survey of 1,347 residents from 41 South Carolina neighborhoods. The authors concluded that "The current research demonstrates the importance of residents seeing the police. Even if the police cannot eliminate crime in a given neighborhood, if residents see the police 'out there trying,' the effort is probably recognized and appreciated by the residents" (Hawdon, Ryan, & Griffin, 2003). The citizens of Fort Worth felt the same way. A responsive police department recognizes that simple reassurance that "we are here" is one of its most important—if unglamorous—roles, whether it reduces crime or not.

Learning Objective

The Role of Patrol in Crime Control

During Compstat meetings, time and again interdiction efforts are described that began with a simple patrol stop of a suspicious vehicle. Indeed, it is almost disconcerting to note how often this occurs. One might think in an era with enhanced technological tools, and after years of effort at structured community contacts, that "leads" would no longer still be so dependent on the alert but relatively random intervention of uniformed patrol officers. One cannot help but worry under such circumstances about how many things are missed by uniformed patrol. Be that as it may be, it is clear that proactive patrol is still a critical component of police crime control efforts.

Learning Objective

The implications for patrol deployment are reasonably clear. Officers should be allocated reasonable amounts of discretionary time to engage in proactive street crime intervention efforts. Famega (2005) indicated that patrol officers have always had, and continue to have, a lot of downtime available for restructuring. The eleven studies reviewed by Famega report results spanning from 1966 to 1998, and find that, on average, 75 percent of a patrol officer's shift is downtime (p. 402). In Chapter 14 it is asserted that patrol is still patrol, notwithstanding a whole series of buzzword forms of "policing." The fundamentals have not changed since vehicle patrol became ubiquitous after World War II. Similarly, the fundamentals of teaching first graders to read have not changed for sixty years either. Debates may rage regarding phonics versus whole reading, but the reality is that early elementary children must be taught to first recognize letters, then words, then sentences, then paragraphs. Patrol officers must still gas up the patrol car, respond to calls-for-service, and remain available on emergency standby status.

But that is not to say that during emergency standby status patrol officers should not be engaging in proactive street crime intervention efforts. With rare exception, officers can remain available for dispatch to a genuine 911 emergency during proactive patrol endeavors; it is not the same as checking out of service for a sophisticated problem project or meeting with a community group. While engaged in proactive crime-specific patrol, officers are still in a marked patrol unit, in uniform within their beat, and can be called off of proactive patrol efforts with very short notice for dispatch to true emergencies. The creation or staffing of specialist units, whether focused directly on crime reduction or more ephemeral community contact and engagement efforts, should not be done at the expense of eliminating proactive patrol efforts by regular beat officers.

A second issue pertaining to the issue of patrol deployment is the use of temporary assignment of patrol officers to tactical response. In agencies employing such a response, officers are taken from regular patrol assignments for periods ranging from a week to a month and placed in tactical mode, usually in uniform but not necessarily always. Managers in agencies employing this technique indicate that motivation among such officers is extremely high. The managers also note that regular tactical officers assigned to this role on a full-time basis do not show the same level of enthusiasm and commitment as regular patrol officers temporarily assigned to tactical response. This is hardly surprising—any job becomes routine after a period of time. The observation generally made is that the motivation of temporarily assigned officers to tactical patrol more than compensates for the lack of experiential tactical depth. It is not that full-time assignments to tactical units should not exist. There is a need for some stability and an immediately available response that only a full-time tactical unit can provide. However, the number of officers with regular tactical assignments should be minimized. Instead of a large contingent of regularly assigned tactical officers, an agency should rotate temporary assignments drawn from regular patrol.

Learning Objective

The Future of Community Policing

In an agency where crime control comes first, community policing specialists are not in one orbit and officers responsible for crime control in another. For example, this author observed a crime reduction strategy meeting where there was discussion of the surge in thefts from autos at a particular housing complex. Certain gang members who lived in the housing complex had previous arrests for thefts from autos, and were strongly suspected in the current series of thefts. A commander asked "Is our police area representative (community policing specialist) involved?" The response from the substation commander, "Yes, he is. He is working with the apartment manager to evict the subjects." Similar scenarios occur in every jurisdiction.

The irony may be that although community policing was regarded as the antithesis of Compstat by almost everyone who was involved in the New York Police Department (NYPD) effort, structured crime reduction may yet turn out to be the saving grace of community policing. If the crime reduction process pulls

Learning Objective

community policing specialists away from broad social service efforts several steps removed from anything reasonably defined as police mission, and refocuses them upon crime control, the process may serve to "save them from extinction." Commenting upon the success of the Chicago Police Department in reducing homicides, retired superintendent Philip J. Cline emphasized, "The relationships with the minority community built by Terry Hilliard [former superintendent] were necessary to the effectiveness of the aggressive tactics to combat gangs, guns, and drugs" (Cline, 2007). Agencies implementing vigorous crime reduction efforts generally feel that community policing specialists can make a valuable contribution in their role as neighborhood liaisons and problem-solving officers.

Learning Objective

Indeed, from interviews with community policing specialists in such agencies, there appears to be a new policing role emerging. Community policing specialists in crime-specific agency environments certainly engage in structured community contact, but within limited bounds. The majority of their time is spent on efforts that are directly linked to ongoing crime problems. Indeed, as noted earlier, some have become investigators without caseloads. Free of the burden of frivolous follow-up on innumerable cases that cannot be solved, they are able to concentrate on problem people and places known to be actively engaged in criminal endeavors. The issue may be identity theft one week, theft from autos the next, and a problematic domestic violence case the next.

The forty-three departments that constitute the police service of the United Kingdom (UK) likewise experimented with just such a role. They implemented a class of senior constables dubbed by both the police service itself and the British media as "super-cops." Officially called "advanced skills officers," their salaries were nearly double that of a standard constable. Their function and role resembled very closely what has emerged in American police agencies that have integrated their community policing specialists into crime reduction operations. The UK advanced skills officers consisted of a selected number of constables in each force that had a proven track record in solving crimes and were trained as investigation specialists. Each "super-cop" had a team of standard-pay colleagues for assistance, and each also directed the activities of police community support officers employed to assist the police. Reportedly, senior police officials in Britain hoped that the reform would transform traditional policing, solve more crimes, and reduce public disorder in the streets.

IMPLICATIONS FOR STRATEGY—AND A PERSONAL NOTE

The focus of a crime reduction strategy meeting of the North Division of the Fort Worth Police Department observed by this author was the offense of auto theft. The conversation focused on the centralized auto theft unit operations in the North Division, including efforts to shut down chop shops, addressing the problem of false reporting as thefts of automobile "loaners" associated with drug deals and prostitution, and apprehension of a group of professional auto thieves. The auto theft unit had recently taken down a chop shop in the North Division, but had failed to inform anyone in the division of the operation. There had apparently been some concern that if patrol were informed, a careless officer might "blow" the undercover effort. The conversation between Captain Bill

Read and representatives of the auto theft unit was decidedly pointed on this issue. Assurances were given that North Division personnel would be kept better informed in the future. Following those assurances, Captain Read brought the conversation to a comfortable and humorous close by gesturing to the patrol officers in the room and saying "They may look dumb, but they're not." There was the predictable laughter. At that juncture, a crime response officer seated close to me laughingly said, "Captain, he is writing that down." (During the entire meeting this author was taking prolific notes.) At that point I promised the patrol officers of the North Division that their legacy in the law enforcement literature base, distributed nationwide, would be that *"The patrol officers of the Fort Worth Police Department, North Division, may look dumb, but they're not."* So I am keeping my promise—here it is in print.

The exchange is described here for reasons beyond keeping a lighthearted promise to the patrol officers of Fort Worth's North Division. There are two points to be made—crime control as teamwork and the motivational engagement of patrol. First, Captain Read's humorous comment has profound implications for crime control macro-strategy. Crime control is teamwork. Crime control in a police agency should never be exclusively the function of specialists, no matter how dedicated those specialists may be. Crime control includes coordinated efforts by crime response teams, divisional detectives, investigative specialists, gang units, narcotics units, community policing specialists, and—most important—by patrol.

Learning Objective

Second, there is the issue of motivating patrol officers to be fully engaged. Patrol's role in crime control is as much about values and motivation as it is strategy. The point was poignantly driven home during the Fort Worth North Division meeting. There was extensive discussion of the **M/O** of a professional car thief with the street name "New York." He was truly professional. He was never behind the wheel of a stolen vehicle. He had a cadre of "dope hoods" working for him. He always used intermediaries to negotiate deals; hence using confidential informants was difficult if not impossible. There was discussion in the room of techniques needed to apprehend him. At one point, it was noted that the state of Georgia had misdemeanor warrants for his arrest but would not extradite him. There was actually serious discussion about whether it might be cost-effective to purchase an airplane ticket and deliver him to the doorstep of the Georgia State Patrol. At some point during the conversation, there was a comment by one of the crime response officers: "I'll tell you what bothers the Captain; he is beating us." There was a serious response from Captain Read, "You're right, this guy is a scumbag and he is beating us." Present in the room at the time were not only the Baker District lieutenant and sergeants, but neighborhood patrol officers, crime response officers, and regular patrol officers as well—probably a total of thirty-five police personnel. Scanning the officers' faces around the room as Captain Read spoke, this author could not help but experience a flashback to his days as a patrol officer in Lansing, Michigan. Looking back, as a twenty-two-year-old officer sitting in that room, if I had heard the divisional captain say, "You're right, this guy is a scumbag and he is beating us," I can assure you that night I'd have been doing everything I could to nail New York. And indeed, when I walked out of the Baker District substation building thirty minutes after the meeting had ended, on the way to my car in the parking lot, there was still a group of patrol officers standing in a circle talking. As I walked by, I could catch enough of the conversation to know that they were not talking about the Dallas Cowboys—they were talking about how to nail New York.

M/O
Stands for *modus operandi* or method of operation; refers to particular techniques or characteristics employed by an offender; for burglary, includes time of day, types of locations targeted, means to gain entry, behaviors once inside, and what is typically stolen.

SUMMARY

- Structured crime intervention strategies require layers of discretionary resources. Effective interdiction requires that immediate redeployment of resources be possible. Even in an agency with extensive community policing programs in place, citizens still demand basic services, including immediate response to genuine emergencies, reasonable response time to nonemergencies, and some level of visibility to provide feelings of security.
- Fort Worth, Texas, provides an illustration of the need for police visibility. Although neighborhood patrol officers, citizens on patrol, citizens' police academies, school programs, and an array of other community responsiveness efforts were strongly supported by the community, the primary issue among citizens was visibility in neighborhoods. Citizens simply wanted to see patrol units drive by. Observations in Fort Worth are reinforced by findings from a survey of residents in South Carolina neighborhoods who rated very high the need to simply see the police drive by.
- Proactive patrol is still a critical component of police crime control efforts. Officers should be allotted reasonable amounts of discretionary uncommitted time to engage in proactive street crime interdiction efforts. Importantly, officers can remain available for dispatch to a genuine 911 emergency during proactive crime interdiction endeavors.
- The use of temporary assignment of patrol officers to tactical response has been successful in a number of agencies. Motivation among officers so assigned is high and compensates for the lack of experiential tactical depth. Instead of a large contingent of regularly assigned tactical officers, agencies should consider rotating temporary assignments drawn from regular patrol.
- Ironically, it may be that although Compstat was regarded as the antithesis of community policing by almost everyone who was involved in the NYPD effort, structured crime reduction may yet turn out to be the saving grace of community policing. Agencies implementing vigorous crime reduction efforts generally report that community policing specialists make a valuable contribution.
- Refocusing community policing specialists on crime control has resulted in the emergence of a new policing role. In many instances, community policing specialists in Compstat environments have become investigators without caseloads, concentrating on problem people and places known to be actively engaged in criminal endeavors.
- Patrol is the core of any agency's broad crime reduction approach. Although specialist units should certainly be involved, care should be taken that generalist patrol is fully informed of their activities. The import of deployment for crime control transcends strategy. Full integration of generalist patrol is a strong motivating force. Challenged to respond to a specific problem, patrol officers will "rise to the occasion."

REVIEW QUESTIONS

1. It is suggested that while citizens do not want to give up the police department's community policing initiatives, delivery of basic police services remains a concern. What are basic police services?
2. Evidence exists that random police patrol has little or no effect upon crime. This might imply that merely driving around a jurisdiction is a waste of resources. What are the arguments counter to this position?
3. It is asserted that proactive patrol is a critical component of police crime control efforts. This is reinforced by the fact that during Compstat meetings the discovery of an offense series is often attributed to an initial simple patrol stop of a suspicious vehicle. What does this imply for patrol deployment?
4. It is suggested that it is ironic that although Compstat was regarded as the antithesis of community policing by almost everyone involved in the NYPD effort, structured crime reduction may yet turn out to be the saving grace of community policing. Given the validity of the assertion, describe how Compstat may serve as the "saving grace" of community policing.

5. What new policing role is emerging from the engagement of community policing specialists in crime-specific interdiction strategies? What is the parallel role being tried experimentally in the United Kingdom (Britain)?

REAL-WORLD SCENARIOS

1. As director of the planning and research division of a major agency, you are asked by the chief of police to assess the adequacy of current patrol deployment. List the metrics that might be employed to assess the adequacy of patrol services. Stated differently, what quantifiable measurements might be made that would be indicative of the adequacy of patrol deployment?
2. In both Fort Worth and South Carolina, citizen expectations of their police department were obtained at least partially from surveys (questionnaires). Construct a ten-item survey that would measure citizens' expectations of their police agency.
3. Since the implementation of Compstat, the role of community policing specialists in your agency has changed dramatically. Community engagement and problem solving remain their core functions, but the nature of both endeavors has been reoriented to directly address issues of crime and disorder. Write an organizational position description for the new role, including both the substance of activities and the needed behavioral requisites.

APPLICATION ACTIVITIES

1. Locate a text focused on community policing, such as *Community Policing: Partnerships for Problem Solving* by Miller, Hess, and Orthmann. Using the text as a resource, write a brief generic description of each of the seven community policing programs conducted by the Fort Worth Police Department.
2. The use of tactical units, also called crime response teams, is discussed in this chapter. Construct a descriptive list of criteria that might be employed to ascertain where such teams should be deployed. Your list should include a minimum of five considerations that might be taken into account.
3. An innovative program being conducted by the British Police Service is mentioned in this chapter. Go to the website of the British National Policing Improvement Agency (http://www.npia.police.uk/). Using the links provided, find five additional examples of innovations in policing in the United Kingdom. Provide a one-paragraph description of each.

COURSEMATE

This available CourseMate has an interactive eBook and interactive learning tools, including flash cards, quizzes, and more. To learn more about this resource and access free demo CourseMate resources, go to **www.cengagebrain.com**, and search for this book. To access CourseMate materials that you have purchased, go to **login.cengagebrain.com.**

REFERENCES

Cline, P. J. (2007). Policing divided communities. Paper presented at the Police Executive Research Forum Annual Meeting—Panel Discussion.

Famega, C. N. (2005). Variation in officer downtime: A review of the research. *Policing: An International Journal of Police Strategies & Management, 28*(3), 388–414.

Hawdon, J. E., Ryan, J., & Griffin, S. P. (2003). Policing tactics and perceptions of police legitimacy. *Police Quarterly, 6*(4).

Hoover, L. T., et al. (2002). *Fort Worth Police Department operations analysis.* Huntsville, TX: Justex Systems Inc.

CHAPTER 14

Limitations on the Police Role

© SVLuma/www.Shutterstock.com

The late Professor Ralph Turner, an icon of the School of Criminal Justice at Michigan State University, was fond of saying "There is nothing new under the sun." The youngest faculty typically dismissed his statement as the musing of "an ole prof." However, as the years went by, the one-time neophytes first mellowed to "Maybe 'Uncle Ralph' was right about some things," and finally they found themselves uttering to the newest generation of faculty that same homily, "There is nothing new under the sun." Professor Turner recognized, of course, that some things do indeed change. His point, however, was that for most human endeavors the fundamentals remain constant. That is the case in policing, and it creates significant limitations on agencies' organization and operations.

Learning Objective

Let's take two examples from occupations very different from policing to illustrate the durability of organizational fundamentals. William Clay Ford, Jr. served as chief executive officer of Ford Motor Company from 2001 through

KEY TERMS

Conflict management

In-service status

Uncommitted patrol time

LEARNING OBJECTIVES

After completing this chapter, you should be able to:

- ➤ Compare the fundamental nature of police patrol today to its character in previous decades.
- ➤ Explain the relevance to policing of the persistence of fundamentals in both the automotive industry and K—12 teaching.
- ➤ Cite the reason mental health professionals sometimes believe the police are callous about persons with mental illness, and explain why patrol officers sometimes appear callous about persons with mental illness.
- ➤ Describe the evidence for the effect of rapid response on citizen satisfaction and apprehension probability.
- ➤ Describe the relationship between the need to maintain availability for emergencies and quality handling of incidents.
- ➤ Identify the factors that must be considered in determination of patrol deployment.
- ➤ Compare attitudes toward firefighters versus police officers being on emergency standby.
- ➤ Cite the effect on patrol deployment of the need to maintain availability for true 911 emergencies.
- ➤ Describe appropriate policy relevant to structured use of emergency standby time by patrol.
- ➤ Cite the linkage between the need for stress recovery time and patrol deployment.
- ➤ Describe the role of professional judgment in determining patrol allocation and deployment.
- ➤ Explain why immediate availability, rapid response, and visibility should be a part of democratic policing philosophy.

2006. He was the great-grandson of Henry Ford, the company's founder (credited with being the inventor of the assembly line). Were his responsibilities in managing the auto giant fundamentally any different in 2001 than the responsibilities of his great-grandfather in 1901? There are, of course, enormous differences of both scale and sophistication. A 2001 Ford Taurus is a far cry from the Model T. But the fundamentals requiring management in 2001 still matched the fundamentals a century earlier:

- Materials acquisition
- Manufacturing/assembly
- Distribution

- Advertising
- Sales/dealerships
- Providing repair service (parts availability)
- Fuel efficiency
- Vehicle performance, comfort, and safety
- Consumer preferences
- Dealing with labor issues—the United Auto Workers
- Competition monitoring

Scale, sophistication, and even breakthrough technology did not alter the fundamentals.

A second illustration is from the public sector—first-grade teaching. By 1940 the one-room rural schoolhouse was a thing of the past, and the K—12 public school system in the United States had evolved to the three-tier model—elementary, junior high, and high school. Each school was in turn divided into classrooms, organized by grade level in elementary schools and by subject at the junior and high school levels. A first-grade teacher was assigned twenty children in September, and they were "hers" (always a "her" in 1940) for six and a half hours a day through the end of May. The educational mandate was the three R's, especially reading. The six-year-olds learned to read from *Dick and Jane* readers, first recognizing single words, then sentences, then storylines. Three-quarters of a century later, what is different? In terms of the fundamentals, not much. The three-tier model endures, albeit with junior high renamed middle school; we still organize elementary schools by grade level; a first-grade teacher still has an individual classroom with twenty or so six-year-olds assigned for a full year; and children still learn to read by building recognition of individual words into sentences, then storylines. Debate may rage about one style of teaching reading versus another; electronics are slowly filtering into classrooms; we are more sensitive to cultural differences; and so forth, but the fundamentals remain unchanged.

Learning Objective

The relevance to policing is straightforward. Enduring fundamentals of the role beget enduring organizational and operational dynamics that persist over time—not because that is the way we have always done things, but because that is the way we have to do things. At the very core of what police agencies must do is to deploy patrol units geographically dispersed to be on emergency standby, and that deployment model imposes significant limitations on the police role.

The Import of Emergency Standby

The import of emergency standby is addressed by first telling a war story—not from the street, but from this author's own academic world. The author was part of the faculty at a conference sponsored by the Illinois Law Enforcement Training and Standards Board addressing police interaction with persons with mental illness. The conference was a mix of plenary sessions and breakout workgroups. The genesis of the conference was the commitment of the former director of the Illinois Board, Dr. Thomas Jurkanin, to developing cooperative agreements between police agencies and mental health service providers. Like the author, his family had been struck with mental illness. Like the author, he was concerned with inadequate or inappropriate response by police agencies to persons experiencing mental health crises.

The author was assigned to one of the workgroups that consisted entirely of mental health professionals. During the discussion among the mental health professionals, allusion was made on two or three occasions to how mental health professionals might engender greater empathy on the part of the police toward persons with mental illness. Statements were made in such a way as to make it clear that the mental health professionals were under the impression that law enforcement officers did not care at all about persons so afflicted—this was not a discussion about how mental health professionals could cause the police to care more; it was about how to persuade the police to show even a modicum of concern.

The author's personal experience did not indicate that law enforcement officers are uncaring. Yes, there are a few callous officers, and yes, one hears in police locker room conversations terminology referring to persons with mental illness that are inappropriate. But an overwhelming percentage of law enforcement officers do show concern, do have empathy, and generally observe that "it shouldn't be us dealing with these people"—that it ought to be medical professionals. The mental health professionals were asked why they were so convinced that the police did not care. They indicated that when the police took a mentally ill person into custody, the only thing officers cared about was "getting rid of them." Further inquiry was made as to whether anyone in the room had ever witnessed the police abusing, either orally or physically, a person suffering from mental illness. The unanimous answer was "no"—their perception of police callousness was derived solely from the fact that officers did not want to take time to deal with the suffering person.

Learning Objective

The mental health professionals were correct in their observation—that the primary concern of a patrol officer is to "get rid of" a person with mental illness—but wrong in their attribution of callousness as the reason. The conversation in the small group caused the issue to be addressed in a later plenary session. In the plenary session, discussion occurred regarding how few patrol units were available in a typical jurisdiction, and thus the importance to a police agency for officers to remain on **in-service status**. That is, it is a significant strain in almost all jurisdictions whenever an officer is taken out-of-service for two to three hours to process a medical commitment for a person suffering from mental illness. Like other citizens, mental health professionals grossly overestimated the number of patrol units on the street at any particular time (Jurkanin, Hoover, & Sergevnin, 2007).

Learning Objective

in-service status
Status of a patrol unit indicating that the unit is available for dispatch to a call-for-service; in-service status implies concurrent engagement in preventive patrol, traffic enforcement, visibility, and simply being on emergency standby.

The issue of the need to stay in service triggered an exchange between the police and mental health representatives that was one of the most useful at the conference. Indeed, although the goal of the conference was to engender development of interagency agreements between police agencies and mental health service providers for emergency response by mental health professionals to crisis situations, considerable discussion followed on expediting "handover arrangements" when a person with mental illness was taken into custody by the police.

THE RESPONSE TIME MANDATE

The need to "get back in service" is driven by the need to maintain rapid response to the constant flow of citizens' request for assistance. Rapid response time to calls-for-service is an important factor affecting citizen satisfaction with police. McEwen, Connors, and Cohen (1984) indicated that evaluations point toward delayed response reducing citizen satisfaction. Other studies have also noted that rapid response time is an important component of victims' evaluation of police (Cihan, Zhang, & Hoover, 2012). Although evidence consistently indicates that rapid response enhances citizen satisfaction, the effect on apprehension probability is mixed. Analysis of response time conducted in conjunction with the Kansas City Preventive Patrol Experiment (Kelling, Pate, Dieckman, & Brown, 1974) suggests that response time is not related to arrest rates. However, more recent research indicates that rapid response does increase the probability of apprehension in burglary cases (Blake & Coupe, 2001; Cihan et al., 2012; Coupe & Blake, 2005).

Learning Objective

Regardless of the effect on apprehension, police are expected to respond to individual citizen demand within a "reasonable" period when the phone rings (Kessler, 1993). However, other goals of patrol frequently conflict with the ability to rapidly respond to calls-for-service (Cihan et al., 2012). For example, citizens want police visibility in residential neighborhoods (Liederbach, Fritsch, Carter, & Bannister, 2007), but patrolling residential areas from which rapid exit is not possible reduces response time. An additional illustration is traffic control. A unit charged with traffic law enforcement and/or taking collision reports is not optimally placed for rapid response to generic calls-for-service. More important, there is a constant strain between maintaining availability and quality handling of incidents (Hoover, 1996). More time spent on calls-for-service equate to less time on other patrol functions. As a general principle, deployment of patrol resources must be done considering the multiple purposes of patrol—including rapid response, visibility, traffic control, citizen engagement, quality handling of calls-for-service, and crime control.

Learning Objective

Beyond issues of citizen satisfaction and apprehension probability, it is important to also note that some 911 calls are genuinely life-and-death situations. Although most involve the concurrent dispatch of emergency medical service or fire suppression units, rapid police arrival can still make a difference. Then there are the circumstances involving assailants—robberies, road-rage incidents, home invasions (Hoover, 2010). Hence agencies still factor rapid response time into deployment plans; in Los Angeles, for example, it is seven minutes to emergency calls (Gascón, 2005).

Emergency Standby as an Organizational Fundamental

Policing is not the only organization for which emergency standby is a core function. Perhaps the quintessential example emanates from the cold war, the Strategic Air Command. From 1946 to 1992, this branch of the U.S. Air Force maintained a twenty-four-hour vigil as a deterrent to a preemptive strike on the United States by the Soviet Union. At the peak of its standby mission, the Strategic Air Command kept several B-52 Stratofortresses constantly in the air, flying circular routes that kept them within range for instant retaliatory nuclear strikes. Emergency standby was not just one of the core functions, it was the only function.

There are a number of organizational roles for which emergency standby consumes a substantial majority of the organization's budget. The U.S. Coast Guard is an illustration. Although the Coast Guard's role since 9/11 has changed, being on emergency standby for search and rescue still governs allocation and deployment. Indeed, to some extent all military branches are emergency standby entities. The era of extended combat in Iraq and Afghanistan is the exception. For most of history, during nineteen years of every twenty-year period, the U.S. military has been simply poised for combat, not engaged in combat.

Emergency standby is likewise inherent in all public safety roles. Both firefighters and emergency medical services personnel (ambulances) spend most of a typical day merely in a state of readiness. The inactivity is condoned because it is recognized that neither firefighters nor EMTs can be performing other public service endeavors and still be available to immediately get emergency apparatus on the way to a scene. In contrast, there is insufficient recognition that "mere" emergency standby is a core role of policing as well. It is not a waste of taxpayer dollars to support patrol units simply being "at the ready" for a genuine life-threatening 911 call, any more than it is a waste of taxpayer dollars to support 24/7 staffing at a fire station. There are at least two principles that are derived from this observation.

Learning Objective

First, availability to respond to genuine 911 emergencies dictates patrol deployment. Patrol units are dispersed geographically across jurisdictional boundaries for this purpose and this purpose alone. It is true that geographically dispersed deployment accomplishes other purposes. To whatever extent that police presence serves to deter criminal behavior, we certainly want to provide that service equitably throughout a jurisdiction. Stated differently, every neighborhood pays taxes, and every neighborhood deserves police presence—hence geographic dispersion. The same premise holds for mere citizen reassurance provided by visibility—equity requires dispersion. Geographic dispersion is also necessary for traffic enforcement to occur. And we could add to this list. The point, however, is that regardless of other purposes served, geographic dispersion is required to provide rapid response to 911 emergency calls.

Learning Objective

This leads to the second principle. Availability to respond to emergency calls-for-service imposes severe limitations on the role of patrol officers. It was noted in Chapter 3 that structured community engagement (community policing) as well as problem solving (problem-oriented policing) have evolved to become specialist functions. The primary reason is that it just has not proved feasible to take regular patrol units out of emergency standby status, removing them from the patrol car, to engage either in structured community contact or problem solving. That is why this chapter is entitled "Limitations on the Police Role," not "New Paradigms in Policing." The fundamentals of managing the Ford Motor Company have not changed in a century, the fundamentals of first-grade teaching have not changed in seventy-five years, and the fundamentals of policing likewise have remained constant since about 1940. For law enforcement, the core fundamental is availability for 911 emergency responses, and that places real restrictions on engaging regular patrol units in crime control interdiction.

It should be noted that there are other fundamentals in policing. Most calls-for-service involve dispute resolution—domestics, landlord–tenet arguments, neighbor disputes, merchant–customer conflicts, and so forth. That has been the case since the creation of police agencies in the 1800s. Unlike their sister public safety agencies, fire and EMS, police departments are expected to perform multiple functions—crime control, traffic regulation, dispute resolution, short-term safety tasks (e.g., standing by downed power lines), crowd control, welfare checks, and so on. That has always been the case, and is not going to change any time soon. However, more than any other "fundamental," the need to be on emergency standby imposes limitations on engaging patrol officers in crime control.

Those who are determined to create new "eras" in policing heralded by a new set of buzzwords are fond of employing the term "paradigm shift." Although there is no standard definition of what extent of change is necessary to be classified as a paradigm shift, it is clear that most claims of paradigm shifts are exaggerated. When officers left walking beats to patrol in motor vehicles, it was undoubtedly a paradigm shift. The introduction of the two-way radio certainly qualifies—it likewise changed the fundamentals of policing. Compstat was described by some advocates as a paradigm shift. Not quite. Compstat begat changes that were both substantial and noteworthy, but not a paradigm shift. More recently, the change in approach to crime analysis described by the term "intelligence-led policing" is described by some as a paradigm shift. But the constituent element of intelligence-led policing, integrated and expanded data analysis, does not change any of the fundamentals of policing.

At the same time it needs to be noted that innovation and experimentation are essential to responsible management of police agencies, whether the innovation evolves to a paradigm shift or not. The fundamentals of the police role create significant limitations, but those limitations are not an excuse to forego organizational and operational development. Chapter 15 includes elaboration of the need for experimentation accompanied by careful evaluation.

Learning Objective

By extension, the limitations on use of **uncommitted patrol time** created by the need for maintaining availability to respond quickly to 911 emergency calls-for-service does not preclude making better use of the uncommitted time. The point is made elsewhere that crime control is most effective if all elements of an agency are involved, including regular patrol. At a minimum, patrol officers should be provided current and detailed crime analysis and offender intelligence information. Further, extended proactive targeting efforts, whether geographic, offense, or offender, may require interventions by specialized units, but that does not preclude participation by regular patrol. Patrol is often referred to as the eyes and ears of policing. Indeed, it is. Specialized unit deployment is no substitute for astute observation and intervention by patrol units deployed 24/7 across a jurisdiction.

uncommitted patrol time
Time that a patrol unit is not engaged in responding to calls-for-service and administrative duties; the time available for generalist patrol functions.

The Human Factor—Recovery Time

Learning Objective

There is yet one other consideration that needs to be noted here. Handling citizen calls-for-service is inherently stressful. The police deal overwhelmingly with **conflict management**. Repeatedly jumping from one conflict situation to another takes a psychological toll. It may simply not be realistic to have an expectation that officers can do this night after night, week after week, month after month, without a break. The uncommitted patrol time that we are trying to recover might also be regarded as recovery time for officers. They need some time to calm down, regroup, think through what has just occurred, and prepare psychologically for the next conflict that will have to be refereed. Again drawing upon the firefighter comparison, we would not expect firefighters to literally run from one conflagration to another. First of all it would obviously be extraordinarily physically demanding. But beyond the physical demand is the psychological one.

There are professions, albeit very few, where practitioners do indeed move steadily from one stressful situation to another. Emergency medical technicians in very busy districts are one example, and emergency room physicians are another. But there is an element in policing that these professionals do not need to deal with—the ever-present threat of personal assault. Policing is inherently far more dangerous than statistics indicate. The only reason we do not have a far greater number of officers injured or killed than we do is because we train and retrain to use strong precaution. It is an overlay of stress against handling what are already inherently stressful situations that we do not talk about enough. Uncommitted time is also recovery time.

conflict management
The police role in calls-for-service that involve mediating disputes among citizens; the most common disputes requiring police intervention include family domestic relations, traffic/parking, landlord–tenet, merchant–customer, and neighbor (usually noise and animal complaints) issues.

The Need for Professional Judgment

Learning Objective

Professional judgment is a critical component of allocation and deployment decision making. Providing mere visibility illustrates the need for professional judgment. Visibility may or may not deter crime, but citizens nevertheless want it (Hawdon, Ryan, & Griffin, 2003). However, visibility is just one of many demands upon patrol services. The desire for simple visibility should not displace other, more poignant needs. Neighborhood associations occasionally exert considerable pressure for more patrol presence. But "squeaky wheel" associations have no business deploying a police department within any style of policing. Citizen input is just that—citizen input. It is not citizen control. Control is exercised by elected legislative bodies in our representative democracy. Presumably well-run city councils or their equivalent appoint professionals and defer to the judgment of those professionals for the daily operations of various governmental departments. It is a relationship, of course, with inherent tension. Volumes have been written in the public administration literature about the relative independence of units of the executive branch of government. But there is universal agreement that there is some balance point between policy setting by elected governing bodies and the overlay of professional judgment by public managers.

Learning Objective

Responsiveness is a critical component of a well-run police agency. If the citizen request is "give us immediate availability, rapid response, and visibility," then those goals must be balanced against vigorous, directed crime control efforts. Demands for more visibility from entities such as neighborhood associations should not be ignored, but professional judgment on resource allocation needs to be an overlay. The exercise of professional judgment in managing allocation and deployment is one of the inherent complexities of policing a democracy.

IMPLICATIONS FOR STRATEGY

In every jurisdiction, police budgets represent a substantial proportion of public expenditure. Every patrol unit is expensive. Every dispatch to a 911 call consumes scarce public resources. More important than any other point is that patrol allocation and deployment are first and foremost policy decisions—not computer-generated statistics. As public administrators, police managers cannot escape responsibility for these public policy decisions. Embedded in these decisions are the enduring purposes of patrol—visibility, rapid response time, and the need to maintain units always available on emergency standby. Yes, the new generation of deployment variables should also be considered—structured community contact, problem solving, and crime control initiatives. Use of emergency standby time for crime control initiatives has proven more flexible than either community or problem-oriented endeavors. But there is no new "type" of policing that substitutes for balance in allocating patrol resources. The core of deployment should be deployment without buzzwords.

SUMMARY

- The fundamentals of police patrol remain constant over time. That does not imply that we should be cynical about innovations conducted under the auspices of community policing, problem-oriented policing, hot spot saturation, or Compstat. Rather, it is simply recognition that, regardless of fresh approach or innovation, patrol units are still deployed across the jurisdiction to provide reasonably rapid response to citizen requests for service, remain on emergency standby during uncommitted time, and engage in a combination of traffic enforcement and investigation of suspicious circumstances during emergency standby time.
- The relevance to policing of persistence of fundamentals in both the automotive industry and K—12 teaching is straightforward. Enduring fundamentals of the role beget enduring organizational and operational dynamics that persist over time—not because that is the way we have always done things, but because that is the way we have to do things. At the very core of what police agencies must do is to deploy patrol units geographically dispersed to be on emergency standby, and that deployment model imposes significant limitations on the police role.
- The need to maintain patrol units available for true 911 emergency response has both philosophical and pragmatic implications. An illustration is the attitude expressed by mental health professionals that patrol officers are callous about persons with mental illness. When examined closely, the source of their attitude turned out to be patrol officers' desire to "hand off" the person with mental illness to someone else. From the police perspective, the reason is not callousness, but rather the need to "get back in service"—to return to emergency standby status. The phenomenon has ramifications for how the police handle a wide range of calls-for-service. There is constant stress between quality handling of calls-for-service and the need to remain on emergency standby.
- Evidence is mixed on the linkage between rapid response and probability of apprehension for in-progress crime calls. Regardless, reasonably rapid response is still important. First, there are indeed instances when rapid response is life and death; they are rare but they do occur. Second, citizens who find themselves in stressful situations want rapid police response—even, for instance, to a fender bender traffic collision.
- There is a constant strain between maintaining availability and quality handling of incidents. More time spent on calls-for-service equates to less time on other patrol functions.
- As a general principle, deployment of patrol resources must be done considering the multiple purposes of patrol—including rapid response, visibility, traffic control, citizen engagement, quality handling of calls-for-service, and crime control.
- The public and its elected government officials are in fact more understanding of the need to "simply" be on emergency standby than are police professionals themselves. We are certainly tolerant and understanding

of the phenomenon in, for example, firefighting. On the one hand, agencies should make every effort to engage generalist patrol officers in crime interdiction efforts. On the other hand, the profession needs to recognize that simply being on emergency standby is not a waste of government expenditure.

- Availability to respond to genuine 911 emergencies dictates patrol deployment. Patrol units are dispersed geographically across jurisdictional boundaries for this purpose and this purpose alone. It is true that geographically dispersed deployment accomplishes other purposes, including criminal deterrence, citizen reassurance provided by visibility, and traffic enforcement. Regardless of other purposes served, geographic dispersion is required to provide rapid response to 911 emergency calls.
- The limitations on use of uncommitted patrol time created by the need for maintaining availability to respond quickly to 911 emergency calls-for-service does not preclude making better use of the uncommitted time. At a minimum, patrol officers should be provided current and detailed crime analysis and offender intelligence information. Further, extended proactive targeting efforts, whether geographic, offense, or offender, may require interventions by specialized units, but that does not preclude participation by regular patrol. Patrol is often referred to as the eyes and ears of policing. Indeed, it is. Specialized unit deployment is no substitute for astute observation and intervention by patrol units deployed 24/7 across a jurisdiction.
- It is widely recognized that policing is a psychologically stressful occupation. Periods of uncommitted patrol time between calls-for-service may be justified in order to provide officers "recovery time." Officers need some time to calm down, regroup, think through what has just occurred, and prepare psychologically for the next conflict that will have to be refereed.
- Police resources are always strained, and not every expectation can be fully met. As public administrators, police managers cannot escape responsibility for policy decisions. Embedded in these decisions are the enduring purposes of patrol—immediate availability, rapid response, and visibility. However, there is a need for professional judgment as an overlay.
- Immediate availability, rapid response, and visibility remain important goals of police agencies. They are important goals because citizens demand them. An agency that practices community policing should take these fundamental citizen expectations into account in making patrol deployment decisions as part of a democratic policing philosophy.

REVIEW QUESTIONS

1. Comparisons are drawn in the chapter to two other public service occupations, K—12 teaching and firefighting. Describe the characteristics of each that are relevant to policing.
2. Responding to assistance calls involving persons in a mental health crisis is challenging for patrol officers on several levels. One of these is the inordinate amount of time that is typically consumed for adequate response to these situations. Explain why this is problematic for police agencies.
3. There are several occupations for which emergency standby is an accepted part of the role. Examples include firefighting, emergency medical assistance (ambulance crews), and the U.S. Coast Guard. The issue appears to be problematic only for policing. Why?
4. Numerous studies of the nature of citizen calls-for-service indicate that a very high proportion involves conflict management in one form or another. What does this imply for patrol deployment, and more particularly for the use of uncommitted patrol time?
5. What are the administrative ramifications for citizen expectations of immediate availability, reasonably rapid response, and neighborhood visibility?

REAL-WORLD SCENARIOS

1. Your department has just installed a new computer dispatch system that provides analytic information not previously available. One type of analytic information is the amount of time spent on various calls-for-service. The data are available in several formats—by type of call in aggregate, by type of call and time of day, by type of call and a particular patrol shift, and by type of call and individual patrol officers. You note that there is considerable variance in the average amount of time individual officers are spending in response to domestic dispute calls. List the steps you would take to attempt to ascertain what the "appropriate" amount of time should be to handle such calls.
2. The same enhanced computer dispatch system also provides you with detail on committed versus uncommitted patrol time. You recognize that there will be less uncommitted patrol time on a busy Friday evening than on a quiet Sunday morning. Nonetheless, you wish to maximize the amount of uncommitted patrol time during the days and hours when it is most fruitful for officers to engage in crime interdiction activities. Construct a spreadsheet that has the days of week down the vertical axis and the twenty-four hours in a day across the horizontal. In each cell indicate the level of uncommitted patrol time desirable as high, medium, or low for the purpose of engaging in crime interdiction activities. There must be an even distribution of high, medium, and low—fifty-six cells each. Additionally, the distribution must be in eight-hour blocks—the length of a given patrol shift.
3. The ramifications of psychological stress in law enforcement have been well documented. Both social and physiological indicators confirm that policing is a stressful profession. List performance factors that you might examine that would serve as an early warning that an officer is not coping well.

APPLICATION ACTIVITIES

1. The problematic nature of police interaction with persons in a mental health crisis concerns every responsible police administrator. Widely replicated by other agencies is a model developed by the Memphis (Tennessee) Police Department. The shorthand description has come to be the "Memphis model." Using library resources, locate descriptive information regarding the Memphis model (it is widely available) and write a synopsis of its characteristics.
2. It is suggested that patrol deployment needs to take into account that there are indeed instances when rapid response is a life-and-death issue. List and describe five situations for which rapid police response might make a difference in a citizen's survival. Note that a police patrol unit is usually dispatched to serious fire and medical calls.
3. On numerous occasions reference is made in the text to "limited resources" in policing. Discussion in this chapter includes citing the fact that as public administrators, police managers are responsible for making professional judgments regarding differential allocation of resources. Describe three expectations either of the general public or a specific element of the public that for all intents and purposes could consume an infinite amount of police resources.

COURSEMATE

This available CourseMate has an interactive eBook and interactive learning tools, including flash cards, quizzes, and more. To learn more about this resource and access free demo CourseMate resources, go to **www.cengagebrain.com,** and search for this book. To access CourseMate materials that you have purchased, go to **login.cengagebrain.com.**

REFERENCES

Blake, L., & Coupe, R. T. (2001). The impact of single and two officer patrols on catching burglars in the act. *British Journal of Criminology, 41*, 381–396.

Cihan, A., Zhang, Y., & Hoover, L. T. (2012). Police response time to in-progress burglary: A multilevel analysis. *Police Quarterly, 15*(3).

Coupe, R. T., & Blake, L. (2005). The effects of patrol workloads and response strength on arrests at burglary emergencies. *Journal of Criminal Justice, 33*, 239–255.

Gascón, G. (2005). Compstat in Los Angeles. Presentation to the Law Enforcement Management Institute of Texas (Major Cities Chiefs Program), Austin, TX.

Hawdon, J. E., Ryan, J., & Griffin, S. P. (2003). Policing tactics and perceptions of police legitimacy. *Police Quarterly, 6*(4).

Hoover, L. T. (2010). Rethinking our expectations. *Police Practice and Research, 11*(2), 160–165.

Hoover, L. T. (Ed.). (1996). *Quantifying quality in policing*. Washington, DC: Police Executive Research Forum.

Jurkanin, T. J., Hoover, L. T., & Sergevnin, V. A. (Eds.). (2007). *Improving police response to persons with mental illness: A progressive approach*. Springfield, IL: Charles C. Thomas.

Kelling, G. L., Pate, T., Dieckman, D., & Brown, C. E. (1974). *The Kansas City Preventive Patrol Experiment: A summary report*. Washington, DC: Police Foundation.

Kessler, D. A. (1993). Integrating calls-for-service with community and problem-oriented policing: A case study. *Crime and Delinquency, 39*(4), 485–508.

Liederbach, J., Fritsch, E. J., Carter, D. L., & Bannister, A. (2007). Exploring the limits of collaboration in community policing: A direct comparison of police and citizen views. *Policing: An International Journal of Police Strategies and Management, 31*(2), 271–291.

McEwen, J. T., Connors, E. F., & Cohen, M. I. (1984). *Evaluation of the differential police response field test*. Alexandria, VA: Research Management Associates, Inc.

CHAPTER 15

Evaluating Strategic Impact

© Kevork Djansezian/Getty Images

Learning Objective

We need to jump-start science in policing. There is too little research on strategy. Effectiveness in policing depends on a combination of philosophical approach, policy, programs, strategy, and tactics. The right combination is likely dependent upon the totality of the environment. That is, no combination of approach, policy, program, strategy, and tactics works in every political system, in every cultural environment, in all socioeconomic settings, and in every era. Replication of the Minneapolis Domestic Violence Experiment (Sherman & Berk, 1984) is instructive. Although arrests in domestic violence cases resulted in fewer subsequent instances of violence in Minneapolis in the original study, the outcome did not hold up in a replication. The evaluation of arrests as an alternative in Milwaukee, Omaha, Dade County, and Colorado Springs indicated mixed results—with arrest sometimes being the worst alternative (Berk, Campbell, Klap, & Western, 1992). The authors note ". . . there is no simple 'bottom line' to the question of whether a given city would be better off or worse off on the average with any particular policy for arrest in spousal violence incidents" (p. 707).

Learning Objective

KEY TERMS

Golden Era of the Police Foundation
Political or social advocacy
"When the phone rings, we will come"

LEARNING OBJECTIVES

After completing this chapter, you should be able to:

- Identify the characteristics appropriately affecting choice of strategy.
- Explain the import of the replication of the Minnesota Domestic Violence Experiment for strategy research.
- Describe the evolution to date of the "state of the art" in strategy research.
- Identify the cause of strategy evaluations being effectively frozen for 25 years.
- Identify the program that generated the "thaw" of the strategy research deep-freeze.
- Describe why research replication is an important element of the development of police science.
- Explain why political or social advocacies for a particular strategic approach should be completely separated from the science of policing.
- Explain the phrase that captures a guiding principle of equitable police service in a democracy.
- Identify the maturation term that best captures the current status of the discipline of police science.

This chapter reviews the issues involved in engendering a needed jump-start of research on police strategy effectiveness. It begins by reviewing the obvious; crime is a complex social behavior that is difficult to categorize. The import of research is, however, enormous. A broad agenda awaits neutral, scientific evaluation. Replication is one element, but some arenas remain virtually unexplored, particularly the efficacy of investigations. To be true to science, police researchers must not slip into the role of advocacy for a particular approach. We witnessed this phenomenon poignantly with community policing. There are warning signs that history is repeating itself among evaluators of hot spot interventions. Finally, we need to look to the more mature research in the physical sciences for guidance. Among the characteristics of physical scientists is respect for those who have gone before—whether their conclusions ultimately proved valid or not.

Learning Objective

Crime Complexity

Domestic violence illustrates an axiom of police crime interdiction efforts. There is no formula, no checklist of what works or does not work, for every criminal offense. First, to state the obvious, but a fact that is often forgotten, common crime categories frequently represent totally unrelated social behaviors. A domestic violence incident may involve a psychologically disturbed chronic and dangerous offender. Or it may merely be a case where both parties are drunk and irrationally quarrelling. A youth grabbing and running away with a six-pack from a convenience store does not equate to a professional high-dollar shoplifter, albeit both are in the *Uniform Crime Reports* (UCR) category of theft. Additionally, chronic domestic violence is a far more complex social behavior than simple theft by juveniles.

Complexity is also illustrated by McCabe's analysis of the relationship between drug arrests and crime rates in Queens, New York City, between 1995 and 2001—within the Compstat era. Results indicated that the rate of marijuana arrests correlated with a reduction in crime, but the rate of controlled substance arrests correlated positively with crime (McCabe, 2008). In yet another illustration, the complexity of intervention technique reaches even to the amount of time spent on field interview stops in hot spot locations. Koper (1995) found that stop duration had to reach a threshold of ten minutes to generate greater deterrence than just driving through an area. And, of course, there is the "perplexing" findings of the Indianapolis "north-versus-east" beat intervention (McGarrell, Chermak, Weiss, & Wilson, 2001). There are no simple formulae, no simple answers. The task ahead is enormous. We have barely scratched the surface.

Golden Era of the Police Foundation
The period roughly from 1972 to 1980 that saw Police Foundation sponsorship of several landmark experimental evaluations of strategic approaches, including the Kansas City Preventive Patrol Experiment and the San Diego Field Interrogation Experiment.

The Import of Research

The drop in crime in New York City that followed the implementation of Compstat underscores the importance of the issue. Unlike better cancer treatment that flows from solid research, we will never know the names of the victims saved by the effectiveness of Compstat. There are tearful moments when cancer survivors are pronounced free of the disease. There will be no such moments for the otherwise victims of murder in New York City who are still enjoying life. But even unknown, they are real people nevertheless, not statistics. Crime destroys whole neighborhoods, whole cities. Finding more effective police strategy is not a trivial social issue.

Learning Objective

Learning Objective

With the close of the **Golden Era of the Police Foundation**, research on strategy slowed to a crawl. A review of the major experimental design research efforts in the area of policing strategy reflects a twenty-five-year gap. Undue optimism regarding the promise of problem-oriented and community policing was at the core of the hiatus. It took the resounding success of New York's Compstat model to thaw the freeze. This situation is strikingly parallel to that of the U.S. space program. In eight years, NASA went from John F. Kennedy's challenge to actually putting men on the moon. Since then, NASA has been going in circles around the Earth. Experimental research on police strategy was launched with a rapid-fire succession of blockbuster studies in the five years between 1972 and 1977. Until roughly the year 2000, we were circling, discussing where to go next. (Yes, a slight exaggeration, but not much of one.) Since 2000 the pace of structured research has increased enormously. Most sophisticated current evaluations, however, focus overwhelmingly on one approach to crime control—hot spot saturation. Although we have come a long way, we have a very long way to go.

An Agenda

Learning Objective

There is an array of strategy research waiting to be completed. First on the agenda might be replication. No scientist conducts a single experiment in a single setting, and then pronounces the findings as a law of science. We might start with the San Diego Field Interrogation Experiment—particularly in light of the current popularity of "broken windows" strategies. Replication is a worthwhile investment. Then there is the Compstat phenomenon. It is really an array of philosophical approach (the police can and do make a difference), policy (unit commander accountability), programs (regular crime reduction strategy meetings), strategy (proactive, even aggressive, enforcement), and tactics (broken windows enforcement). What combination of components apply in what environments remains unknown. We need to systematically explore variation in problem-solving strategy—going beyond telling only the success stories at the annual Problem-Oriented Policing Conference every autumn. Then there is genuine unbiased analysis of expanded community engagement—the core of community policing. And in case no one has noticed, alternative approaches to criminal investigations are an unexplored scientific wilderness. Current funding of the National Institute of Justice is grossly inadequate. If federal funds are to be allocated to state and local law enforcement, they ought to be directed to evaluation, not hiring more officers or buying new radio systems.

Academics should spend more time telling students what we do not know in contrast to telling them what we do know. The current status of policing research compares to the study of chemistry before the brilliant decoding of the Periodic Table by Dmitri Mendeleev on February 17, 1869. There were mathematical patterns in elements that had similar properties, but no one could make sense of it—or make predictions of chemical reactions based upon those patterns (Moore, 2002). Police research has identified patterns—focused interdiction efforts are more effective than those broadly constituted—but reliable prediction of the effect of a particular strategy in a given environment eludes us.

Although there are patterns to what seems to work in police strategies, no one has close to a model, much less something akin to Mendeleev's theoretical framework. The "Evidence-Based Policing Matrix" developed at George Mason University is a start (Lum, 2009). But even in this instance, "evidence" is almost exclusively focused upon a singular approach—hot spot saturation. Importantly, it should be recognized that we will never discover a "one best way" scientific framework. In the physical sciences, uncertainty or chance has been difficult to accept as inherent in nature. Einstein's famous quote, "God does not play dice with the universe" exemplifies the slow acceptance of the Uncertainty Principle. (Even the greatest genius of our era can be wrong.) Cutler notes that while Newton's "clockwork" universe is more comforting, ". . . we now understand that chance and probability are inherent in biology, thermodynamics, cosmology, quantum physics—indeed all of science" (Cutler, 2000, p. 26). This truth in the physical sciences certainly applies to police science.

political or social advocacy
The process of being a proponent of a particular approach or strategy that is perceived as "competing" with alternative approaches.

Separating Science from Advocacy

Learning Objective

Above all, we need to separate science from **political or social advocacy**. No matter how attractive a political or social vision of policing might be, the criteria for police scientists must be "what demonstrably works." Yes, there are some givens. What works may not trample on human rights. The police in democracies must be both representative and responsive to the communities they serve. There must be formal review mechanisms, and the police must be held accountable. But the fact that the police must adhere to basic democratic ideals does not dictate a given model of policing among many that are all consistent with those ideals. The preconceived idea that we are going to demonstrate that community policing is the way to go—or problem-oriented policing, or Compstat—must be abandoned in favor of nonpolitical assessments, nonadvocacy evaluations, of what works if we are to ever develop a respectable discipline of police science. As stated well by Balick and Frank: "New information ultimately up-ends the best of theories in every field of research. That is the nature of progress. Discovery is often disruptive. It clears out old niches and prepares the way for big (and often disorienting) leaps forward. Scientific theories are built to be used, but they must be mistrusted, tested and improved" (2004).

Now we are visited with intelligence-led policing and evidence-based policing. And the next form of "fill-in-the-blank" policing is, quite certainly, just around the corner. There are times when inappropriate rhetorical style does real harm. This is one of those occasions. Elsewhere it is argued that we need to ban the term "uncommitted (or free) patrol time" from our vocabulary. Likewise, we need to ban the use of the term "policing" attached to a descriptive adjective describing an approach, or strategy, or even a focused tactic. There is only one form of policing worthy of being called "policing"—and that is democratic policing—a term coined decades ago. Police agencies should be representative and responsive to the communities they serve. End of mantra. After that, there are approaches, strategies, and tactics. Depending on the circumstances, one approach among many may be more appropriate than others. In most circumstances a mix of approaches, strategies, and tactics is most appropriate.

For administrators the approach should reflect current thought in organizational theory—knowledge management. The concept of knowledge management was beget by the information age. However, knowledge management does not imply a particular strategic approach. More information is never complete information. Strategy is dependent on evolving circumstance.

Repeatedly in previous chapters it is suggested that the use of various philosophical approaches, such as community engagement, problem solving, or focused enforcement, may be appropriate depending on circumstance. Within the context of broad approaches, various strategies may be appropriate; any given strategy might subsume more than one tactic. In turn, approaches, strategies, and tactics are operationalized by policies and programs. But the decision tree relating to crime control is not the sum and total of "policing." The police serve multiple purposes in society, begetting multiple goals. Traffic enforcement is only tangentially discussed herein. Order maintenance is reviewed only in a context of linkage to crime control, but order maintenance is a purpose in its own right. Mediation of disputes is a purpose in its own right. One of the hallmarks of American police service is its democratic nature—**"when the phone rings, we will come"**. The callers are not asked their economic status, how much they paid in taxes last year, whom they know at city hall, or whether they live in the "right" area of town. Yet universal response to requests for service is often regarded as nothing but interference with the "real" role of the police—crime control. Above all, upholding individual rights—the right to free speech, the right to assemble (to protest), the right to be free of undue government interference—are among the most important functions of democratic policing. Indeed, for emphasis it should be observed that when officers raise their right hand and take an oath, they do not swear to engage the community, problem

Learning Objective

"When the phone rings, we will come" A phrase that captures an important philosophical underpinning of democratic policing—that all citizens merit equal access to police services.

solve, or reduce crime; they swear to uphold the Constitution of the United States. Upholding human rights is the first purpose of democratic policing.

Indeed, it is premature to talk about models of policing at all from a scientific analysis perspective. Isolation of variables in terms of approach, policy, program, strategy, or tactic should be the guiding principle. This is not easy. Shermer (2009) notes that science begins with the null hypothesis, which assumes that the claim under investigation is not true unless demonstrated otherwise. He goes on to remind us that the null hypothesis means that the burden of proof is on the person making a positive claim, not on the skeptics to disprove it.

Some would argue that a social science effort cast in the maelstrom of a volatile subset of public administration is far more complex than controlled experimentation in the physical sciences. There is general consensus that experimentation is the best approach available, but that other practical reasons impede researchers from using this methodology (Lum & Yang, 2005). It is even suggested that the physical sciences do not provide viable models. But is our task really that much more difficult than discerning the motion of the planets with the instrumentation available in 1543? Is it that much more challenging than deciphering the Periodic Table of the Elements in 1869, particularly given that Mendeleev had no concept of the structure of the atom? Have you looked at the Periodic Table of the Elements since your first-year chemistry class? Does it look inherently intuitive to you? Surely we are capable of sorting through the political and social overlays to better establish contextual principles of police effectiveness. But we can sort through those political and social overlays only if we are not advocates ourselves. Objectivity and neutrality are absolute requisites of science. Kuhn (1996) correctly points out that all science operates from a paradigm, a set of assumptions about how the world operates. However, science does not attempt to "prove" the derivatives of such assumptions; it tests the validity of the derivatives.

Respecting Our Heritage

We need to develop at least a modicum of respect for each other and our predecessors as explorers of a neophyte science. The Police Section of the Academy of Criminal Justice Sciences (ACJS) sponsors an annual O. W. Wilson award given to those who are assessed as making contributions to police science. A few years ago at the ACJS conference, this author congratulated that year's recipient of the award. His response was a cuttingly snide remark about O. W. Wilson and the outmoded professional model. As scientists, we can do better than that. The professional model has its shortcomings. The "principles approach" to administration has been supplanted. But as a recipient of the award a few years later, this author felt honored to receive an award that is a namesake for O. W. Wilson.

A mature academic discipline does not bash scientists of a different era with more limited instrumentation and experimental groundwork. Isaac Newton gave us the first model of gravity and space in *Principia Mathematica*, published in 1687 (Hawking, 2001). Physicists today do not castigate Isaac Newton for his failure to recognize the relativity of time and space, or that gravity is, in fact, a warp in the fabric of time/space. Einstein did not begin his treatise on relativity with a slap at Isaac Newton. Niels Bohr was not held up to ridicule by his contemporaries for his hypothesis of "allowed orbits" of electrons when it became clear that quantum mechanics was a better explanation for the subatomic observations then being made (Wynn & Wiggins, 1997). Biologists do not rile about the lack of insight of the Swedish botanist Carolus Linnæus, developer of the Linnæan hierarchy, because he failed to recognize evolution years before Darwin and Wallace (Mayr, 2001). Indeed, today's members of the Linnæan Society bear affiliation with the Society's namesake with pride. Science progresses in a heuristic process. Those who follow respect those who preceded them, even if their hypotheses have long since been rendered obsolete. Isaac Newton's famous quote—that his work was possible only because he stood on the shoulders of giants—was not only appropriately humble, but reflects the values of true science.

Not all of the "insights" of the sociologists who discovered policing in the late 1960s will bear the test of time. But that does not detract from their contributions. The findings of much of the macro strategy research of the 1970s may not stand up to replication, but that will not demean the integrity of the researchers. O. W. Wilson bashing is misplaced at best. Wilson wrote a magnificent book with no other books to guide him. He promulgated what, for its era, was a groundbreaking work. The book contains minimal citations because there was little to cite. Wilson sat down with a blank pad of paper and started writing. A police agency run by the principles set out by O. W. Wilson would still be a well-run police agency today. The principles he articulated in *Police Administration* (1950) remain a necessary condition of good police management. They are perhaps not a sufficient condition, but they remain a necessary condition. Most of the principles promulgated in *Police Administration* are as true today as they were in 1950. If one was to start picking up the pieces of an agency in disarray, a good place to start would be the 300-item checklist at the back of O. W.'s book.

Most important, Wilson's book sets as an assumption that the police are there to equitably serve all citizens. The guiding principle of equitable service is carried out in a way that we now so take for granted in democracies that we forget how really profound it is. That guiding principle is *"when the phone rings, we will come"*—the ultimate democratic response in policing. It is a response premised upon the equality of the citizenry and equal protection of the law. It is a principle not practiced worldwide; in many places whether the police will respond or not depends upon who you are, where you live, or whom you know. Those who criticize O. W. Wilson for creating a system of "deployment by the telephone" would do well to consider the fact that deployment by the telephone is at the core of community responsiveness—no matter who you are, no matter what neighborhood you live in, when you punch in a mere three numbers, the police will come.

Learning from the Physical Sciences

Learning Objective

Considerable attention is given here to the O. W. Wilson issue because it relates so closely to the final and most important issue in the development of a science of policing. We need to keep a truly open mind about what works. Our discipline, police science, is literally in its infancy. We do not have an ultimate, definitive, "this is it for sure" model of democratic policing. Victor Strecher addressed the issue poignantly in his *Histories and Futures of Policing: Readings and Misreadings of a Pivotal Present* (Strecher, 1991).

Scientists who are lured onto the intellectual trail leading to final answers will assuredly ultimately take the wrong fork in the road. Science never ever says never, and never ever says always. For example, the rotation speed of galaxies suggests far more matter (mass) in the universe than is visible—if Newton's laws of motion are correct. Newton's laws have always been correct up to now (given the special circumstances of relativity). But try as they might, physicists cannot find the elusive dark matter. It may be that matter comes in a form not yet discernible. Or Newton's laws of motion and mass may not hold on cosmological scales. There is an alternative—Modified Newtonian Dynamics (MOND Theory) suggests that Newton's laws fail in extremely low-density environments. MOND can explain the notion of stars in the outer regions of disk galaxies without the presence of dark matter (Anderson, 2009). Alternatively again, Peter Hořava of the University of California has proposed that if physicists "snip the threads" that bind time to space at the high energy of the big bang, quantum gravity emerges—eliminating the need for either dark matter or dark energy. A fluctuating graviton interacting with normal matter makes gravity pull more strongly than expected in general relativity—which in turn makes galaxies appear to "need" more matter than is visible (Merali, 2009). Be it dark matter or alternatives, any physicist worthy of the name has an open mind—dark matter may yet be there, or Newton's laws may have to be adjusted, or time may not always be intertwined with space. There may be accepted theories, but there are no absolutes in science.

From the perspective of the scientific method, one would never suggest that a particular approach is a universal law of policing for all times, all governmental systems, all cultures, and all social/economic circumstances. If we are not very careful, police science will be burdened with the equivalent of a convoluted Ptolemaic solar system keeping the sun and planets circling the Earth with compounded circles.

To illustrate the point—in 1990–1991, crime in New York City's subways plummeted after the implementation of vigorous broken windows enforcement. The vigorous enforcement included sweeps, banishment of the homeless, physical arrests for petty offenses (particularly fare jumping), harassment of panhandlers, and intimidation of gang members. In that environment the effect appeared to revolve around broken windows enforcement. In short order, felonies declined 75 percent and robberies 64 percent (Kelling & Coles, 1996). However, results reported in Queensland, Australia, (Mazerolle, Rombouts, & McBroom, 2007) and Fort Worth, Texas (Jang, Hoover, & Joo, 2010), although positive, were less dramatic and more limited. Further, in both jurisdictions broken windows enforcement did not play a role in crime reduction. Effective strategy in policing is very much an "it depends" issue.

IMPLICATIONS FOR STRATEGY

The state-of-the-art in police research is cause for optimism. Increasingly, both practitioners and scholars have abandoned the dogma of a "one best way" to seek solid scientific evidence of the blend of strategies that works under various circumstances. The term "evidence based" has replaced "agencies ought to." There is a broad agenda awaiting the application of scientific assessment. Several seminal studies beg for replication. Although some approaches appear to reduce crime, we lack cost-effective analysis. Other police responsibilities have, for all intents and purposes, not been touched.

Research in the physical sciences—astronomy, biology, chemistry, geology, physics—is far more mature. There is much to be learned from the physical sciences. It was once axiomatic that while the physical sciences were characterized by certainty, the social sciences were characterized by probability. But no longer—quantum mechanics leveled the playing field. All science is now characterized by probability.

There are no shortcuts to ascertaining "what works" to control the inherently complex social phenomenon we call crime. The fallacy of succumbing to the temptation to find easy answers is best illustrated by a time-worn joke:

> Late at night, a police officer finds a drunk man crawling around on his hands and knees under a streetlight. The drunk man tells the officer he's looking for his wallet. When the officer asks if he's sure this is where he dropped the wallet, the man replies that he thinks he more likely dropped it across the street. The befuddled officer asks, "Then why are you looking over here?" Because the light's better here, explains the drunk man. (Freedman, 2010, p. 55)

Freedman (2010) refers to the fallacy as the "streetlight effect"—which plagues every field of science. The current emphasis on evaluating hot spot saturation illustrates the phenomenon in police science—it is relatively easy to do versus, say, evaluating a complex problem-oriented intervention. We should be as cautious about currently popular "models" as we are about accepting the universality of models promulgated in the 1980s. The universe of policing is far too complex to fit a schema of a single central model about which everything in that universe revolves. We can do better.

SUMMARY

- Effectiveness in policing depends on a combination of philosophical approach, policy, programs, strategy, and tactics. The right combination is dependent upon the totality of the environment. That is, no combination of approach, policy, program, strategy, and tactics works in every political system, in every cultural environment, in all socioeconomic settings, and in every era.
- The desirability of replication in evaluation of police strategy was brought home by the four-city replication of the Minneapolis Domestic Violence Experiment. Although arrest emerged as the most effective option in the city of Minneapolis in the original study, it actually proved to be the worst option for preventing future violence in two of the four replication cities. Many environmental and instrumental characteristics of a particular jurisdiction may influence the viability of a particular strategy. Replication is an important element of the development of police science.
- There is a poignant need to jump-start research on police strategy effectiveness. There is far too little strategy evaluations. The potential import of research is enormous. A broad agenda awaits neutral, scientific evaluation. Replication is one element, but some arenas remain virtually unexplored, particularly the efficacy of investigations. To be true to science, police researchers must not slip into the role of advocacy for a particular approach. We need to look to the more mature research in the physical sciences for guidance.

- Strategy evaluations were effectively frozen for nearly twenty-five years, from 1975 to 2000, due to a confluence of factors. First, the "nothing-works" research of the early 1970s engendered pessimism regarding the potential for police impact upon crime. Second, two viable alternatives to discretionary use of police resources emerged almost concurrently in the early 1980s—problem-oriented policing and community policing. Although both remain, and should remain, viable strategic options for a police agency, undue optimism regarding their effectiveness led to the assumption that the combination of the two approaches was the only viable option for reducing crime.
- Effectively generating a "thaw" in the twenty-five-year freeze in strategy research was the success of the Compstat approach in New York City in the early 1990s, which brought recognition that, first, the police can have a substantial impact on crime, and second, that options other than community and problem-oriented policing may be viable.
- A hallmark of scientific inquiry is the necessity of replication before acceptance of a cause-and-effect relationship. Stated differently, replication is at the core of the scientific method. Replication is necessary to ascertain whether a strategy or elements of a particular strategy apply in a variety of locations. To illustrate the point, whereas a broken windows approach to street crime interdiction appeared to be an essential part of the New York City approach, it did not prove to be the case in either Fort Worth, Texas, or Queensland, Australia. This underlines the point made earlier concerning replication of the Minnesota Domestic Violence Experiment.
- There is an element of bias in any research. It is often pointed out that the first level of bias is the decision on what it is a researcher will evaluate. That being said, scientists go to great lengths to assure that bias is controlled and does not inappropriately influence conclusions. For that reason political or social advocacy for a particular strategic approach in policing should be completely separated from the science of policing. It is essential to the validity of the scientific process that researchers are open minded and willing to accept results, whether or not those results are "politically desirable" to the researcher.
- "When the phone rings, we will come" is a phrase that captures a guiding principle of equitable police service in a democracy. The underlying premise is equitable access to police service, no matter your social status, race, religion, economic condition, and so forth. It matters not what neighborhood you live in; it matters not whom you know in the police department; it matters not whom you know at city hall. The process of differential response, or suggesting to a citizen that he or she might file a report over the telephone or via the Internet, does not violate the principle as long as the process is applied such that it is only the nature of the complaint or report that determines differential response, not who the citizen is.
- The maturation term that best captures the current status of the discipline of police science is that it is in its infancy. We do not have an ultimate, definitive model of democratic policing.

REVIEW QUESTIONS

1. The 1970s are characterized as the "Golden Era" of police strategy research. What were the constituent characteristics of this Golden Era?
2. Why did the community/problem-oriented movement "freeze" police strategy research for twenty-five years? How do we prevent that from happening again?
3. It is suggested that the current status of police research parallels the status of research in chemistry prior to Mendeleev's decoding of the Periodic Table of the Elements. Explain.
4. It is suggested that the science of policing should be kept separate from political or social advocacy. Stated differently, researchers should not be advocates of a particular strategic approach. Why is this so? Why is it so tempting for researchers to lapse into advocacy status?

5. What is the significance for democratic policing of the catchphrase "when the phone rings, we will come"? Does the principle clash with the widespread practice of differential response? What is the risk of sending a patrol unit to every citizen's request for service?

REAL-WORLD SCENARIOS

1. As the newly appointed police chief, you are acutely aware that patrol resources are stretched thin. During evening hours it is not unusual for every patrol unit to be out on a call-for-service—a dangerous situation for both the public and officers. You decide to immediately implement a differential response program, handling selected offense and nuisance complaints by taking a report over the phone, or directing the complainant to the agency's website for "e-filing" of the report. What procedures and/or policies do you develop to assure that the process is not applied disproportionately to some classes of citizens?
2. As a patrol captain, you are considering concentrated deployment of patrol units to high-crime hot spots. However, you are not certain about the effectiveness of hot spot deployment *per se*, and you are even less certain about the optimal "dosage" (how many extra patrol units are needed to make a difference) or duration (how long concentrated patrol must continue to have an effect). Describe the criteria that should be employed in a literature search to find answers to these questions.
3. At a press conference concerning an enforcement initiative about to be launched, you are asked as the department's public relations officer "How do you know if this will work?" You initially respond that other agencies have reported some success. You are challenged, however, by the "investigative" reporter of a local television station, asserting "Of course they report 'some success'; they spent taxpayer's money on the program. In reality, you are expending precious public funds on a program for which you lack any hard evidence that it will reduce crime." Develop a response drawing upon what you know about state-of-the-art strategy in police science.

APPLICATION ACTIVITIES

1. Numerous streams of research have been described throughout this book. Select one study discussed in this chapter that suggests findings that you would question—"the data may have indicated this, but I am not sure of its universal validity." Develop a research design that would replicate the study in multiple and diverse locations or circumstances.
2. Scientific advocacy is always problematic. There are times, however, when scientists feel compelled to "weigh in" due to overwhelming scientific evidence. A current example is the value of disease vaccinations for children. Describe a topic in policing that you feel would justify advocacy on the part of police researchers.
3. Allusion was made to the fact that the social sciences have much to learn from the more mature physical sciences. However, there are certainly differences. What are some of those differences that impact both methodology and our ability to generalize findings from a particular setting to other environments?

COURSEMATE

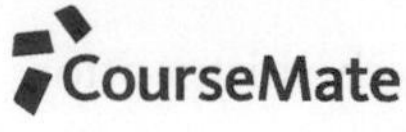

This available CourseMate has an interactive eBook and interactive learning tools, including flash cards, quizzes, and more. To learn more about this resource and access free demo CourseMate resources, go to **www.cengagebrain.com,** and search for this book. To access CourseMate materials that you have purchased, go to **login.cengagebrain.com.**

REFERENCES

Anderson, J. D. (2009). Is there something we don't know about gravity? *Astronomy, 37*(3), 27.

Balick, B., & Frank, A. (2004, July). The extraordinary deaths of ordinary stars. *Scientific American, 291*, 52–59.

Berk, R. A., Campbell, A., Klap, R., & Western, B. (1992). The deterrent effect of arrest in incidents of domestic violence: A Bayesian analysis of four field experiments. *American Sociological Review, 57*(5), 698–708.

Cutler, A. (2000). "New frontiers, new explorations" in Smithsonian Institution. In *Forces of change: A new view of nature* (p. 26). Washington, DC: National Geographic Society.

Freedman, D. H. (2010). The streetlight effect. *Discover Magazine, 31*(6), 55.

Hawking, S. (2001). *The universe in a nutshell*. New York: Bantam Books.

Jang, H. S., Hoover, L. T., & Joo, H. J. (2010). An evaluation of Compstat's effect upon crime: The Fort Worth experience. *Police Quarterly, 13*(4).

Kelling, G. L., & Coles, C. M. (1996). *Fixing broken windows: Restoring order and reducing crime in our communities*. New York: Free Press.

Koper, C. S. (1995). Just enough police presence: Reducing crime and disorderly behavior by optimizing patrol time in crime hot spots. *Justice Quarterly, 12*(4), 649–671.

Kuhn, T. S. (1996). *The Structure of Scientific Revolutions*(3rd ed.). Chicago: University of Chicago Press.

Lum, C. (2009). *Translating police research into practice*. Washington, DC: Police Foundation.

Lum, C., & Yang, S. M. (2005). Why do evaluation researchers in crime and justice choose non-experimental methods? *Journal of Experimental Criminology, 1*, 191–213.

Mayr, E. (2001). *What evolution is*. New York: Basic Books.

Mazerolle, L. G., Rombouts, S., & McBroom, J. (2007). The impact of Compstat on reported crime in Queensland. *Policing: An International Journal of Police Strategies and Management, 30*, 237–256.

McCabe, J. E. (2008). What works in policing? The relationship between drug enforcement and serious crime. *Police Quarterly, 11*(3), 289–314.

McGarrell, E. F., Chermak, S., Weiss, A., & Wilson, J. M. (2001). Reducing firearms violence through directed police patrol. *Criminology & Public Policy, 1*(1), 119–148.

Merali, Z. (2009, December). Splitting time from space. *Scientific American, 301*, 6.

Moore, P. (2002). $E = mc^2$: *The great ideas that shaped our world*. London: Friedman/Fairfax Publishers and Quintet.

Sherman, L. W., & Berk, R. A. (1984). *The Minneapolis Domestic Violence Experiment*. Washington, DC: Police Foundation.

Shermer, M. (2009). I want to believe. *Scientific American, 301*(1), 33–36.

Strecher, V. G. (1991). Histories and futures of policing: Readings and misreadings of a pivotal present. *Police Forum, 1*, 1–9.

Wilson, O. W. (1950). *Police administration*. New York: McGraw-Hill.

Wynn, C. M., & Wiggins, A. W. (1997). *The five biggest ideas in science*. New York: Barnes and Noble Publishing.

Glossary

advocacy books Publications that promote a particular concept or approach. Used herein to describe a series of books describing New York City's implementation of Compstat.

aggressive patrol Patrol activities designed to proactively intervene in the commission of offenses, or preparation for commission. Components include high visibility, frequent stops of suspicious vehicles or persons, and blanket warrant checks.

bait vehicles Vehicles placed by the police in opportune locations for theft; starting the vehicle triggers a geographic positioning system (GPS) device, allowing the police to trace its location.

beat team concept Assignment of a team of officers, usually ten to fifteen, for providing all services to a designated area, typically a cluster of three to five beats; supervised by a sergeant and granted broad leeway to establish its own engagement and problem-solving endeavors.

"broken windows" approach Vigorous enforcement of minor and nuisance offenses as well as intervention in obnoxious behavior to prevent the development of a downward spiral of crime and disorder in stressed neighborhoods.

Bureau of Justice Statistics Federal agency in the U.S. Department of Justice responsible for compiling a range of statistical reports pertaining to state and local criminal justice administration.

buy and bust The process of undercover officers purchasing drugs and immediately arresting the seller.

buy and walk A drug enforcement technique whereby undercover officers purchase drugs but do not immediately make an arrest in favor of either identifying a pattern of sales and/or obtaining search warrants to allow a broadening of the investigation.

buy and warrant A form of buy-and-walk strategy where the goal is focused on obtainment of a search warrant for vehicles or residences.

challenging questioning The practice during crime strategy meetings of aggressively quizzing unit commanders regarding whether they have done everything reasonably possible to interrupt a crime pattern or trend.

chop shops Locations where stolen vehicles are "disassembled" to recover and then market expensive parts.

citizens on patrol Volunteer groups sponsored by police agencies that drive around neighborhoods, usually during evening hours, reporting anything suspicious to police communications; always unarmed with instructions to never attempt intervention.

citizens' police academies Abbreviated versions of police basic training offered to interested citizens to acquaint them with the challenges of a law enforcement role; typically one evening a week for ten weeks.

civil service commissions Official entities of government responsible for administration of personnel policies; typically commissions set standards for employment and competitive promotion of police and fire departments; the purpose of employing commissions is to separate public safety personnel administration from partisan political influence.

clearance by arrest Categorizing an offense as solved, with the perpetrator arrested specifically for the particular case in question.

clearance by exception Categorizing an offense as resolved (not necessarily solved). Most frequently cases are cleared by exception because a suspect admits to committing the offense while being debriefed in the course of arrest for a different offense. The category also includes cases that are determined to be unfounded (although reported as such, an offense did not actually occur) and cases where an offender cannot be arrested because he or she has subsequently died.

community policing A philosophy or orientation that emphasizes engagement with citizens and community groups to address issues of crime and disorder.

Compstat An approach to crime control originating in the New York City Police Department in the early 1990s. Compstat incorporates up-to-the-minute crime analysis, proactive enforcement, and patrol commander accountability.

conflict management The police role in calls-for-service that involve mediating disputes among citizens; the most common disputes requiring police intervention include family domestic relations, traffic/parking, landlord–tenet, merchant–customer, and neighbor issues (usually noise and animal complaints).

consent searches A search of a person, vehicle, or residence with the permission of an authorized agent or owner.

COPS The Community-Oriented Policing Services Office, a federal agency in the U.S. Department of Justice.

court watch programs Informal volunteer efforts to monitor judicial sentencing practices; ostensibly neutral but in practice nearly all court watch programs are premised upon elimination of what is perceived as lenient sentencing practices.

CPTED An acronym representing Crime Prevention Through Environmental Design, or the altering of the physical environment to assist in deterring crime.

crime analysis Plotting of crime patterns and trends, usually employing geographic information systems (GIS).

crime response team Another term for tactical patrol; patrol units freed from normal call-for-service responsibility and charged with concentrated patrol at hot spots.

crime-specific policing Strategies aimed at particular offenses committed by particular offender types at specific times and types of locations.

D.A.R.E.® Registered trademark of Drug Abuse Resistance Education, Inc.; school-based program intended to inculcate an inherent negative attitude toward illegal drug use.

demographic setting An area or neighborhood with given population, housing, and economic characteristics.

differential police response Saving patrol resources by taking minor offense reports over the phone or via the Internet.

diffusion The possibility that geographically focused police intervention efforts will have an effect beyond the boundaries of the area targeted; the opposite phenomenon of displacement.

directed patrol Consists of dispatching patrol vehicles to problematic locations during uncommitted patrol time.

disorderly and nuisance offenses Behaviors such as loitering, obnoxious displays, catcalling, and aggressive begging—creating an atmosphere of dangerousness in public places.

displacement The possibility that enforcement focused on a particular area will simply drive crime to surrounding areas.

division-level meetings Crime strategy meetings conducted at substation (precinct) facilities. These meetings focus only on crime within the division boundaries, and are much more specific than agency-wide sessions.

DNA Abbreviation for deoxyribonucleic acid, the core of a cell that encodes functional instructions for the living organism. DNA fingerprinting is the process of identifying the unique combination of molecules in every person's genetic makeup.

dynamic system Any system that alters response based on environmental changes; in policing, refers to the fact that patrol officers alter the time they spend on certain types of calls-for-service depending on the current call queue.

effectiveness The degree to which objectives are achieved.

efficiency Cost per unit of production; in the public sector, generally regarded as the relative cost of achieving a given objective.

"every officer is a community policing officer" model Hypothetical commitment to having every officer responsible for community engagement; most frequently an emphasis upon a philosophy of neighborhood responsiveness rather than structured positive engagement programs.

evidence-based policing A conceptual framework emphasizing basing crime and disorder interdiction strategies upon structured, sophisticated research regarding the relative effectiveness of alternatives.

fare jumping Leaping over a fare turnstile in subway systems to avoid having to pay the fee.

field interviews Stopping of vehicles or pedestrians triggered by suspicious behavior or unexplained presence in high-crime areas; the primary purposes of field interviews are to run warrant checks on the individuals stopped and/or deter criminal behavior.

focused patrol Directing marked patrol units to proactively intervene in problematic situations; focused patrol may be geographically based, offense based, offender based, or a mixture.

foot patrol Assignment of officers to walking beats; foot patrol beats are employed predominantly in downtowns and problematic strip-center corridors.

general deterrence The propensity of the general public to obey the law out of fear of punishment.

generalist divisional investigators Detectives assigned to substations (precincts) with responsibility for investigating routine offenses such as assault, auto theft, burglary, theft, and sometimes sexual assault and robbery; range of responsibility depends on the extent of centralized specialty investigative units.

geographic information systems (GIS) analysis Use of computerized mapping programs for crime analysis. Most frequently used in policing to depict the locations of given offenses over stipulated time periods.

geographic targeting Focusing crime intervention efforts on a defined area with inordinately high crime rates, ranging from a specific problematic address to three or four square miles. Hot spot concentrated deployment is the most frequent form.

geospatial crime analysis The use of sophisticated GIS analysis to identify linkages among crime patterns or trends. Merged databases are often a component, such as known offender addresses.

GIS Geographic information system, or computerized mapping.

global positioning system (GPS) Satellite-based positioning system now ubiquitous in cell phones, vehicle navigation systems, and other applications.

Golden Era of the Police Foundation The period roughly from 1972 to 1980 that saw Police Foundation sponsorship of several landmark experimental evaluations of strategic approaches, including the Kansas City Preventive Patrol Experiment and the San Diego Field Interrogation Experiment.

hot spot policing Concentrated patrol and other proactive interventions in small geographical areas characterized by inordinately high crime rates or problems of disorder.

incapacitation The inability of confined offenders to commit additional offenses as a result of simply being locked up.

in-service status Status of a patrol unit indicating that the unit is available for dispatch to a call-for-service; in-service status implies concurrent engagement in preventive patrol, traffic enforcement, visibility, and simply being on emergency standby.

intelligence-led policing A broad strategic approach emphasizing, in addition to traditional crime analysis, linkage of known offenders to crime patterns; also incorporates the concept of anticipating crime or security issues by risk assessment.

interactive programs Police interventions that require the engagement of residents or businesses to address problems of crime and disorder.

investigative caseload The number of individual cases assigned to a given detective (or occasionally an investigative unit). The most common accepted way to express caseload is in "new cases assigned per month." Typically that number is about thirty per month for investigators assigned crimes against persons, and thirty-five per month for property crime.

Law Enforcement Assistance Administration (LEAA) A federal agency created in 1968 to provide funding for innovations in state and local law enforcement. The LEAA was superseded in 1982 by the Bureau of Justice Assistance and Bureau of Justice Statistics.

M/O Stands for *modus operandi* or method of operation; refers to particular techniques or characteristics employed by an offender; for burglary, includes time of day, types of locations targeted, means to gain entry, behaviors once inside, and what is typically stolen.

malum in se Term used to describe behavior that is inherently evil or harmful to others.

malum prohibitum Term used to describe offenses that involve behaviors that in and of themselves are not harmful; drinking of alcohol is not inherently harmful to others, but may be so if the individual drinks excessively and then drives a vehicle.

Managing Patrol Operations A training program implemented by the Law Enforcement Assistance Administration designed to train police managers to target patrol resources.

meta-analysis Research that includes scanning all previous related evaluations to ascertain patterns in the findings.

ministerial alliance Volunteer group of ministers sponsored by a police agency as a special point of contact with citizens; employed for both routine community engagement efforts and as a communication medium when community relations problems occur.

moribund Stagnant and unresponsive to change.

National Victimization Survey An annual survey of a sample of households queried regarding household member victimization; conducted by the Bureau of Justice Statistics, a unit of the U.S. Department of Justice.

neighborhood team policing A precursor to community policing, neighborhood team policing involved assigning a group of officers comprehensive full-time responsibility for a small geographic area.

neighborhood watch Volunteer groups sponsored by a police agency that commit to monitoring activity in their own residential vicinity; receiving emphasis is observing neighbors' homes during absences for indications of burglary.

networked adult street gangs Professionally operated criminal enterprises, almost always engaged in drug sales. Such gangs are usually affiliated with other gangs that control drug sales in other neighborhoods. Linkages exist to international drug distribution networks.

Occam's razor One of the core principles of science—the simple explanation is usually correct. Stated differently, all other things being equal, the least complex causative theory is most likely to be true.

offender targeting Focusing repression and/or apprehension efforts upon a given type of offender, for example, gang members.

offense targeting Focusing interdiction efforts on a particular type of crime, for example, auto theft.

open-air drug dealing Engaging in the sale of illegal drugs in outdoor, public places—street corners, parking lots, and so forth.

paradigm A broad conceptual model or approach that serves as a framework for development.

patrol as the backbone of law enforcement A metaphor conveying the premise that the patrol division has been and remains the "core" of a police organization.

pawn shop records submission The process of police compilation of information from pawn shops to identify items being pawned that have been stolen; police also monitor pawn shop records to identify frequent pawners likely disposing of stolen merchandise.

philosophical approach A set of assumptions about the role and function of the police that undergirds strategic decision making.

Police Executive Research Forum (PERF) An association of police chiefs from large agencies and other police professionals; incorporated in 1977; offices in Washington, D.C.

Police Foundation A not-for-profit organization with headquarters in Washington D.C.; its goal is fundamental research on police operations; created by the Ford Foundation in 1970.

police-operated surveillance cameras Cameras placed outdoors in areas of public access, such as street corners, to monitor problematic behaviors; surveillance cameras are most frequently placed at intersections plagued by persistent drug dealing and/or curbside prostitution.

police-to-citizen ratios Proportion of officers to population; typically expressed as number of officers per

1,000 persons; ranges from 4.0 per 1,000 in large East Coast cities to 1.5 per 1,000 in cities west of the Mississippi.

policy A formal directive specifying either what employees of an agency are to do and/or how they are to do it.

political or social advocacy The process of being a proponent of a particular approach or strategy that is perceived as "competing" with alternative approaches.

President's Commission on Law Enforcement and Administration of Justice A national study group convened during Lyndon Johnson's presidency in the 1960s to make recommendations for improvement of policing, court administration, and corrections. Its primary publication is entitled *The Challenge of Crime in a Free Society*.

problem-oriented policing An approach or orientation that entails ascertaining root causes of repetitive crime and disorder patterns and using innovative approaches to permanently resolve the issue by changing underlying conditions.

program A structured intervention with defined participants, characteristics, and goals.

property crime Generally refers to auto theft, burglary, and theft—three of the seven Part 1 offenses included in the FBI's Uniform Crime Reports.

prosecutor acceptance rates The proportion of all arrests by a police agency for which the accused perpetrator is actually charged by a prosecuting attorney.

"pulling-levers" strategy An approach to controlling inter-gang violence initiated by the Boston Police Department. Tactics include direct communication with gangs, which if unsuccessful results in "pulling every available lever" to prosecute.

racial profiling The illegal practice of using race as criteria for vehicle or pedestrian probative stops.

racial proportionality The relative proportion of minorities arrested, stopped, cited, or searched in comparison to their population proportion.

random routine preventive patrol Unstructured, unguided cruising of a patrol beat; associated with the concept of systematically unsystematic patrol.

real-time crime analysis Data regarding crime trends and patterns that are current. Because offense reports must be proofread and approved by a supervisor, "real time" is generally within three days of the present.

referendum A policy or program that is subject to a general election vote.

reintegration Processes involved in an offender reestablishing a legitimate role in the community.

reinventing an organization An approach to organizational growth and renewal that emphasizes comprehensive analysis of purpose, product, and process—amidst a changing environment. Also referred to as reengineering the organization.

reverse sting operations An undercover technique entailing the sale of stolen goods or drugs; a sting involves the police posing as customers to purchase stolen goods or drugs, whereas a reverse sting involves the police posing as illegitimate goods sellers to arrest those who knowingly are buying illegal or stolen goods.

routine activities theory A criminological perspective for which the core concept is the crime triangle of a motivated offender, suitable target, and lack of guardianship.

salvage yard inspections Inspections of businesses engaged in recycling auto parts, typically from inoperable vehicles involved in collisions; police inspections are designed to intercept parts stripped from stolen vehicles for resale.

SARA model A recommended approach to formal problem solving premised upon scanning, analysis, response, and assessment.

saturation patrol Assignment of extra patrol units to a small geographic area; the concentration of multiple marked patrol units in crime hot spots.

simple visibility The process of systematically driving throughout a patrol beat as a form of reassurance to residents that the police are present.

specialist model of community policing Assignment of officers to concentrate on community engagement and problem solving; normally a full-time assignment.

specific deterrence The propensity of a particular potential offender to obey the law out of fear of punishment.

squeegee men Aggressive panhandlers who approach vehicles stopped at an intersection and without permission "wash" the windshield. If demands for a donation are not met, the usual response is to curse the driver.

storefront police stations Small offices usually located in commercial strip centers designed primarily to provide citizens "walk-in" convenience to report issues; staffing levels vary, but typical is a single police agency employee during business hours; patrol units do not deploy from storefronts, but may use the facility to complete reports.

strategy A broad set of interventions related to and complementing one another.

strip-center corridors Street segments dominated by small businesses and/or offices.

suppressible street crime Offenses thought to be directly impacted by concentrated or proactive vehicle patrol; includes auto theft, theft from autos, burglary, robbery, and assaultive behavior in public places.

surgical zero tolerance Saturation patrol with frequent stops of vehicles and pedestrians, but done with care to avoid the inadvertent stopping of law-abiding residents.

tactic A specific type of focused intervention.

tactical patrol Marked patrol units freed from normal call-for-service responsibility; typically assigned to concentrated patrol at hot spots.

The Godfather A 1972 film that depicts the criminal enterprises of the Italian-American Corleone family. Stars Marlon Brando as the family patriarch.

Three Citizens' Model Structured community engagement consisting of citizen advisory groups, citizens' police academies, and citizens-on-patrol programs.

typology A categorization scheme premised upon conceptual attributes of a phenomenon. In contrast, a taxonomy is a categorization scheme premised upon natural attributes—flora and fauna are categorized into taxonomies; organizational patterns typically are typologies.

uncommitted patrol time Time that a patrol unit is not engaged in responding to calls-for-service and administrative duties; the time available for generalist patrol functions.

Uniform Crime Reports (UCR) An annual summary of crimes known to the police published by the Federal Bureau of Investigation.

vice-oriented business clusters Business groupings dominated by adult book stores, strip clubs, liquor stores, low-level bars, and marginal businesses.

victimizing the victims A product of zero-tolerance crackdowns whereby law-abiding residents of a neighborhood are stopped as frequently as offenders; in effect, inadvertent harassment of neighborhood residents innocently caught up in crackdowns.

violent crime Generally refers to murder/manslaughter, aggravated assault, sexual assault, and robbery—four of the seven Part 1 offenses included in the FBI's Uniform Crime Reports.

"when the phone rings, we will come" A phrase that captures an important philosophical underpinning of democratic policing—that all citizens merit equal access to police services.

zero-tolerance crackdowns Saturation patrol in a given area marked by frequent stops of vehicles and pedestrians; stops are made for the most trivial of violations or appearance of suspicious behavior. Most frequently used in areas with concentrated drug trafficking.

References

Abrahamse, A. F., & Ebener, P. A. (1991). An experimental evaluation of the Phoenix repeat offender program. *Justice Quarterly, 8*(2), 141–168.

Anderson, J. D. (2009). Is there something we don't know about gravity? *Astronomy, 37*(3), 27.

Balick, B., & Frank, A. (2004, July). The extraordinary deaths of ordinary stars. *Scientific American, 291*, 52–59.

Bartch, F. (1978). Integrating patrol assignments: Directed patrol in Kansas City. In *Review of patrol operations analysis: Selected readings from ICAP cities*. Washington, DC: U.S. Department of Justice, Law Enforcement Assistance Administration.

Berk, R. A., Campbell, A., Klap, R., & Western, B. (1992). The deterrent effect of arrest in incidents of domestic violence: A Bayesian analysis of four field experiments. *American Sociological Review, 57*(5), 698–708.

Berman, B. (2009). Applying Occam's razor. *Astronomy Magazine*, 14.

Bittner, E. (1967). The police on skid row. *American Sociological Review, 32*(5), 699–715.

Bittner, E. (1970). *The functions of police in modern society*. Washington, DC: U.S. Government Printing Office.

Blake, L., & Coupe, R. T. (2001). The impact of single and two officer patrols on catching burglars in the act. *British Journal of Criminology, 41*, 381–396.

Bloch, P. B., & Bell, J. (1976). *Managing investigations: The Rochester system*. Washington, DC: Police Foundation.

Bloch, P. B., & Specht, D. (1973). *Neighborhood team policing*. Washington, DC: U.S. Government Printing Office.

Bloch, P. B., & Weidman, D. R. (1975). *Managing criminal investigations*. Washington, DC: U.S. Department of Justice.

Boydstun, J. E. (1975). *San Diego field interrogation: Final report*. Washington, DC: Police Foundation.

Boydstun, J. E., & Sherry, M. E. (1975). *San Diego community profile: Final report*. Washington, DC: The Police Foundation.

Braga, A. A. (2001). The effects of hot-spots policing on crime. *Annals of the American Academy of Political and Social Science, 578*, 104–125.

Braga, A. A. (2002). *Problem-oriented policing and crime prevention*. Monsey, NY: Criminal Justice Press.

Braga, A. A. (2005). Hot spots policing and crime prevention: A systematic review of randomized controlled trials. *Journal of Experimental Criminology, 1*, 317–342.

Braga, A. A. (2007). The effects of hot spots policing on crime, a Campbell Collaboration systematic review. Available at http://www.aic.gov.au/campbellcj/reviews/titles.html

Braga, A. A., & Bond, B. J. (2008). Policing crime and disorder hot spots: A randomized controlled trial. *Criminology, 46*(3), 577–607.

Braga, A. A., Kennedy, D. M., Waring, E. J., & Piehl, A. M. (2001). Problem-oriented policing, deterrence, and youth violence: An evaluation of Boston's Operation Ceasefire. *Journal of Research in Crime and Delinquency, 38*, 195–226.

Braga, A. A., Pierce, G. L., McDevitt, J., Bond, B. J., & Cronin, S. (2008). The strategic prevention of gun violence among gang-involved offenders. *Justice Quarterly, 25*(1), 132–162.

Braga, A. A., Weisburd, D., Waring, E. J., Mazerolle, L. G., Spelman, W., & Gajewski, F. (1999). Problem-oriented policing in violent crime places: A randomized controlled experiment. *Criminology, 37*(3), 541–580.

Brandl, S. G., & Frank, J. (1994). The relationship between evidence, detective effort, and the disposition of burglary and robbery investigations. *American Journal of Police, XIII*(3), 149–168.

Brandstatter, A. F., & Radelet, L. A. (1968). *Police and community relations: A sourcebook*. Beverly Hills, CA: Glencoe Press.

Bratton, W., & Knobler, P. (1998). *The turnaround: How America's top cop reversed the crime epidemic*. New York: Random House.

Brennan, C. (2005). Compstat in Philadelphia. Presentation to the Law Enforcement Management Institute of Texas (Major Cities Chiefs Program), Austin, TX.

Brogden, M. (1999). Community policing as apple pie. In R. I. Mawby (Ed.), *Policing across the world* (p. 179). London: University College London Press.

Bulkeley, W. M. (2009, November 17). Chicago's camera network is everywhere. *The Wall Street Journal*. Available at WSJ.com/article/.

Bureau of Justice Statistics. (2002, May). *Special report: Police departments in large cities, 1990–2000*. Washington, DC: U.S. Department of Justice, Bureau of Justice Statistics.

Bureau of Justice Statistics. (2010). *Correctional populations in the United States: Imprisonment rate*. Washington, DC: U.S. Department of Justice, Bureau of Justice Statistics.

Burrows, J., Lewis, H., Stobart, G., & Tyrer, R. (1988). *Directing patrol work: A study of uniformed policing*. London, UK: Her Majesty's Stationery Office.

Cahn, M. F., & Tien, J. M. (1981). *An alternative approach in police response—Wilmington Management of Demand program*. Washington, DC: U.S. Department of Justice.

Canter, D. V., Coffey, T., Huntley, J., & Missen, C. (2000). Predicting serial killers' home base using a decision support system. *Journal of Quantitative Criminology, 16*, 457–478.

Carter, D. L. (1999). *The police and the community*. Upper Saddle River, NJ: Pearson Education, Inc.

Carter, D. L. (2009). *Law enforcement intelligence: A guide for state, local and tribal law enforcement agencies* (2nd ed.). Washington, DC: U.S. Department of Justice, Office of Community Oriented Policing Services.

Carter, D. L., Katz-Bannister, A. J., & Schafer, J. (2001). *Lansing Police Department MATS data: Six month analysis*. Lansing, MI.

Casady, T. (2003). Lincoln police department—specific examples of GIS successes. In M. Leipnik & D. P. Albert (Eds.), *GIS in law enforcement: Implementation issues and case studies*. London: Taylor & Francis.

Cawley, D. F., & Miron, H. J. (1977). *Managing patrol operations—manual*. Washington, DC: U.S. Department of Justice, National Institute of Justice.

Chermak, S., McGarrell, E., & Weiss, A. (2001). Citizens' perceptions of aggressive traffic enforcement strategies. *Justice Quarterly, 18*(21), 365–391.

Chicago Police Department. (2007). *Making Chicago the safest big city in America, Chicago Police Department crime reduction initiatives: 2003–2007*. Chicago, IL: Chicago Police Department.

Chilvers, M., & Weatherburn, D. (2004). The New South Wales Compstat process: Its impact on crime. *Australian and New Zealand Journal of Criminology, 37*(1), 22–48.

Cihan, A., Zhang, Y., & Hoover, L. T. (2012). Police response time to in-progress burglary: A multilevel analysis. *Police Quarterly, 15*(3).

Clarke, R. V. (2002). *Burglary of retail establishments. Problem-oriented guides for police, problem-specific guides series, no. 15*. Washington, DC: U.S. Department of Justice, Office of Community Oriented Policing Services.

Cline, P. J. (2007). Policing divided communities. Paper presented at the Police Executive Research Forum Annual Meeting—Panel Discussion.

Cohen, L. E., & Felson, M. (1979). Social change and crime rate trends: A routine activity approach. *American Sociological Review, 44*, 588–605.

Connell, N. M., Miggans, K., & McGloin, J. M. (2008). Can a community policing initiative reduce serious crime? *Police Quarterly, 11*(2), 127–150.

Conrad, J. P., & Myren, R. A. (1979). *Two views of criminology and criminal justice: Definitions, trends and the future*. Chicago: University of Illinois at Chicago, Joint Commission on Criminology and Criminal Justice Education and Standards.

Cordner, G. (2001). Community policing: Elements and effects. In R. G. Dunham & G. P. Albert (Eds.), *Critical issues in policing: Contemporary readings* (4th ed., pp. 493–510). Prospect Heights, IL: Waveland.

Cordner, G. W. (1981). The effects of directed patrol: A natural quasi-experiment in Pontiac. In J. J. Fyfe (Ed.), *Contemporary issues in law enforcement* (pp. 37–58). Beverly Hills, CA: Sage.

Cordner, G. W. (1996). Evaluating tactical patrol. In L. T. Hoover (Ed.), *Quantifying quality in policing*. Washington, DC: Police Executive Research Forum.

Cordner, G. W., & Biebel, E. P. (2004). *Problem-oriented policing in practice*. Washington, DC: National Criminal Justice Reference Service.

Corman, H., & Mocan, N. (2005). Carrots, sticks and broken windows. *Journal of Law and Economics, 48*, 235–266.

Coupe, R. T., & Blake, L. (2005). The effects of patrol workloads and response strength on arrests at burglary emergencies. *Journal of Criminal Justice, 33*, 239–255.

Cumming, E., Cumming, I., & Edell, L. (1965). Policeman as philosopher, guide and friend. *Social Problems, 12*, 276–286.

Cutler, A. (2000). "New frontiers, new explorations" in Smithsonian Institution. In *Forces of change: A new view of nature* (p. 26). Washington, DC: National Geographic Society.

D'Agnese, J. (2006, September). Book review: Not even wrong and the trouble with physics. *Discover Magazine*, p. 68.

deGuzman, M. C. (2002). The changing roles and strategies of the police in a time of terror. *ACJS Today, 22*(3), 8–13.

DeSimone, D. C. (2003). Federal budget: A mixed bag for state and local governments. *Government Finance Review, 19*(2), 66–69.

Eck, J. E. (1979). *Managing case assignments: The burglary investigation decision model replication*. Washington, DC: Police Executive Research Forum.

Eck, J. E. (1983). *Solving crimes: The investigation of burglary and robbery*. Washington, DC: Police Executive Research Forum.

Eck, J. E. (1996). Rethinking detective management. In L. T. Hoover (Ed.), *Quantifying quality in policing*. Washington, DC. Police Executive Research Forum.

Eck, J. E., Gersh, J., & Taylor, C. (2000). Finding crime hot spots through repeat address mapping. In V. Goldsmith, P. McGuire, J. Mollenkopf, & T. Ross (Eds.), *Analyzing crime patterns: Frontiers of practice*. Thousand Oaks, CA: Sage.

Eck, J. E., & Maguire, E. (2000). Have changes in policing reduced violent crime?: An assessment of the evidence. In A. Blumstein & J. Wallman (Eds.), *The crime drop in America*. Cambridge, England; New York: Cambridge University Press.

Eck, J. E., & Rosenbaum, D. (1994). The new police order: Effectiveness, equity and efficiency in community policing. In D. P. Rosenbaum (Ed.), *Community policing: Testing the promises*. Thousand Oaks, CA: Sage.

Eck, J. E., & Spelman, W. (1987). *Problem-solving: Problem-oriented policing in Newport News*. Washington, DC: Police Executive Research Forum.

Famega, C. N. (2005). Variation in officer downtime: A review of the research. *Policing: An International Journal of Police Strategies & Management, 28*(3), 388–414.

Famega, C. N. (2007). A comparison of patrol officers' and community policing specialists' time allocation. Paper presented at the Academy of Criminal Justice Sciences 2007 meeting.

Fayol, H. (1949, Originally published 1919). *General and industrial management* (C. Stours, Trans.). London: Pitman.

Federal Bureau of Investigation. (Annually). *Crime in the United States, Uniform Crime Reports*. Washington, DC: U.S. Department of Justice.

Fennessy, E. F. (1983). *Police directed patrol—an initial national assessment, June 1983*. Washington, DC: U.S. Department of Justice, National Institute of Justice.

Firman, J. R. (2003). Deconstructing Compstat to clarify its intent. *Criminology & Public Policy, 2*(3), 457–460.

Freedman, D. H. (2010). The streetlight effect. *Discover Magazine, 31*(6), 55.

Fridell, L., & Wycoff, M. A. (2004). *Community policing: The past, present, and future*. Washington, DC: Police Executive Research Forum.

Fritsch, E., Caeti, T., & Taylor, R. (1999). Gang suppression through saturation patrol, aggressive curfew, and truancy enforcement: A quasi-experimental test of the Dallas anti-gang initiative. *Crime and Delinquency, 45*(1), 122–139.

Fritz, R. (1996). *Corporate tides: The inescapable laws of organizational structure.* San Francisco: Berrett-Koehler Publishers.

Gascón, G. (2005). Compstat in Los Angeles. Presentation to the Law Enforcement Management Institute of Texas (Major Cities Chiefs Program), Austin, TX.

Gay, W. G., Day, H. T., & Woodward, J. P. (1977). *Neighborhood team policing, national evaluation program phase I summary report.* Washington, DC: U.S. Government Printing Office.

Gay, W. G., & Schack, S. (1977). *Improving patrol productivity, volume I—routine patrol.* Washington, DC: U.S. Department of Justice, National Institute of Law Enforcement and Criminal Justice.

Goldstein, H. (1979). Improving policing: A problem-oriented approach. *Crime and Delinquency, 25*, 236–258.

Goldstein, H. (1990). *Problem-oriented policing.* New York: McGraw-Hill, Inc.

Goldstein, H. (2003). On further developing problem-oriented policing: The most critical need, the major impediments, and a proposal. *Crime Prevention Studies, 15*, 13–47.

Grassie, R. G., Burrows, J. W., White, S. M., & Waymire, R. V. (1978). *Integrated criminal apprehension program: Manual for the design and implementation of training.* Washington, DC: U.S. Department of Justice, Law Enforcement Assistance Administration.

Greenberg, B., Yu, O., & Lang, K. (1972). *Enhancement of the investigative function: Volume 1—Analysis and conclusions.* Springfield, VA: National Technical Information Service.

Greene, J. R., & Mastrofski, S. D. (Eds.). (1988). *Community policing: Rhetoric or reality.* New York: Praeger.

Greene, J. R., & Taylor, R. (1988). Community based policing and foot patrol: Issues of theory and evaluation. In J. R. Greene & S. D. Mastrofski (Eds.), *Community policing: Rhetoric or reality?* New York: Praeger Press.

Greenwood, P., & Petersilia, J. (1975). *The criminal investigation process—volume I: Summary and policy implications.* Santa Monica, CA: RAND Corp.

Greenwood, P., Petersilia, J., & Chaiken, J. (1977). *The criminal investigation process.* Lexington, MA: D. C. Heath.

Griswold, M. E., & Murphy, G. R. (2010). *It's more complex than you think: A chief's guide to DNA.* Washington, DC: Police Executive Research Forum.

Groff, E., Kearley, B., et al. (2005). A randomized experimental study of sharing crime data with citizens: Do maps produce more fear? *Journal of Experimental Criminology, 1*(1), 87–115.

Gulick, L. H., & Urwick, L. F. (Eds.). (1937). *Papers on the science of administration.* New York: Columbia University, Institute of Public Administration.

Gurwitt, R. (2007). Bratton's Brigade. Governing.com. Available at http://www.governing.com/print/article/brattons-brigade

Halper, A., & Ku, R. (1974). *New York City Police Department street crime unit: An exemplary project.* Washington, DC: U.S. Department of Justice, Law Enforcement Assistance Administration.

Hawdon, J. E., Ryan, J., & Griffin, S. P. (2003). Policing tactics and perceptions of police legitimacy. *Police Quarterly, 6*(4).

Hawking, S. (2001). *The universe in a nutshell.* New York: Bantam Books.

Henry, V. E. (2002). *The Compstat paradigm: Management accountability in policing, business and the public sector.* Flushing, NY: Looseleaf Law Publications, Inc.

Hill, B. (2003). Operationalizing GIS to investigate serial robberies in Phoenix, Arizona. In M. Leipnik & D. P. Albert (Eds.), *GIS in law enforcement: Implementation issues and case studies.* London: Taylor & Francis.

Hoover, L. T. (1975). *Police educational characteristics and curricula.* Washington, DC: U.S. Government Printing Office.

Hoover, L. T. (2002). *Racial profiling data analysis: Final report.* Huntsville, TX: Sam Houston State University.

Hoover, L. T. (2010). Rethinking our expectations. *Police Practice and Research, 11*(2), 160–165.

Hoover, L. T. (Ed.). (1996). *Quantifying quality in policing.* Washington, DC: Police Executive Research Forum.

Hoover, L. T., & Caeti, T. J. (1994). *Crime specific policing in Houston* (Vol. 1). Huntsville, TX: Sam Houston State University. Available at http://www.lemitonline.org/telemasp/index.php#by_volume%201/vol1no9.pdf).

Hoover, L. T., & Lund, D. W. (1977). *Guidelines for criminal justice programs in community and junior colleges.* Washington, DC: American Association of Community and Junior Colleges.

Hoover, L. T., et al. (2002). *Fort Worth Police Department operations analysis.* Huntsville, TX: Justex Systems Inc.

Hornick, J. P., Burrows, B. A., Tjosvold, I., & Phillips, D. M. (1990). *An evaluation of the neighbourhood foot patrol program of Edmonton Police Service.* Edmonton, Canada: Canadian Research Institute of Law and the Family.

Horvath, F., & Meesig, R. T. (2002). *A national survey of police policies and practices regarding the criminal investigation process: Twenty-five years after RAND.* East Lansing, MI: Michigan State University, School of Criminal Justice.

Hubbs, R. (2003). Mapping crime and community problems in Knoxville, Tennessee. In M. Leipnik & D. P. Albert (Eds.), *GIS in law enforcement: Implementation issues and case studies.* London: Taylor & Francis.

Innes, M. (2005). What's your problem? Signal crimes and citizen-focused problem solving. *Criminology & Public Policy, 4*(2), 187–200.

Institute of Judicial Administration. (1973). *Standards relating to the urban police function: Project on standards for criminal justice.* New York: American Bar Association.

Jang, H. S., Hoover, L. T., & Joo, H. J. (2010). An evaluation of Compstat's effect upon crime: The Fort Worth experience. *Police Quarterly, 13*(4).

Jurkanin, T. J., Hoover, L. T., & Sergevnin, V. A. (Eds.). (2007). *Improving police response to persons with mental illness: A progressive approach.* Springfield, IL: Charles C. Thomas.

Kansas City Police Department. (1978). *Response time analysis: Executive summary.* Washington, DC: U.S. Department of Justice.

Katz, C. M., & Webb, V. J. (2006). *Police gangs in America.* New York: Cambridge University Press.

Katz, C. M., Webb, V. J., & Schaefer, D. R. (2001). An assessment of the impact of quality-of-life policing on crime and disorder. *Justice Quarterly, 18*(4), 825–876.

Kelling, G. L. (1981). *The Newark foot patrol experiment.* Washington, DC: Police Foundation.

Kelling, G. L., & Coles, C. M. (1996). *Fixing broken windows: Restoring order and reducing crime in our communities*. New York: Free Press.

Kelling, G. L., Pate, T., Dieckman, D., & Brown, C. E. (1974). *The Kansas City Preventive Patrol Experiment: A summary report*. Washington, DC: Police Foundation.

Kelling, G. L., & Sousa Jr., W. H. (2001). Do police matter? An analysis of the impact of New York City's police reforms. In *Civic report* (Vol. 22). New York: Manhattan Institute for Policy Research.

Kennedy, D. M. (1998). Pulling levers: Getting deterrence right. *National Institute of Justice Journal 7*, 2–8.

Kennedy, D. M., & Braga, A. A. (1998). Homicide in Minneapolis: Research for problem solving. *Homicide Studies, 2*, 263–290.

Kessler, D. A. (1993). Integrating calls for service with community and problem-oriented policing: A case study. *Crime and Delinquency, 39*(4), 485–508.

Koper, C. S. (1995). Just enough police presence: Reducing crime and disorderly behavior by optimizing patrol time in crime hot spots. *Justice Quarterly, 12*(4), 649–671.

Kubrin, D. E., Messner, S. F., Deane, G., McGeever, K., & Stucky, T. D. (2010). Proactive policing and robbery rates across U.S. cities. *Criminology and Public Policy, 48*, 57–91.

Kuhn, T. S. (1996). *The structure of scientific revolutions* (3rd ed.). Chicago: University of Chicago Press.

La Vigne, N. G., Lowry, S. S., Dwyer, A. M., & Markman, J. A. (2011). *Using public surveillance systems for crime control and prevention: A practical guide for law enforcement and their municipal partners*. Washington, DC: U.S. Department of Justice, Urban Institute Justice Policy Center, Office of Community Oriented Policing Services.

LaFave, W. (1965). *Arrest: The decision to take a suspect into custody*. Boston: Little, Brown and Company.

Langton, L. (2010). *Gang units in large local law enforcement agencies, 2007*. Washington, DC: Bureau of Justice Statistics.

Larson, R. C., & Cahn, M. F. (1981). *Synthesizing and extending the results of police patrol studies*. Washington, DC: U.S. Department of Justice, National Institute of Justice.

LaVigne, N. G., Solomon, A. L., Beckman, K. A., & Dedel, K. (2006). *Prisoner reentry and community policing: Strategies for enhancing public safety*. Washington, DC: U.S. Department of Justice, Urban Institute Justice Policy Center, Office of Community Oriented Policing Services.

LaVigne, N., & Wartell, J. (2001). *Mapping across boundaries: Regional crime analysis*. Washington, DC: Police Executive Research Forum.

Lawton, B. A., Taylor, R. B., & Luongo, A. J. (2005). Police officers on drug corners in Philadelphia, drug crime, and violent crime: Intended, diffusion, and displacement impacts. *Justice Quarterly, 22*(4), 427–451.

Leipnik, M., & Albert, D. (2003). *GIS in law enforcement: Implementation issues and case studies*. London: Taylor & Francis.

Levitt, S. D. (2004). Understanding why crime fell in the 1990s: Four factors that explain the decline and six that do not. *Journal of Economic Perspectives, 18*(1), 163–190.

Lewis, L. (2006, April). Organized retail crime: Retail's no. 1 security issue. *California Grocer*, 2–11.

Liederbach, J., Fritsch, E. J., Carter, D. L., & Bannister, A. (2007). Exploring the limits of collaboration in community policing: A direct comparison of police and citizen views. *Policing: An International Journal of Police Strategies and Management, 31*(2), 271–291.

Lindblom, C. E. (1959). The science of "muddling through." *Public Administration Review, XIX*(2), 79–88.

Lum, C. (2009). *Translating police research into practice*. Washington, DC: Police Foundation.

Lum, C., Koper, C. S., & Telep, C. W. (2010). The evidence-based policing matrix. *Journal of Experimental Criminology, 7*, 3–26.

Lum, C., & Yang, S. M. (2005). Why do evaluation researchers in crime and justice choose non-experimental methods? *Journal of Experimental Criminology, 1*, 191–213.

MacDonald, J. M. (2002). The effectiveness of community policing in reducing urban violence. *Crime & Delinquency, 48*(4), 592–617.

Maguire, M. (2000). Policing by risks and targets: Some dimensions and implications of intelligence-led crime control. *Policing and Society: An International Journal of Research and Policy, 9*(4), 315–336.

Manning, P. K. (1971). The police: Mandate, strategies and appearances. In J. D. Douglas (Ed.), *Crime and justice in America*. Indianapolis: Bobbs, Merrill.

Manning, P. K. (1972). Observing the police: Deviants, respectables and the law. In J. D. Douglas (Ed.), *Research on deviance* (pp. 213–268). New York: Random House.

Manning, P. K. (1977). *Police work*. Cambridge, MA: MIT Press.

Manning, P. K. (2003). Personal communication during International Police Studies Conference, Eastern Kentucky University. Richmond, KY.

Maple, J., & Mitchell, C. (1999). *The crime fighter*. New York: Doubleday.

Martin, S. E., & Sherman, L. W. (1986). *Catching career criminals: The Washington, D.C., repeat offender project*. Washington, DC: Police Foundation.

Martinson, R. (1975). The effectiveness of correctional treatment: A survey of treatment evaluation studies. In *The State of Corrections*, American Correctional Association.

Mayr, E. (2001). *What evolution is*. New York: Basic Books.

Mazerolle, L. G., Ready, J., Terrill, W., & Waring, E. J. (2000). Problem-oriented policing in public housing: The Jersey City evaluation. *Justice Quarterly, 17*(1), 129–158.

Mazerolle, L. G., Rombouts, S., & McBroom, J. (2007). The impact of Compstat on reported crime in Queensland. *Policing: An International Journal of Police Strategies and Management, 30*, 237–256.

McCabe, J. E. (2008). What works in policing? The relationship between drug enforcement and serious crime. *Police Quarterly, 11*(3), 289–314.

McDonald, P. P. (2002). *Managing police operations: Implementing the New York crime control model—Compstat*. Australia: Wadsworth Thomson Learning.

McEwen, J. T., Connors, E. F., & Cohen, M. I. (1984). *Evaluation of the differential police response field test*. Alexandria, VA: Research Management Associates, Inc.

McGarrell, E. F., Chermak, S., Wilson, J. M., & Corsaro, N. (2006). Reducing homicide through a "level-pulling" strategy. *Justice Quarterly, 23*(2), 214–231.

McNamara, J. H. (1967). Uncertainties in police work: The relevance of police recruits' backgrounds and training. In D. J. Bordua (Ed.), *The police: Six sociological essays* (pp. 163–252). New York: John Wiley and Sons.

Merali, Z. (2009, December). Splitting time from space. *Scientific American, 301*, 6.

Monk, K. M., Heinonen, J. A., & Eck, J. E. (2010). *Street robbery*. Problem-oriented guides for police, problem-specific guides series, No. 59. Washington, DC: U.S. Department of Justice, Office of Community Oriented Policing Services.

Moore, M. H. (2003). Sizing up Compstat: An important administrative innovation in policing. *Criminology & Public Policy, 2*(3), 469–494.

Moore, P. (2002). *E = mc²: The great ideas that shaped our world*. London: Friedman/ Fairfax Publishers and Quintet.

Mugging Compstat: Assault on NYPD crime-tracking program is wrongheaded. (2010, February 11). *New York Daily News*. Available at http://www.nydailynews.com/fdcp?1265997016418

Muir, W. K. (1977). *Police: Streetcorner politicians*. Chicago, IL: University of Chicago Press.

National Advisory Commission on Civil Disorders. (1968). *Report*. New York: Bantam Books.

National Advisory Commission on Criminal Justice Standards and Goals. (1973). *Report on police*. Washington, DC: U.S. Government Printing Office.

Niederhoffer, A. (1969). *Behind the shield: Police in urban society*. New York: Anchor Books.

Novak, K. J., Hartman, J. L., Holsinger, A. M., & Turner, M. G. (1999). The effects of aggressive policing of disorder on serious crime. *Policing: An International Journal of Police Strategies and Management, 22*(2), 171–190.

Nunn, S., Quintet, K., Rowe, K., & Christ, D. (2006). Interdiction day: Covert surveillance operations, drugs, and serious crime in an inner-city neighborhood. *Police Quarterly, 9*(1), 73–99.

O'Keefe, J. (2004). Personal interview with the former director of the NYPD Academy, now on the faculty at St. John's University in New York City.

Pasciuto, A., et al. (1978). *Managing patrol operations—program test design*. Washington, DC: U.S. Department of Justice, National Institute of Law Enforcement and Criminal Justice.

Pate, A. M., & Annan, S. O. (1989). *The Baltimore Community Policing Experiment: Technical report*. Washington, DC: Police Foundation.

Pate, T., Bowers, R. A., & Parks, R. (1976). *Three approaches to criminal apprehension in Kansas City: An evaluation report*. Washington, DC: Police Foundation.

Paulsen, D. J. (2004). Map or not to map: Assessing the impact of crime maps on police officer perceptions of crime. *International Journal of Police Science & Management, 6*(4), 234–246.

Paulsen, D. J. (2006). Human versus machine: A comparison of the accuracy of geographic profiling methods. *Journal of Investigative Psychology and Offender Profiling, 3*, 77–89.

Peters, T., & Waterman, R. (1982). *In search of excellence*. New York: Harper and Row.

Pooley, E. (1996, January). One good apple. *Time*, 55–56.

Potchak, M. C., McGloin, J. M., & Zgoba, K. M. (2002). A spatial analysis of criminal effort: Auto theft in Newark, New Jersey. *Criminal Justice Policy Review, 13*, 257–285.

President's Commission on Campus Unrest. (1971). *The report of the President's Commission on Campus Unrest*. New York: Avon Books.

President's Commission on Law Enforcement and Administration of Justice. (1967). *The challenge of crime in a free society*. Washington, DC: U.S. Government Printing Office.

Public Safety Research Institute. (1975). *Full-service neighborhood team policing: Planning for implementation*. St. Petersburg, FL: Public Safety Research Institute Inc.

Radelet, L. A. (1973). *The police and the community* (1st ed.). Encino, CA: Glencoe Press.

Ratcliffe, J. H. (2007). *Integrated intelligence and crime analysis: Enhanced information management for law enforcement leaders*. Washington, DC: U.S. Department of Justice, Police Foundation and Office of Community Oriented Policing Services.

Ratcliffe, J. H., Groff, E., Wood, J., Taniguchi, T., Johnson, L., McGuire-Taylor, C., et al. (2010). *The Philadelphia Foot Patrol experiment: Research brief*. Philadelphia, PA: Temple University and Philadelphia Police Department.

Ratcliffe, J. H., Taniguchi, T., & Taylor, R. B. (2009). The crime reduction effects of public CCTV cameras: A multi-method spatial approach. *Justice Quarterly, 26*, 746–770.

Reaves, B. A. (2010). *Local police departments, 2007*. Washington, DC: U.S. Department of Justice, Office of Justice Programs, Bureau of Justice Statistics.

Reiss Jr., A. J. (1971). *The police and the public*. New Haven: Yale University Press.

Retired officers raise questions on crime data. (2010, February 7). *New York Times*.

Roman, J. K., Dunworth, T., & Marsh, K. (Eds.). (2010). *Cost-benefit analysis and Crime control*. Washington, DC: The Urban Institute Press.

Rosenbaum, D. (1989). Community crime prevention: A review and synthesis of the literature. *Justice Quarterly, 5*(3), 323–395.

Rosenbaum, D. P., & Stephens, C. (2005). *Reducing public violence and homicide in Chicago: Strategies and tactics of the Chicago Police Department*. Chicago: University of Illinois at Chicago, Center for Research in Law and Justice.

Rossmo, D. K. (2000). *Geographic profiling*. New York: CRC Press.

Sampson, R., & Cohen, J. (1988). Deterrent effects of the police on crime: A replication and theoretical extension. *Law and Society Review, 22*, 163–189.

San Jose Police Department. (1999). *Vehicle stops demographic study*. San Jose, CA: San Jose Police Department.

San Miguel, C. (2005). *An analysis of neighborhood watch programs in Texas*. Huntsville, TX: Sam Houston State University.

Sanders, W. B. (1977). *Detective work: A study of criminal investigations*. New York: Free Press.

Saunders Jr., C. B. (1970). *Upgrading the American police*. Washington, DC: The Brookings Institution.

Schack, S., & Gay, W. G. (1977). *Improving patrol productivity, volume II—specialized patrol*. Washington, DC: U.S. Department of Justice, National Institute of Law Enforcement and Criminal Justice.

Schmerler, K. (2005). *Disorder at budget motels. Problem-oriented guides for police*. Problem-Specific Guides Series, No. 30. Washington, DC: U.S. Department of Justice, Office of Community Oriented Policing Services.

Schmidt, J. D., & Sherman, L. W. (1993). Does arrest deter domestic violence? *American Behavioral Scientist, 36*(5), 601–609.

Scott, M. S. (2003). *The benefits and consequences of police crackdowns*. Problem-Oriented Guides for Police Response Guides Series, No. 1. Washington, DC: U.S. Department of Justice, Office of Community Oriented Policing Services.

Scott, M. S., & Dedel, K. (2006). *Assaults in and around bars—2nd edition.* Problem-Oriented Guides for Police Problem-Specific Guides Series, No. 1. Washington, DC: U.S. Department of Justice, Office of Community Oriented Policing Services.

Sherman, L. W. (1978). *The quality of police education.* San Francisco: Jossey-Bass.

Sherman, L. W. (1990). Police crackdowns: Initial and residual deterrence. In M. Tonry & N. Morris (Eds.), *Crime and justice: An annual review of research* (Vol. 12). Chicago: University of Chicago Press.

Sherman, L. W., & Berk, R. A. (1984). *The Minneapolis domestic violence experiment.* Washington, DC: Police Foundation.

Sherman, L. W., Gartin, P. R., & Buerger, M. E. (1989). Hot spots of predatory crime: Routine activities and the criminology of place. *Criminology, 27*(1), 27–56.

Sherman, L. W., & Milton, C. H. (1973). *Team policing—seven case studies.* Washington, DC: Police Foundation.

Sherman, L. W., & Rogan, D. P. (1995). Effects of gun seizures on gun violence: "Hot spots" patrol in Kansas City. *Justice Quarterly, 12*, 673–694.

Sherman, L. W., Rogan, D. P., Edwards, T., Whipple, R., Shreve, D., et al. (1995). Deterrent effects of police raids on crack houses: A randomized controlled experiment. *Justice Quarterly, 12*(4), 755–781.

Sherman, L. W., Shaw, J. W., & Regan, D. P. (1995). *The Kansas City Gun Experiment.* Washington, DC: National Institute of Justice.

Sherman, L. W., & Weisburd, D. (1995). General deterrent effects of police patrol in crime "hot spots": A randomized, controlled trial. *Justice Quarterly, 12*(4), 625–648.

Shermer, M. (2009). I want to believe. *Scientific American, 301*(1), 33–36.

Shi, L. (2009). The limit of oversight in policing: Evidence from the 2001 Cincinnati riot. *Journal of Public Economics, 93*, 99–113.

Silverman, E. B. (1999). *NYPD battles crime: Innovative strategies in policing.* Boston, MA: Northeastern University Press.

Skogan, W. G. (1990). *Disorder and decline.* New York: Free Press.

Skolnick, J. H. (1966). *Justice without trial: Law enforcement in a democratic society.* New York: John Wiley and Sons.

Smith, M. R. (2001). Police-led crackdowns and cleanups: An evaluation of a crime control initiative in Richmond, Virginia. *Crime and Delinquency, 47*(1), 60–83.

Smith, M. R., & Petrocelli, M. (2001). Racial profiling? A multivariate analysis of police traffic stop data. *Police Quarterly, 4*(1), 4–27.

Sparrow, M. K., Moore, M., & Kennedy, D. M. (1992). *Beyond 911: A new era for policing.* New York: Basic Books.

Spelman, W. (1995). Criminal careers of public places. In J. E. Eck & D. Weisburd (Eds.), *Crime and place: Crime prevention studies 4.* Monsey, NY: Willow Tree Press.

Stephens, D. (2000). Personal interview.

Strecher, V. G. (1991). Histories and futures of policing: Readings and misreadings of a pivotal present. *Police Forum, 1*, 1–9.

Stroud, M. (2011). Fighting crime in an era of belt-tightening. *The Atlantic Cities.* Available at http://www.theatlanticcities.com/neighborhoods/2011/09/fighting-crime-era-belt-tightening/112/

Sumrall, R. O., Roberts, J., & Farmer, M. T. (1981). *Differential police response strategies.* Washington, DC: Police Executive Research Forum.

Sutherland, E. (1947). *Principals of criminology.* Chicago: J. B. Lippincott Co.

Sutton, M. (2010). *Stolen goods markets.* Problem-oriented guides for police, problem-specific guides series, No. 57. Washington, DC: U.S. Department of Justice, Office of Community Oriented Policing Services.

Taylor, B., Koper, C. S., & Woods, D. J. (2011). A randomized controlled trial of different policing strategies at hot spots of violent crime. *Journal of Experimental Criminology, 7*, 149–181.

Taylor, R. B. (2001). *Breaking away from broken windows: Baltimore neighborhoods and nationwide fight against crime, grime, fear and decline.* Boulder, CO: Westview Press.

Tenney Jr., C. W. (1971). *Higher education programs in law enforcement and criminal justice.* Washington, DC: U.S. Government Printing Office.

Tien, J., Simaon, J., & Larson, R. (1978). *An alternative approach in police patrol: The Wilmington split-force experiment.* Washington, DC: U.S. Government Printing Office.

Trojanowicz, R., & Bucqueroux, B. (1990). *Community policing: A contemporary perspective.* Cincinnati, OH: Anderson Publishing Co.

Trojanowicz, R. J. (1982). *An evaluation of the Neighborhood Foot Patrol Program in Flint, Michigan.* East Lansing: Michigan State University.

Uchida, C., Forst, B., & Annan, S. O. (1992). *Modern policing and the control of illegal drugs: Testing new strategies in two American cities.* Washington, DC: National Institute of Justice.

Urwick, L. F. (1944). *Elements of administration.* New York: Harper.

von Drehle, D. (2010, February 22). Why crime went away: The murder rate in America is at an all-time low. Will the recession reverse that? *TIME Magazine.*

Walsh, W. F. (2001). Compstat: An analysis of an emerging police managerial paradigm. *Policing: An International Journal of Police Strategies and Management, 24*(3), 347–361.

Ward, R. H., & Webb, V. J. (1984). *Quest for quality.* New York: University Publications.

Warren, J., Forst, M., & Estrella, M. (1979). Directed patrol: An experiment that worked. *The Police Chief, 48*, 78.

Webb, K. W. (1977). *Specialized patrol projects, phase 1: Summary report.* Washington, DC: U.S. Department of Justice, National Institute of Law Enforcement and Criminal Justice.

Weisburd, D. (2005). Hot spots policing experiments and criminal justice research: Lessons from the field. *Annals of the American Academy of Political and Social Science, 599*(5), 220–245.

Weisburd, D., & Braga, A. A. (2006). Hot spots policing as a model for police innovation. In *Police innovation: Contrasting perspectives* (pp. 225–244). New York: Cambridge University Press.

Weisburd, D., Bushway, S., Lum, C., & Yang, S. M. (2004). Trajectories of crime at places: A longitudinal study of street segments in the city of Seattle. *Criminology, 42*(2), 283–320.

Weisburd, D., & Eck, J. E. (2004). What can police do to reduce crime, disorder, and fear? *Annals of the American Academy of Political & Social Science, 593*(5), 42–65.

Weisburd, D., & Green, L. (1995). Policing drug hot spots: The Jersey City drug market analysis experiment. *Justice Quarterly, 12*(4), 711–734.

Weisburd, D., Groff, E., & Morris, N. (2011). *Hot spots of Juvenile crime: Findings from Seattle*. Washington, DC: U.S. Department of Justice, Office of Justice Programs, Office of Juvenile Justice and Delinquency Prevention.

Weisburd, D., & Lum, C. (2005). The diffusion of computerized crime mapping in policing: Linking research and practice. *Police Practice and Research, 6*(5), 419–434.

Weisburd, D., Mastrofski, S. D., McNally, A. M., Greenspan, R., & Willis, J. J. (2003). Reforming to preserve: Compstat and the strategic problem solving in American policing. *Criminology & Public Policy, 2*(3), 421–456.

Weisburd, D., & Mazerolle, L. G. (2000). Crime and disorder in drug hotspots: Implications for theory and practice in policing. *Police Quarterly, 3*(3), 331–349.

Weisburd, D., Morris, N. A., & Ready, J. (2008). Risk-focused policing at places: An experimental evaluation. *Justice Quarterly, 25*(1), 163–200.

Weisburd, D., Telep, C. W., Hinkle, J. C., & Eck, J. E. (2008). *The effects of problem-oriented policing on crime and disorder*. Manassas, VA: Campbell Systematic Reviews, George Mason University.

Weisburd, D., Wyckoff, L. A., Ready, J., Eck, J. E., Hinkle, J. C., & Gajewski, F. (2006). Does crime just move around the corner? A controlled study of spatial displacement and diffusion of crime control benefits. *Criminology, 44*(3), 549–591.

Wexler, C. (2011). Police leaders at PERF/BJA meeting discuss Compstat: Best practices and future outlook. In C. Fischer (Ed.), *Subject to debate* (Vol. 25, No. 2). Washington, DC: Police Executive Research Forum.

Willis, J. J. (2011). *First-line supervision under Compstat and community policing*. Washington, DC: U.S. Department of Justice, Office of Community Oriented Policing Services.

Willis, J. J., Mastrofski, S. D., Weisburd, D., & Greenspan, R. (2003). *Compstat and organizational change in the Lowell Police Department*. Washington, DC: Police Foundation.

Wilson, J. Q. (1968). *Varieties of police behavior: The management of law and order in eight communities*. Cambridge, MA: Harvard University Press.

Wilson, J. Q. (1978). *The investigators: Managing FBI and narcotic agents*. New York: Basic Books.

Wilson, J. Q. (2011). Hard times, fewer crimes. *Wall Street Journal*. Available at, http://online.wsj.com/article/SB10001424052702304066504576345553135009870.html

Wilson, J. Q., & Boland, B. (1978). The effect of police on crime. *Law and Society Review, 12*(3), 367–390.

Wilson, J. Q., & Kelling, G. L. (1982). Broken windows: The police and neighborhood safety. *Atlantic Monthly, 249*(March), 29–38.

Wilson, O. W. (1950). *Police administration*. New York: McCraw-Hill.

Worden, R. E. (1993). Toward equity and efficiency in law enforcement: Differential police response. *American Journal of Police, 12*(1), 1–32.

Wycoff, M. A., & Skogan, W. G. (1986). Storefront police offices: The Houston field test. In D. Rosenbaum (Ed.), *Community crime prevention: Does it work?* Beverly Hills, CA: Sage.

Wynn, C. M., & Wiggins, A. W. (1997). *The five biggest ideas in science*. New York: Barnes and Noble Publishing.

Zimring, F. E. (2007). *The great American crime decline*. New York: Oxford University Press.

Zimring, F. E. (2011). How New York beat crime: With its judicious use of cops and innovative methods, the Big Apple is a model for how to stem homicides, muggings and other ills. *Scientific American, 305*(2), 75–79.

Index